ABCs of
Microsoft Office 97
Small Business Edition

ABCs of
Microsoft® Office 97
Small Business Edition

Guy Hart-Davis

SYBEX®

San Francisco • Paris • Düsseldorf • Soest

Associate Publisher: Amy Romanoff
Acquisitions Manager: Kristine Plachy
Acquisitions & Developmental Editor: Sherry Bonelli
Editor: Marilyn Smith
Project Editor: Alison Moncrieff
Technical Editor: Dale Wright
Book Designer: Catalin Dulfu
Electronic Publishing Specialists: Robin Kibby, Kate Kaminski, and Dina F. Quan
Production Coordinator: Duncan J. A. Watson
Proofreader: Katherine Cooley
Indexer: Ted Laux
Cover Designer: Design Site
Cover Illustrator/Photographer: Design Site

Screen reproductions produced with Collage Complete.

Collage Complete is a trademark of Inner Media Inc.

SYBEX is a registered trademark of SYBEX Inc.

TRADEMARKS: SYBEX has attempted throughout this book to distinguish proprietary trademarks from descriptive terms by following the capitalization style used by the manufacturer.

The author and publisher have made their best efforts to prepare this book, and the content is based upon final release software whenever possible. Portions of the manuscript may be based upon pre-release versions supplied by software manufacturer(s). The author and the publisher make no representation or warranties of any kind with regard to the completeness or accuracy of the contents herein and accept no liability of any kind including but not limited to performance, merchantability, fitness for any particular purpose, or any losses or damages of any kind caused or alleged to be caused directly or indirectly from this book.

Library of Congress Card Number: 97-61956
ISBN: 0-7821-2178-0

Manufactured in the United States of America

10 9 8 7 6 5 4 3 2 1

This book is dedicated to Rhonda.

Acknowledgments

I'd like to thank the following people for their help and support with this book: Amy Romanoff for increasing the page count; Sherry Bonelli for making the book happen; Lee Ann Pickrell and Marilyn Smith for careful editing; Juanita Tischendorf and Dale Wright for reviewing the manuscript; Dina F. Quan, Kate Kaminski, and Robin Kibby for typesetting the book; Duncan Watson for coordinating the production of the book; and Ted Laux for creating the Mega-Index.

Finally, thanks go to Hawkwind for "The Golden Void" and to Bruce Spatz for providing me with a dangerously loud subwoofer system through which to enjoy it.

Contents at a Glance

Table of Contents

Chapter 20: Working in Publications 375

Chapter 24: Pushpins, Points of Interest, and WebLinks 443

PART 7: OUTLOOK 455

Chapter 25: Getting Started with Outlook 457

Introduction

Microsoft Office 97 Small Business Edition for Windows 95 and Windows NT is a version of Office designed to fulfill the needs of the small-business and individual market. It includes the following applications: Word, the word processor; Excel, the spreadsheet application; Small Business Financial Manager, an Excel add-on for working with accounting information; Publisher, the desktop-publishing and Web-publishing application; Outlook, the desktop information manager application; Automap Streets Plus, mapping software that can take you to just about any street address in the United States; and Internet Explorer, Microsoft's Web browser.

NOTE   If you're using Office 97 Professional Edition or Office 97 Standard Edition, look for *The ABCs of Office 97 Professional Edition*, which covers Word, Excel, PowerPoint, Access, and Outlook.

What Will You Learn from This Book?

This book is designed to get you quickly up to speed with Microsoft Office 97 Small Business Edition in as short a time as possible. It will show you the most useful features of the Office applications and teach you to use them productively and efficiently without burdening you with arcane and useless information.

The Office applications offer so many features that it can take a while to figure out what you really need to know as opposed to what is so specialized that you'll seldom need to know it even exists. This book discusses only those features that you're likely to use the most. If you eventually need to learn to use the esoteric features that the Office applications offer, the knowledge you gain from this book will stand you in good stead for puzzling out what each command or feature does or for rooting determinedly through the Help file for information.

What Do You Need to Know Already?

For concision, this book assumes that you know a few things about Windows 95 or Windows NT (whichever you're using):

- How to use Windows and navigate its interface enough to start up an application, either with the keyboard or with your mouse

---

NOTE   **In this book, *mouse* is a generic term that refers to any mouse, trackball, touchpad, pointing stick, joystick, finger-ring mouse, 3-D motion sensor, foot-roller, infrared head-tracker, speech-driven cursor, or other pointing device you may be using.**

- How to use Windows programs—how to start them and how to exit them; how to use the menus and dialog boxes to make choices; and how to get help whenever you need it by pressing the F1 key or clicking any convenient Help button
- That you click toggle buttons (such as those for boldface and italic) to select them, and that they'll appear to be pushed in when they've been selected
- That you *select* a check box for an item by clicking in it to place a check mark there, and that you *clear* a check box by clicking to remove the check mark from it
- That you normally click the left (or primary) mouse button to choose an item or to perform an action on it, and that you click the right (or nonprimary) mouse button in or on an item to access a shortcut menu (or *context* menu) of commands suited to that item
- How to navigate through Windows's windows and dialog boxes, double-clicking items to drill down through them and clicking the Up One Level button (or pressing Backspace) to move back up through them
- That many Windows applications let you open multiple documents at the same time, and that you can switch among them using the Window menu

How to Use This Book

This book is set up so that you can go straight to the topic you want and instantly learn what you need to know to get the current task done. *The ABCs of Office 97 Small Business Edition* is divided into seven parts:

- Part 1 examines the common elements of Microsoft Office, from the basics of working with applications and files to object linking and embedding.
- Part 2 introduces you to Web browsing with Internet Explorer and discusses how to configure Internet Exporer security and performance options.
- Part 3 discusses Word—everything from entering text and formatting it to performing mail merges, to creating macros, to customizing your work environment.
- Part 4 deals with Excel and the Small Business Financial Manager. You will learn how to create spreadsheet workbooks that use formulas and charts and how to customize Excel with macros and menus. I'll also discuss how to use the Small Business Financial Manager to import and analyze your accounting data.
- Part 5 shows you how to use Publisher to create publications ranging from tri-fold brochures to full-scale Web sites.
- Part 6 discusses Automap Streets Plus, from locating addresses and points of interest to importing sets of pushpins from your address book so that you can pinpoint your customers and calculate the distance you'll need to travel between appointments.
- Part 7 tackles Outlook, the new desktop information manager that takes over from Schedule+. You will learn how to manage your appointments, track projects and tasks, maintain an effective database of contacts, and send and receive e-mail to and from all and sundry.

Within the seven parts, chapters divide the material by topic, and within each chapter, sections divide the material into easily accessible segments. For specific information, you should be able to dive right into a section and find exactly what you need.

The Appendix looks at installing Office 97 Small Business Edition on your computer—both installing from scratch and installing extra pieces that, for whatever reason, were not included in the original installation.

NOTE   **Notes, Tips, and Warnings, each identified clearly with the appropriate keyword, give you extra guidance with specific topics.**

Conventions Used in This Book

This book uses a number of conventions to convey information:

- A flush-right arrow (➤) designates choosing a command from a menu. For example, "choose File ➤ Open" means that you should pull down the File menu and choose the Open command from it.
- Plus (+) signs indicate key combinations. For example, "press Ctrl+Shift+F9" means you should hold down the Ctrl and Shift keys, and then press the F9 key. Some of these key combinations are visually confusing (for example, "Ctrl++" means that you should hold down Ctrl and press the + key; that is, hold down Ctrl and Shift and press the = key), so you may need to read them carefully.
- Up (↑), down (↓), left (←), and right (→) arrows represent the arrow keys that should appear in some form on your keyboard. The important thing to note is that ← is *not* the Backspace key (which on many keyboards bears a deceptively similar arrow). The Backspace key is referred to as "Backspace" or "the Backspace key."
- **Boldface** indicates items that you may want to type in letter for letter.
- *Italics* indicate either new terms being introduced or variable information (such as a drive letter that will vary from computer to computer and that you'll need to establish on your own).

Part 1

Microsoft Office

Chapter 1

GETTING STARTED WITH THE OFFICE APPLICATIONS

FEATURING

- **Introducing the applications in Microsoft Office**
- **Starting and exiting the Office applications**
- **Creating and saving files**
- **Opening files**
- **Managing files**

In this chapter, we'll run through the basics of working with the applications contained in Microsoft Office 97 Small Business Edition. You'll learn what these applications do, and how to start them and exit from them.

You'll also learn how to create, save, and manipulate files. These techniques apply to Word documents, Excel spreadsheets (including Small Business Financial Manager reports and analyses), and Publisher publications. Outlook works a little differently, so we'll look at the techniques used in that application in detail in the chapters on Outlook in Part 7. (Automap Streets Plus does not create files.)

The Applications in Microsoft Office

Microsoft Office 97 comes in four versions: Office 97 Small Business Edition, Office 97 Standard Edition, Office 97 Professional Edition, and Office 97 Professional Developer Edition. Office 97 Small Business Edition, which this book covers, contains the following applications:

- Word, a powerful word processor capable of generating anything from a typewriter-style letter to a fully formatted book like this one.
- Excel, a spreadsheet and charting application capable of performing extremely complex mathematical and financial analysis.
- Small Business Financial Manager, a set of Excel templates that work with your accounting data to produce financial reports and what-if analyses.
- Outlook, a desktop information management application for improving your work life. Outlook, which is new in Office 97, combines a personal information manager and contact manager with a full-featured e-mail package and work-management utilities.
- Publisher, a desktop-publishing program for creating everything from change-of-address postcards to complex Web sites suitable for a small business.
- Automap Streets Plus, a mapping program that can show you the location of any address in the United States to within a couple of yards, and which can create pushpins on a map for each address in your address list.
- Microsoft Internet Explorer, the browser for exploring not just the World Wide Web and any available intranet, but also the contents of your local hard drive.

NOTE Office 97 Professional Edition and Office 97 Standard Edition both contain the core Office components: Word, Excel, and Outlook. Neither contains Small Business Financial Manager, Publisher, or Automap Streets Plus; these components are specific to Office 97 Small Business Edition. Office 97 Standard Edition adds PowerPoint, the presentation designer, to the core Office components. Office 97 Professional adds Access, the relational database application, as well. Office 97 Professional Developer Edition has the same components as Office 97 Professional Edition, with some additional tools for application developers.

The applications in Microsoft Office are intimately connected to each other: Not only can you share information among applications (for example, by inserting part of an Excel spreadsheet in a Word document or by using data from an address list to build a set of pushpins in Automap Streets Plus), but the main applications also share tools, such as spelling dictionaries and AutoCorrect entries.

If you have questions about how the Office applications work, you will have no problem getting answers. Microsoft's Office Assistant pops up with help either when you hesitate or when you explicitly summon it. You then have the choice of either following the tips the Office Assistant provides or searching for specific information by using *natural-language queries*—queries phrased in normal, everyday language (such as, "How do I make this list into a table?") rather than stilted computer jargon. If you find the Office Assistant intrusive or bothersome, you can modify its behavior so that it appears only when you call it or only in response to certain topics. You can choose from nine different Office Assistant characters, each of which has a different virtual personality and performs different actions.

Starting and Exiting the Office Applications

You can start an Office application in several ways. One of the easiest ways is to use the Windows Start menu, as follows:

1. Click the Start button to display the Start menu.
2. Click the Programs item to display the Programs submenu.
3. Click the name of the application you want to start (for example, click Microsoft Word), or click the folder that contains the item, and then click the application name (for example, click the Microsoft Reference folder, and then click the Automap Streets Plus item).

Word 97
If you've created a shortcut for an Office application on the Desktop, you can start the application by double-clicking the icon for the shortcut.

You can also start one of the Office applications that create files by opening a file associated with the application or by starting a new file associated with the application. We'll look at these techniques later in this chapter.

To exit an Office application, choose File ➤ Exit (open the application's File menu and select the Exit command), click the Close button in the upper-right corner of the application's window, or press Alt+F4 (hold down the Alt key while you press the F4 function key). If any of the files open in the application contain unsaved changes, the application will prompt you to save them.

> **NOTE** In Auto Streets Plus, you'll find the Exit command on its Options menu (choose Options ➤ Exit Streets Plus).

Creating a New File

To create a new file based on the default template (Blank Document in Word, Workbook in Excel, and Full Page Blank Page in Publisher) from within a running application, click the New button on the Standard toolbar or press Ctrl+N. Word opens a new document named Document*x* (Document1, Document2, Document3, and so on); Excel opens a new spreadsheet named Book*x*; and Publisher opens a new publication named Unsaved Publication.

To create a new file based on a template other than the default:

1. Choose File ➤ New to display the New dialog box for the application. (In Publisher, choose File ➤ Create New Publication to display the Microsoft Publisher 97 dialog box.) Figure 1.1 shows the New dialog box that you will see in Word.

2. In the New dialog box, choose the tab that contains the type of document you want to create. In Excel, click the Spreadsheet Solutions tab; in Word, choose from General, Letters & Faxes, Memos, Reports, Legal Pleadings, Publications, Other Documents, or Web Pages; and in Publisher, choose from the types of publications offered on the PageWizard and Blank Page tabs.

   - To see a preview of a template in Word or Excel, click the template. The preview will appear in the box on the right side of the New dialog box.

> **NOTE** A *template* is a special type of file that you use as a basis for producing similar files. Take a look at the Preview box in Word and Excel as you click each template to get an idea of the different document designs you can use with templates.

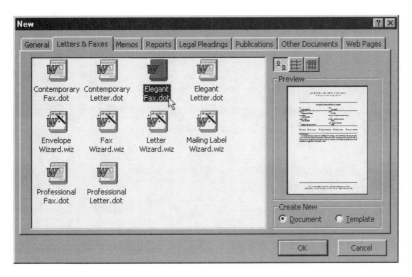

FIGURE 1.1:   To create a new file based on a different template, choose File ➤ New
and select the template in the New dialog box.

- In Word and Excel, you can choose between three views of the templates available by
  clicking one of the three buttons above the Preview box. The leftmost button gives the
  Large Icons view, the second gives the List view, and the third gives the Details view.
  Details view offers the most information of the three views. In Details view, you can sort
  the templates by name, size, type, or date last modified by clicking the buttons at the top
  of the columns.
3. To start a file based on the template you've chosen, double-click the icon or
   listing for the template, or click the icon or listing once and then click the OK
   button.

NOTE   **When you start Publisher, by default it displays the Microsoft
Publisher 97 dialog box, which lets you choose whether to create a
new publication or open an existing one. When you start Word or
Excel, the application opens a new file for you based on the default
template.**

Saving a File

The first time you save a file, you assign it a name and choose the folder in which to save it. Thereafter, when you save the file, the application uses that name and folder and does not prompt you for changes, unless you decide to save the file under a different name. In that case, you need to use the File ➤ Save As command rather than File ➤ Save.

Saving a File for the First Time

To save a file for the first time:

1. Choose File ➤ Save to display the Save As dialog box (see Figure 1.2). Alternatively, click the Save button on the Standard toolbar or press Ctrl+S, Shift+F12, or Alt+Shift+F2 to display the dialog box.

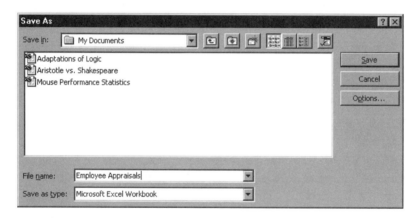

FIGURE 1.2: In the Save As dialog box, choose the folder in which to save your file, and then enter a name for the file and click the Save button.

2. In the Save In box at the top of the Save As dialog box, choose the folder in which to save the document.

   • Navigate the Save As dialog box in the same way that you would move through folders in a typical Windows 95 or Windows NT dialog box: Click the Up One Level button (or press the Backspace key with the focus in the main area of the dialog box) to move up one level of folders, or double-click the folders displayed in the main area to move down through them to the folder you want.

- Use the Look in Favorites button to quickly display the list of Favorite folders. (Publisher's Save As dialog box does not have this button.) Click the button again if you need to return to the folder you were in before you displayed the list of Favorites.

3. In the File Name text box, enter a name for your file.

- With Windows 95's and Windows NT's long file names, you can enter a thorough and descriptive name of up to 255 characters, including the path to the file (the *path* is the name of the folder or folders in which to save the file).

- You cannot use the following characters in file names (if you do try to use one of these, the application will advise you of the problem): colon (**:**), semicolon (**;**), backslash (****), forward slash (**/**), greater-than sign (**>**), less-than sign (**<**), asterisk (*****), question mark (**?**), double quotation mark (**"**), vertical bar or "pipe symbol" (**|**).

4. Click the Save button to save the file.

5. If the application displays a Properties dialog box for the document, enter any identifying information on the Summary tab (see Figure 1.3). (Publisher does not use a Properties dialog box.)

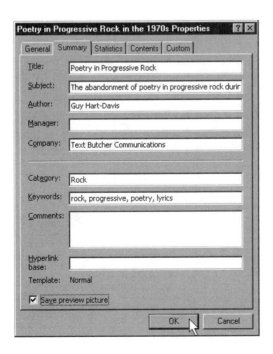

FIGURE 1.3:
If a file you're saving displays a Properties dialog box, enter any appropriate identifying information on the Summary tab, then click the OK button to close the dialog box.

NOTE Whether or not the Properties dialog box appears depends on a setting in the Options dialog box (Tools ➤ Options). In Word, this setting is called Prompt for Document Properties and is on the Save tab; in Excel, it's called Prompt for Workbook Properties and is on the General tab. Select this check box to have the application prompt you for properties.

- In the Title box, Word will display the first paragraph of the file (or part of it) if it deems that text a likely candidate as a title. You'll often want to change this. Excel doesn't usually suggest a title.
- In the Author text box, the application displays the user name from the User Info tab of the Options dialog box.
- In the Company text box, it displays the company information with which you registered the application.
- Use the Subject box to describe the subject of the document.
- Enter any keywords that will help you remember the document in the Keywords box.
- Fill in any other boxes as necessary to help you identify the document later, then click the OK button to close the Properties dialog box and save the file.

Saving a File Again

To save a file that you've saved before, choose the Save command by using one of the methods given in the previous section:

- Click the Save button on the Standard toolbar.
- Choose File ➤ Save.
- From the keyboard, press Ctrl+S, Shift+F12, or Alt+Shift+F2.

The application will save the file without consulting you about the location or file name.

NOTE With the database portions of Outlook, you don't need to save material explicitly, because Outlook saves information for you the moment you finish entering it into a field and move to another field. We'll look at this in more detail in the Outlook chapters in Part 7.

Saving a File under Another Name

One of the easiest ways to make a copy of an open file is to open it and save it under a different name. This technique can be particularly useful if you're working on a file and have made changes to it, but you don't want to replace the original file. For example, you might save the file under another name if you think you may need to revert to the original file and you forgot to make a backup before making your changes. The Save As command also can be useful for copying a file to a different folder or drive. For example, you can use this command if you want to copy a document to a floppy drive or to a network drive.

To save a file under a different name or to a different folder:

1. Choose File ➤ Save As to display the Save As dialog box.
2. Enter a different name for the file in the File Name box, or choose a different folder in the Save In drop-down list.
3. Click the Save button to save the file. If the folder you've chosen already contains a file with the same name, the application will ask whether you want to overwrite it, as shown here (the wording on the warning message box varies from application to application). Choose Yes

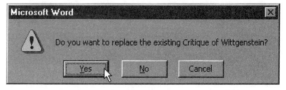

or No. If you choose No, the application will return you to the Save As dialog box, so you can choose a different name or different folder.

Saving a File in a Different Format

In addition to letting you open files saved in different formats, Word and Excel also let you save files in formats other than their own so that you can use the files with other applications. (Publisher offers more complex file-saving options that we'll examine in the Publisher chapters in Part 5.)

NOTE   For this procedure to work, you must have the appropriate file converters installed so that the application can translate the file to the appropriate format. If you don't, you'll need to install them. To install another converter, run the Setup program again (as described in the Appendix) and choose to install the appropriate converter.

To save an existing file in a different format:

1. Choose File ➤ Save As to display the Save As dialog box.
2. Scroll down the Save as Type drop-down list, and choose the file type you want to save the current file as.
3. If you want, enter a different file name for the file. In most cases, you don't need to enter a different name, because the file will get the new extension for the file type you chose in step 2, and will not overwrite the existing file. The exception is when you save the file in a different format that uses the same file extension as the current format.
4. Click the Save button or press Enter.

NOTE   **If you haven't saved the file before, you can choose File ➤ Save instead of File ➤ Save As to open the Save As dialog box. You'll also need to specify a name for the file (unless you want to accept the default name that Word or Excel suggests for it).**

Opening a File

To open a file in the current application:

1. Click the Open button on the Standard toolbar, choose File ➤ Open, or press Ctrl+O to display the Open dialog box (see Figure 1.4). (In Publisher, this dialog box is called Open Publication.)
2. If you're already in the folder that contains the file you want to open, proceed to step 3. If not, use the Look In drop-down list to navigate to the folder holding the file that you want to open.
   - Move through the folders using standard Windows navigation techniques: Click the Up One Level button (or press the Backspace key with the focus in the main area of the dialog box) to move up one level of folders or double-click a folder to move down through it.

   - Click the Look in Favorites button (the left of the two buttons shown here) to display your list of favorite folders. Click the Add to Favorites button (the right button) to add a folder to that list.

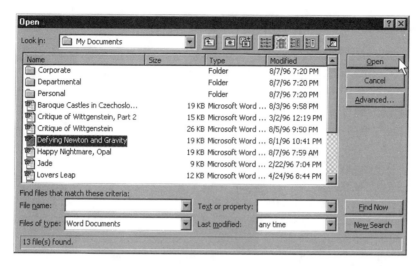

FIGURE 1.4: In the Open dialog box (or Open Publication dialog box in Publisher), use the Look In box to navigate to the folder that contains the file you want to open, and then select the file and click the Open button.

3. Choose the file to open, then click the Open button. You can use the List, Details, Properties, and Preview buttons (shown here from left to right) to help make sure you're picking the right file.

- The List button lists the names of the files and nothing more.
- The Details button lists the files, together with their size, type (such as Microsoft Excel Worksheet), and the date and time they were last modified.
- The Properties button displays a panel containing the file's properties.
- The Preview button displays a small preview of the first page (you can scroll down to see more).

TIP

To open several files at once in Word and Excel, click the first one in the Open dialog box to select it. Then, to select contiguous files, hold down Shift and click the last file in the sequence to select it and all the ones between it and the first file. To select noncontiguous files, or to select other files after selecting a contiguous sequence, hold down Ctrl and click each file you want to open. When you've selected all the files you want to open, click the Open button.

Opening a File Using Windows 95 and NT Techniques

Windows 95 and Windows NT 4 offer several ways to open a file quickly. If you've used the file recently, click the Start button to display the Start menu, choose Documents, and select the file from the list of the 15 most recently used files. If the application with which the file is associated is already open, Windows will open the file for you; if the application isn't open, Windows will start it and open the file at the same time.

If you need to open a file frequently but can't be sure that it will always be among your 15 most recently used files on the Start menu's Document menu, create an icon for it on the Desktop. There are two easy ways to create a shortcut:

- Right-click (click with the mouse's right button) the Desktop and choose New ➤ Shortcut to display the Create Shortcut dialog box. Then click the Browse button to identify the file.

- Open an Explorer window or My Computer window, find the file you want to keep handy, and right-drag it (drag with the right mouse button held down) to the Desktop. Windows will invite you to create a shortcut to the file; go right ahead.

To quickly open one of the files you worked on most recently from inside Word, Excel, or Publisher, pull down the File menu and choose one of the most recently used files listed at the bottom of the menu. By default, Word, Excel, and Publisher list four files, but you can change this in Word and Excel (Publisher doesn't allow you to change the number of recently used files or turn off the display of the recently used files list). Choose Tools ➤ Options to display the Options dialog box, then select the General tab. Under Recently Used File List, change the number in the Entries text box (from 1 to 9). Alternatively, you can turn off the display of recently used files by clearing the Recently Used File List check box.

Finding a File

The Open dialog box in Word and Excel also lets you quickly search your computer for files that match a certain description. This can be useful when you need to find a file whose name or location you've forgotten but whose contents you can remember.

NOTE **Publisher offers different features for finding publications, which are described in Chapter 20. Outlook offers some special ways to find files. For example, you can quickly find a file by locating a Journal entry associated with it. We'll look at those techniques in the chapters on Outlook in Part 7.**

Finding a File from a Known Word

To find a file using a word you remember from the text of the file:

1. In the Open dialog box, navigate to the folder you think the file is in. (If you don't remember that, start with the drive you think the file is on.)
2. Make sure the File Name text box is blank. If it's not, click the New Search button to clear it.
3. Make sure the Files of Type drop-down list shows the type of file you're looking for, such as Word Documents (*.doc) for Word documents or Microsoft Excel File (*.xl*; *.xls; *.xlt) for Excel workbooks.
4. In the Text or Property drop-down list box, enter the text to search for.
5. Click the Find Now button to start the search. If the application finds the file, it will highlight it in the dialog box. (If the application finds several files containing the text, you'll need to decide which one you want.)
6. Click the Open button to open the file.

Finding a File from Other Information

In Word and Excel, you can also search for a file using other known information, such as its contents, author, company, or the last time it was modified or printed. To find a file using information about the file:

1. Click the Advanced button to display the Advanced Find dialog box (see Figure 1.5).
2. In the Find Files That Match These Criteria box, check that the application is showing only appropriate criteria, such as Files of Type is Word Documents (*.doc). To remove inappropriate criteria, select them and click the Delete button.
3. In the Define More Criteria group box, leave the And option button selected and choose the item to search for in the Property drop-down list: Application Name, Author, Category, Company, Hyperlink Base, Last Printed, and so on. You'll recognize most of these as properties from the Properties dialog box.
4. In the Condition drop-down list, choose from the options available for the property you chose. For example, if you chose Author in the Property drop-down list, you could choose Is (Exactly) or Includes Words from the Condition drop-down list to search by the whole author name or by part of it. If you choose a time-related property such as Last Printed, you can choose from Yesterday, Today, Last Week, and so on.

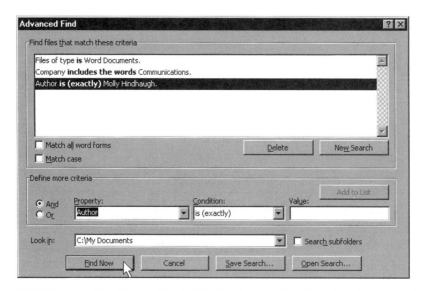

FIGURE 1.5: The Advanced Find dialog box lets you find files using almost any piece of information you can remember about them.

5. In the Value box, enter the item you're searching by. For example, when searching for a file by author, specify the author's name here (or part of it, if you're using Includes Words). For a time-related property, you don't enter a value.

6. Click the Add to List button to add this criterion to the list.

7. Add more criteria if necessary by repeating steps 3 through 6.

8. In the Look In drop-down list, specify the folder in which to start the search for the missing file. If the folder has subfolders that you want to search as well, check the Search Subfolders box to the right of the Look In drop-down list.

9. Click the Find Now button to have the application search for the file. If it finds the file, it will display it in the Open dialog box, where you can open it as usual. (If the application finds several files that meet your criteria, you'll need to decide which one you want.)

TIP **You can save search criteria by clicking the Save Search button in the Advanced Find dialog box. To open a saved search, click the Open Search button.**

Opening a File Created in Another Application

Word, Excel, and Publisher can open files saved in a number of other formats:

- Word can open anything from plain-text ASCII files to spreadsheets (for example, Lotus 1-2-3) to calendar and address books.
- Excel can open various types of spreadsheets, including 1-2-3 and Quattro Pro formats.
- Publisher can open files in various text formats (including HTML) and spreadsheet formats.

NOTE To open a file saved in another application's format, you need to have installed the appropriate converter so the Office application can read the file. Generally speaking, the easiest way to tell if you have the right converter installed for a particular file format is to try to open the file; if the application cannot open it, you probably need to install another converter. Run the application's Setup program again and choose to install the appropriate converter (see the Appendix for information about installing the applications).

To open a file saved in another application's format:

1. Select File ➤ Open to display the Open dialog box.
2. Choose the folder containing the file you want to open.
3. Click the drop-down list button on the Files of Type list box. From the list, select the type of file you want to open. If the application doesn't list the file you want to open, choose All Files (*.*) from the drop-down list to display all the files in the folder. If the Files of Type drop-down list contains no entry for the type of file you want to open, you may need to install the converter file for it.
4. Choose the folder in the main window of the Open dialog box, select the file to open, then click the Open button or press Enter to open the file.

Closing a File

To close the current file, choose File ➤ Close, press Ctrl+F4, or click the Close button on the file window. If the file contains unsaved changes, the application will prompt you to save them, and will close the file when you've saved the file or chosen not to save it.

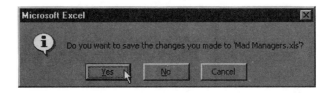

If the file has been saved before and if there are no new changes, the application will simply close the file.

To close all open files at once in Word or Excel, hold down the Shift key while you use the mouse to choose File ➤ Close All.

Exiting the Application

When you've finished working in the application, exit it to get back to the Windows Desktop. When you do this, the application will remove from your computer's hard disk any temporary files that it created while it was doing your bidding.

Choose File ➤ Exit or click the Close button at the top-right corner of the application's window. If you have unsaved files, the application will prompt you to save them (save them as described earlier in this chapter in the section "Saving a File"). If you have open files that you've saved before but have subsequently changed without saving, the application will prompt you to save those changes.

Managing Your Files with the Office Applications

Like other Windows applications, the Office applications provide file-management capabilities in their common dialog boxes, such as the Open dialog box and the Save dialog box.

Renaming a File or Folder

To rename a file or folder in a common dialog box, right-click it and choose Rename from the context menu. (Alternatively, click the file or folder once to select it, wait a second, then click again.) Type the new name for the file or folder in the resulting expanded box (drag through

a word or part of a word to select it if you don't want to change the whole name). Then press Enter or click elsewhere in the dialog box to apply the new name.

Copying or Moving a File or Folder

To copy a file or folder quickly in a common dialog box, right-click it and choose Copy from the context menu. Then navigate to the folder into which you want to place the copy of the file or folder, right-click in it (or on its icon), and choose Paste from the context menu.

NOTE **You can also paste a copy of a file back into the same folder. The copy will be identified as *Copy of* plus the original file name. You can then rename the copy as described in the previous section.**

To move a file or folder in a common dialog box, right-click it and choose Cut from the context menu. Then navigate to the folder into which you want to move the file or folder, right-click it (or its icon), and choose Paste from the context menu.

Deleting a File or Folder

To delete a file in a common dialog box, right-click it, hold down Shift, and choose Delete from the context menu. The application will ask you to confirm the deletion; click the Yes button. (When you delete a file this way, you will not be able to restore it.)

To send a file to the Recycle Bin from a common dialog box, right-click it and choose Delete from the context menu. The application will ask you to confirm the deletion; click the Yes button.

TIP **If you send a file to the Recycle Bin, it will remain there until you empty the Recycle Bin or until the Recycle Bin gets full and is emptied automatically. If you discover you've accidentally sent something valuable to the Recycle Bin, retrieve it immediately.**

Checking a File's Properties

To check a file's properties from a common dialog box (for example, to help identify a file), right-click it and choose Properties from the context menu to display the Properties dialog box. Click the OK button to close the Properties dialog box when you're finished.

Creating a Shortcut to a File or Folder

To create a shortcut to a file, right-click the file and choose Create Shortcut from the context menu. The application will create a shortcut to the file in the same folder and will name it *Shortcut to* plus the file's original name (unless the combination will be more than 255 characters including the path, in which case the application will truncate the name accordingly). You can then move the shortcut to wherever you need it by using the techniques described in "Copying or Moving a File or Folder."

TIP   **To create a shortcut on the Windows Desktop to a file, open an Explorer or My Computer window, right-click the file, and right-drag it to the Desktop. Then choose Create Shortcut Here from the context menu that Windows displays.**

Searching for a File

Windows and Office provide several ways of searching for files that you know exist but can't locate. In the "Finding a File" section earlier in this chapter, we looked at how to locate a file by building as elaborate a list of its details as you can, but Windows Find dialog box offers the simplest way to assemble a list of files matching certain criteria. Choose Start ➤ Find ➤ Files or Folders to display the Windows Find dialog box (see Figure 1.6).

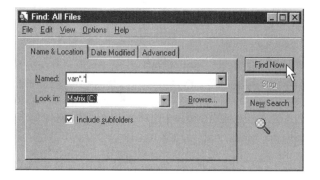

FIGURE 1.6:
Use the Windows Find dialog box to find files matching certain criteria.

In the Named box on the Name & Location tab, enter the closest approximation of the name of the file you want to find. For example, enter ***.doc** if you're looking for Word documents with any name, or **My*.pub** if you're looking for Publisher publications that have names starting with *My*. In the Look In drop-down list, choose the drive on which to search for the file. To specify a folder on the drive, click the Browse button, choose the folder in the Browse for Folder dialog box, and then click the OK button.

On the Date Modified tab, choose either to find All Files or to Find All Files Created or Modified within a certain time range. Specify the time range for the second option in the boxes underneath the option.

On the Advanced tab, choose advanced options as necessary:

- In the Of Type drop-down list, choose the type of file you're looking for, such as 1-2-3 Worksheet or DeScribe Word Processor 5.
- In the Containing Text text box, enter the text you know the file contains, such as **Acme Industries Contract**.
- In the Size Is drop-down list, choose At Least or At Most, then specify the minimum or maximum file size in kilobytes in the KB box. For example, you could specify At Least 2048KB to find files larger than 2MB.

Click the Find Now button to find the files that match the criteria you've specified. Windows will display the found files in the Find window. To open one, double-click it.

Chapter 2

USING SHARED TOOLS IN THE OFFICE APPLICATIONS

- **Using the menu bars and key combinations**
- **Displaying and customizing toolbars**
- **Using Undo and Redo**
- **Using the Spelling checker and AutoCorrect**
- **Using Find and Replace**
- **Linking and embedding objects**

In this chapter, we'll look at the elements (such as menu bars, key combinations, and toolbars) and the tools common among the various Office applications. By examining them as a common unit rather than as a feature of each application in turn, we can save a great deal of time (and a large number of pages in the book).

In this chapter, you'll find that Word and Excel share the most common elements, but Publisher also shares many of the features, and Outlook shares some. Because it is a different type of application, Automap Streets Plus shares relatively few of the features beyond the key combinations for operations, such as Cut, Copy, and Paste.

Key Combinations

As well as the shared menus with their common access keys (Alt+F for the File menu, Alt+E for the Edit menu, and so on), the Office applications have common key combinations for operations, such as:

- Cut (Ctrl+X)
- Copy (Ctrl+C)
- Paste (Ctrl+V)
- Undo (Ctrl+Z)
- Print (Ctrl+P)
- Save (Ctrl+S)

Cut, Copy, and Paste

The Cut, Copy, and Paste commands work smoothly between the various Office applications. You can copy, say, a telephone number from a spreadsheet or an e-mail message and paste it into the contact-management part of Outlook, or you can cut a number of paragraphs from a Word document and paste them into a Publisher publication.

Cut, Copy, and Paste use the *Clipboard,* which is an area of reserved memory in Windows. The Clipboard can hold only one item at a time, so every time you cut or copy something new, that item replaces the previous one. When you paste an item, however, you paste in a *copy* of the newest item from the Clipboard; the item remains on the Clipboard until supplanted by another item, so you can paste it more than once if you wish.

You can access the Cut, Copy, and Paste commands in a number of ways:

- By clicking the Cut, Copy, and Paste toolbar buttons (shown here in that order, from left to right)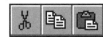
- By choosing the menu commands Edit ➤ Cut, Edit ➤ Copy, or Edit ➤ Paste
- By using the Cut (Ctrl+X), Copy (Ctrl+C), and Paste (Ctrl+V) keyboard shortcuts
- By right-clicking in the item you want to cut or copy, or in the location where you want to paste the item, and choosing Cut, Copy, or Paste from the context menu (in Publisher, these commands will be modified to suit the element you're working with: Cut Text, Cut Picture Frame, Cut Table, and so on)

Drag-and-Drop Editing

Word, Excel, Publisher, and Outlook support *drag-and-drop* editing. This feature allows you to not only move an item in an application by selecting it and dragging the selection, but also to select an item in one application and drag it to another application to move it there. For example, you can select a table in Word, drag it to an Excel window, and drop it there; and Excel will take in the information as cells.

Interapplication drag-and-drop works best with plain text or with items that work in similar ways in the different applications (such as the Word table and the Excel cells mentioned in the previous paragraph), but you can also use drag-and-drop to move items such as graphics and tables between Publisher publications and Word documents (and vice versa).

TIP **If you hold down Ctrl when dragging, you'll copy the item rather than move it.**

Menu Bars and Toolbars

The next major point of similarity among the Office applications is their menu bars and toolbars.

You'll see that most of the menus in Word and Excel are the same. They each have File, Edit, View, Insert, Format, Tools, Window, and Help menus, but the menu between Tools and Window is different (Table in Word and Data in Excel). Publisher shares many of these menus, adding an Arrange menu and a Mail Merge menu. (Outlook has different commands and so has different menus.)

This commonality of menus makes it easy to find the commands you need when working in the Office applications. You can also customize the menu bar in Word and Excel, and you can move the menu bar to different places in the application window in Word, Excel, and Outlook.

Likewise, all the Office applications use multiple toolbars to allow you to easily execute the most useful commands. Word and Excel provide a plethora of toolbars; Publisher and Outlook provide only a couple. By default, the applications display the most widely used toolbar or toolbars, but you can easily choose to display other toolbars. Alternatively, you can hide all the toolbars to give yourself more on-screen room to work in. You can also customize the toolbars in Word and Excel so that they contain the commands you need most; and in Word, Excel, and Outlook, you can move the toolbars to wherever you want them in the application window.

The following sections illustrate the general steps for working with menu bars and toolbars.

Displaying Toolbars

To display and hide toolbars in Word, Excel, and Outlook, right-click anywhere in the menu bar or in a displayed tool-bar, or choose View ➤ Toolbars, to display a list of toolbars. Check marks appear next to the toolbars that are currently displayed. Click next to a displayed toolbar to hide it or next to a hidden toolbar to display it. With the keyboard, use ↓ and ↑ to move the highlight to the displayed toolbar you want to hide or the hidden toolbar you want to display, then press ↵.

In Publisher, right-click anywhere in a displayed toolbar (including the toolbar to the left of the workspace) to display the context menu of toolbars. Alternatively, choose View ➤ Toolbars and Rulers to display the Toolbars and Rulers dialog box, and select the check boxes for the tool-bars you want to display.

Moving and Reshaping Toolbars and the Menu Bar

Word, Excel, and Outlook can display their toolbars and menu bar as either *docked* panels attached to one side of the screen or as free-floating panels that you can drag anywhere on your screen (see Figure 2.1).

To move a toolbar or the menu bar from its current position, click on the move han-dle at its left end (or its top end, if the bar is positioned vertically) and drag it to where you want it—either to one of the edges, in which case it will snap into position, or to the middle of the screen. (The move handle is the two wrinkles at the left end of a toolbar.)

TIP You can undock a docked toolbar (but not the menu bar) by double-clicking its move handle. To redock a floating toolbar (or the float-ing menu bar), double-click its title bar.

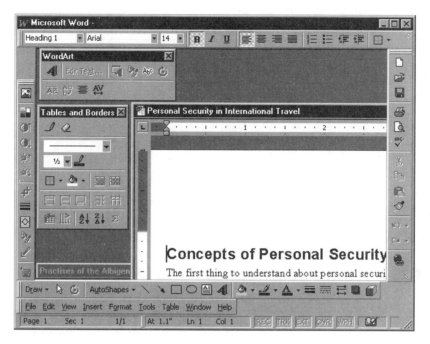

FIGURE 2.1: You can display your toolbars and the menu bar at any extremity of the screen or place them plumb in the middle.

To reshape a floating toolbar or floating menu bar, move the mouse pointer over one of its borders until the pointer turns into a double-ended arrow, then click and drag to resize the toolbar. Because of the shape of their buttons or menu names, toolbars and the menu bar resize in jumps rather than smoothly like windows.

Customizing Toolbars and the Menu Bar in Word and Excel

You can customize the toolbars and menu bar in Word and Excel. Not only can you create new toolbars that contain the macros or commands most important to you, but you can also modify your own toolbars or the existing ones. You can delete your own toolbars, but not the built-in toolbars or the menu bar. You can create new menus, add commands to menus, and remove commands from menus. By customizing toolbars and the menu bar, you can put the commands you need for using an application right at your fingertips.

Creating a New Toolbar

To create a new toolbar in Word or Excel:

1. Right-click in the menu bar or in any displayed toolbar and choose Customize from the list of toolbars to display the Customize dialog box.
2. On the Toolbars tab, click the New button to display the New Toolbar dialog box.
3. Enter a name for the new toolbar in the Toolbar Name text box.

NOTE In Word, if you want to make the toolbar available only to the current template, choose the template's name in the Make Toolbar Available To drop-down list in the Customize dialog box. Otherwise, make sure All Documents (Normal.dot) is selected in the Make Toolbar Available To drop-down list.

---

4. Click the OK button to close the New Toolbar dialog box and create the toolbar. The application will display the new toolbar (with space for just one button and most of its name truncated), along with the Customize dialog box.

After you've created your new toolbar, you'll want to add commands to it. To do this, skip ahead to "Adding, Moving, and Removing Toolbar and Menu Commands."

Renaming a Toolbar To rename a toolbar you've created, right-click in the menu bar or in any displayed toolbar and choose Customize from the context menu to dis-

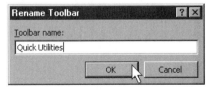

play the Customize dialog box. On the Toolbars tab, highlight the toolbar you want to rename, and then click the Rename button to display the Rename Toolbar dialog box. After entering the new name for the toolbar in the Toolbar Name text box, click the OK button to rename the toolbar. Click the Close button to close the Customize dialog box.

NOTE You cannot rename the built-in toolbars in Word and Excel.

Choosing Toolbar Options   You can choose the following options on the Options tab of the Customize dialog box:

- Select the Large Icons check box to have the toolbar buttons appear in a much larger size.
- Select the Show ScreenTips on Toolbars check box to have the ScreenTips information boxes pop up when you move the mouse pointer over a toolbar button.
- In Word, you can select the Show Shortcut Keys in Screen-Tips check box to have the ScreenTips include any key combination defined for the command linked to the toolbar button (as shown on the ScreenTip here).
- In the Menu Animations drop-down list, choose whether to have the application use one of the three animation effects when producing menus: Slide, Unfold, or Random. To best assess the resulting effects, click one menu with the mouse to display it, then move the mouse pointer along the menu bar to display the other menus rapidly in turn.

TIP   You can also set toolbar options in Outlook and Publisher. In Outlook, choose Tools ➤ Options and select the Large Toolbar Icons check box on the General tab of the Options dialog box. In Publisher, choose View ➤ Toolbars and Rulers, and select the Large Buttons or Show ToolTips check box in the Toolbars and Rulers dialog box.

Creating a New Menu

To create a custom menu in Word and Excel:

1. Right-click in the menu bar or in any displayed toolbar and choose Customize from the context menu to display the Customize dialog box.
2. Click the Commands tab to display it (unless it's already displayed).
3. In the Categories list box, select New Menu (it's at the end of the list).
4. In the Commands list box, click the New Menu item and drag it to the menu bar or to any displayed toolbar. You can place it among the existing menus, or before or after them, or among the buttons on a toolbar. The heavy black I-beam indicates where the new menu will appear when you drop the New Menu item. The application will add a new menu named New Menu.
5. Right-click the New Menu menu to display the context menu. Then drag through the text in the Name text box, enter the name you want the menu to have, and press ↵ or click elsewhere.

> **TIP** Enter an ampersand in the menu name before the letter you want to use as the *access key* for the menu. When you press Alt plus the access key (the underscored letter), you can quickly access that particular menu (for example, you can access the built-in File menu by pressing Alt+F). Make sure that the letter you assign isn't already used as an access key by another menu. (If the letter has already been used, the menu it was assigned to first will be activated when you press the key combination once; a second press will activate the second menu that uses the letter.)

After you've created a new menu, you can add commands to it, as described in the next section.

Adding, Moving, and Removing Toolbar and Menu Commands

To add, move, or remove commands from a toolbar or menu in Word and Excel:

1. Click the Commands tab of the Customize dialog box to display it.
2. From the Categories list, select the type of command you're looking for. The categories vary with the application but include most of the regular menus (File, Edit, and so on).
3. The available commands (and their associated buttons) for most categories appear in the Commands list box. In Word, if you choose All Commands, Macros, Fonts, AutoText, or Styles, you see a list of commands, macros, fonts, AutoText entries, or styles. To see a description of a command, select it and click the Description button.
4. Click the item you want, then drag it to the toolbar or menu you want it to appear on. The position of the heavy black I-beam or heavy black horizontal I-beam indicates where the command will land when you drop it (see Figure 2.2).
5. Optionally, you can change the appearance or name of the item you just added to the toolbar or menu. Right-click it to display the context menu.
   - If the command has an image, you can select Change Button Image and select one of the application's available buttons from the submenu (see Figure 2.3), or you can select Edit Button Image to display the Button Editor dialog box, in which you can modify the image on the button or draw a new button from scratch; click the OK button to close the Button Editor dialog box when you're finished.

FIGURE 2.2:
Drag a command from the Commands list box to a toolbar or menu to add it. The heavy black I-beam or horizontal beam indicates where the command will appear on the menu or toolbar.

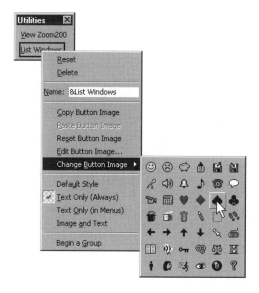

FIGURE 2.3:
You can quickly change a toolbar or menu command from the context menu.

- You can borrow an existing button image by right-clicking the button that has the image and choosing Copy Button Image from the context menu, then right-clicking the button to which you want to add the image and choosing Paste Button Image from the context menu.

- If the command has a text name, you can change its name. Select the name in the Name text box, make your changes, and press ↵ or click elsewhere on the screen when you're finished.

6. To rearrange the commands on a toolbar or menu, or to move items from one toolbar or menu to another, drag and drop them while the Customize dialog box is open. Watch the heavy black I-beam or heavy black horizontal I beam to see where the command will land when you drop it, as shown here.

7. To remove a command from a toolbar or menu, drag it off and drop it somewhere on the document or the Customize dialog box; drop it anywhere except on a toolbar or on the menu bar.

8. Click the Close button in the Customize dialog box when you've finished customizing your toolbars and menus.

Modifying a Toolbar Quickly

To modify an existing toolbar in Word and Excel, display it on screen by right-clicking the menu bar or a displayed toolbar and selecting it from the context menu. Then add, move, copy, or remove buttons as appropriate:

- To remove a button from the toolbar or menu bar, hold down Alt and drag the button off the toolbar or menu bar and into an open space in a document. Drop it there, and it will disappear.

WARNING   **Custom buttons (ones that you've created) are stored only on tool-bars or the menu bar; you can't save them in a separate location. So if you remove a custom button from a toolbar or from the menu bar, the application will delete the details of the button, and you'll need to re-create it if you want to use it again. If you want to store your custom buttons safely, create a toolbar as described in the previous section and use it to safely store custom buttons for future use.**

- To move a button from one toolbar to another, hold down Alt and drag the button from one toolbar to the other. You can also rearrange the buttons on a toolbar (and add spaces between them) by holding down Alt and dragging the buttons. This also works for buttons you've put on the menu bar, but not for menu items (pressing Alt with a menu open closes the menu).

- To copy a button from one toolbar to another, hold down Ctrl and Alt, then drag the button from one toolbar to the other. Again, this also works for buttons on the menu bar, but not for menu items.
- To add buttons to a toolbar or to the menu bar, display the toolbar, then right-click the menu bar or any displayed toolbar to display the Customize dialog box. Add the buttons to the toolbar as described in the previous section, and click the Close button to close the Customize dialog box when you've finished.

Deleting a Toolbar or Menu

To delete a toolbar you've created, right-click in the menu bar or in any displayed toolbar and choose Customize from the context menu to display the Customize dialog box. On the Toolbars tab, highlight the toolbar to delete and click the Delete button. Confirm the deletion in the message box that appears, and then click the Close button to close the Customize dialog box.

NOTE You can delete only toolbars you've created. You cannot delete any of the applications' built-in toolbars.

You don't need to display the Customize dialog box to delete a menu. Just hold down the Alt key and drag the menu off the menu bar or toolbar and drop it in open space (anywhere in the application window except on a toolbar or the menu bar).

Displaying and Hiding the Status Bar and Scroll Bars

The status bar at the bottom of the screen provides details about the Office application you're working in. The scroll bars let you quickly access other parts of your document, spreadsheet, or publication. Although both of these are useful, they also take up valuable space on screen. To toggle the display of the status bar and scroll bars in Word and Excel:

1. Choose Tools ➤ Options to display the Options dialog box.
2. If the View tab is not displayed, select it.
3. The View tab includes check boxes for the Status Bar, Horizontal Scroll Bar, and Vertical Scroll Bar. Select the check boxes to display these elements; clear the check boxes to hide them. In Excel, you can also choose to display or hide the Formula bar.
4. Click the OK button to close the Options dialog box and apply your choices.

In Publisher, right-click any displayed toolbar and then click the Status Line entry in the context menu to toggle the status bar on and off. Alternatively, choose View ➤ Toolbars and Rulers to display the Toolbars and Rulers dialog box, select or clear the Status Line check box, and click the OK button.

Undo and Redo

All the Office 97 Small Business Edition applications have Undo and Redo capabilities for undoing an action you've just performed and for redoing an action you've just undone. Publisher and Outlook can undo and redo only one action. Word and Excel can undo and redo a number of actions.

- To undo the last action, click the Undo button, press Ctrl+Z, or choose Edit ➤ Undo. To undo more than one action in Word or Excel, click the arrow to the right of the Undo button and choose the number of actions to undo from the drop-down list.
- To redo an action in Excel or Word, click the Redo button. To redo more than one action in Word or Excel, click the arrow to the right of the Redo button and choose the number of actions to redo from the drop-down list. To redo an action in Outlook or Publisher, click the Undo button again (to undo the undo, so to speak).

Spell Checking

The Office Spelling checker can be a great tool for making sure your documents, spreadsheets, publications, and messages contain no embarrassing typos. However, the Spelling checker is limited in what it can actually do for you. It simply tries to match words you type against the lists in its dictionary files, flagging any words it does not recognize and suggesting replacements that seem to be close in spelling. It does not consider the word in context beyond making sure that a word does not match the word immediately preceding it (it questions the second instance of a repeated word).

The Spelling checker is shared among the Office applications, but Word also offers on-the-fly spell-checking and can flag any offending word just microseconds after you type it.

> **NOTE** The AutoCorrect feature in Word and Excel offers another form of spell-checking. We'll look at AutoCorrect later in this chapter.

Regular Spell Checking

To start the Spelling checker in Word, click the Spelling button, choose Tools ➤ Spelling and Grammar, or double-click the Spelling indicator on the status bar. In Excel and Outlook, choose Tools ➤ Spelling. In Publisher, choose Tools ➤ Check Spelling.

If you have selected a portion of a file (such as some words or paragraphs in Word or Publisher, or a range or cells in Excel), the Spelling checker assumes that you want to spell-check the selection. After the Spelling checker has finished checking the selection, in Word and Outlook, it displays a message box asking if you want to spell-check the rest of the document; in Excel it displays a message box saying that it has finished checking the range of cells; and in Publisher, it goes ahead and finishes checking the rest of the item.

If you have not selected anything, the Spelling checker will automatically start spell-checking from the insertion point and, on reaching the end, will ask if you want to continue from the beginning of the file or item.

> **NOTE** If the Spelling checker does not find any words that it does not recognize, in Word, Outlook, and Excel, it will display a message box telling you that the spell-check is complete.

As soon as the Spelling checker encounters a word that does not match an entry in its dictionary, it displays the Spelling dialog box. Figure 2.4 shows the Spelling dialog box you'll see in Excel. You will see slightly different Spelling dialog boxes in the other Office applications, but they work in almost exactly the same way.

The dialog box has three main areas:

- The Not in Dictionary area shows the offending word.
- The Change To box shows the Spelling checker's best guess at the word you intended.
- The Suggestions box contains other words that the Spelling checker considers close to what you typed (you may disagree).

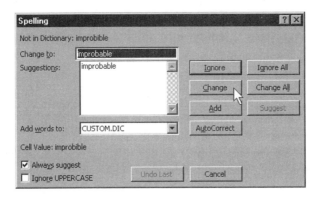

FIGURE 2.4: The Spelling dialog box appears when the Spelling checker finds a word that ins't in its dictionary.

You now have several choices:

- Click the Ignore button to skip the word if it's correct and is the only instance in the document.
- Click the Ignore All button to have the Spelling checker skip all instances of this word. Use this button for names, technical terms, or foreign words that will appear in only one document and which you don't want to add to your custom dictionaries.
- Click the Change button to change this instance of the word in the Not in Dictionary box to the word in the Change To box (or one of the suggested words—highlight it before clicking Change).
- Click the Change All button to change all instances of the word in the Not in Dictionary box to the word you've chosen.
- Click the Add button to add the word in the Not in Dictionary box to the custom dictionary currently selected in the Add Words To drop-down list box (see "Creating a Custom Dictionary"). Once you've added the word to the dictionary, the Spelling checker will not flag it again. (To select another dictionary, choose one from the Add Words To drop-down list.)
- If the Spelling checker has found a typo you feel you're likely to repeat, click the AutoCorrect button to add the Not in Dictionary word and the Change To word to the list of AutoCorrect entries (see "AutoCorrect").
- Click the Undo Last button to undo the last spell-checking change you made.
- Click the Suggest button to have the Spelling checker suggest words in the Suggestions box. (This option is available only if you have turned off the

Always Suggest Corrections option that the application offers in the Options dialog box.)

- Click the Cancel button to stop the spell-check.

On-the-Fly Spell-Checking and Grammar-Checking in Word

Word's on-the-fly spell-checking and grammar-checking offer you the chance to correct each spelling error and grammatical error the moment you make it or to highlight all the spelling errors and grammatical errors in a document and deal with them one by one. This is one of those partially great features that isn't right for everybody. The Spelling checker in particular can be intrusive and distracting, especially when you're typing like a maniac trying to finish a project on time; nonetheless, try leaving it enabled and see how you do. (If you've just installed Office, the Spelling checker is enabled by default.)

To enable Word's on-the-fly spell-checking and grammar-checking:

1. In Word, choose Tools ➤ Options to display the Options dialog box, or right-click the Spelling indicator on the status bar and choose Options from the context menu.
2. Click the Spelling & Grammar tab to bring it to the front.
3. In the Spelling area, select the Check Spelling as You Type check box.
4. In the Grammar area, select the Check Grammar as You Type check box.
5. Click the OK button to close the Options dialog box.

The Spelling checker will now put a squiggly red line under any word that doesn't match an entry in its dictionary. To spell-check one of these words quickly, right-click in it. Word will display a spelling menu with suggestions for spelling the word (or what it thinks the word is) along with four options:

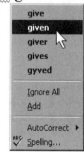

Ignore All Ignores all instances of this word.

Add Adds the word to the spelling dictionary currently selected (we'll get to dictionaries in a minute).

AutoCorrect Lets you quickly define one of Word's suggestions as an AutoCorrect entry for this word (we'll get to AutoCorrect a bit later in this chapter).

Spelling Fires up the full-fledged Spelling checker (as described in the previous section).

Once you have chosen Add or Ignore All for one instance of a word that the Spelling checker has flagged, Word removes the squiggly red underline from all other instances of that word. (If you have chosen another spelling for a flagged word, Word doesn't change all instances of that word.)

If you type the same word twice in immediate succession, Word will flag that, too, and offer you a different menu when you right-click in the word. This menu has the options Delete Repeated Word, Ignore, and Spelling. (In this case, if you choose Spelling, the Spelling and Grammar dialog box will appear to tell you that you've repeated the word.)

WARNING Text formatted with the *(no proofing)* language choice (which we'll look at in the "Language Formatting" section in Chapter 7) will not be spell-checked and will not display the squiggly red lines. If you find the Spelling checker apparently failing to catch blatant spelling errors, check the language formatting of the text in question.

The Grammar checker will put a squiggly green line under any word or construction that runs afoul of the rules that the Grammar checker is currently using. To see what the Grammar checker thinks is wrong with one of these words, right-click it and see what suggestions Word offers from the context menu.

The grammar suggestion may consist of a single word, as it does here. In other instances, Word may suggest a way to rewrite the whole sentence, or simply warn you that you've written an exceptionally long sentence.

The Spelling indicator on the status bar shows the status of spell-checking and grammar-checking. While you're typing (or inserting text), the icon will show a pen moving across the book; when Word has time to check the text, you'll see a check mark on the right page of the book if everything's fine, and a cross on the page if Word thinks there's one or more mistakes. You can double-click the Spelling indicator to start the Spelling checker, and you can right-click it to display a context menu of choices, including a quick way to hide and display spelling and grammatical errors.

WARNING   The Grammar checker often takes quite a while to identify mistakes, especially if you're running Word on anything less macho than a Pentium 166 or equivalent, and especially when you're inputting text at high speed. Check the Spelling indicator on the status bar when you take a break, and you may find that the Grammar checker, grumbling along in the background, has taken exception to something you wrote much earlier in the document.

Working with Dictionaries

The Office Spelling checker comes with a built-in dictionary of words that it uses for spell-checking. You can't change this dictionary—to save you from yourself, perhaps—but you can add words to the Office custom dictionary from all the applications. Word and Excel also allow you to create your own custom dictionaries. You can open and close your dictionaries as needed for the particular documents you're working on, but the more dictionaries you have open, the slower spell-checking will be.

The Default Custom Dictionary

Office starts you off with a default custom dictionary named Custom.dic, typically located in either the \Windows\MSApps\Proof\ folder or the \Program Files\Microsoft Office\Office\ folder. Whenever you run the Spelling checker, it adds any words that you select to the currently selected custom dictionary.

- To have Word add words to a different dictionary, click the Options button to display the Spelling & Grammar tab of the Options dialog box and choose the dictionary you want to use from the Custom Dictionary drop-down list.
- To have Excel add words to a different dictionary, select the dictionary in the Add Words To drop-down list in the Spelling dialog box.

TIP   When adding words to your custom dictionary, use lowercase letters unless the words require special capitalization. If you enter a word in lowercase, the Spelling checker will recognize it when you type it in uppercase or with an initial capital letter. If you enter a word with an initial capital letter, the Spelling checker will not recognize it if you type it using all lowercase letters.

Creating a Custom Dictionary

Using Word and Excel, you can create custom dictionaries for special uses. For example, you may want to create a dictionary for foreign words you use in your English documents, spreadsheets, or publications (as opposed to foreign words you use in your foreign-language documents, spreadsheets, or publications), or for technical terms that you don't want to keep in Custom.dic.

To create a new custom dictionary in Word:

1. Choose Tools ➤ Options to display the Options dialog box and then click the Spelling & Grammar tab. Alternatively, click the Options button in the Spelling dialog box in Word if you're in the middle of spell-checking.
2. Click the Dictionaries button to display the Custom Dictionaries dialog box.
3. Click the New button to open the Create Custom Dictionary dialog box.
4. Enter a name for the dictionary in the File Name text box and then click the Save button. Word will return you to the Custom Dictionaries dialog box, where you will see the new dictionary in the Custom Dictionaries list box.
5. Make sure that a check mark appears next to the name of the new dictionary to indicate that it has been selected, then click the OK button to close the Custom Dictionaries dialog box.
6. Click the OK button in the Options dialog box to close it.

To create a new custom dictionary in Excel, type the name for the custom dictionary into the Add Words To drop-down list box in the Spelling dialog box and press ↵. Excel will create the new custom dictionary and will set it as the default dictionary for the addition of new words.

Adding Custom Dictionaries from Other Folders

If you have custom dictionaries stored in folders other than the \proof\ folder or \Office\ folder (for example, you might share dictionaries with colleagues via a network), you need to tell the Spelling checker where they are:

1. In Word, choose Tools ➤ Options to display the Options dialog box, then click the Spelling tab. Alternatively, click the Options button in the Spelling dialog box if you are in the middle of spell-checking in Word.
2. Click the Dictionaries button to display the Custom Dictionaries dialog box.
3. Click the Add button to display the Add Custom Dictionary dialog box, which you'll recognize as a variant of the Open dialog box.
4. Navigate to the folder containing the custom dictionary you want to add using standard Windows navigation techniques.
5. Select the dictionary to add, then click the OK button. Word will add the

dictionary to the list of custom dictionaries, and then return you to the Custom Dictionaries dialog box.

6.   Make sure a check mark appears next to the new dictionary in the Custom Dictionaries list box, then click the OK button to close the Custom Dictionaries dialog box.

7.   Click the OK button in the Options dialog box to close it and return to your document or to the Spelling checker.

NOTE   **To remove a custom dictionary from the Custom Dictionaries list in the Custom Dictionaries dialog box, select the dictionary you want to remove and then click the Remove button. (This option just removes the dictionary from the list; it does not delete the dictionary file.)**

Editing a Custom Dictionary

One way to add the words you need to your custom dictionaries is to click the Add button whenever you run into one of those words during a spell-check. However, you can also open and edit your custom dictionaries in Word. This is particularly useful when you have added a misspelled word to a dictionary, and the Spelling checker is now merrily accepting a mistake in every document you write.

To edit a custom dictionary:

1.   In Word, choose Tools ➤ Options to display the Options dialog box, then click the Spelling tab.

2.   Click the Custom Dictionaries button to display the Custom Dictionaries dialog box.

3.   In the Custom Dictionaries list box, choose the dictionary you want to edit and click the Edit button. Word will display a warning telling you that it is about to turn off automatic spell-checking, and then it will open the dictionary as a Word file.

4.   Edit the dictionary as you would any other document, making sure you have only one word per line.

5.   Choose File ➤ Save to save the dictionary.

6.   Choose File ➤ Close to close the dictionary and return to your document.

7.   Choose Tools ➤ Options to display the Options dialog box, and turn automatic spell-checking back on by checking the Automatic Spell Checking check box on the Spelling tab. Click the OK button to close the Options dialog box.

AutoCorrect

The AutoCorrect tool in Word and Excel offers a number of features that help you quickly enter your text in the right format. AutoCorrect works similarly to Word's on-the-fly Spelling checker (which we looked at in the previous section), but AutoCorrect has far greater potential for improving your working life. Every time you finish typing a word and press the spacebar, Tab, Enter, or type any form of punctuation (comma, period, semicolon, colon, quotation marks, exclamation point, question mark, or even a % sign), AutoCorrect checks it for a multitude of sins and, if it finds it guilty, takes action immediately.

NOTE In Excel, pressing ←, →, ↑, ↓, Home, or End to move to another cell activates AutoCorrect as well.

The first four of AutoCorrect's features are straightforward; the fifth is a little more complex:

Correct TWo INitial CApitals   Stops you from typing an extra capital at the beginning of a word. If you need to type technical terms that need two initial capitals, clear the check box to turn this option off.

Capitalize First Letter of Sentence   Does just that.

Capitalize Names of Days   Does just that, too.

Correct Accidental Usage of cAPS lOCK Key   A neat feature that works most of the time. If AutoCorrect thinks you've got the Caps Lock key down and you don't know it, it will turn Caps Lock off and change the offending text from uppercase to lowercase and vice versa. AutoCorrect usually decides that Caps Lock is stuck when you start a new sentence with a lowercase letter and continue with uppercase letters; however, the end of the previous sentence may remain in the wrong case.

Replace Text as You Type   The best of the AutoCorrect features. We'll look at it in detail in the next section.

Replacing Text as You Type

AutoCorrect's Replace Text as You Type feature keeps a list of AutoCorrect entries. Each time you finish typing a word, AutoCorrect scans this list for that word. If the word is on the list, AutoCorrect substitutes the replacement text for the word.

Replace Text as You Type is a great way of fixing typos you make regularly, and in fact, Office 97 ships with a decent list of AutoCorrect entries already configured. If you type *awya* instead of *away* or *disatisfied* instead of *dissatisfied*, AutoCorrect will automatically fix the typo for you. But AutoCorrect is even more useful for setting up abbreviations for words, phrases, titles, or even names that you use frequently in your day-to-day work, saving you not only time and keystrokes, but also the effort of memorizing complex spellings or details. For example, you could create an AutoCorrect entry called *myadd* that contained your full address and zip code, or you could create an entry called *cme* that expanded to "Please do not hesitate to contact me if you have any questions about this matter." See "Adding AutoCorrect Entries Manually" for more details about using this feature.

You can add AutoCorrect entries to the list in three ways: automatically while running a spell-check; automatically during on-the-fly spell-checking (in Word only); or manually at anytime.

Adding AutoCorrect Entries While Spell-Checking

Adding AutoCorrect entries while spell-checking a document is a great way to teach AutoCorrect the typos you make regularly. When the Spelling checker finds a word it doesn't like, make sure the appropriate replacement word is highlighted in the Change To box; if the word in the Change To box isn't the appropriate one, type in the right word. Then click the AutoCorrect button in the Spelling dialog box. AutoCorrect will add the word from the Not in Dictionary box to the Replace list in AutoCorrect and the word from the Change To box to the With list in AutoCorrect. This way, you can build an AutoCorrect list tailored precisely to your typing idiosyncrasies.

Adding AutoCorrect Entries while On-the-Fly Spell-Checking

In Word, you can add AutoCorrect entries during an on-the-fly spell-check. Instead of accepting a suggestion from the top of the Spelling context menu, select the AutoCorrect menu item and choose the correct word from the submenu. Word will create the new AutoCorrect entry for you and correct the typo at the same time.

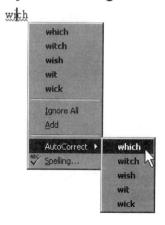

Adding AutoCorrect Entries Manually

Adding AutoCorrect entries while spell-checking is great for building a list of your personal typos but of little use for setting up AutoCorrect with abbreviations that will increase your typing speed dramatically. For that, you need to add AutoCorrect entries manually.

To add AutoCorrect entries manually:

1. If the replacement text for the AutoCorrect entry is in the current document or spreadsheet, select it.

TIP   **Word supports AutoCorrect entries that contain formatting, such as bold, italic, or paragraph formatting; Excel does not support formatting in AutoCorrect entries. To create an AutoCorrect entry that contains formatting, select the formatted text in a Word document before opening the AutoCorrect dialog box.**

---

2. Choose Tools ➤ AutoCorrect to display the AutoCorrect dialog box. Figure 2.5 shows the AutoCorrect dialog box for Word (the AutoCorrect dialog box for Excel is similar).

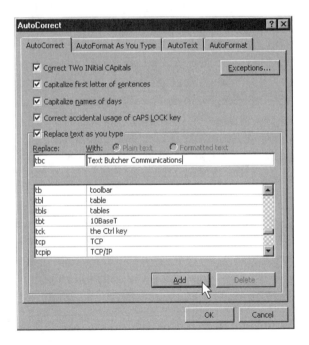

FIGURE 2.5:
Choose settings in the AutoCorrect dialog box to save yourself time and typos. This is the AutoCorrect dialog box for Word; it has a couple more options than the AutoCorrect dialog box for Excel.

3. Make sure that the Replace Text as You Type check box has been selected.
4. Enter the typo or abbreviation to replace in the Replace box.

> **TIP**
>
> When choosing the Replace text for an abbreviated AutoCorrect entry, avoid using a regular word that you might type and not want to have replaced. Try reducing the word or phrase to an abbreviation that you'll remember; for example, omit all the vowels and include only the salient consonants. If you doubt you will remember the right abbreviation, set up several AutoCorrect entries for the same Replace text; for example, set up *thr*, *thru*, *throgh*, and *thrugh* for *through*, and you can hardly go wrong.

5. Enter the replacement text in the With box.
   - If you selected text before opening the AutoCorrect dialog box, that text will appear in the With box.
   - In Word, if the text needs to retain its formatting, make sure the Formatted Text option button is selected. (The Formatted Text option button also needs to be selected if your selection contains a paragraph mark or tab character, because these count as formatting.)
6. Click the Add button or press Enter to add the AutoCorrect entry to the list. If there already is an AutoCorrect entry stored for that Replace text, the Add button will be replaced with a Replace button. When you press Enter or click this button, AutoCorrect will display a confirmation dialog box to make sure you want to replace the current entry.
7. To add another AutoCorrect entry, repeat steps 3 to 6.
8. To close the AutoCorrect dialog box, click the OK button.

> **TIP**
>
> You can include graphics, frames, borders, and so on in AutoCorrect entries for Word. For example, you can easily include your company's logo in an AutoCorrect entry for the company address for letterhead. Be imaginative— AutoCorrect can save you plenty of time. One other thing: Unless you create truly massive numbers of AutoCorrect entries (say, several thousand), you shouldn't need to worry about AutoCorrect slowing your computer down any more than Office 97 already does.

Deleting AutoCorrect Entries

To delete an AutoCorrect entry, open the AutoCorrect dialog box by choosing Tools ➤ AutoCorrect and select the entry from the list box at the bottom of the dialog box.

(You can also type the first few letters of an entry's Replace designation in the Replace box to scroll to it quickly.) Then click the Delete button. You can then delete additional AutoCorrect entries at the same time or click the OK button to close the AutoCorrect dialog box.

WARNING   **Remember that Word and Excel (and PowerPoint and Access, if you have them) share the AutoCorrect entries, so if you delete an entry while in Excel, it will no longer be available in Word. The only exception is that Excel can have AutoCorrect entries that have the same Replace designations as formatted AutoCorrect entries in Word. If you're planning to use duplicate AutoCorrect entries like this, be very careful when creating and deleting AutoCorrect entries.**

Find and Replace

Word, Excel, and Publisher have Find and Replace features, and Outlook includes a Find feature. Find and Replace lets you search for any *string* of text (a letter, several letters, a word, or a phrase) and replace chosen instances or all instances of that string with another string. For example, you could replace all instances of *dangerous* with *unwise,* or you could replace selected instances of *this fearful lunatic* with *the Vice President of Communications.* You can also use Find independent of Replace to locate strategic parts of your files quickly.

To find and replace text:

1. Choose Edit ➤ Replace to display the Replace dialog box (or, from the Find dialog box, click the Replace button). Figure 2.6 shows the Replace dialog box for Excel. The Replace dialog box in Publisher is a little different, and the Replace dialog box in Word is much more complex, but the principles are the same.

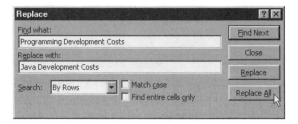

FIGURE 2.6:
The Replace dialog box for Excel. The Replace dialog boxes for Word and Publisher are similar but contain other features as well.

2. In the Find What box, enter the text to find. To find text you've searched for before in the current session, click the arrow at the right end of the Find What box and choose the text from the drop-down list.

3. In the Replace With box, enter the text you want to replace the found text with. To reuse replacement text from the current session, click the arrow at the right end of the Replace With box and choose the text from the drop-down list.

4. If applicable, choose a search direction from the Search drop-down list. Word offers Down, Up, or All. Excel offers By Rows or By Columns. (Publisher doesn't offer any choice of direction.)

5. Choose Replace options as appropriate:

- Match Case makes Find pay attention to the capitalization of the word in the Find What box. For example, with Match Case selected and **indolence** entered in the Find What box, Find will ignore instances of *Indolence* in the document and find only *indolence.*

- Find Whole Words Only (or Match Whole Words Only in Publisher) makes Find look only for the exact word entered in the Find What box and not for the word when it is part of another word. For example, by checking Find Whole Words Only, you could find *and* without finding *land*, *random*, *mandible*, and so on. In Word, Find Whole Words Only is not available if you type a space in the Find What box (for example, if you enter *and a*). Excel has a feature similar to Find Whole Words Only called Find Entire Cells Only.

6. Start the Replace operation by clicking the Find Next button, the Replace button, or the Replace All button:

- The Find Next button will find the next instance of the text in the Find What box. Once you've found it, click the Find Next button to skip to the next occurrence of the text without replacing it with the contents of the Replace With box.

- The first time you click the Replace button (if you haven't used the Find Next button first), it will find the next instance of the text in the Find What box. The second time you click the Replace button, it will replace the found instance of the text in the Find What box with the contents of the Replace With box and then find the next instance of the Find What text.

- The Replace All button will replace all instances of the text in the Find What box with the text in the Replace With box.

7. When you've finished your Replace operation, click the Close button or Cancel button to close the Replace dialog box.

NOTE **Word has much more powerful Find and Replace features than the other Office applications. We'll look at these features in Chapter 11.**

Help and the Office Assistants

The Office applications also come with a sophisticated Help system designed to solve all your problems (or at least the Office-related ones) swiftly and smoothly. You can get help in several ways:

- Turn to the ever-present Office Assistant for help. (To summon the Office Assistant if it's hiding, press F1 or click the Office Assistant button on the Standard toolbar.) Click in the Office Assistant window to display a Search box, as shown here. In the "What Would You Like to Do?" box, enter a question and press ↵ or click the Search button. Choose a suitable topic from the list that the Office Assistant retrieves.

- Choose Help ➤ Contents and Index to display the Index tab of the Help Topics dialog box (see Figure 2.7). Enter the first few letters of the word describing the topic in the first text box. Then choose the index entry in the list box and click the Display button to display information about that topic.

FIGURE 2.7:
On the Index tab of the Help Topics dialog box, enter the first few letters of the word describing the topic you're looking for, and then choose the index entry and click the Display button.

- Display the Help Topics dialog box, click the Contents tab for an overview of the Help topics available, then move down through the topics that interest you until you find the information that you want.
- Display the Help Topics dialog box and click the Find tab. Enter the word describing the topic you're looking for in the first box; select matching words from the second box to narrow the search. Then choose a topic in the third box and click the Display button.
- To get help in a dialog box, click the Help button (the button bearing the question mark in the upper-right corner of the dialog box) so the mouse pointer changes into a question mark.

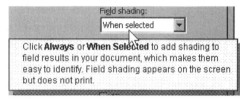

Click the question mark on the part of the dialog box that puzzles you, and the application will display an explanation of that item (and remove the question mark from the mouse pointer).

NOTE   **Publisher offers a sophisticated Help system that we'll explore in Chapter 19.**

Templates and Wizards

Word, Excel, Publisher, and Outlook come with *templates*, which are special files on which you can base different types of documents, spreadsheets, or publications:

- Word has templates for faxes, reports, memos, and more.
- Excel has templates for invoices, car loans, budgets, and so on.
- Publisher has templates for many different sizes and types of publications, including various Web pages.
- Outlook has templates for e-mail messages.

Word and Publisher also have *Wizards,* which are powerful macros that help you choose templates, enter information in them in the appropriate places, make formatting decisions, and generally produce professional-looking documents in a short amount of time. For example, when you run the Newsletter Wizard, Word will shepherd you through the creation of a newsletter in either a classic style or a modern style, with your choice of columns (from one to four) and contents.

We'll look at how to use templates easily and efficiently in the chapters that deal with each application.

Word and Excel share a common macro language, Visual Basic for Applications (VBA for short), that you can use to write macros that can range from the very simple (but useful) to the extremely complex and powerful. *Macros* are sequences of commands that can save you time and keystrokes. We'll look at macros in the chapters on Word (Part 3) and Excel (Part 4).

Object Linking and Embedding

Object Linking and Embedding (OLE) gives you two ways to include an *object* (information) created in one application in files created in other applications. By *linking* an object from, say, an Excel spreadsheet to a Word document, you can have the object automatically updated whenever you open or print the document (or any time you choose to update the object manually). By *embedding* the Excel object in the Word document, you can make that object part of the document, so you can change that object even when you don't have access to the Excel spreadsheet file. For example, you can include data from an Excel spreadsheet in a Word document, transfer the document to your laptop, and then hit the road.

***Object* is one of those great computer terms whose meaning people can never quite agree on. For the moment, think of an object as being a chunk of information (data) that knows which application it was created in—for example, a group of spreadsheet cells that knows it was created in Excel.**

Linking

Linking connects an object from one application (the *source* application) to a file created in another application (the *destination* application). The object appears in the destination application but stays connected to its source application. This way, if you change the object in the source application, the destination application automatically updates the object as well. For example, by linking the sales figures in an Excel spreadsheet to a Word document, you can make sure the document always has the latest sales figures in it.

Here's how to link information from another application to a Word document:

1. Start the source application for the object you want to link to a Word document.

2. Open the file containing the object.

TIP   **Linking objects to your documents makes your files only a little larger—not nearly as much larger as embedding. To keep your files as small as possible, choose linking over embedding when you have the choice.**

---

3. Select the object to insert. For example, if you're inserting a group of cells from a spreadsheet, select those cells.

4. Right-click in the selection and choose Copy from the context menu (or choose Edit ➤ Copy, or click the Copy button in that application, or choose Ctrl +C) to copy the object to the Clipboard.

5. Switch back to Word (or start Word if it isn't already running) by clicking the Microsoft Word icon on the Taskbar or by pressing Alt+Tab until the Word icon is selected in the task-switching list.

6. Position the insertion point where you want the linked item to appear in the Word document.

7. Choose Edit ➤ Paste Special to display the Paste Special dialog box (see Figure 2.8).

8. Select the Paste Link option on the left side of the dialog box.

9. In the As list box, choose the option that describes the item you're linking as *Object*. In Figure 2.8, the selected option is Microsoft Excel Worksheet Object because Excel is the source application. With other source applications, you'll see different descriptions.

10. To have the item display as an icon rather than at its full size, select the Display as Icon check box. To change the icon, click the Change Icon button and select a different icon in the Change Icon dialog box; then click the OK button. The Change Icon button appears when you select the Display as Icon check box.

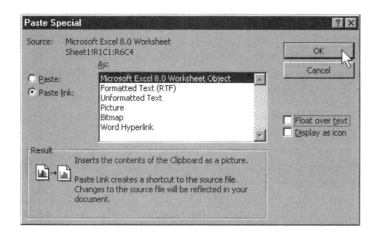

FIGURE 2.8:
To link information, select the Paste Link option in the Paste Special dialog box and choose the option that describes the item as *Object* from the As list box; here it's Microsoft Excel Worksheet Object.

11. To have the item appear in the *drawing layer* (a separate layer from the layer the text is in), so you can superimpose the object on the text (or text on the object), select the Float over Text check box. Otherwise, make sure this check box is cleared.

12. Click the OK button to insert the object in your document. Figure 2.9 shows an example of linked Excel spreadsheet cells inserted in a Word document.

Employee Update

We are glad to welcome the following employees:

ID	First Name	Last Name	Position
4401	Jerome	Frizzell	Accounting Clerk
4402	Leslie	Garland	Payroll Supervisor
4403	Katie	Russo	Receptionist
4404	Amir	Salindong	Sales Representative
4405	Susan	Santillan	Support Technician

FIGURE 2.9:
The cells from the Excel spreadsheet inserted in the document.

You can now format the linked object. For example, you can add borders and shading (which we'll discuss in Chapter 7) or place the object in a text box or frame (text boxes and frames are discussed in Chapter 5).

TIP To open the source file for the linked object in the application that created it, double-click the linked object (or the icon for it) in your document.

Updating and Deleting Links

You can update links manually, or update them automatically so that the link is updated every time you open the document that contains it or every time the source file is updated (when the document containing the link is open). In Word, you can also lock a link, so that it cannot be updated.

To set updating for links:

1. Open the document containing the links. Here we'll look at updating a Publisher publication that contains data from Excel and from Word.

2. Choose Edit ➤ Links to display the Links dialog box (see Figure 2.10).

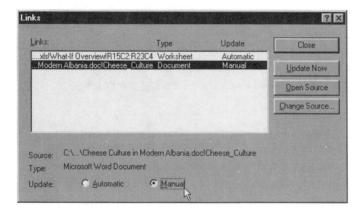

FIGURE 2.10:
Choose how to update your links in the Links dialog box.

3. In the list box, select the link or links you want to affect. (Use Shift+click to select several adjacent links or Ctrl+click to select nonadjacent links.)

4. Choose how the link or links should be updated by selecting the Automatic option button or the Manual option button. (When you want to update a link manually, click the Update Now button.)

NOTE
To lock the link or links in Word, click the Locked check box. Word will then dim the Automatic option button and the Manual option button to indicate the choices are not available. To unlock a link, select it in the list box and clear the Locked check box.

---

5. Click the Close button to close the Links dialog box.

To delete a linked object, click it to select it and then press the Delete key, or choose Edit ➤ Clear.

Breaking Links in Word

If you no longer need to be able to update a link or if you're planning to share a document with someone who won't have the linked information available, you can break the link in Word. This essentially turns the linked information into embedded information.

To break a link:

1. Choose Edit ➤ Links to display the Links dialog box.
2. Select the link or links in the list box.
3. Click the Break Link button. Word will display a message box to make sure that you want to break the link.
4. Click the Yes button to break the link.
5. Click the OK button or the Close button to close the Links dialog box.

WARNING **Once you've broken a link, you cannot restore it (except by reinserting the linked information, thus creating the link again).**

Embedding

To embed an object in a document, you follow a similar procedure to linking, but the result is completely different. Instead of creating a connection from the object in the destination file to its source file in the source application, the destination application saves in the file all the information needed to edit the object in place. Because the object is not connected to the source file, you cannot update the object in the destination file, but you can edit the object in the destination file to your heart's content without worrying about changing the source file.

TIP **The advantage of embedding over linking is that you can edit the embedded information even if you don't have the source file for the information on your computer. The disadvantage is that embedding objects makes the destination files much larger than linking objects does because all the information needed to edit the object is stored in the destination file (instead of just the information pointing to the source file).**

Embedding an Existing Object

To embed an existing object in a document:

1. Start the source application for the object you want to embed.

2. Open the file containing the object.

3. Select the object to embed. Here, we'll select a Word table to include in a Publisher publication.

Region	Highlights
Western	• Five new offices opened
	• 28% increase in revenue
South	• Implemented rightsizing
	• 53% reduction in costs
Central	• Active community outreach program

4. Right-click in the selection and choose Copy from the context menu (or choose Edit ➤ Copy, or click the Copy button in that application, or choose Ctrl+C) to copy the object to the Clipboard.

5. Switch to the destination application (in this case, Publisher) by using the Taskbar or by pressing Alt+Tab. (Start the destination application if it isn't yet running.)

6. Position the insertion point where you want to embed the object.

7. Choose Edit ➤ Paste Special to display the Paste Special dialog box.

8. Select the Paste option button.

9. In the As list box, choose the option that describes the item you're embedding as *Object*. In this case, the selected option is Microsoft Word Document Object because Word is the source application. With other source applications, you'll see different descriptions.

10. Click the OK button to insert the object in your document.

So far, this all seems singularly similar to linking. But you'll notice the difference when you double-click the embedded object: It displays a border from its source application (in this case, Word) and the toolbars and menus change to those of the source application, so you can edit the object within Publisher as if you were working in the source application, Word (see Figure 2.11).

TIP   **To edit a sound clip or video clip, right-click the object and choose the Edit option (for example, Edit Wave Sound Object) from the context menu. Double-click an embedded sound or video clip to run it.**

To delete an embedded object, select it by clicking it and pressing the Delete key, or choose Edit ➤ Clear.

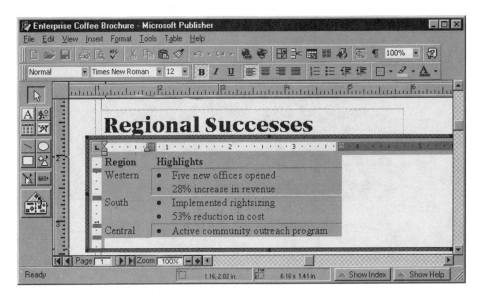

FIGURE 2.11:   Double-click an embedded object to edit it in place. The destination application will display the menus and toolbars from the source application. Here, Publisher is displaying Word's menus and toolbars.

Embedding a New Object

You can also create a new object and embed it at the same time. For example, you could insert a sound clip in your document like this:

1. Choose Insert ➤ Object to display the Object dialog box.
2. In Word or Excel, click the Create New tab to bring it to the front of the dialog box (unless it's already there). In Publisher, make sure the Create New option button is selected.
3. From the Object Type list, choose the type of object you want to insert.
4. Check the Display as Icon box if you want the object to display as an icon in the document. To change the icon for the object, click the Change Icon button (which will appear when you select the Display as Icon check box) and select a different icon in the Change Icon dialog box; click the OK button to return to the Object dialog box.
5. Click the OK button. The destination application will start the source application you chose.
6. Create the object as usual in that application.
7. Choose File ➤ Exit and Return to *Document Name* to close the source application and return to the destination application. The destination application will insert the object, which you can then position and format as necessary.

Part 2

Internet
Explorer

Chapter 3

BROWSING WITH INTERNET EXPLORER

FEATURING

- **Using the Internet Explorer interface**
- **Opening documents on the Web**
- **Changing your start page, search page, and Quick Links**
- **Dealing with error messages**

Internet Explorer, the Microsoft Web browser, is part of the ValuPack included with Office 97 Small Business Edition. (For instructions on setting up Internet Explorer, see the Appendix.) Internet Explorer provides full browsing capabilities that you can use on the World Wide Web or a corporate intranet.

In this chapter, I will discuss how to browse with Internet Explorer and how to set two of the most useful options for browsing. I will assume that you already have an Internet connection configured, either through a dial-up connection (via a modem) or through a local area network. In the next chapter, I will discuss how to configure Internet Explorer for maximum performance and for appropriate levels of security.

Using the Internet Explorer Interface

The Internet   To run Internet Explorer, double-click the icon named The Internet or Internet Explorer on the Desktop, or choose Start ➤ Programs ➤ Internet Explorer. You should see something like Figure 3.1.

The status bar shows information on the current operation (for example, *Connecting to site www.microsoft.com*) or information on any hyperlink the insertion point is pointing to.

As you can see in the figure, Internet Explorer provides a three-part toolbar for navigating the Web and Internet. When you start Internet Explorer, the Address bar is displayed as the lower layer of the toolbar, with the Links bar reduced to just a button at the right end of the Address bar. You can customize the size and position of the three parts of the Internet Explorer toolbar by clicking and dragging the toolbar handles at the left end of each toolbar. For example, you can drag the toolbar handles of the Links bar to the left from their default position to display more of the Links bar and less of the Address bar. Alternatively, you could drag the Links bar down to display it below the Address bar.

Here's how to use the buttons on the toolbar in Internet Explorer:

- Click the Back button to move to the previous page you were on.
- Click the Forward button to move forward to a page you were on before you clicked the Back button. (Until you have clicked the Back button, the Forward button will be dimmed and unavailable.)
- Click the Stop button to stop Internet Explorer from pursuing a jump that's in progress. (For example, if the jump has stalled or if the page is loading very slowly, you might want to stop it.)
- Click the Refresh button to have Internet Explorer reload the current page. You may want to do this if part of the page fails to transfer properly.
- Click the Home button to jump to your home page.
- Click the Favorites drop-down list button to display a menu of your Favorites. (I'll discuss what Favorites are later in this chapter.)

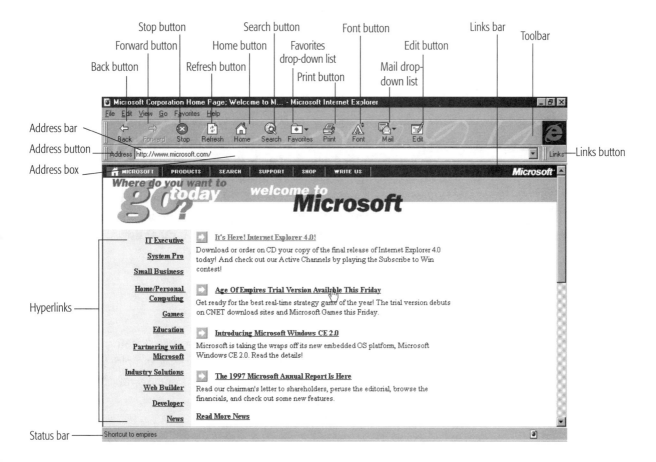

FIGURE 3.1: The main features of Internet Explorer

- Click the Print button to display the Print dialog box, which you can use to print the current page.
- Click the Font button one or more times to adjust the font for easy reading. Internet Explorer will cycle the display through five different font sizes.
- Click the Mail drop-down list button to display a menu of the Internet Explorer components, such as the optional newsreader, you have installed on your computer. You can move to one of these components by choosing it from the menu. For example, to move to your current mail program, choose the Read Mail item. (Internet Explorer will start the mail program if it is not already running.)

- Click the Edit button to display the current page in your currently designated HTML-editing software (typically, Word).
- Click either the Address button or the Links button to display the Links bar (when the Address bar is displayed) or the Address bar (when the Links bar is displayed).

TIP   **You can run two or more Internet Explorer windows at once, allowing you to download a page or a file in one window while continuing to browse in another. To start another Internet Explorer window, choose File ➤ New Window or press Ctrl+N. Be aware that both windows (or all windows) will be sharing your modem connection or network connection, so that they will slow each other down.**

Opening a Document

Each Web site or Web page is identified by a Uniform Resource Locator, or URL (usually pronounced "earl," sometimes spelled out as "U-R-L"). For example, the URL for the Microsoft Web site is `http://www.microsoft.com`. By pointing your browser at this URL, you can access the Microsoft Web site.

To open a document on the Web or on an intranet:

1. Choose File ➤ Open to display the Open dialog box (see Figure 3.2).

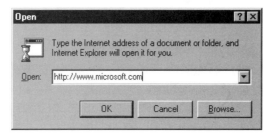

FIGURE 3.2:
To open a document on the Web, choose File ➤ Open, enter the address in the Open text box, and click the OK button.

2. In the Open text box, enter the address for the document or file you want to open, using any of the following three methods:

   - Type the name of the document or file into the Open text box.
   - To open a document or file you've accessed recently, click the down-arrow button at the right end of the Open text box and select the file from the drop-down list.
   - Click the Browse button to display the larger Open dialog box (see Figure 3.3), then select the file and click the Open button to place the file's name and path in the Open text box.

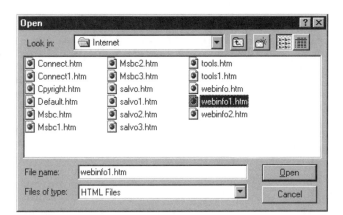

FIGURE 3.3:
Click the Browse button to display the larger Open dialog box so that you can select a file to open.

TIP   **You can also click in the Address box on the Address bar, type in the address of the document, and press Enter to access it.**

---

3. Click the OK button in the smaller Open dialog box to open the file.

You can also use Internet Explorer to open other types of documents, such as Word documents or Excel spreadsheets. To do so, enter the path and name of the document in the Open text box in the Open dialog box. Alternatively, click the Browse button to display the larger Open dialog box, choose All Files in the Files of Type drop-down list, select the file you want to open, and click the Open button. Then click the OK button in the smaller Open dialog box. Internet Explorer will open the file, using object linking and embedding (discussed in the previous chapter) as necessary.

Jumping to a Hyperlink

Many Web documents contain *hyperlinks*, which are jumps to other locations. Hyperlinks are typically displayed as underlined text, graphical objects, or pictures. (For example, Figure 3.1 contains a large number of hyperlinks, several of which are labeled.)

When you move the mouse pointer over a hyperlink, the mouse pointer takes on the shape of a hand with a finger pointing upward (also shown in Figure 3.1). To jump to the hyperlinked location, click the hyperlink.

Returning to a Previous Document

Because you often will access dead ends or pages that do not offer the information you need, you will often need to return to the previous document you accessed. There are several ways to move back to a document you've visited before:

- Click the Back button on the toolbar, as described earlier in the chapter.
- Click the down-arrow at the right end of the Address box and choose the document from the drop-down list.
- Choose one of the items listed in the Go menu.
- Choose Go ➤ Open History Folder to display an Explorer window containing a complete list of the pages you've visited. Double-click the item you want to return to.

Saving a Document

Although you cannot create new documents in Internet Explorer, you can use Internet Explorer to save documents to your computer. For example, you might want to save a copy of a Web page or intranet page to your hard disk so that you can examine it when your computer is offline.

To save the current page, choose File ➤ Save As File. Internet Explorer will display the Save As dialog box. Choose a location for the file as usual, specify a file name, and click the Save button.

Using Favorites

Internet Explorer lets you designate URLs as "Favorites," which allows you to access them quickly using the Favorites menu on the menu bar or the Favorites drop-down menu on the toolbar. (Most other Web browsers call these "bookmarks.")

To add the current URL (the site that Internet Explorer is currently displaying) to the Favorites menu, choose Favorites ➤ Add to Favorites. Internet Explorer will display the Add to Favorites dialog box (see Figure 3.4). In the Name box, enter the name by which to identify the Favorite. (You will often need to change the default name, which will be the title of the page.) Click the OK button to create the Favorite.

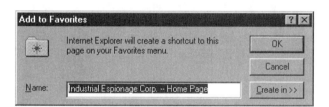

FIGURE 3.4:
To add a URL to your list of Favorites, choose Favorites ➤ Add to Favorites, enter a name, and click the OK button.

If you want to create the Favorite in a different folder, click the Create In button in the Add to Favorites dialog box to display an additional part of the dialog box. Select the folder in the Create In list box and click the OK button. (You can click the New Folder button to create a new subfolder of the current folder.) This will produce an entry on the Favorites menu that displays a submenu of the contents of the folder.

To organize your favorites, choose Favorites ➤ Organize Favorites. Internet Explorer will display the Organize Favorites dialog box. You can then move, rename, or delete a Favorite by selecting it and clicking the Move, Rename, or Delete button. When you're finished working with your Favorites, click the Close button to close the Organize Favorites dialog box.

Customizing Your Start Page and Quick Links

Apart from Favorites, Internet Explorer provides several features for quickly accessing particular sites. These include your start page, your search page, and Quick Links buttons.

Your *start page* (also called a *home page*) is the page that Internet Explorer automatically opens when you start Internet Explorer and when you click the Home button on the toolbar. You'll usually want to change your start page from the default setting to the site you want to see first in every Internet Explorer session.

Your *search page* is the page that Internet Explorer displays when you click the Search button on the toolbar. You'll usually want to set your search page to your favorite Internet or intranet directory—perhaps an Internet site, such as Yahoo or AltaVista, or a local corporate directory page.

The Links bar provides five *Quick Links* to regularly updated Microsoft sites, typically named Best of the Web, Today's Links, Web Gallery, Product News, and Microsoft. (The names of these Quick Links vary a little in different versions of Internet Explorer.) You can access any of these sites by clicking its button on the Links bar.

You can change your start page or search page, or change the Quick Links buttons to point to different sites as follows:

1. Navigate to the page you want to make your start page, search page, or into a Quick Link page.
2. Choose View ➤ Options to display the Options dialog box, then click the Navigation tab to display it.
3. In the Page drop-down list, choose Start Page, Search Page, or Quick Link #1 to Quick Link #5, as appropriate.
4. Click the Use Current button to set the start page, search page, or Quick Link page to the current page.
5. Click the OK button to close the Options dialog box.

To change your start page, search page, or Quick Links page (or pages) back to the default setting, repeat the above procedure and click the Use Default button.

CONFIGURING INTERNET EXPLORER

- **Choosing how Internet Explorer runs**
- **Guarding against malevolent programs**
- **Using the Content Advisor to screen objectionable content**
- **Clearing your viewing history and temporary files**

In this chapter, I'll discuss the most important of the many options that Internet Explorer offers for controlling how it runs. You can configure most aspects of its behavior—everything from the font size Internet Explorer uses to display text, to security, to improving performance over a slow Internet connection.

The Options Categories

To choose options for Internet Explorer, select View ➤ Options to display the Options dialog box. Internet Explorer divides the options into six categories—General, Connection, Navigation, Programs, Security, and Advanced—each of which occupies one tab in the Options dialog box. We'll look at each tab in turn in this chapter.

I should mention one thing before we start: Internet Explorer 3 has been through several different versions in a remarkably short time. The version you're using may have slightly different features that those shown here, and some features may be on a different tab in the Options dialog box.

General Options

The options on the General tab of the Options dialog box (see Figure 4.1) control most of what you'll see on screen in Internet Explorer:

- The Multimedia group box lets you choose whether to have Internet Explorer display pictures, play sounds, and play videos. Pictures, sounds, and video files take more time to download than text, so if you have a slow connection, consider clearing the check box for any of the three that you can dispense with. Pictures tend to be integral to Web pages, while sound and video are easier to do without.
- The Colors group box lets you select colors for text and the background in Internet Explorer. To choose colors, clear the Use Windows Colors check box, click the Text button or Background button to display the Color dialog box, select the color, and click the OK button.
- The Links group box lets you set the color for links you've visited and links you haven't visited. Click the Visited button or the Unvisited button to display the Color dialog box, select the color, and click the OK button. You can also clear the Underline Links check box if you don't want Internet Explorer to underline links.
- In the Toolbar group box, select or clear the check boxes for display options for the toolbar: Standard Buttons (the toolbar buttons from Back through Edit), Address Bar, Links (the Links bar), Text Labels (the text on the buttons), and Background Bitmap (the scrawled pattern across the toolbar buttons).
- To change the fonts Internet Explorer uses, click the Font Settings button and choose fonts in the Proportional Font drop-down list and the Fixed-Width Font drop-down list in the Fonts dialog box.

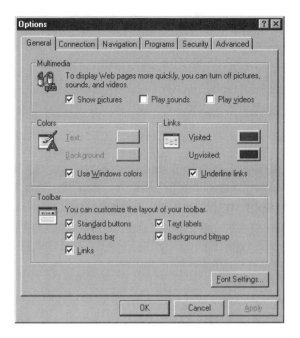

FIGURE 4.1:
The General tab of the Options dialog box

Connection Options

The Connection tab provides options for controlling your connection to the Internet:

- To have Internet Explorer connect automatically to the Internet as necessary, select the Connect to the Internet as Needed check box and specify the appropriate dial-up connection in the Use the Following Dial-Up Networking Connection drop-down list. When this check box is selected, Internet Explorer will automatically start your Internet connection when you request a Web page.

- Select the Disconnect If Idle for *XX* Minutes check box and set a suitable value in the text box if you want Internet Explorer to automatically terminate your Internet connection after a number of minutes passing without your using it. This is most useful for dial-up Internet connections that cost you money, either for the phone line or for connect time.

- Select the Perform System Security Check before Dialing check box if you want Internet Explorer to security-check your password information before connecting to the Internet. This is most useful when your computer is connected to a local area network.

- Select the Connect through a Proxy Server check box if you need to connect to the Internet through a proxy server rather than directly. Click the Settings button to display the Proxy Settings dialog box, and then enter the necessary information. (You may need to consult your network administrator for this information.)

NOTE   **A *proxy server*, often used on a local area network, is a computer that stores frequently requested information so that it can deliver it quickly upon request. A proxy server can also restrict access to certain addresses; for example, a proxy server on a company network might ban access to sports sites or sex sites. The disadvantage to using a proxy server is that the information on the pages it stores may not be up-to-the-minute.**

Navigation Options

The Navigation tab of the Options dialog box lets you control your start page, search page, Quick Links, and browsing history.

Use the options in the Customize group box to set your start page, search page, and Quick Links pages, as discussed in the previous chapter.

Your history, a record of the Web sites you visited, enables you to navigate with the Back and Forward buttons, but it also enables other people to see which sites you've been accessing. In the History group box, you can click the View History button to display your History folder in an Explorer window. You can then double-click an item to visit that site, or select an item and press the Delete key to delete it. Close the History folder when you've finished with it. You can also click the Clear History button to purge the record that Internet Explorer keeps of the sites you've visited. Do this when you need to protect yourself from security threats or embarrassment. Internet Explorer will display the Internet Properties dialog box to confirm the deletion; click the Yes button to proceed.

Programs Options

The Programs tab of the Options dialog box lets you specify which e-mail and news-reader applications to use, and which applications to use for viewing files that Internet Explorer itself cannot display or play (such as particular formats of graphics or sounds).

- If you've installed Outlook, Microsoft Outlook should be selected in the Mail drop-down list. (If you use a different e-mail application, make sure that application is selected instead.)
- If you have a newsreader application installed, select it in the News drop-down list if it does not already appear there.

TIP **Microsoft provides a free newsreader in the Internet Mail and News package, which is available for download in the Internet Explorer area of the Microsoft Web site at http://www.microsoft.com/ie.**

- To configure viewers, click the File Types button to display the File Types dialog box, and specify the file type and application as usual. (For details on configuring file types, consult the Help files or a book such as *Mastering Windows 95*.)
- The Internet Explorer Should Check to See Whether It Is the Default Browser check box controls whether Internet Explorer makes sure it's the default browser whenever you run it, to ensure that Windows knows Internet Explorer is the application associated with certain types of files. Unless you have installed or run another browser (for example, Navigator), Internet Explorer will be the default browser. In any case, leave this check box selected.

Security Options

The Security tab of the Options dialog box contains some of the most important options for browsing the Web: the Content Advisor and Active Content.

Content Advisor

The Content Advisor feature enables you to set up content screening based on the ratings of the Recreational Software Advisory Council rating service for the Internet (RSACi). To do so, click the Enable Ratings button. The first time you do this, Internet Explorer will display the Create Supervisor Password dialog box. Enter the password in the Password text box and the Confirm Password text box, then click the OK button. Internet Explorer will display the Content Advisor dialog box (see Figure 4.2).

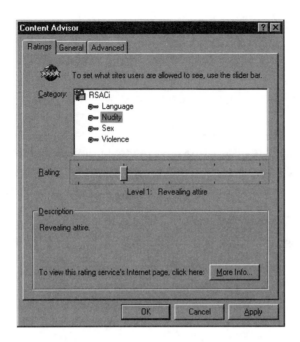

FIGURE 4.2:
Use the Content Advisor dialog box to screen out objectionable content

On the Ratings tab, select the item in the Category list box and drag the Rating slider to a suitable level. Each of the items has five levels, ranging from 0 (none of the offensive item) to 4 (lots of it). For example, the Violence levels are No Violence (0), Fighting (1), Killing (2), Killing with Blood and Gore (3), and Wanton and Gratuitous Violence (4). The Language levels are Inoffensive Slang (0), Mild Expletives (1), Moderate Expletives (2), Obscene Gestures (3), and Explicit or Crude Language (4).

Internet Explorer will display a Content Advisor message box telling you that Content Advisor has been installed. Click the OK button to return to the Options dialog box, where the Enable Ratings button will have changed to Disable Ratings.

To adjust the settings for Content Advisor, click the Settings button. Internet Explorer will display the Supervisor Password Required dialog box. Enter your password and click the OK button to display the Content Advisor dialog box, then change the settings and click the OK button.

To disable ratings again, click the Disable Ratings button. Internet Explorer will display the Supervisor Password Required dialog box. Enter your password and click the OK button. Internet Explorer will display a Content Advisor message box telling you that Content Advisor has been turned off.

Active Content

The Active Content group box lets you choose whether to download certain types of active content. The Allow Downloading of Active Content controls whether Internet Explorer downloads animations, multimedia files, and the like. The Enable ActiveX Controls and Plug-Ins check box and the Run ActiveX Scripts check box control whether Internet Explorer uses ActiveX, Microsoft's active content. The Enable Java Programs check box controls whether Internet Explorer runs programs written in Java, a popular programming language.

Click the Safety Level button and choose an appropriate level of safety (High, Medium, or None) in the Safety Level dialog box. Usually, you'll want the High setting unless all the content you access is on a secure intranet and known to be harmless, in which case you might choose None.

Advanced Options

The Advanced tab of the Options dialog box contains a large number of options, most of which you should know about.

The options in the Warnings group box specify when Internet Explorer should warn you about a potentially insecure action you're about to perform. Usually, you'll want to keep these check boxes selected:

- Select the Warn before Sending over an Open Connection if you want Internet Explorer to warn you when you are sending information over a connection that is not secure. (Others might be able to intercept the information you send.) Choose the Only When I'm Sending More than One Line of Text option button or the Always option button as appropriate. The former option button is useful when you're often specifying small amounts of text without concerns about security. For example, when you're using an Internet search engine to locate information, you don't want Internet Explorer to keep warning you that you're transmitting text over an unsecure connection.
- Select the Warn if Changing between Secure and Unsecure Mode check box to have Internet Explorer warn you when you move from a secure Web site to an unsecure one, or vice versa. At a secure Web site, you can be sure that nobody is intercepting information you send; at an unsecure Web site, your information is potentially in jeopardy.

- Select the Warn about Invalid Site Certificates check box to have Internet Explorer warn you when the URL in a certificate is not valid. Certificates allow you to ensure that certain content comes from the person, site, or publisher it claims to be coming from. For example, if you download an application from a company you don't know about, you might choose to view its certificate to make sure the company is bona fide.
- Select the Warn before Accepting "Cookies" check box to have Internet Explorer warn you when a Web site sends your computer a cookie. Cookies are files containing information that sites use to identify your computer. For many sites, they are useful and beneficial, but they represent a potential security hazard that you should be aware of.

The two buttons in the Temporary Internet Files group box let you control the temporary Internet files in which Internet Explorer stores information while you're browsing:

- To display an Explorer window containing the files in the temporary folder, click the View Files button.
- Click the Settings button to display the Settings dialog box, where you can adjust the amount of disk space to use for storing the temporary files. You can also choose when Internet Explorer should check for new versions of stored pages: Every Visit to the Page (typically the most useful option), Every Time You Start Internet Explorer, or Never. To delete all the temporary files, click the Empty Folder button in the Settings dialog box, and then click the Yes button in the Internet Properties dialog box that Internet Explorer displays.

Usually, you'll want to have these four options at the bottom of the Advanced tab selected:

- The Show Friendly URLs check box controls whether Internet Explorer shows the full URL for a site on the status bar.
- The Highlight Links when Clicked check box controls whether Internet Explorer places an emphasis on links when you click them.
- The Use Smooth Scrolling check box controls whether Internet Explorer scrolls Web pages in jerks or at a steady speed.
- The Use Style Sheets check box controls whether Internet Explorer uses style sheets to interpret Web pages.

Finally, the Enable Java JIT Compiler check box controls whether Internet Explorer uses its just-in-time (JIT) compiler to compile and run Java programs at sites you visit.

Part 3

Word

Chapter 5

GETTING STARTED IN WORD

FEATURING

- **Setting up the Word screen**
- **Entering text, graphics, and frames**
- **Moving the insertion point**
- **Selecting items**
- **Using Word's different views**

In this chapter, we'll race through the basics of creating documents with Word—setting up the screen so you have on it what you need, entering the text (and illustrations) of your document, moving the insertion point and selecting items, and using the different views that Word provides for working with your documents.

Setting Up Your Screen

First, let's quickly look at how Word appears on the screen (see Figure 5.1).

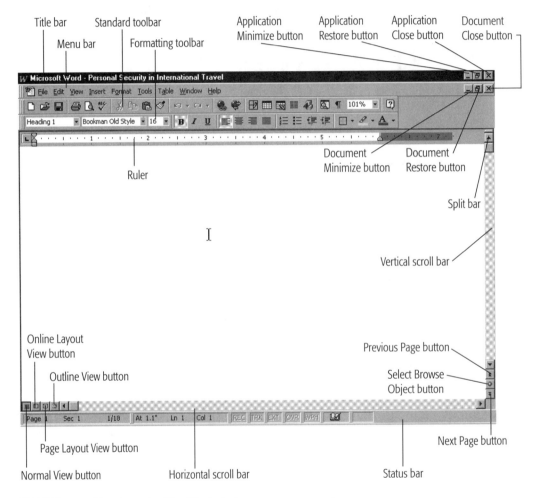

FIGURE 5.1: The elements of the Word window

Before you start working in Word, you may want to customize your screen. At a minimum, consider maximizing the Word window by clicking the Maximize button on the title bar and then maximizing the document you're working on within the Word window by clicking the Document Maximize button. Once you've maximized the Word window or the document window, Word will replace the Application Maximize button with an Application Restore button or the Document Maximize button with the Document Restore button; click a restore button to restore the window to its pre-maximized size.

You may also want to use Zoom to enlarge or shrink the display. If so, skip ahead to "Zooming the View" later in this chapter.

Displaying and Hiding the Rulers

To help you position your text optimally on the page, Word offers a horizontal ruler in Normal view and both horizontal and vertical rulers in Page Layout view and Print Preview.

You can either display the ruler on-screen or keep it hidden but available. To toggle the display of the ruler on and off, choose View ➤ Ruler.

To pop up the horizontal ruler momentarily, move the insertion point to the thin bar at the top of the current document window.

The ruler will appear automatically.

The ruler will disappear when you move the insertion point away.

To pop up the vertical ruler in Page Layout view or Print Preview, move the insertion point to the thin bar at the left edge of the current document window. The vertical ruler will appear automatically, and it will disappear when you move the insertion point away again.

NOTE **You cannot display the ruler continuously in Online Layout view, but you can pop it up when you need it.**

If the rulers will not pop up, select Tools ➤ Options to display the Options dialog box. Click the General tab and select the Provide Feedback with Animation check box. Click the OK button to close the Options dialog box.

Working with Text, Graphics, and Text Boxes

As with most word-processing applications, the basic unit Word thinks in is the paragraph. These aren't paragraphs as people generally understand them: A *paragraph* in Word consists of a paragraph mark (made by pressing Enter) and any text (or graphic) between it and the previous paragraph mark (or the beginning of the document). In other words, a paragraph consists of anything (text, a graphic, space, or even nothing at all) that appears between two paragraph marks, up to and including the second paragraph mark. This seems a strange way to describe it, but a paragraph mark with nothing between it and the previous paragraph mark is considered a full paragraph. You can treat each paragraph as a unit for formatting with styles (which we'll look at in Chapter 7) or for moving and copying.

TIP

If you don't see paragraph marks on your screen, click the ¶ button on the Formatting toolbar. This is the Show/Hide button, and it toggles the display of spaces, tabs, paragraph marks, and the like. Some people find it easier to work with these marks displayed; others find them distracting. You can also display and hide these marks by pressing Ctrl+Shift+8.

Entering Text

To enter text in your document, simply position the insertion point where you want the text to appear and type it in. Word will automatically wrap text as it reaches the end of a line. Press Enter to start a new paragraph.

If you want to move to a new line without starting a new paragraph—for example, so there is no space between lines—press Shift+Enter to start a new line within the same paragraph.

When you reach the end of a page, Word will automatically break text onto the next page. If you want, you can start a new page at any point by inserting a page break. To do so, press Ctrl+Enter.

Insert and Overtype Modes

Word offers two modes for adding text to your documents: *Insert mode* and *Overtype mode*. In Insert mode (the default mode), characters you type are inserted into the text to the left of the insertion point, pushing any characters to the right of the insertion point farther to the right. If you want to replace existing text in Insert mode, select the text using either the mouse or the keyboard and type in the text you want to insert in its place. In Insert mode, the OVR indicator on the status bar is dimmed.

In Overtype mode, any character you type replaces the character (if any) to the immediate right of the insertion point. When Word is in Overtype mode, the OVR indicator on the status bar is active (darkened).

To toggle between Insert mode and Overtype mode, double-click the OVR indicator on the status bar.

Moving the Insertion Point

In Word, you move the insertion point using either the mouse or the keyboard.

Using the Mouse

To position the insertion point using the mouse, simply move the mouse pointer to where you want it and click.

Use the vertical scroll bar or the roller on the IntelliMouse to move up and down through your document (as you drag the box in the scroll bar in a multipage document, Word will display a small box showing you which page you're on). Use the horizontal scroll bar to move from side to side as necessary.

TIP   **If you're continually scrolling horizontally in Normal view to see the full width of your documents, turn on the Wrap to Window option, which makes the text fit into the current window size, regardless of the window's width. To turn on Wrap to Window, choose Tools ➤ Options, click the View tab, and select the Wrap to Window check box. Click OK to close the Options dialog box.**

Click the Next Page and Previous Page buttons to move to the next page and previous page, respectively. Make sure these buttons are black, which indicates that Word is browsing by page. If they're blue, that means Word is browsing by a different item, such as sections or comments. To reset Word to browse by page, click the Object Browser button between the Next and Previous Page buttons and choose the Browse by Page button in the Object Browser list, as shown here.

Using Keyboard Shortcuts

Word offers a number of keystrokes and key combinations to move the insertion point swiftly through the document. Besides ← to move left one character, → to move right one character, ↑ to move up one line, and ↓ to move down one line, you can use the following keystrokes and combinations:

Keystroke	Action
Ctrl+→	One word to the right
Ctrl+←	One word to the left
Ctrl+↑	To the beginning of the current paragraph or (if the insertion point is at the beginning of a paragraph) to the beginning of the previous paragraph
Ctrl+↓	To the beginning of the next paragraph
End	To the end of the current line
Ctrl+End	To the end of the document
Home	To the start of the current line
Ctrl+Home	To the start of the document
PageUp	Up one screen's worth of text
PageDown	Down one screen's worth of text
Ctrl+PageUp	To the first character on the current screen
Ctrl+PageDown	To the last character on the current screen

TIP   **You can quickly move to the last three places you edited in a document by pressing Shift+F5 (Go Back).**

Selecting Text

In Word, you can select text using the keyboard, the mouse, or the two in combination. You'll find that some ways of selecting text work better than others with certain equipment; experiment to find which are the fastest and most comfortable methods for you.

Selecting Text with the Mouse

The simplest way to select text with the mouse is to position the insertion point at the beginning or end of the block you want to select and click and drag to the end or beginning of the block.

TIP

Word offers an automatic word selection feature to help you select whole words more quickly with the mouse. When this feature is switched on, as soon as you drag from one word to the next, Word will select the whole of the first word and the whole of the second; when the mouse pointer reaches the third, it selects that, too. To temporarily override automatic word selection, hold down the Alt key before you click and drag. To turn off automatic word selection, choose Tools ➤ Options to display the Options dialog box. Click the Edit tab, and clear the When Selecting, Automatically Select Entire Word check box to turn it off. Then click OK. To turn automatic word selection on, select the When Selecting, Automatically Select Entire Word check box.

You can also select text with multiple clicks:
- Double-click in a word to select it.
- Triple-click in a paragraph to select it.
- Ctrl+click in a sentence to select it.

In the selection bar on the left side of the screen (where the insertion point turns from an I-beam to an arrow pointing up and to the right), you can click to select the following text:
- Click once to select the line the arrow is pointing at.
- Double-click to select the paragraph the arrow is pointing at.
- Triple-click (or Ctrl+click once) to select the entire document.

Selecting Text with the Keyboard

To select text with the keyboard, hold down the Shift key and move the insertion point by using the keyboard shortcuts given in the "Using Keyboard Shortcuts" section earlier in the chapter.

You can also select text by using Word's Extend Selection feature, though I wouldn't recommend it—it takes longer than the other ways. Press the F8 key once to enter Extend Selection mode; EXT will appear undimmed on the status bar. Press F8 a second time to select the current word, a third time to select the current sentence, a fourth time to select the current paragraph, and a fifth time to select the whole document. Then press the Esc key to turn off Extend Selection mode. The F8 key also works in the following manner: To select a sentence, press F8 at the beginning of the sentence and then press the punctuation mark that appears at the end of the sentence. If you wish to select a portion of text, position the insertion point at the beginning of that text, press F8, and then press the letter up to which you want to select; if there is another instance of the letter before the one you want to select, press the letter again. Select a paragraph by placing the cursor at the start of the paragraph and pressing F8 and then the Enter key.

Selecting Text with the Mouse and Keyboard

Word also lets you select text using the mouse and keyboard together. These techniques are well worth trying out, as you can quickly select awkward blocks of text—for example, you can select a few sentences from a paragraph or several columns of characters.

To select a block of text using the mouse and the keyboard, position the insertion point at the start (or end) of a block and click. Then move the insertion point to the end (or start) of the block—scroll if necessary with the IntelliMouse roller or with the scroll bar, but don't use the keyboard—hold down the Shift key, and click again.

To select columns of characters, hold down the Alt key, and click and drag from one end of the block to the other (see Figure 5.2). This technique can be very useful for getting rid of extra spaces or tabs that your colleagues have used to align text.

NOTE Selecting text in a table works a little differently from selecting regular text; we'll discuss that in Chapter 9.

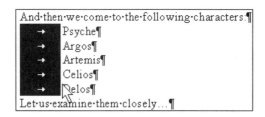

FIGURE 5.2:
To select columns of characters without selecting whole lines, hold down the Alt key and drag through the block.

Deleting Text

Word lets you delete text swiftly and easily:

- To delete the character to the left of the insertion point, press Backspace.
- To delete the character to the right of the insertion point, press Delete.
- To delete a block of text, select it and press the Delete key.
- To delete the word to the right of the insertion point, press Ctrl+Delete. (This deletes from the insertion point to the beginning of the next word—or the end of the line, if the current word is the last one in the line—so if the insertion point is in a word when you press Ctrl+Delete, you will delete only the remainder of the word.)
- To delete the word to the left of the insertion point, press Ctrl+Backspace. (Again, if the insertion point isn't at the end of the word, only the part of the word to the left of the insertion point will be deleted.)

TIP   **You can also delete selected text by choosing Edit ➤ Clear or by right-clicking in the selection and choosing Cut from the context menu that appears. (Some context menus—which are different for different elements of Word documents—don't have a Cut command.)**

Inserting and Sizing Pictures

You can easily insert pictures of various types into Word documents. Once you've inserted them, you can resize them and crop them as necessary.

Inserting a Picture

To insert a picture at the insertion point:

1. Choose Insert ➤ Picture to display the Picture submenu.
2. Choose from the six options for inserting a picture: Clip Art, From File, AutoShapes, WordArt, From Scanner (if one is available), or Chart. Here we'll choose From File and look at inserting a picture you have in a file. Word displays the Insert Picture dialog box (see Figure 5.3).
3. Navigate to the folder containing the picture you want using standard Windows techniques. Click the Up One Level button (or press the Back-space key) to move up one level of folders, or double-click the folders displayed in

the main window to drill down through them to the folder you want. Word starts off by displaying all the types of pictures it knows, but you can restrict the display to certain types of graphics by choosing them from the Files of Type drop-down list.

4. Choose the picture file to insert in the main list box. Click the Preview button to display the Preview box to make sure you've got the right file.

5. Click the Insert button to insert the picture in your document.

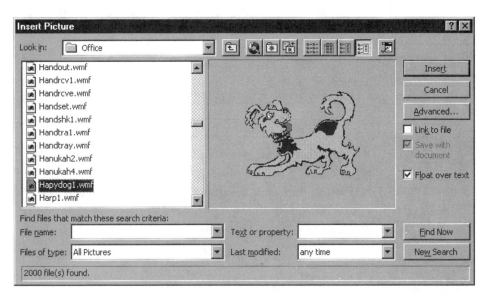

FIGURE 5.3: In the Insert Picture dialog box, choose the picture to insert and click the Insert button.

Resizing and Cropping Pictures

To resize a picture quickly, first click it to select it. Word will display the Picture toolbar (see Figure 5.4) and will display an outline around the picture with eight handles, one at each corner and one in the middle of each side. Drag a corner handle to resize the image proportionally; drag a side handle to resize the image only in that dimension (horizontally or vertically).

To crop a picture quickly (cutting off part of it), click the picture to select it, and then click the Crop button to select the cropping tool. The mouse pointer will take on the cropping handles. Move the mouse pointer over one of the picture's handles, and drag inwards or outwards to crop the picture. Click the Crop button again or press Esc to restore the mouse pointer.

To resize or crop a picture more precisely:

1. Click the picture to display the outline and handles around it.
2. Click the Format Picture button or choose Format ➤ Picture to display the Format Picture dialog box (see Figure 5.5).
3. To crop a picture, make sure the Picture tab is displayed (click on it if it isn't). Enter how much to crop in the Left, Right, Top, and Bottom boxes in the Crop From area.
4. To resize the picture, click on the Size tab to display it. Then either set Width and Height percentages in the Scale area, or enter the desired width and height, such as 5.46" by 5.74", in the Width and Height boxes in the Size and Rotate group box. The Lock Aspect Ratio check box in the Scale area controls whether the Height and Width boxes act in concert or independently.
5. Click OK to close the Format Picture dialog box and apply your changes.

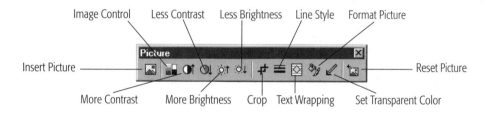

FIGURE 5.4: The Picture toolbar contains buttons for manipulating pictures quickly.

Inserting, Positioning, and Formatting Text Boxes

To position a picture precisely in a document, use a *text box*. A text box is a container that Word uses to position items (pictures, text, and other elements) exactly on the page. You can position a text box relative to a paragraph (so it moves with the text) or relative to the margin or page (so it remains in place even if the text moves). The advantage of positioning a text box relative to the page rather than relative to the margin is that you can adjust the margins without the text box moving. Text boxes are held in place by *anchors*.

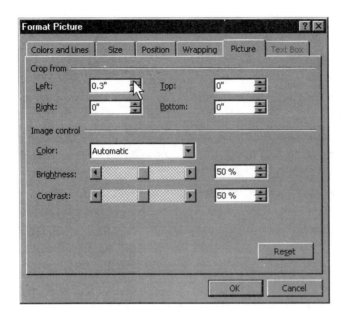

FIGURE 5.5:
The Format Picture dialog box lets you resize and crop pictures precisely.

Inserting a Text Box

To insert a text box:

1. Choose Insert ➤ Text Box. Word will change the insertion point to a large + sign and will switch you into Page Layout view if you are in Normal view or Outline view. (We'll look at the different views Word offers in "Viewing the Document" later in this chapter.)

2. Click and drag in the document to create a text box of the size you want, as shown here. The text box will appear with a thick shaded border, and Word will display the Text Box toolbar.

Now you can click inside the text box and insert a picture in it as described earlier in this chapter.

Sizing and Positioning a Text Box

To resize a text box quickly, click in it to display the text box border, and then drag one of the sizing handles.

To position a text box quickly:

1. Click inside the text box to display the text box border and handles.

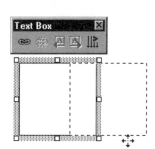

2. Move the mouse pointer onto the shaded border of the text box, so the pointer changes into a four-headed compass arrow attached to the usual mouse-pointer arrow.

3. Click and drag the text box to wherever you want to place it on the page. Here, I'm dragging a text box and its contents.

To resize and position a text box exactly:

1. Right-click on the border of the text box and choose Format Text Box from the context menu to display the Format Text Box dialog box (see Figure 5.6).

2. To resize the text box, click the Size tab to display it. You can then set the Height and Width either by entering measurements in the Height and Width boxes in the Size and Rotate area or by entering percentages in the Height and Width boxes in the Scale area. To resize the image proportionally, select the Lock Aspect Ratio check box; to resize the image independently in each dimension, clear the check box.

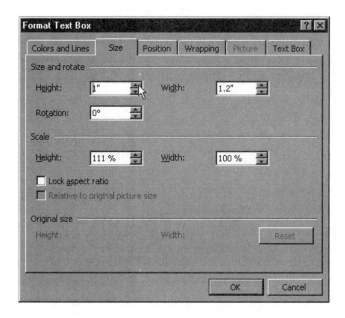

FIGURE 5.6:
Choose the text box's position on the page in the Format Text box dialog box.

3. To reposition the text box, click the Position tab to display it. Specify a horizontal position by entering a measurement in the

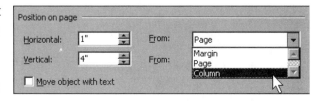

Horizontal box and specifying in the upper From drop-down list whether this is from the Margin, the Column, or the Page. Then specify a vertical position by setting a measurement in the Vertical box and specifying in the lower From drop-down list whether this is from the Margin, the Page, or the current Paragraph.

4. To allow a text box to move when the text it is attached to moves, select the Move with Text check box. For example, if you position a text box relative to a paragraph, click to put a check mark in this box; if you position a text box relative to the page, clear the check mark.

5. To lock the text box to the paragraph it is with (so you can't move it to another paragraph accidentally), select the Lock Anchor check box.

6. Click OK to close the Format Text Box dialog box and apply the settings to the text box.

Removing a Text Box

To delete a text box, select it by clicking on its border, and then press the Delete button. This deletes both the text box and any contents it has. To preserve the contents of the text box, copy and paste them into the document before deleting the text box.

Viewing the Document

Word offers six different ways to view your documents, each of which has its strengths and its weaknesses:

- Normal view
- Online Layout view
- Page Layout view
- Print Preview
- Outline view
- Split-Screen view

Normal View

Normal view provides the easiest view of the text and other elements on screen and is probably the Word view you'll spend most of your time using. In Normal view,

Word approximates the fonts and other formatting that you'll see when you print your document but adapts the document so you can see as much of it as possible on screen. In Normal view, you don't see the margins of the paper, or the headers and footers, or the footnotes and annotations. Word can wrap the text horizontally to the size of the window so no text disappears off the side of the screen.

 To switch the document to Normal view, choose View ➤ Normal or click the Normal View button at the left end of the horizontal scroll bar.

NOTE   **Another Word option that's almost a separate view is Draft Font view, a relic of the Draft View of Word versions 2 and earlier. Draft Font view, located in the Show area on the Options dialog box's View tab, is now an option that you choose for Normal or Outline view. Draft Font view uses standard fonts (with underline to indicate any form of emphasis, such as bold or italic) in order to speed up the display of text; for most purposes, it's hardly worth using in Word 97.**

Online Layout View

Online Layout view, which is new in Word 97, is designed for creating and reading online documents. Online Layout view (see Figure 5.7) shows a left pane—the document map—that displays the structure of the document (its headings) and a right pane that displays the text at an easily readable size, with features such as animated text and hyperlinks.

To switch to Online Layout view, choose View ➤ Online Layout or click the Online Layout View button on the horizontal scroll bar. To display the document map in another view, choose View ➤ Document Map.

Page Layout View

Page Layout view is useful for getting a rough idea of how your documents will look when you print them. In Page Layout view, Word shows you the margins of the sheet or sheets of paper you're working on, any headers or footers, and any footnotes or annotations. Word doesn't wrap text to the size of the window because doing so would change the page from its printable format.

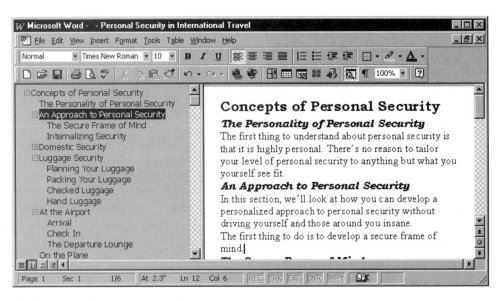

FIGURE 5.7: Online Layout view provides special features for working with online documents.

To switch to Page Layout view, choose View ➤ Page Layout or click the Page Layout View button on the horizontal scroll bar. You'll see an approximation of your document's layout, complete with margins (see Figure 5.8). If necessary, zoom to a more appropriate zoom percentage (see the section "Zooming the View," a couple of blocks south of here).

Print Preview

Print Preview provides a way for you to scan your documents on screen for formatting howlers before you immortalize them on dead trees. Print Preview shows you, as closely as Word knows how, the effect you'll get when you print your document on the currently selected printer. We'll look at Print Preview in detail in Chapter 8.

Outline View

Outline view lets you collapse your documents to a specified number of heading levels—for example, you could choose to view only the first-level heads in your documents or the first three levels of heads. Outline view is useful for structuring long documents and is somewhat more complex than the other views. We'll examine it in detail in Chapter 11.

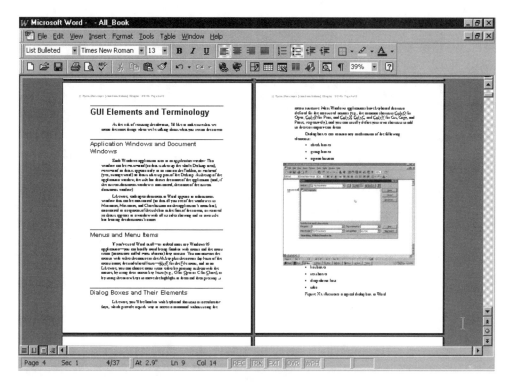

FIGURE 5.8:   Page Layout view shows you where each element in your document will really appear.

Split-Screen View

Word also offers split-screen view, in which the screen is divided into two panes. You can use a different view in each pane and can zoom each pane to a different zoom percentage.

To split the screen, choose Window ➤ Split. The mouse pointer will change to a double-headed arrow pointing up and down and dragging a thick gray line. Move the line up or down the screen to where you want to split it; then click to place the line. Figure 5.9 shows a split window.

To remove the split screen, choose Window ➤ Remove Split.

TIP   **To split the window in half quickly, double-click the split bar, the tiny horizontal bar at the top of the vertical scroll bar. Double-click the split bar again to remove the split screen.**

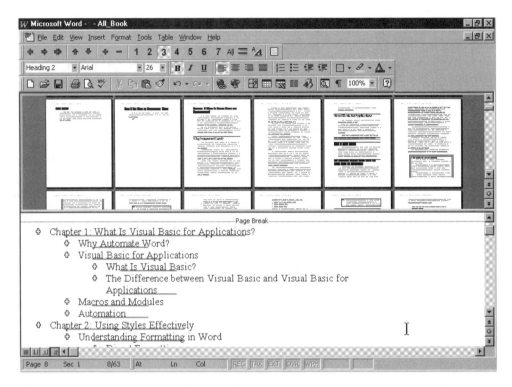

FIGURE 5.9: Choose Window ➤ Split to split the screen into two panes. You can then work in a different view or at a different zoom percentage in each pane.

Zooming the View

In any of Word's views, you can use the Zoom feature to increase or decrease the size of the display to make it easily visible. Word lets you set any zoom percentage between 10% and 500% of full size.

You can use either the Zoom box on the Standard toolbar or the Zoom dialog box to set the zoom percentage.

Zooming with the Zoom Box on the Standard Toolbar

To zoom the view with the Zoom box on the Standard toolbar:

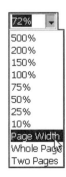

1. Display the Standard toolbar if it isn't visible.
2. Click the button to the right of the Zoom box to display a drop-down list of zoom percentages.
3. Choose a zoom percentage from the drop-down list or type in a different percentage (between 10% and 500%).

Zooming with the Zoom Dialog Box

To zoom the view with the Zoom dialog box:

1. Choose View ➤ Zoom to display the Zoom dialog box (see Figure 5.10).

2. In the Zoom To box, choose the zoom percentage you want:

   - To zoom to 200%, 100%, 75%, Page Width, or Whole Page (which is available only in Page Layout view and Print Preview), click the appropriate option button in the Zoom To box.

   - To display more than one page at a time (only in Page Layout view and Print Preview), click on the monitor button under the Many Pages option button and drag it through the grid that appears to indicate the configuration of pages you want to view: 2×2 pages, 2×3 pages, and so on (see Figure 5.10).

   - To display the page or pages at a precise zoom percentage of your choosing, adjust the setting in the Percent box in the lower-left corner of the Zoom dialog box.

3. Click the OK button to apply the zoom percentage you've selected.

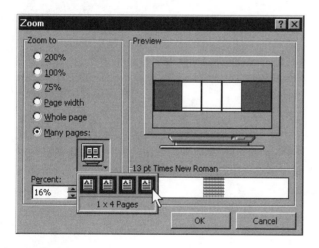

FIGURE 5.10:
In the Zoom dialog box, choose the zoom percentage you want to work at and click the OK button.

Chapter 6

SIMPLE FORMATTING

- **Formatting characters and words**
- **Formatting paragraphs**
- **Setting indents and line spacing**
- **Setting and using tabs**

Word supplies you with enough formatting options to typeset a long work of moderate complexity. The basic types of options start with *character* formatting—how the individual letters look—and move through *paragraph* formatting—how paragraphs appear on the page—to *style* formatting—which combines character and paragraph formatting, among other types—and finally, *page setup*. In this chapter, we'll look at character and paragraph formatting; in the next chapter, we'll look at the more advanced types of formatting.

Character Formatting

Character formatting is formatting that you can apply to one or more characters. Character formatting consists of

- Character attributes, such as bold, italic, underline, and strikethrough (among others)
- Fonts, such as Courier New, Times New Roman, and Arial
- Point size—the size of the font
- Character spacing, such as *superscripts* and *subscripts* (vertical spacing), and *kerning* (horizontal spacing)

You can apply character formatting in several ways: using the Font dialog box, using keyboard shortcuts, or using the Formatting toolbar. Each of these has advantages and disadvantages depending on what you're doing when you decide to start applying formatting and how much of it you need to apply. Let's look at each of them in turn.

Character Formatting Using the Font Dialog Box

The Font dialog box offers you the most control over font formatting, providing all the character-formatting options together in one handy location.

To set character formatting using the Font dialog box:

1. Select the text whose formatting you want to change. If you want to change the formatting of just one word, place the insertion point inside it.
2. Right-click in the text and choose Font from the context menu, or choose Format ➤ Font, to display the Font dialog box (see Figure 6.1). If the Font tab isn't displayed, click it to bring it to the front of the dialog box.
3. Choose the formatting options you want from the Font tab:
   - In the Font list box, choose the font (or *typeface*) for the text.
   - In the Font Style list box, choose the font style: Regular, Italic, Bold, or Bold Italic.

TIP   **Watch the Preview box at the bottom right corner of the dialog box to see approximately how your text will look.**

- In the Size box, choose the font size you want. To choose a font size between two of the sizes Word offers, type it into the top Size box—for example, enter **13** to produce 13-point text. (Word offers 12-point and 14-point options in the list box.)

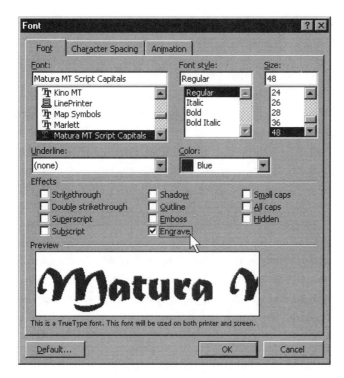

FIGURE 6.1:
The Font dialog box gives you quick access to all the character-formatting options Word offers.

- In the Underline box, choose the underlining style you want. The styles are mostly self-explanatory, with the possible exception of these two: None removes any existing underline, while Words Only adds a single underline underneath words and no underline underneath spaces.
- Select any special effects you want in the Effects group box by selecting the check boxes for Strikethrough, Double Strikethrough, Superscript, Subscript, Shadow, Outline, Emboss, Engrave, Small Caps, All Caps, or Hidden. (Hidden text is invisible under normal viewing conditions and does not print unless you choose to include it.)
- Choose a color for your text from the Color drop-down list. This will affect the text on screen—and on printouts if you have a color printer.

4. For special effects, try adjusting the settings on the Character Spacing tab of the Font dialog box.
- The Spacing option controls the horizontal placement of letters relative to each other—closer to each other or farther apart. From the Spacing drop-down list, you can choose Expanded or Condensed and then use the up and down spinner arrows in the By box to adjust the degree of expansion or condensation. (Alternatively, simply click the spinner

arrows and let Word worry about making the Spacing drop-list match your choice.) Again, watch the Preview box for a simulation of the effect your current choices will have.

- The Position option controls the vertical placement of letters relative to the baseline they're theoretically resting on. From the Position list, you can choose Normal, Raised, or Lowered, and then use the spinner arrows in the By box to raise or lower the letters—or simply click the spinner arrows and let Word determine whether the text is Normal, Raised, or Lowered.
- To turn on automatic kerning for fonts above a certain size, select the Kerning for Fonts check box and adjust the point size in the Points and Above box if necessary.

NOTE Kerning is the adjustment of space between letters so no letter appears too far from its neighbor. For example, if you type WAVE in a large font size without kerning, Word will leave enough space between the W and the A, and the A and the V, for you to slalom a small truck through. With kerning, you'll only be able to get a motorcycle through the gap.

5. To really enliven a document, try one of the six options on the Animation tab of the Font dialog box. Use these in moderation for best effect.
6. When you've finished making your choices in the Font dialog box, click the OK button to close the dialog box and apply your changes to the selected text or current word.

Setting a New Default Font

To set a new default font for all documents based on the current template, make all your choices on the Font and Character Spacing tabs (and, in extreme cases, on the Animation tab as well) of the Font dialog box, and then click the Default button (on any tab). Word will display a message box to confirm that you want to change the default font.

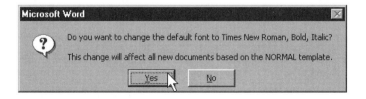

Click Yes to make the change.

Character Formatting Using the Formatting Toolbar

The Formatting toolbar offers a quick way to apply some of the most used character formatting options: font, font size, bold, italic, underline, highlighting, and font color (see Figure 6.2).

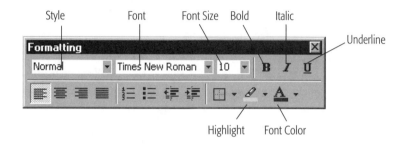

FIGURE 6.2:   The Formatting toolbar provides a quick way to apply formatting to your documents.

To change the font with the Formatting toolbar, select the text you want to affect, click the drop-down list button on the Font box, and select the new font from the list that appears.

- The fonts you've used most recently will be listed at the top of the list, with an alphabetical listing of all the fonts underneath those.
- To move quickly down the list of fonts to the one you want, type the first letter of the font's name.

To change font size, select the text to change, click the drop-down list button on the Font Size box, and select the font size from the list that appears.

TIP   **To change the font or font size of just one word, you don't need to select it—just placing the insertion point within the word does the trick.**

Click the Bold, Italic, or Underline button on the Formatting toolbar to apply bold, italic, or underline to the text you want to emphasize. When you've applied one of these attributes, the relevant button will appear to be pushed in.

    To apply highlighting to one instance of text, select the text, then click the Highlight button.

> **NOTE** To remove bold, italic, or underline, select the emphasized text, and then click the Bold, Italic, or Underline button again to remove the formatting.

To apply highlighting to several instances of text easily, click the Highlight button before selecting any text. Your mouse pointer will grow a little highlighter pen. Drag this over text to highlight it. Click the Highlight button again or press the Esc key to turn the highlighting off.

If you want to change the color of the highlighting, click the drop-down list arrow next to the Highlight button and choose another color from the list. (The default color for highlighting is the classic fluorescent yellow—Enhanced French Headlamp, as it's known in the trade—beloved of anyone who has ever had a highlighter pen break in their shirt pocket.)

To remove highlighting, drag the highlighter pen over the highlighted text.

To change the font color, click the Font Color drop-down palette button and choose the color you want from the palette. You can then apply that color quickly to selected text by clicking the Font Color button.

Character Formatting Using Keyboard Shortcuts

Word offers the following keyboard shortcuts for formatting text with the keyboard. For all of them, select the text you want to affect first, unless you want to affect only the word in which the insertion point is currently resting.

Action	Keyboard Shortcut
Increase font size (in steps)	Ctrl+Shift+.
Decrease font size (in steps)	Ctrl+Shift+,
Increase font size by 1 point	Ctrl+]
Decrease font size by 1 point	Ctrl+[
Change case (cycle)	Shift+F3
All capitals	Ctrl+Shift+A
Small capitals	Ctrl+Shift+K
Bold	Ctrl+B
Underline	Ctrl+U
Underline (single words)	Ctrl+Shift+W

Action	Keyboard Shortcut
Double-underline	Ctrl+Shift+D
Hidden text	Ctrl+Shift+H
Italic	Ctrl+I
Subscript	Ctrl+=
Superscript	Ctrl+Shift+= (i.e., Ctrl++)
Remove formatting	Ctrl+Shift+Z
Change to Symbol font	Ctrl+Shift+Q

Paragraph Formatting

With paragraph formatting, you can set a number of parameters that influence how your paragraphs in Word look:

- Alignment
- Tabs
- Indents
- Line spacing
- Text flow

The following sections of this chapter discuss each of these paragraph-formatting options in turn.

Setting Alignment

Word offers you several ways to set paragraph alignment: You can use the alignment buttons on the Formatting toolbar, or the keyboard shortcuts, or the options in the Paragraph dialog box. Using the buttons on the Formatting toolbar is the easiest way, and the one you'll probably find yourself using most often, so we'll look at that first.

Setting Alignment Using the Formatting Toolbar

To set alignment using the Formatting toolbar, place the insertion point in the paragraph that you want to align. To align more than one paragraph, select all the paragraphs. Then, click the Align Left, Center, Align Right, or Justify button on the Formatting toolbar (see Figure 6.3).

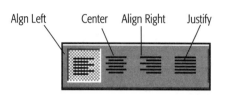

Algn Left   Center   Align Right   Justify

FIGURE 6.3:
To align the current paragraph or selected text quickly, click the appropriate button on the Formatting toolbar.

Setting Alignment Using Keyboard Shortcuts

When you're typing, the quickest way to set the alignment of paragraphs is by using these keyboard shortcuts:

Effect	Keyboard Shortcut
Align left	Ctrl+L
Center	Ctrl+E
Align right	Ctrl+R
Justify	Ctrl+J

Setting Alignment Using the Paragraph Dialog Box

The third way to set alignment—and usually the slowest—is to use the Paragraph dialog box. Why discuss this? Because often you'll need to make other formatting changes in the Paragraph dialog box, so sometimes you may find it useful to set alignment there, too.

To set alignment using the Paragraph dialog box:

1. Place the insertion point in the paragraph you want to align. To align several paragraphs, select them.
2. Right-click and choose Paragraph from the context menu, or choose Format ➤ Paragraph, to display the Paragraph dialog box (see Figure 6.4).
3. Choose the alignment you want from the Alignment drop-down list on the Indents and Spacing tab.
4. Click the OK button to close the Paragraph dialog box.

Setting Tabs

To align the text in your documents, Word offers five kinds of tabs: left-aligned, centered, right-aligned, decimal-aligned, and bar.

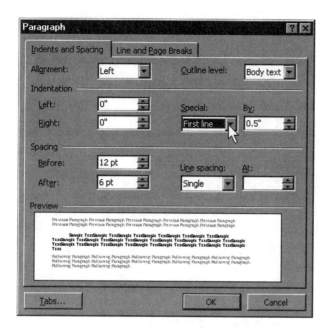

FIGURE 6.4:
In the Paragraph dialog box, you can set many paragraph-formatting options, including alignment.

Setting Tabs Using the Ruler

The quickest way to set tabs for the current paragraph or for a few paragraphs is to use the ruler. Choose View ➤ Ruler to display the ruler if it isn't visible, or simply pop it up by sliding the mouse pointer onto the thin bar at the top of the screen once you've selected the paragraphs you want to work on. (If the ruler won't pop up, select the Provide Feedback with Animation check box on the General tab of the Options dialog box, as discussed in Chapter 12.)

Adding a Tab

To add a tab, display the ruler if necessary, and then:

1. Select the paragraph or paragraphs to which you want to add the tab.
2. Choose the type of tab you want by clicking the tab selector button at the left end of the ruler to cycle through left tab, center tab, right tab, and decimal tab.
3. Click in the ruler where you want to add the tab. The tab mark will appear in the ruler.

TIP

When adding a tab, you can click with either the left or the right mouse button. For moving or removing a tab, only the left button works. Don't ask.

Moving a Tab

To move a tab, display the ruler if necessary, and then click the tab marker and drag it to where you want it.

Removing a Tab

To remove a tab, display the ruler if it's not visible, and then click the marker for the tab you want to remove and drag it into the document. The tab marker will disappear from the ruler.

Setting Tabs Using the Tabs Dialog Box

When you need to check exactly where the tabs are in a paragraph or if you set too many tabs in the ruler and get confused, turn to the Tabs dialog box to clear everything up.

First, select the paragraphs whose tabs you want to change, then choose Format ➤ Tabs to display the Tabs dialog box (see Figure 6.5) and follow the procedures described in the following sections.

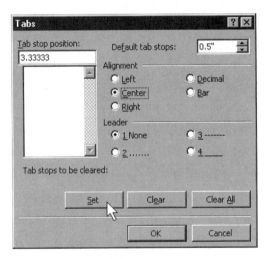

FIGURE 6.5:
The Tabs dialog box gives you precise control over the placement and types of tabs in your document.

TIP   To quickly display the Tabs dialog box, double-click on an existing tab in the bottom half of the ruler. (If you double-click in an open space in the bottom half of the ruler, the first click will place a new tab for you; if you double-click in the top half of the ruler, Word will display the Page Setup dialog box.) You can also get to the Tabs dialog box quickly by clicking the Tabs button on either panel of the Paragraph dialog box.

Setting Default Tabs

To set a different spacing for default tabs, adjust the setting in the Default Tab Stops box at the top of the Tabs dialog box. For example, a setting of 1" will produce tabs at 1", 2", 3", and so on.

Setting Tabs

To set tabs:

1. Enter a position in the Tab Stop Position box.
   - If you're using the default unit of measurement set in the copy of Word you're using, you don't need to specify the units.
   - If you want to use another unit of measurement, specify it: 6.3" (or 6.3 in—Word recognizes both), 11 cm, 22 pi, 128 pt.
2. Specify the tab alignment in the Alignment box: Left, Center, Right, Decimal, or Bar. (Bar inserts a vertical bar "|"at the tab stop.)
3. In the Leader box, specify a tab leader, if you want one—periods, hyphens, or underlines—leading up to the tabbed text. (Periods are often used as tab leaders for tables of contents, between the heading and the page number.)
4. Click the Set button.
5. Repeat steps 1 through 4 to specify more tabs if necessary.
6. Click the OK button to close the Tabs dialog box and apply the tabs you set.

Clearing Tabs

To clear a tab, select it in the Tab Stop Position list and click the Clear button. Word will list the tab you chose in the Tab Stops to Be Cleared area at the bottom of the Tabs dialog box. Choose other tabs to clear if necessary, and then click the OK button.

To clear all tabs, simply click the Clear All button, and then click the OK button.

Moving Tabs

To move tabs using the Tabs dialog box, you need to clear them from their current position and then set them elsewhere—you can't move them as such. (To move tabs easily, use the ruler method described earlier in this chapter.)

Setting Indents

As with setting alignment and tabs, you can set indents in more than one way. Again, the quickest way is with the ruler, but you can also use the Paragraph dialog box and some obscure keyboard shortcuts.

Setting Indents Using the Ruler

To set indents using the ruler, click and drag the indent markers on the ruler (see Figure 6.6).

- The first-line indent marker specifies the indentation of the first line of the paragraph (including a hanging indent, if any).
- The left-margin marker specifies the position of the left margin.

NOTE To move the left-margin marker and first-line indent marker together, drag the left-margin marker by the square box at its base rather than by the upward-pointing mark. Dragging by the upward-pointing mark moves the left-margin marker but leave the first-line indent marker in place.

- The right-margin marker specifies the position of the right margin.

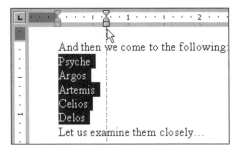

FIGURE 6.6:
Click and drag the indent markers on the ruler to change the indentation of the current paragraph or selected paragraphs.

Setting Indents Using Keyboard Shortcuts

Here are the keyboard shortcuts for setting indents:

Action	Keyboard Shortcut
Indent from the left	Ctrl+M
Remove indent from the left	Ctrl+Shift+M
Create (or increase) a hanging indent	Ctrl+T
Reduce (or remove) a hanging indent	Ctrl+Shift+T
Remove paragraph formatting	Ctrl+Q

Setting Indents Using the Paragraph Dialog Box

Depending on whether you have a graphical or literal mind-set, you may find setting indents in the Paragraph dialog box easier than setting them with the ruler.

To set paragraph indents with the Paragraph dialog box:

1. Place the insertion point in the paragraph for which you want to set indents. To set indents for several paragraphs, select them.

2. Right-click and choose Paragraph from the context menu, or choose Format ➤ Paragraph, to display the Paragraph dialog box.

3. Make sure the Indents and Spacing tab is selected (if it's not visible, click it to bring it in front of the Line and Page Breaks tab).

4. In the Left box, enter the distance to indent the paragraph from the left margin.

5. In the Right box, enter the distance to indent the paragraph from the right margin.

6. In the Special box, choose from (none), First Line, and Hanging (Figure 6.7 illustrates the different types of indentation Word provides for paragraphs):

(none)	Formats the paragraph as a regular paragraph with indents controlled solely by the Left and Right settings.
First Line	Adds an indent to the first line of the paragraph. This indent is on top of the Left setting. For example, if you choose a Left setting of 0.5" and a First Line setting of 0.5", the first line of the paragraph will be indented one inch. By using a first-line indent on paragraphs, you can avoid having to start them with a tab.
Hanging	Makes the first line of the paragraph hang out to the left of the rest of the paragraph. (Excessively logical people call this an outdent.) Hanging indents are great for bulleted or numbered paragraphs–the bullet or number hangs way out to the left of the paragraph, and the wrapped lines of the paragraph align neatly with the first line.

7. If you chose a Special setting of First Line or Hanging, enter a measurement in the By box.

8. Click the OK button to close the Paragraph dialog box.

TIP

When setting indents, you can use negative values for Left and Right indents to make the text protrude beyond the margin. Negative indents can be useful for special effects, but if you find yourself using them all the time, you probably need to adjust your margins. One other thing—for obvious reasons, you can't set a negative hanging indent, no matter how hard you try.

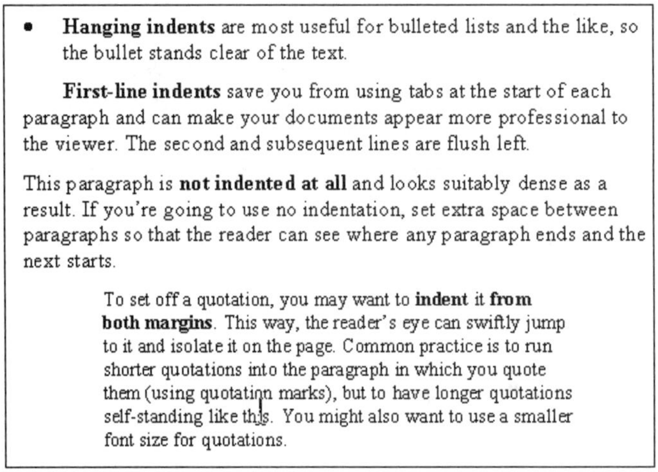

• **Hanging indents** are most useful for bulleted lists and the like, so the bullet stands clear of the text.

First-line indents save you from using tabs at the start of each paragraph and can make your documents appear more professional to the viewer. The second and subsequent lines are flush left.

This paragraph is **not indented at all** and looks suitably dense as a result. If you're going to use no indentation, set extra space between paragraphs so that the reader can see where any paragraph ends and the next starts.

> To set off a quotation, you may want to **indent** it **from both margins**. This way, the reader's eye can swiftly jump to it and isolate it on the page. Common practice is to run shorter quotations into the paragraph in which you quote them (using quotation marks), but to have longer quotations self-standing like this. You might also want to use a smaller font size for quotations.

FIGURE 6.7:
Word provides these different types of indentation for formatting paragraphs.

Choosing Measurement Units

You may have noticed that the measurement units (inches, centimeters, and so on) in the Paragraph dialog box on your computer are different from those in the screens shown here—for example, you might be seeing measurements in centimeters or picas rather than in inches.

If so, don't worry. Word lets you work in any of four measurements: inches, centimeters, points, and picas. Points and picas—$\frac{1}{72}$ of an inch and $\frac{1}{6}$ of an inch, respectively—are most useful for page layout and typesetting, but if you're not doing those, you might want to switch between inches and centimeters. (Sooner or later, we'll all be using centimeters, I'm told.)

To change your measurement units:

1. Choose Tools ➤ Options to display the Options dialog box.
2. Click the General tab to bring it to the front.
3. Choose Inches, Centimeters, Points, or Picas as your measurement unit in the Measurement Units drop-down list.
4. Click the OK button to close the Options dialog box.

Setting Line Spacing

You can change the line spacing of your documents by using either the Paragraph dialog box or keyboard shortcuts.

1. Select the paragraphs whose line spacing you want to change. To select the whole document quickly, choose Edit ➤ Select All, or hold down the Ctrl key and click once in the selection bar at the left edge of the Word window.

Alternatively, press Ctrl+5 (that's the *5* on the numeric keypad, not the *5* in the row above the letters *R* and *T*).

2. Right-click in the selection and choose Paragraph from the context menu, or choose Format ➤ Paragraph, to display the Paragraph dialog box (shown earlier in Figure 6.4).

3. If the Indents and Spacing tab isn't at the front of the Paragraph dialog box, click it to bring it to the front.

4. Use the Line Spacing drop-down list to choose the line spacing you want:

Line Spacing	Effect
Single	Single-spacing, based on the point size of the font.
1.5 lines	Line-and-a-half spacing, based on the point size of the font.
Double	Double-spacing, based on the point size of the font.
At least	Sets a minimum spacing for the lines, measured in points. This can be useful for including fonts of different sizes in a paragraph, or for including in-line graphics.
Exactly	Sets the exact spacing for the lines, measured in points.
Multiple	Multiple line spacing, set by the number in the At box to the right of the Line Spacing drop-down list. For example, to use triple-spacing, enter **3** in the At box; to use quadruple-spacing, enter **4**.

5. If you chose At Least, Exactly, or Multiple in the Line Spacing drop-down list, adjust the setting in the At box if necessary.

6. Click the OK button to apply the line spacing setting to the chosen text.

TIP   To set line spacing with the keyboard, press Ctrl+1 to single-space the selected paragraphs, Ctrl+5 to set 1.5-line spacing, and Ctrl+2 to double-space paragraphs.

Setting Spacing Before and After Paragraphs

As well as setting the line spacing within any paragraph, you can adjust the amount of space before and after any paragraph to position it more effectively on the page. So instead of using two blank lines (two extra paragraphs with no text) before a heading and one blank line after, you can adjust the paragraph spacing to give the heading plenty of space without using any blank lines at all.

TIP The easiest way to set consistent spacing before and after paragraphs of a particular type is to use Word's styles, which we'll discuss in the next chapter.

To set the spacing before and after a paragraph:

1. Place the insertion point in the paragraph whose spacing you want to adjust, or select several paragraphs to adjust their spacing all at once.
2. Right-click and choose Paragraph from the context menu, or choose Format ➤ Paragraph, to display the Paragraph dialog box (shown earlier in Figure 6.4).
3. Make sure the Indents and Spacing tab is foremost. If it isn't, click it to bring it to the front.
4. In the Spacing box, choose a Before setting to specify the number of points of space before the selected paragraph. Watch the Preview box for the approximate effect this change will have.
5. Choose an After setting to specify the number of points of space after the current paragraph. Again, watch the Preview box.

NOTE The Before setting for a paragraph adds to the After setting for the paragraph before it; it does not change it. For example, if the previous paragraph has an After setting of 12 points, and you specify a Before setting of 12 points for the current paragraph, you'll end up with 24 points of space between the two paragraphs (on top of the line spacing you've set).

6. Click the OK button to close the Paragraph dialog box and apply the changes.

TIP To quickly add or remove one line's worth of space before a paragraph, press Ctrl+0 (Ctrl+zero).

Using the Text Flow Options

Word offers six options for controlling how your text flows from page to page in the document. To select them, click in the paragraph you want to apply them to or select a number of paragraphs. Then choose Format ➤ Paragraph to display the Paragraph dialog box, click the Line and Page Breaks tab to bring it to the front of the dialog box (unless it's already at the front), and select the options you want to use:

Widow/Orphan Control	A *widow* (in typesetting parlance) is when the last line of a paragraph appears on its own at the top of a page; an *orphan* is when the first line of a paragraph appears by itself at the foot of a page. Leave the Widow/Orphan Control box checked to have Word rearrange your documents to avoid widows and orphans.
Keep Lines Together	Tells Word to prevent the paragraph from breaking over a page. If the whole paragraph will not fit on the current page, Word moves it to the next page.

WARNING   **If you write long paragraphs, choosing the Keep Lines Together option can produce painfully short pages.**

Keep with Next	Tells Word to prevent a page break from occurring between this paragraph and the next. This option can be useful for making sure that a heading appears on the same page as the paragraph of text following it or that an illustration appears together with its caption, but be careful not to set Keep with Next for body text paragraphs.
Page Break Before	Tells Word to force a page break before the current paragraph. This is useful for making sure that, for example, each section of a report starts on a new page.
Suppress Line Numbers	Tells Word to turn off line numbers for the current paragraph. This applies only if you are using line numbering in your document.
Don't Hyphenate	Tells Word to skip the current paragraph for automatic hyphenation.

When you've chosen the options you want, click the OK button to apply them to the paragraph or paragraphs.

Chapter 7

PAGE LAYOUT AND STYLES

- **Using language formatting**
- **Applying borders and shading**
- **Creating and using styles**
- **Setting up the page**
- **Using Word's AutoFormat options**
- **Creating headers and footers**

In this chapter, we'll look at the more advanced formatting features that Word offers. You can format text as being in one language or another (which is useful for spelling checks); you can add borders and shading to paragraphs or other elements; you can use styles to apply complex formatting quickly to different paragraphs; and you can set up Word to use various sizes of paper.

Language Formatting

You can format text as being written in a language other than English. This is formatting, not translation—it doesn't mean that the text *is* in another language, just that you're telling Word that it is. For example, you could enter text in Swahili and then format it as Norwegian (Bokmal or Nynorsk); the text would still be in Swahili, but Word would tag it with the Norwegian Bokmal (or Norwegian Nynorsk) language formatting. Not only can you then spell-check the text written in other languages, but you can also use the Find feature to search for text formatted in those languages for quick reference. (Chapter 2 discusses spell-checking, while Chapter 11 discusses the Find feature.)

To format selected text as another language:

1. Choose Tools ➤ Language ➤ Set Language to display the Language dialog box (see Figure 7.1).

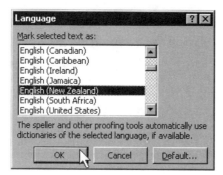

FIGURE 7.1:
In the Language dialog box, choose the language in which to format the selected text, and then click OK.

2. In the Mark Selected Text As list box, choose the language you want to format the text as.

3. Click OK to apply the language formatting to the selected text.

NOTE   **The (no proofing) language choice tells Word not to spell-check the text. This can be very useful for one-shot technical terms that you don't want to add to your custom dictionaries (which we looked at in Chapter 2). But if you find the Spelling checker apparently failing to catch blatant spelling errors, check the language formatting of the text in question.**

Borders and Shading

If a part of your text, or a picture, or indeed the whole page, needs a little more emphasis, you can select it and add borders and shading:

1. Choose Format ➤ Borders and Shading to display the Borders and Shading dialog box (see Figure 7.2).

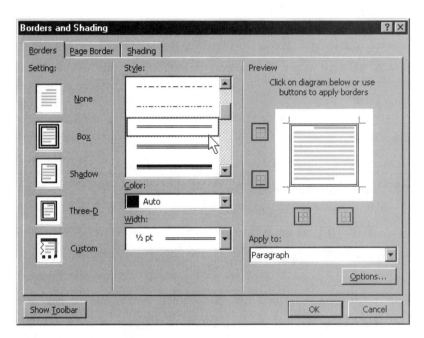

FIGURE 7.2:   Apply borders and shading to items from the Borders and Shading dialog box.

2. On the Borders tab, choose the type of border you want to add from the options displayed:

- In the Setting area, choose one of the settings—None, Box, Shadow, Grid (for tables and cells), Three-D (not for tables and cells), or Custom. Watch the effect in the Preview box.
- Select the type of line you want from the Style list, and choose a color from the Color drop-down list and a weight from the Width drop-down list if you want. To change one of the lines, click the appropriate icon in the Preview area to apply it or remove it.
- For text, you can choose Text or Paragraph in the Apply To drop-down list below the Preview area. If you apply the border to a paragraph, you can specify the distance of the

border from the text by clicking the Options button and specifying Top, Bottom, Left, and Right settings in the Border and Shading Options dialog box, and then clicking OK.

3. On the Page Border tab, choose the type of border you want to add to the page. The controls on this tab work in the same way as those described in step 2. The important difference is that the Apply To drop-down list allows you to choose between Whole Document, This Section, This Section—First Page Only, and This Section—All Except First Page. Again, clicking the Options button displays the Border and Shading Options dialog box, which allows you to place the border precisely on the page.

4. On the Shading tab, choose the type of shading to add:
    - Choose the color for the shading from the Fill palette.
    - Choose a style and color for the pattern in the Style and Color drop-down list boxes in the Patterns area.
    - Use the Apply To list to specify whether to apply the shading to the paragraph or just to selected text.

WARNING   **Any shading over 20 percent will completely mask text on most black-and-white printouts (even if it looks wonderfully artistic on screen).**

5. Click OK to close the Borders and Shading dialog box and apply your changes to the selection.

To remove borders and shading, select the item, and then choose Format ➤ Borders and Shading to display the Borders and Shading dialog box. To remove a border, choose None in the Setting area on the Borders tab; to remove a page border, choose None in the Setting area on the Page Border tab; and to remove shading, choose None in the Fill palette and Clear in the Style drop-down list on the Shading tab. Click OK to close the Borders and Shading dialog box.

Style Formatting

Word's *paragraph styles* bring together all the formatting elements discussed so far in the last two chapters—character formatting, paragraph formatting (including alignment), tabs, language formatting, and even borders and shading. Each style contains complete formatting information that you can apply with one click of the mouse or one keystroke.

NOTE Word also offers character styles, which are similar to paragraph styles but contain only character formatting. Character styles are suitable for picking out elements in a paragraph formatted with paragraph styles.

Using styles not only gives your documents a consistent look—every Heading 1 paragraph will appear in the same font and font size, with the same amount of space before and after it, and so on—but also saves you a great deal of time in formatting your documents.

You can either use Word's built-in styles—which are different in Word's various predefined templates—or create your own styles. Every paragraph in Word uses a style; Word starts you off in the Normal style unless the template you're using dictates otherwise.

Applying Styles

To apply a style, place the insertion point in the paragraph or choose a number of paragraphs, and then click the Style drop-down list button on the Formatting toolbar and choose the style you want from the list (as shown here).

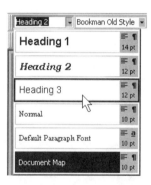

You can also apply a style by choosing Format ➤ Style to display the Style dialog box (see Figure 7.3). Select a style from the Styles list box and click the Apply button.

TIP Some of the most popular styles have keyboard shortcuts: Ctrl+Shift+N for Normal style, Ctrl+Alt+1 for Heading 1, Ctrl+Alt+2 for Heading 2, Ctrl+Alt+3 for Heading 3, and Ctrl+Shift+L for List Bullet style.

To tell which style paragraphs are in, you can display the *style area*, a vertical bar at the left side of the Word window that displays the style name for each paragraph:

Heading 1	**Concepts of Personal Security**
Heading 2	*The Personality of Personal Security*
Main Text	The first thing to understand about personal security is that it is your level of personal security to anything but what you yourse

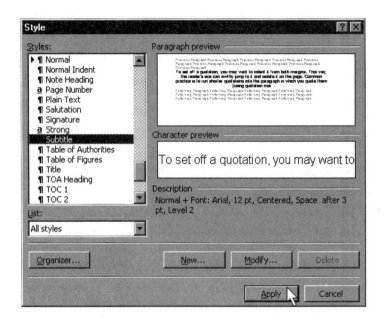

FIGURE 7.3:
To apply a style, choose it in the Styles list box in the Style dialog box and click the Apply button.

If you want to display the style area, choose Tools ➤ Options to display the Options dialog box and click the View tab to bring it to the front. Enter a measurement in the Style Area Width box in the Window group box, and then click OK.

You can also alter the width of the style area once you've displayed it by clicking and dragging the dividing line. To remove it, drag the dividing line all the way to the left of the Word window (or reset the Style Area Width box to zero).

NOTE You cannot display the style area in Online Layout View, Page Layout view, or Print Preview.

Creating a New Style

As you can see in the Styles list box, shown in Figure 7.3, Word's templates come with a number of built-in styles. If they're not enough for you, you can create your own styles in three ways: by example, by definition, and by having Word do all the work for you.

Creating a New Style by Example

The easiest way to create a style is to set up a paragraph of text with the exact formatting you want for the style—character formatting, paragraph formatting, borders

Digression	▾

and shading, bullets or numbers, and so on. Then click the Style drop-down list button on the Formatting toolbar, type the name for the new style in the box, and press Enter. Word will create the style, which you can immediately select from the Style drop-down list and apply to other paragraphs as necessary.

Creating a New Style by Definition

The more complex way to create a style is by definition:

1. Choose Format ➤ Style to display the Style dialog box.
2. Click the New button. Word will display the New Style dialog box (see Figure 7.4).
3. Set the information for your new style:
    - In the Name box, enter a name for the style. Style names can be a decent length—Word will accept over 100 characters—but you'll do better to keep them short enough to fit in the Style box on the Formatting toolbar. If your style name is over 20 characters long, you should probably rethink your naming convention.
    - In the Based On drop-down list box, choose the style on which you want to base the new style. Bear in mind that if you change the other style later, the new style will change, too. The Preview box will show what the Based On style looks like.
    - In the Style Type box, choose whether you want a paragraph style or a character style.
    - In the Style for Following Paragraph box (which is not available for character styles), choose the style that you want Word to apply to the paragraph immediately after this style. For example, after the Heading 1 style, you might want Body Text, or after a Figure paragraph, you might want a Caption paragraph. But for many styles you'll want to continue with the style itself.
4. To adjust the formatting of the style, click the Format button and choose Font, Paragraph, Tabs, Border, Language, Frame, or Numbering from the drop-down list. This will display the dialog box for that type of formatting. When you've finished, click the OK button to return to the New Style dialog box.

NOTE   Some of these dialog boxes, such as Character, Paragraph, and Tabs, we looked at in Chapter 6; others we'll examine in subsequent chapters.

5. Repeat step 4 as necessary, selecting other formatting characteristics for the style.

FIGURE 7.4:
Creating a new style
in the New Style
dialog box.

6. Select the Add to Template check box to add the new style to the template.
7. Select the Automatically Update check box if you want Word to automatically update the style when you change it. (We'll look at this more in a minute.)
8. To set up a shortcut key for the style, click the Shortcut Key button. Word will display the Customize Keyboard dialog box. With the insertion point in the Press New Shortcut Key box, press the shortcut key combination you would like to set, click the Assign button, and then click the Close button.

WARNING   **Watch the Currently Assigned To area of the Customize Keyboard dialog box when selecting your shortcut key combination. If Word has already assigned that key combination to a command, macro, or style, it will display its name there. If you choose to assign the key combination to the new style, the old assignment for that combination will be deactivated.**

9. In the New Style dialog box, click the OK button to return to the Style dialog box.
10. To create another new style, repeat steps 2 through 9.
11. To close the Style dialog box, click the Apply button to apply the new style to the current paragraph or current selection, or click the Close button to save the new style without applying it.

Having Word Create Styles Automatically

Creating styles yourself can get tedious—why not have Word create them for you? And when you change the formatting of a paragraph that has a certain style, you can have Word update the style for you, so that every other paragraph with the same style takes on that formatting, too.

To have Word automatically create styles for you:

1. Choose Tools ➤ AutoCorrect to display the AutoCorrect dialog box.
2. Click the AutoFormat As You Type tab to display it.
3. In the Automatically As You Type area at the bottom of the tab, select the Define Styles Based on Your Formatting check box. (This is selected by default.)
4. Click the OK button to close the AutoCorrect dialog box.

Once you've set this option, Word will attempt to identify styles you're creating and will supply names for them. For example, if you start a new document (with paragraphs in the Normal style, as usual) and bold and center the first paragraph, Word may define that bolding and centering as a Title style; if you simply increase the font size, Word may call that paragraph Heading 1 instead. This sounds creepy but works surprisingly well, and if it doesn't suit you, you can easily turn it off by clearing the Define Styles Based on Your Formatting check box once more.

Modifying a Style

You can modify a style by example and by definition. You can also have Word automatically identify and apply changes you make to the style.

Modifying a Style by Example

To modify a style by example, change the formatting of a paragraph that currently has the style assigned to it, and then choose the same style again from the Style drop-down list. Word will display the Modify Style dialog box (see Figure 7.5). Make sure the Update the Style to Reflect Recent Changes option button is selected, and then click the OK button to update the style to include the changes you just made to it. If you want Word to automatically update the style without displaying this dialog box when you make changes in the future, select the Automatically Update the Style from Now On check box first.

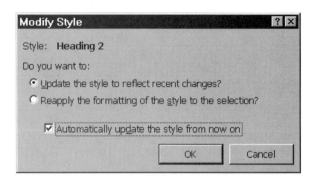

FIGURE 7.5:
In the Modify Style dialog box, choose OK to update the style to reflect changes you just made to it. If you want Word to auto-matically update the style in the future, select the Automatically Update the Style from Now On check box first.

Modifying a Style by Definition

Modifying a Word style by definition is similar to creating a new style, except that you work in the Modify Style dialog box, which offers one fewer option than the New Style dialog box does—you don't get to choose whether the style is a paragraph or character style because Word already knows which it is.

Open the Style dialog box by choosing Format ➤ Style, and then choose the style you want to work on from the Styles list. (If you can't see the style you're looking for, make sure the List box at the bottom-left corner of the Style dialog box is showing All Styles rather than Styles in Use or User-Defined Styles.)

Click the Modify button. Word will display the Modify Style dialog box—not the Modify Style dialog box shown in Figure 7.5, but a mutated version of the New Style dialog box shown in Figure 7.4. From there, follow steps 3 to 9 in the "Creating a New Style by Definition" section (except for selecting the style type) to modify the style and step 11 to leave the Style dialog box.

Removing a Style

To remove a style, open the Style dialog box by choosing Format ➤ Style, select the style to delete in the Styles list, and click the Delete button. Word will display a message box asking you to confirm that you want to delete the style; click the Yes button.

You can then delete another style the same way, or click the Close button to leave the Style dialog box.

NOTE   **Two things here: You can't delete a Heading style once you've started using it. Second, when you delete a style that's in use (other than a Heading style), Word applies the Normal style to those paragraphs.**

Using the Style Gallery

Word provides the Style Gallery to give you a quick overview of its many templates and the myriad styles they contain. To open the Style Gallery, choose Format ➤ Style Gallery. Word will display the Style Gallery dialog box (see Figure 7.6).

To preview a template in the Preview Of box, select it in the Template list box. Then choose the type of preview you want in the Preview group box:

- Document shows you how your current document looks with the template's styles applied.
- Example shows you a sample document that uses the template's styles.
- Style Samples shows each of the styles in the document.

To apply the template you've chosen to your document, click the OK button. Alternatively, click the Cancel button to close the Style Gallery without applying a template.

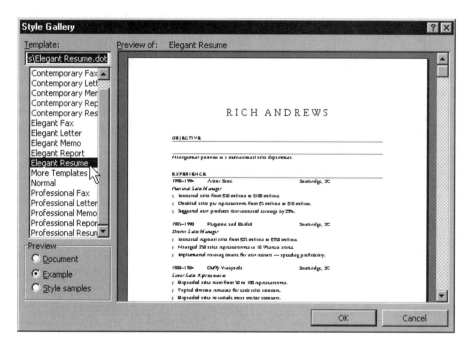

FIGURE 7.6: The Style Gallery dialog box gives you a quick view of the styles in Word's templates.

Page Setup

If you're ever going to print a document, you need to tell Word how it should appear on the page. You can change the margins, the paper size, the layout of the paper, and even which printer tray it comes from (which we'll look at in Chapter 8, "Printing a Document").

> **NOTE** The best time to set paper size is at the beginning of a project. While you can change it at any time during a project without trouble, having the right size (and orientation) of paper from the start will help you lay out your material.

To alter the page setup, double-click in the top half of the horizontal ruler (not in the bottom half—double-clicking there will display the Tabs dialog box) or anywhere in the vertical ruler, or choose File ➤ Page Setup, to display the Page Setup dialog box. Then follow the instructions for setting margins, paper size, and paper orientation in the next sections. If you want to change the page setup for only one section of a document, place the insertion point in the section you want to change before displaying the Page Setup dialog box. Alternatively, you can choose This Point Forward from the Apply To drop-down list on any tab of the Page Setup dialog box to change the page setup for the rest of the document.

Setting Margins

To set the margins for your document, click the Margins tab in the Page Setup dialog box (see Figure 7.7). In the boxes for Top, Bottom, Left, and Right margins, use the spinner arrows to enter the measurement you want for each margin; alternatively, type in a measurement.

> **NOTE** The unit of measurement is controlled by the Measurement Units setting on the General tab of the Options dialog box. You can choose inches, points, centimeters, or picas. (In case you've forgotten, a point is $1/72$ of an inch, and a pica is twelve points, or $1/6$ of an inch.)

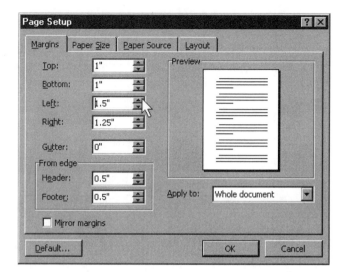

FIGURE 7.7:
The Margins tab of the Page Setup dialog box

If you're typesetting documents (rather than simply using the word processor to put them together), you may want to select the Mirror Margins check box. This makes the two inner-margin measurements the same as each other and the two outer-margin measurements the same as each other, and changes the Left and Right settings to Inside and Outside, respectively.

The Gutter measurement is the space that your document will have on the inside of each facing page. For example, if you're working with mirror-margin facing pages, you could choose to have a Gutter measurement of 1" and Inside and Outside margins of 1.25". That way, your documents would appear with a 1.25-inch left margin on left-hand pages, a 1.25-inch right margin on right-hand pages, and a 2.25-inch margin on the inside of each page (the gutter plus the margin setting).

TIP

Use gutters for documents you're planning to bind. That way, you can be sure you won't end up with text bound unreadably into the spine of the book.

Use the Preview box in the Page Setup dialog box to give you an idea of how your document will look when you print it.

Setting Paper Size

Word lets you print on paper of various sizes, offering a Custom option to allow you to set a peculiar paper size of your own, in addition to the various standard paper and envelope sizes.

To change the size of the paper you're printing on, click the Paper Size tab of the Page Setup dialog box (see Figure 7.8).

In the Paper Size drop-down list box, choose the size of paper you'll be working with (for example, Letter 8½×11 in). If you can't find the width and height of paper you want, use the Width and Height boxes to set the width and height of the paper you're using; Word will automatically select Custom Size in the Paper Size box.

Setting Paper Orientation

To change the orientation of the page you're working on, click the Paper Size tab of the Page Setup dialog box (shown in Figure 7.8) and choose Portrait or Landscape in the Orientation group box. (*Portrait* is taller than it is wide; *Landscape* is wider than it is tall.)

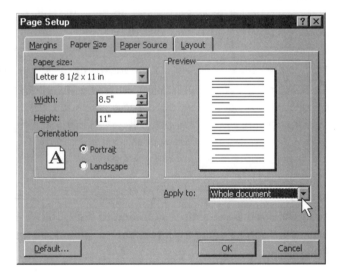

FIGURE 7.8:
The Paper Size tab of the Page Setup dialog box

Section Formatting

Often you'll want to create documents that use different page layouts, or even different sizes of paper, in different parts. Word handles this by letting you divide documents into *sections*, each of which can have different formatting characteristics. For example, you could use sections to set up a document to contain both a letter and an envelope or to have one-column text and then multicolumn text.

Creating a Section

To create a section:

1. Place the insertion point where you want the new section to start.
2. Choose Insert ➤ Break. Word will display the Break dialog box (see Figure 7.9).

FIGURE 7.9:
In the Break dialog box, choose the type of section break to insert, and then click the OK button.

3. Choose the type of section break to insert by clicking one of the option buttons in the Section Breaks area:

Next Page   Starts the section on a new page. Use this when the formatting changes drastically between sections–for example, when you have an envelope on one page and a letter on the next.

Continuous   Starts the section on the same page as the preceding paragraph. This is useful for creating layouts with differing numbers of columns on the same page.

Even Page   Starts the section on a new even page.

Odd Page   Starts the section on a new odd page. This is useful for chapters or sections that should start on a right-hand page for consistency.

4. Click the OK button to insert the section break. It will appear in Normal view and Outline view as a double dotted line across the page containing the words *Section Break* and the type of section break:

Section Break (Continuous)

The Sec indicator on the status bar will indicate which section you're in.

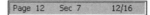

You can change the type of section break on the Layout tab of the Page Setup dialog box: Place the insertion point in the relevant section, choose File ➤ Page Setup, select the type of section you want from the Section Start drop-down list on the Layout tab, and click the OK button.

Deleting a Section

To delete a section break, place the insertion point at the beginning of the section break (or select it) and press the Delete key.

When you delete a section break, the section before the break will take on the formatting characteristics of the section after the break.

Using AutoFormat

To automate the creation of documents, Word offers two types of automatic formatting with its AutoFormat features: AutoFormat, which applies styles when you choose the Format ➤ AutoFormat command, and AutoFormat As You Type, which applies automatic formatting to paragraphs as you finish them.

To set AutoFormat or AutoFormat As You Type options:

1. Choose Tools ➤ AutoCorrect to display the AutoCorrect dialog box.
2. Click the AutoFormat tab or AutoFormat As You Type tab.
3. In the Apply or Apply As You Type area, select the check boxes next to the AutoFormatting options you want to use. For AutoFormat: Headings, Lists, Automatic Bulleted Lists, and Other Paragraphs; and for AutoFormat As You

Type: Headings, Borders, Tables, Automatic Bulleted Lists, and Automatic Numbered Lists. Here's what the options do:

Headings	Word applies Heading 1 style when you type a short paragraph, starting with a capital letter and not ending with a period, and press Enter twice, and Heading 2 when that paragraph starts with a tab.
Automatic Numbered Lists	Word creates a numbered list when you type a number followed by a punctuation mark (such as a period, hyphen, or closing parenthesis) and then a space or tab and some text.
Automatic Bulleted Lists	Word creates a bulleted list when you type a bullet-type character (e.g., a bullet, an asterisk, or a hyphen) and then a space or tab followed by text.
Borders	Word adds a border to a paragraph that follows a paragraph containing three or more dashes, underscores, or equal signs: Dashes produce a thin line, underscores produce a thick line, and equal signs produce a double line.
Tables	Word creates a table when you type an arrangement of hyphens and plus signs (e.g., +−+−+−+) and press Enter. Here, each +−+ becomes a column, producing a three-column table. This is one of the more bizarre and inconvenient ways to create a table; we'll look at better ways in Chapter 9.
Other Paragraph	Word applies styles based on what it judges your text to be.

TIP **You can stop the automatic numbered or bulleted list formatting by pressing Enter twice.**

4. Choose Replace or Replace As You Type options as necessary.
5. In the Automatically As You Type area of the AutoFormat As You Type tab, select the Format Beginning of List Item Like the One Before It check box if you want Word to try to mimic your formatting of lists automatically. Select the Define Styles Based on Your Formatting check box if you want Word to automatically create styles whenever it feels appropriate.
6. In the Always AutoFormat area of the AutoFormat tab, select the Plain Text WordMail Documents check box if you want Word to automatically format plain-text e-mail in WordMail.

7. Click the OK button to close the AutoCorrect dialog box.

AutoFormat As You Type options will now spring into effect as you create your documents.

If you decide to use the regular AutoFormat feature instead of AutoFormat As You Type, create your document and then choose Format ➤ AutoFormat. Word will display an AutoFormat dialog box (see Figure 7.10), which lets you access the AutoFormat tab of the AutoCorrect dialog box to refine your predefined AutoFormat settings if necessary. Choose a type of document from the drop-down list, and then click the OK button to start AutoFormatting.

FIGURE 7.10:
In the AutoFormat dialog box, choose a type of document and whether you want to review the changes Word proposes, and then click the OK button.

NOTE **You can also use AutoFormat to create automatic hyperlinks in Word. See Chapter 28, "Office and the Web," for details.**

Headers and Footers

Headers and footers give you an easy way to repeat identifying information on each page of your document. For example, in a *header* (across the top of each page), you might include the title of a document and the author, while in a *footer* (across the bottom of each page) you might include the file name, the date, and the page number out of the total number of pages in the document (for example, *Page 1 of 9*).

You can repeat headers and footers throughout all the pages of your document, or you can vary them from page to page. For example, if a proposal has two different authors, you might want to identify in the header which author wrote a particular part of the proposal. If you want to identify the different part titles in the header, you can easily display that, too. You can also arrange for odd pages to have different headers and footers from those on even pages or for the first page in a document to have a different header and footer than subsequent pages.

Setting Headers and Footers

To include a header in your document:

1. Choose View ➤ Header and Footer. Word will display the page in Page Layout view and will display the Header and Footer toolbar (see Figure 7.11).

NOTE **You can work with headers and footers only in Page Layout view and Print Preview. If you choose View ➤ Header and Footer from Normal view or Outline view, Word will switch you to Page Layout view. When you leave the header or footer area, Word will return you to the view you were in before.**

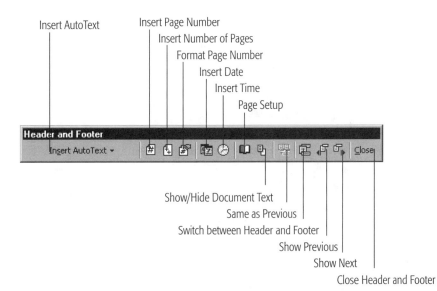

FIGURE 7.11: The Header and Footer toolbar offers 12 buttons that help you produce headers and footers quickly and easily–and a Close Header and Footer button to get you out of the header or footer.

2. Enter the text (and graphics, if you like) for the header in the Header area at the top of the page. Use the buttons on the Header and Footer toolbar to speed your work.

Insert AutoText	Provides a drop-down menu of canned header and footer text, including the file name and path, and *Page X of Y* (e.g., *Page 3 of 34*).
Insert Page Number	Inserts a code for the current page number at the insertion point.
Insert Number of Pages	Inserts a code for the number of pages in the document.
Format Page Number	Displays the Page Number Format dialog box (see Figure 7.12). In the Number Format drop-down list, choose the type of numbering you want: 1, 2, 3; a, b, c; etc. If you want to include chapter numbers in the page numbering, select the Include Chapter Number check box, and then choose the Heading style with which each chapter in the document starts in the Chapter Starts with Style drop-down list and a separator character for the numbering from the Use Separator drop-down list. Finally, in the Page Numbering area, choose whether to continue the page numbering from the previous section of the document (if there is a previous section) or to start at a page number of your choosing. Click the OK button when you've made your selections.

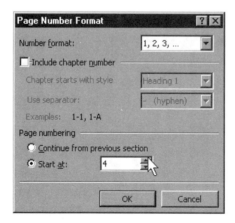

FIGURE 7.12:
In the Page Number Format dialog box, choose formatting and numbering options for the page numbers.

Insert Date	Inserts a code for the current date in the document.
Insert Time	Inserts a code for the current time in the document.
Page Setup	Displays the Page Setup dialog box with the Layout tab at the front.
Show/Hide Document Text	Displays and hides the document text. Its purpose is a little esoteric: You probably won't want to hide your document's text unless you're trying to place a header or footer behind the text. For example, you might want to add a watermark behind the text on a business letter or a brochure.

WARNING Unwittingly clicking the Show/Hide Document Text button can lead you to think you've lost all the text in your document. If your text suddenly disappears under suspicious circumstances, check to see if the Show/Hide Document Text button is selected. If it is, restore the display of the document text by clicking the Show/ Hide Document Text button again. (If the Show/Hide Document Text button isn't the culprit and your text has really vanished, try choosing Edit ➤ Undo, or pressing Ctrl+Z, or closing the document without saving changes.)

Same as Previous	Makes the current header or footer the same as the header or footer in the previous section (if there is one; we'll get into this in a minute) or page (if you're using a different header and footer on the first page). If there is no previous section, this button will not be available.
Switch between Header and Footer	Moves the insertion point between the header and footer. (Alternatively, you can use the up and down arrow keys to move between the two.)
Show Previous	Moves the insertion point to the header or footer in the previous section (if there is one) or page (if you're using a different header and footer on the first page).
Show Next	Moves the insertion point to the header or footer in the next section (if there is one) or page (if you're using a different header and footer on the first page).
Close Header and Footer	Hides the Header and Footer toolbar, closes the header and footer panes, and returns you to whichever view you were using before.

3. To return to your document, click the Close Header and Footer button or choose View ➤ Header and Footer again. You can also double-click anywhere in the main document as long as the Show/Hide Document Text button is not selected.

Formatting Headers and Footers

Despite their special position on the page, headers and footers contain regular Word elements (text, graphics, text boxes, and so on), and you work with them as described in the previous chapters.

By default, Word starts you off with the Header style in the header area and the Footer style in the Footer area. You can modify these styles (as described earlier in this chapter), choose other styles (including Header First, Header Even, and Header Odd, which Word provides in some templates) from the Styles drop-down list on the Formatting toolbar (or by choosing Format ➤ Style and using the Styles dialog box), or apply extra formatting.

> **TIP** Headers and footers aren't restricted to the header and footer areas that appear on your screen—you can also use headers and footers to place repeating text anywhere on your page. While in the header or footer area, insert a text box at a suitable location on the page, and then insert text, graphics, and so on inside the text box. (Chapter 5 discusses how to work with text boxes.)

Producing Different Headers and Footers

Often you'll want different headers and footers on different pages of your documents. Word gives you three options to choose from:

- A different header and footer on the first page of a document
- Different headers and footers on odd and even pages (combined, if you like, with a different header and footer on the first page)
- Different headers and footers in different sections (combined, if you like, with the previous two options for those sections)

Different First-Page Headers and Footers

To produce different headers and footers on the first page of a document:

1. Choose File ➤ Page Setup to display the Page Setup dialog box; click the Layout tab to bring it to the front.
2. In the Headers and Footers box, select Different First Page.
3. Click the OK button to close the Page Setup dialog box.

After setting up your header and footer for the first page of the document, move to the second page and set up the header and footer for it and subsequent pages.

Different Headers and Footers on Odd and Even Pages

To create different headers and footers on odd and even pages, first bring up the Page Setup dialog box (File ➤ Page Setup), and then select the Different Odd and Even check box in the Headers and Footers group box on the Layout tab. Move the insertion point to an odd page and set its header and footer, and move to an even page and set its header and footer.

Different Headers and Footers in Sections

To set different headers and footers in the different sections of a document, create the document and divide it into sections as described in "Section Formatting" earlier in this chapter. To adjust the header or footer for any section, click in that section, and then choose View ➤ Header and Footer to display the Header area of the document.

By default, when a document consists of more than one section, Word sets the header and footer for each section after the first to be the same as the header and footer in the previous section, so the Same as Previous button on the Header and Footer toolbar will appear pushed in, and the legend Same as Previous will appear at the top- right corner of the Header or Footer area. To change this, click the Same as Previous button on the Header and Footer toolbar, and then enter the new header or footer in the Header or Footer area.

To move through the headers or footers in the sections of your document, click the Show Previous and Show Next buttons on the Header and Footer toolbar.

Chapter 8

PRINTING A DOCUMENT

- **Using Print Preview**
- **Printing documents**
- **Printing envelopes**
- **Printing labels**

Once you've written, set up, and formatted your documents, you'll probably want to print them. As with its other features, Word offers a wealth of printing options. Printing can be as simple as clicking one button to print a whole document or as complicated as choosing which parts of your document to print, what to print them on, how many copies to print, and even what order to print them in.

In this chapter, we'll first look at how to use Word's Print Preview mode to nail down any glaring deficiencies in your text before you print it. After that, we'll tackle straightforward printing and then move on to the tricky stuff.

Using Print Preview

Before you print any document, use Word's Print Preview mode to make sure the document looks the way you want it to look. Choose File ➤ Print Preview to display the current document in Print Preview mode (see Figure 8.1).

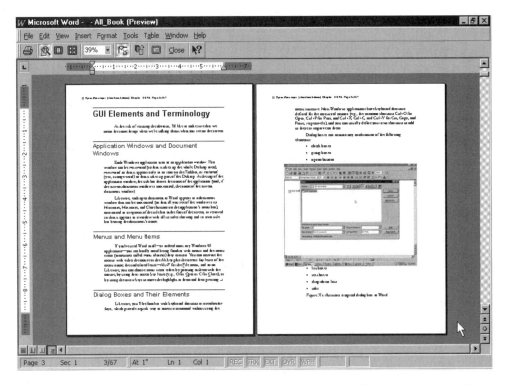

FIGURE 8.1: In Print Preview mode, Word displays your document as it will appear when you print it— to the best of Word's ability.

In Print Preview mode, Word displays the Print Preview toolbar (see Figure 8.2), which offers the following buttons:

Print	Prints the current document using the default print settings.
Magnifier	Switches between Magnifier mode and Editing mode. In Magnifier mode, the mouse pointer appears as a magnifying glass containing a plus sign (when the view is zoomed out) or a minus sign (when the view is zoomed in). In Editing mode, the mouse pointer appears at the insertion point; use it to edit as usual.

One Page	Zooms the view to one full page.
Multiple Pages	Zooms the view to multiple pages. When you click the Multiple Pages button, Word displays a small grid showing the display combinations possible—one full page; two pages side-by-side; three pages side-by-side; two pages, one on top of the other; four pages, two on top, two below, etc. Click and drag through the grid to choose the arrangement of pages you want.
Zoom Control	Lets you choose the zoom percentage that suits you.
View Ruler	Toggles the display of the horizontal and vertical rulers on and off.
Shrink to Fit	Attempts to make your document fit on one fewer page (by changing the font size, line spacing, and margins). This is useful when your crucial fax strays a line or two on to a second or third page, and you would like to shrink it down.
Full Screen	Removes the menus, status bar, scroll bars, etc., from the display. This is useful for clearing more screen real estate to see exactly how your document looks before you print it.
Close Preview	Closes Print Preview, returning you to whichever view you were in before.
Help	Adds a question mark to the mouse pointer, so you can click any screen element and receive pop-up help.

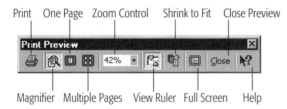

FIGURE 8.2:
The Print Preview toolbar offers quick access to the Print Preview features.

I'll let you explore Print Preview on your own, but here's one thing to try: Display the rulers (by choosing View ➤ Ruler), and then click and drag the gray margin borders on the rulers to quickly adjust the page setup of the document.

TIP

Print Preview will show you how the document will look on the current printer. If you're using Print Preview to check that your document looks okay before you print it, make sure you've already selected the printer you're going to use.

To exit Print Preview, click the Close Preview button on the Print Preview toolbar or choose File ➤ Print Preview again to return to the view you were in before Print Preview.

Printing a Document

Once you've checked a document in Print Preview and made any necessary adjustments, you're ready to print it. Next, you need to decide whether you want to print the whole document at once or just part of it.

Printing All of a Document

The easiest way to print a document in Word is simply to click the Print button on the Standard toolbar. This prints the current document without offering you any options—to be more precise, it prints one copy of the entire document in page-number order (1, 2, 3) to the currently selected printer.

Printing from the Print Dialog Box

If you want to print only part of a document, don't click the Print button. Instead, choose File ➤ Print or press Ctrl+P to display the Print dialog box (see Figure 8.3).

To print from the Print dialog box:

1. Make sure the printer named in the Name drop-down list is the one you want to use. If it's not, use the drop-down list to select the right printer.

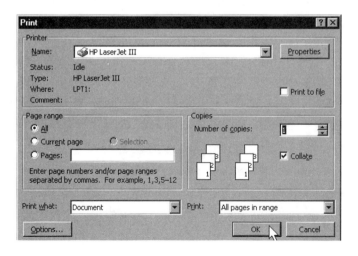

FIGURE 8.3: In the Print dialog box, choose the printer you want to use, which pages you want to print, and the number of copies you want. Then click the OK button to print.

2. Choose which pages to print in the Page Range group box by clicking one of the option buttons:

All Prints the whole document.

Current Page Prints the page where the insertion point is currently.

Selection Prints only the selected text in your document. If you haven't selected any text, this option button will be dimmed.

Pages Lets you print individual pages by number or by range (or ranges) of pages. Use commas to separate the page numbers (for example, **1, 11, 21**) and a hyphen to separate page ranges (for example, **31-41**). You can also combine the two: **1, 11, 21-31, 41-51, 61**.

TIP **To print from a particular page to the end of the document, you don't need to know the last page number of the document—simply enter the page number you want to print from followed by a hyphen (for example, 11-).**

---

3. If you want to print only odd pages or even pages, use the Print drop-down list at the bottom-right corner of the Print dialog box to specify Odd Pages or Even Pages.
4. Choose how many copies of the document you want to print by using the Number of Copies box in the Copies group box. You can also choose whether to collate the pages or not—if you collate them, Word prints the first set of pages in order (1, 2, 3, 4, 5) and then prints the next set and subsequent sets; if you don't collate them, Word prints all the copies of page 1, then all the copies of page 2, and so on.
5. When you've made your choices in the Print dialog box, click the OK button to send the document to the printer.

Printing on Different Paper

So far we've looked only at printing on your default-sized paper (for example, 8½x11" paper). Sooner or later you're going to need to print on a different size of paper, be it to produce a manual, an application to some bureaucracy, or a birthday card. This section discusses how to proceed.

Not only can you use various sizes of paper with Word, but also you can use different sizes of paper for different sections of the same document, as discussed in Chapter 7.

The first thing to do when you want to print on paper of a different size is to set up your document suitably—paper size, margins, and orientation. (Look back to the "Page Setup" section of Chapter 7 for more details on this if you need to.)

Next, choose the paper source for each section of your document.

Choosing a Paper Source

If you're writing a letter or a report, you may want to put the first page on special paper. For example, the first page of a letter might be on company paper that contains the company's logo, name, and address, while subsequent pages might be on paper that contains only the company's name and logo.

To choose the paper source for printing the current section of the current document:

1. Choose File ➤ Page Setup. In the Page Setup dialog box, click the Paper Source tab.

2. In the First Page list box, choose the printer tray that contains the paper for the first page. (If your printer has only one tray, choose Manual Feed.)

3. In the Other Pages list box, choose the printer tray that contains the paper you want to use for the remaining pages of the document. Usually, you'll want to choose the Default Tray here, but on occasion you may want to use another tray or Manual Feed for special effects.

4. In the Apply To drop-down list box, choose the section of the document that you want to print on the paper you're choosing. The default is Whole Document unless the document contains sections, in which case the default is This Section. You can also choose This Point Forward to print the rest of the document on the paper you're choosing, the page the insertion point is on being the "first page" and the rest of the document being the "other pages."

5. Click the OK button to close the Page Setup dialog box; it will automatically save your changes.

To set the paper source for other sections of the document, click in a section and repeat these steps.

Setting a Default Paper Source

If you always print from a different paper tray than your copy of Word is set up to use, you should change the default. This might happen if you always need to use letterhead on a networked printer that has a number of paper trays, and your colleagues keep filling the default paper tray with unflavored white bond.

To set your default paper source:

1. Choose File ➤ Page Setup to display the Page Setup dialog box.
2. On the Paper Source tab, make your selections in the First Page list box and Other Pages list box.
3. Choose an option from the Whole Document drop-down list if necessary.
4. Click the Default button. Word will display a message box asking you to confirm your choice.
5. Click Yes. Word will close the Page Setup dialog box and change the default.

Printing Envelopes

Printing envelopes has long been the bane of the computerized office. Envelopes have been confusing to set up in word-processing applications and—worse—they tend to jam in laser printers (and that's not even mentioning what dot-matrix printers think of envelopes). There have been four traditional ways of avoiding these problems: handwrite the labels, use a typewriter, use window envelopes, or use sheets of labels. If these methods don't appeal to you, read on.

To print an envelope:

1. Choose Tools ➤ Envelopes and Labels. Word will display the Envelopes and Labels dialog box (see Figure 8.4). If Word finds what it identifies as an address in the current document, it will display it in the Delivery Address box. If you don't think Word will find the address hidden in the document—for example, if the document contains more than one address or the address is not broken over several lines into a typical address format—highlight the address before choosing Tools ➤ Envelopes and Labels.
2. If Word hasn't found an address in the document, you'll need to choose it yourself.
   - To include a recently used address, click the Insert Address drop-down list button in the Envelopes and Labels dialog box and choose the name from the drop-down list.

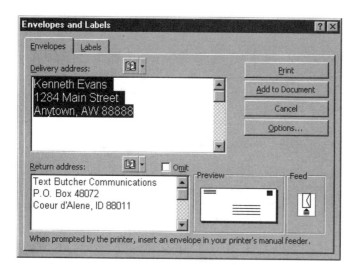

FIGURE 8.4:
Word displays any address it finds in the document—or the address you selected—in the Delivery Address box on the Envelopes and Labels dialog box.

- To include an address from an address book, click the Insert Address button and choose the address book from the Show Names From The drop-down list in the Select Name dialog box. If you aren't logged on to e-mail, you will be prompted to choose a messaging profile before the Select Name dialog box is displayed. Then choose the name, either by typing the first characters of the name into the Type Name or Select from List text box or by selecting it from the list box. Click the OK button to insert the name in the Delivery Address box on the Envelopes and Labels dialog box.

- Alternatively, type the name and address into the Delivery Address box.

3. Verify the return address that Word has inserted in the Return Address box. Word automatically picks this information out of the User Info tab of the Options dialog box. If the information is incorrect, you can correct it in the Return Address box, but it's a better idea to correct it in the Options dialog box if you regularly work with the computer you're now using. (Choose Tools ➤ Options, and then click the User Info tab.)

- You can also use the Insert Address button's drop-down list to insert a recently used address or click the Insert Address button and choose a name in the Select Name dialog box.

- Alternatively, you can omit a return address by checking the Omit check box.

4. Next, check the Preview box to see how the envelope will look and the Feed box to see how Word expects you to feed it into the printer. If either of these is not to your liking, click the Options button (or click the Preview icon or the Feed icon) to display the Envelope Options dialog box (see Figure 8.5).

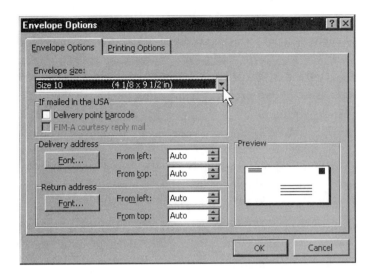

FIGURE 8.5:
In the Envelope Options dialog box, use the Envelope Options tab to set the size of the envelope and the fonts for the delivery address and return address. Use the Printing Options tab to set the feed method you want to use with your printer.

5. On the Envelope Options tab of the Envelope Options dialog box (yes, this gets weird), use the Envelope Size drop-down list to choose the size of envelope you're using. (Check the envelope box for the size before you get out your ruler to measure the envelopes.)

6. If you want to customize the look of the addresses, use the options in the Delivery Address box and Return Address box. The Font button in these boxes opens a version of the Font dialog box, which you'll recognize from Chapter 6. Choose the font and effects you want; then click the OK button. Use the From Left and From Top boxes in the Delivery Address box and Return Address box to set the placement of the address on the envelope. Watch the Preview box to see how you're doing.

7. On the Printing Options tab, Word offers options for changing the envelope feed method—you have the choice of six different envelope orientations, the choice of placing the envelope Face Up or Face Down in the printer, and the choice of Clockwise Rotation. Again, choose the options you want. Click the OK button when you're satisfied.

8. You now have the option of printing the envelope you've set up by clicking the Print button in the Envelopes and Labels dialog box or adding it to the current document by clicking the Add to Document button.

WARNING Don't mess with the printing options unless you have to; if you've set your printer up correctly, Word should be able to make a fair guess at how you'll need to feed the envelope for the printer to print it correctly. You probably won't need to change the settings on the Printing Options tab of the Envelope Options dialog box unless you find that Word won't print your envelopes correctly.

If you choose the Add to Document button, Word places the envelope on a new page at the start of the document and formats the page to require a manual envelope feed. When you print the document, you'll need to start the printer off with a manually fed envelope; once the envelope has printed, Word will resume its normal feeding pattern for the rest of the document (unless that, too, has abnormal paper requirements).

Printing Labels

If you don't want to mess with feeding envelopes into your printer and betting that it won't chew them up, sheets of labels are a good alternative. What's more, Word makes it easy to set up labels.

NOTE In this section, we'll look at how to set up labels for one addressee— either a single label or a whole sheet of labels with the same address on each. For sheets of labels with a different address on each label, see Chapter 10, "Mail Merge."

1. If the current document contains the address you want to use on the label, select the address.

2. Choose Tools ➤ Envelopes and Labels to display the Envelopes and Labels dialog box, and click the Labels tab to display it. If you selected an address in step 1, Word will display it in the Address box.

3. First, choose the type of labels you want. The current type of label is displayed in the Label box in the bottom-right corner of the dialog box. To choose another type of label, click the Options button. You'll see the Label Options dialog box.

- Choose the type of printer you'll be using: Dot Matrix or Laser. (Laser includes ink-jets, bubble-jets, and the like.)
- Choose the printer tray where you'll put the label sheets using the Tray drop-down list.
- Choose the category of label in the Label Products drop-down list: Avery Standard, Avery Pan European, or Other. (Other includes labels by manufacturers other than Avery.)
- In the Product Number list box, choose the type of labels you're using—it should be on the box of labels. The Label Information group box will show the details for the type of labels you've selected in the Product Number list box.
- For more details on the labels you've chosen or to customize them, click the Details button to display the Information dialog box. Click OK when you're done.
- Click the OK button in the Label Options dialog box to return to the Envelopes and Labels dialog box. It will now display the labels you've chosen in the Label box.

4. Add the address (if you haven't already selected one):
   - To include an address from your current address book, click the Insert Address drop-down list button and choose the name from the drop-down list.
   - To include an address from another address book, click the Insert Address button and choose the address book from the Show Names From The drop-down list in the Select Name dialog box. If you aren't logged on to e-mail, you will be prompted to choose a messaging profile before the Select Name dialog box is displayed. Then choose the name, either by typing the first characters of the name into the Type Name or Select from List text box or by selecting it from the list box. Click the OK button to insert the name in the Address box of the Envelopes and Labels dialog box.
   - Alternatively, type the name and address into the Address box.

5. In the Print group box, choose whether to print a full page of the same label or a single label. If you choose to print a single label, set the Row and Column numbers that describe its location on the sheet of labels.

6. If you chose to print a full page of the same label, click the New Document button to create a new document containing the labels, and then print it and save it for future use. Alternatively, click the Print button to print the sheet of labels. (If you chose to print a single label, Word offers only the Print button.)

TIP   If you want to customize your labels, choose the New Document button, and then add any formatting that you'd like. You can also add graphics using Word's Insert ➤ Picture command.

Chapter 9

COLUMNS, TABLES, AND SORTING

FEATURING

- Creating, formatting, and deleting columns
- Creating and inserting tables
- Editing and formatting tables
- Converting tables to text
- Arranging your data suitably for sorting
- Sorting your data
- Using Word's sorting options

In this chapter, we'll look at two ways to create multicolumn documents in Word without using large numbers of tabs. Word's *columns* provide a quick way to create newspaper-style columns of text. *Tables* are for laying out text (or data) in columns made up of rows of cells—and, if necessary, for sorting that text or data.

Columns

To create columns in a document, you can either convert existing text to columns, or you can create columns and then enter the text in them.

Word uses sections (discussed in Chapter 7) to separate text formatted in different numbers of columns from the rest of the document. If a whole document contains the same number of columns, Word doesn't use section breaks, but if the document contains one-column and two-column text, Word will divide the text with section breaks; likewise, two-column text will be separated from three-column text, three-column text from four-column text from two-column text, and so on, as shown in Figure 9.1.

Anytown·Mine·to·Close·Next·Year¶

by·Molly·Hindhaugh¶··Section Break (Continuous)···················

| The·rural·community·of· Anytown·was·thrown·into· shock·yesterday·by·the·news· that·its·renowned·copper· mine·will·close·next·year,· five·years·earlier·than·had· been·anticipated.¶ | In·a·wide-reaching·imple- mentation·of·the·budget·cuts· agreed·on·at·last·week's·Council· meeting,·Anytown·plans·to· close·the·mine·without·further· investigation·of·opportunities·to· extend·its·life.¶ | Anytown·Copper·Works·currently· employs·369·people,·all·of·whose· livelihoods·depend·on·the·copper· mine.·While·the·Copper·Works·may· be·able·to·continue·operating·under· special·circumstances·agreed·upon·by· *(continued·on·page·4·col.·5)¶*········ |

Local·Boy·Saves·Dog¶

by·our·Special·Correspondent¶··Section Break (Continuous)···················

| By·diving·into·a·roaring·stream·swollen·with· the·runoff·from·spring·downpours·to·rescue·a· sheepdog·swept·off·a·bridge,·Mark·Frazer· claimed·the·respect·of·the·Anytown·community· on·Monday.¶ | Mark,·13,·played·down·his·feat·with·the·modesty· that·has·made·him·a·favorite·among·his·schoolmates·at· Anytown·Junior·School.¶ "I·just·saw·the·dog·and·did·it·without·thinking,"·he· explained.¶············Section Break (Continuous)··········· |

FIGURE 9.1: Word uses section breaks to separate the sections of text that have different numbers of columns from each other.

NOTE   **Word displays column layouts only in Page Layout view and in Print Preview. In Normal view, Online Layout view, and Outline view, Word won't indicate how the columns in your document will look.**

Creating Columns Quickly with the Columns Button

To create columns quickly, without worrying about formatting details:

1. To create columns from existing text, select it. To create columns in only one part of your document, select that part.

2. Click the Columns button on the Standard toolbar and drag down and to the right over the grid that appears to indicate how many columns you want. Release the mouse button, and Word will create the columns.

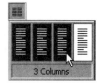

Creating Columns with the Columns Dialog Box

For more control over the columns you create, use the Columns dialog box instead of the Columns button:

1. To create columns from existing text, first select the text. To create columns in only one part of your document, select that part.

2. Choose Format ➤ Columns to display the Columns dialog box (see Figure 9.2).

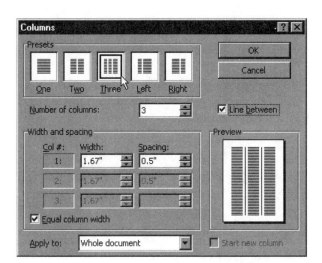

FIGURE 9.2:
The Columns dialog box gives you fine control over the number of columns and their formatting.

3. Choose the number of columns you want to create, either by clicking one of the buttons in the Presets group box or by entering a number in the Number of Columns box. (These settings affect each other.) Watch the Preview box as you choose the settings for your columns.

4. If need be, adjust the column width and spacing in the Width and Spacing group box.
   - If you chose One, Two, or Three columns from the Presets box and want to produce columns of varying widths, clear the Equal Column Width check box.
   - In the Width box for each column, enter the column width you want. In the Spacing box, enter the amount of space you want between this column and the column to its right.
5. To add a line between each column on your page, select the Line Between check box.
6. Click the OK button to close the Columns dialog box and create the columns with the settings you chose.

Changing the Number of Columns

Once you've created columns in a document, you can change the number of columns by selecting the relevant text and using either the Columns button or the Columns dialog box:

- Click the Columns button on the Standard toolbar and drag the grid that appears until you've selected the number of columns you want.
- Choose Format ➤ Columns to make adjustments to the columns as described in the previous section, "Creating Columns with the Columns Dialog Box."

Starting a New Column

To start a new column at the top of the page:

1. Place the insertion point at the beginning of the text that will start the new column.
2. Choose Format ➤ Columns to display the Columns dialog box.
3. In the Apply To drop-down list, choose This Point Forward.
4. Select the Start New Column check box.
5. Click the OK button to close the Columns dialog box. Word will create a new column from the insertion point forward.

Removing Columns from Text

You don't really remove columns from text—you adjust the number of columns. For example, to "remove" two-column formatting from text, you change the text to a single-column layout.

The easiest way to switch back to a single-column layout is to click the Columns button on the Standard toolbar and drag through the resulting grid to select the one-column bar; then release the mouse button. Alternatively, choose Format ➤ Columns to display the Columns dialog box, choose One from the Presets group box, and then click the OK button.

To switch only part of a document back to a single-column format, select that part first. To switch only a section, place the insertion point anywhere within that section.

Tables

Word's tables give you a way to present complex information in vertical columns and horizontal rows of cells. Cells can contain text—a single paragraph or multiple paragraphs—or graphics.

You can create a table from existing text, or you can create a table first and then enter your text into it. Once you've created a table, you can add further columns or rows, or merge several cells in the same row to make one cell.

To embellish your tables, you can use borders, along with font formatting (bold, italic, underline, highlight, and so on), paragraph formatting (indents, line spacing and so on), and style formatting—not to mention Word's Table AutoFormat feature. We'll briefly look at formatting tables in this section.

Word provides the Tables and Borders toolbar (see Figure 9.3) for working with tables.

Here's what the buttons on the Tables and Borders toolbar do:

- The Draw Table button turns the mouse pointer into a pen that you can click and drag to draw table cells in a document. Click the button again to restore the mouse pointer.
- The Eraser button turns the mouse pointer into an eraser that you can drag to erase the borders of cells. Click the button again to restore the mouse pointer.
- The Line Style button displays a drop-down list of available line styles. Select one for the cells you're about to draw.
- The Line Weight button displays a drop-down list of available line weights for the current line style.

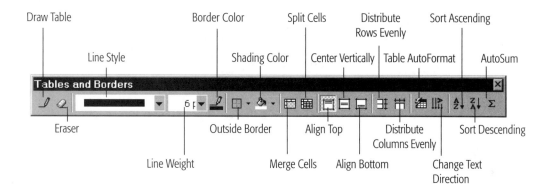

FIGURE 9.3: The Tables and Borders toolbar

- The Border Color button displays a palette of available border colors.
- The Outside Border button applies the current border to the selection or to tables or cells you draw. To change the current border, click the drop-down list button and choose a type of border from the palette.
- The Shading Color button applies the current shading color to the selection. To change the current shading color, click the drop-down list button and choose a color from the palette.
- The Merge Cells button merges the contents of selected cells.
- The Split Cells button displays the Split Cells dialog box for splitting the selected cell into two or more cells.
- The Align Top button, the Center Vertically button, and the Align Bottom button control the vertical alignment of selected cells.
- The Distribute Rows Evenly button and the Distribute Columns Evenly button adjust row height and column width, respectively, to equal the tallest cell in the row or the widest cell in the column.
- The Table AutoFormat button displays the Table AutoFormat dialog box. We'll look at autoformatting later in the chapter.
- The Change Text Direction button rotates the text in the selected cell in 90-degree jumps.
- The Sort Ascending button and the Sort Descending button are for quick sorting.
- The AutoSum button inserts a formula for adding the contents of a row or column.

Drawing a Table with the Draw Table Button

To quickly design your own table, use the Draw Table feature:

1. First, display the Tables and Borders toolbar if it's not displayed. (Click on the menu bar or on any displayed toolbar, and choose Tables and Borders from the drop-down list of toolbars.)

2. Verify the settings in the Line Style and Line Weight drop-down lists and the color on the Border Color button to make sure they're suitable for the table you want to draw.

3. Click the Draw Table button on the Tables and Borders toolbar. (Display the Tables and Borders toolbar if it's not displayed.) The mouse pointer will turn into a pen.

4. Click and drag in the document to create the shape for the table.

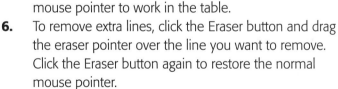

5. Click and drag across the table to create rows; click and drag down to create columns. Word will adjust the row height to make the rows the same height. Click the Draw Table button again when you need to restore the normal mouse pointer to work in the table.

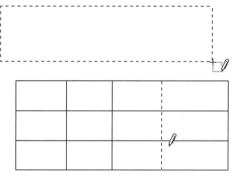

6. To remove extra lines, click the Eraser button and drag the eraser pointer over the line you want to remove. Click the Eraser button again to restore the normal mouse pointer.

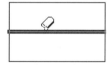

Inserting a Table Quickly with the Insert Table Button

The easiest way to insert a table is to click the Insert Table button on the Standard toolbar. Drag the mouse pointer down and to the right over the grid that appears to select the format of table (number of rows and columns) you want to create, and then release the mouse button. Word will create the table and apply borders to it.

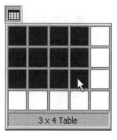

3 x 4 Table

To create the table from existing text, select the text before clicking the Insert Table button. Word will not display the grid when you click the button but will convert the text to an appropriate table configuration. For example, if you have three columns laid out with tabs, Word will create a three-column table when you click the Insert Table button.

Inserting a Table with the Insert Table Command

You can also insert a table by choosing Table ➤ Insert Table and then choosing the details of the table in the Number of Columns, Number of Rows, and Column Width boxes in the Insert Table dialog box (see Figure 9.4).

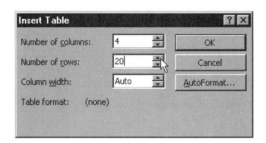

FIGURE 9.4
In the Insert Table dialog box, set up the table you want to create.

Using Table Autoformatting

Formatting your tables can be a slow business, so Word offers a Table AutoFormat feature that can speed up the process. To create a new table and autoformat it, choose Table ➤ Insert Table and click the AutoFormat button in the Insert Table dialog box. Word will display the Table AutoFormat dialog box (see Figure 9.5).

If you're not sure what shape and layout your table will take on as you create it, you can also apply autoformatting after creating the table—just click inside the table and click the Table AutoFormat button on the Tables and Borders toolbar, or choose Table ➤ Table AutoFormat, or right-click in the table and choose Table Auto-Format from the context menu. Alternatively, you can format the table manually, as we'll see in "Formatting a Table."

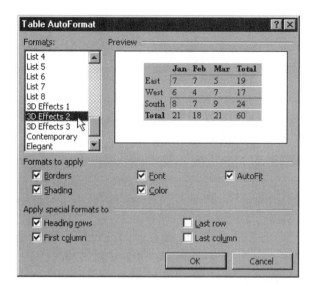

FIGURE 9.5
The Table AutoFormat dialog box offers quick access to a veritable plethora of predefined table formats and options to customize them.

Use the Formats list box and the adjacent Preview box to choose the format that suits your table best. You'll find that some of the formats (for example, Elegant and Professional) fail to live up to their names, but others (such as 3D Effects 2) might be satisfactory.

In the Formats to Apply area, choose whether you want Word to apply Borders, Shading, Font, and Color formatting to the table by selecting or clearing the check boxes. Watch the Preview box again to see the effects your changes will have. The most important of these formatting options is AutoFit, which causes Word to adjust the column width to suit the text in your table rather than blindly allotting an inappropriate width to each column.

In the Apply Special Formats To area, select the check boxes to choose which rows and columns you want Word to apply special formatting to: Heading Rows, First Column, Last Row, and Last Column. The last two choices are good for emphasizing totals or conclusions.

Once you've made your choices, click the OK button. If you're creating a table, Word will return you to the Insert Table dialog box, where you again click OK to dismiss the dialog box. Word will create the table with the formatting you've chosen; if you're running AutoFormat on a table already created, Word will apply the formatting you chose to the table.

Converting Existing Text to a Table

If you've already got the material for a table in a Word document, but it's laid out with tabs, paragraphs, commas, or the like, you can quickly convert it to a table:

1. First, select the text.

2. Choose Table ➤ Convert Text to Table. Word will display the Convert Text to Table dialog box (see Figure 9.6) with its best guess about how you want to separate the text into table cells:

   • If the selected text consists of apparently regular paragraphs of text, Word will suggest separating it at the paragraph marks, so each paragraph will go into a separate cell.

   • If the selected text appears to contain tabbed columns, Word will suggest separating it at each tab, so each tabbed column will become a table column.

   • If the selected text appears to have commas at regular intervals in each paragraph—as in a list of names and addresses, for example—Word will suggest separating the text at each comma. This is suitable for database-output information (such as names and addresses) separated by commas.

   • If the selected text appears to be divided by other characters (such as hyphens), Word will suggest dividing it at each hyphen (or whatever).

3. If necessary, change the setting in the Separate Text At box. This may change the number of columns and rows that Word has suggested. If you choose Other, enter the separator character in the Other box. This can be any character or any letter.

4. If necessary, manually adjust the number of columns and rows by changing the number in the Number of Columns box; the number of rows will adjust automatically.

5. Adjust the setting in the Column Width box if you want to. Auto usually does a reasonable job, and you can adjust the column widths later if you need to.

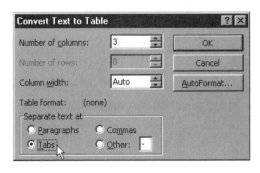

FIGURE 9.6

In the Convert Text to Table dialog box, choose the options for converting existing text into a Word table.

6. Click the OK button to convert the text to a table, or click the AutoFormat button to have Word walk you through formatting the table. If you choose AutoFormat, click OK when Word returns you to the Convert Text to Table dialog box after formatting.

Selecting Parts of a Table

When manipulating your tables, first you need to select the parts you want to manipulate. While you can just click and drag with the mouse (or use the keyboard or the Shift+click technique discussed in Chapter 5), Word also offers shortcuts for selecting parts of tables.

- To select one cell, move the mouse pointer into the thin cell-selection bar at the left edge of the cell. You'll know when it's in the right place because the insertion point will change to an arrow pointing north-northeast. Then click once to select the cell (including its end-of-cell marker).
- To select a row, move the mouse pointer into the table selection bar to the left of the row and then click. Alternatively, double-click in the cell selection bar at the left edge of any cell in the row.
- To select multiple rows, click in the table selection bar and drag up or down.
- To select a column, Alt+click in it. Alternatively, move the mouse pointer to just above the topmost row of the column, where it will turn into a little black arrow pointing straight down, and then click.
- To select multiple columns, click just above the topmost row of any column and drag left or right.
- To select the whole table, Alt+double-click anywhere in it.

TIP   One of the keys to understanding how Word selects cells is the hidden end-of-cell marker that each cell contains. Once you drag past this to another cell, you've selected both that cell and the other. The end-of-cell marker is a little circle with pointy corners. To display end-of-cell markers, choose Tools ➤ Options to display the Options dialog box and select the Paragraphs check box in the Nonprinting Characters area on the View tab, or click the Show/Hide button on the Standard toolbar.

Word also offers menu options for selecting parts of tables: Table ➤ Select Column, Table ➤ Select Row, and Table ➤ Select Table. Place the insertion point in the appropriate row or column (or drag through the rows or columns to select cells in multiple rows or columns), and then choose the appropriate command.

Navigating in Tables

You can move easily through tables using the mouse, the arrow keys, or the Tab key: ← moves you backwards through the contents of a cell, character by character, and then to the end of the previous cell; → moves you forwards and then to the start of the next cell; ↑ moves you up through the lines and paragraphs in a cell and then up to the next row; and ↓ moves you downwards. Tab moves you to the next cell, selecting any contents in the process; Shift+Tab moves you to the previous cell and also selects any contents in the cell.

Adding and Deleting Cells, Rows, and Columns

Often you'll need to change the layout of your table after you create it—for example, you might need to add a column or two, or delete several rows, so your information is presented most effectively.

TIP	Word distinguishes between deleting the contents of a cell, row, or column and deleting the cell, row, or column itself. When you delete the contents of a cell, row, or column, the cell, row, or column remains in place, but when you delete the cell, row, or column, both it and any contents in it disappear. To delete just the contents of a cell, row, or column, select your victim and press Delete.

Adding Cells

To add cells to a table, select the cells above which or to the right of which you want to insert the new cells, and then right-click and choose Insert Cells from the context menu or choose Table ➤ Insert Cells. In the Insert Cells dialog box, choose Shift Cells Right or Shift Cells Down to specify how the selected cells should move, and then click the OK button.

Deleting Cells

To delete cells and their contents from a table, select the cells, right-click, and choose Delete Cells from the context menu or choose Table ➤ Delete Cells. Word will display the Delete Cells dialog box, offering to move the remaining cells up or to the left to fill the space left by the cells you're deleting. If necessary, choose Shift Cells Left or Shift Cells Up and then click the OK button.

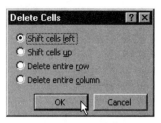

Adding Rows

You can add a row or rows to a table in several ways:

- To add a row to the end of a table instantly, position the insertion point in the last cell of the table and press Tab.
- To add a row to a table, click in the row above which you want to add the new row; then right-click and choose Insert Rows from the context menu or choose Table ➤ Insert Rows.
- To insert multiple rows, select the same number of existing rows, right-click, and choose Insert Rows from the context menu or choose Table ➤ Insert Rows. For example, to add three rows, select three rows.
- Alternatively, after selecting a cell or cells in a number of rows, choose Table ➤ Insert Cells, select the Insert Entire Row option in the Insert Cells dialog box, and then click OK.

TIP **The Insert Table button on the Standard toolbar changes into an Insert Rows button when the insertion point is inside a table and into an Insert Columns button when you've selected one or more columns in a table.**

Deleting Rows

To delete a row of cells from a table, right-click in the row you want to delete and choose Delete Cells from the context menu, or click in the row and choose Table ➤ Delete Cells. In the Delete Cells dialog box, choose Delete Entire Row and click the OK button.

You can skip the Delete Cells dialog box by first selecting the row. Then either right-click and choose Delete Rows from the context menu, or choose Table ➤ Delete Rows.

To delete multiple rows, select the rows you want to delete; then either right-click and choose Delete Rows from the context menu, or choose Table ➤ Delete Rows.

Adding Columns

To add a column to a table, select the column to the left of the new column you want to add, and then right-click and choose Insert Columns from the context menu, or choose Table ➤ Insert Columns.

To insert multiple columns, select the same number of existing columns to the left of the ones you want to add, and then right-click and choose Insert Columns from the context menu, or choose Table ➤ Insert Columns. For example, to add three columns, select three columns.

Deleting Columns

To delete a column of cells from a table, right-click in the column and choose Delete cells from the context menu, or choose Table ➤ Delete Cells. In the Delete Cells dialog box, choose Delete Entire Column and click the OK button.

You can skip the Delete Cells dialog box: first, select the column, and then right-click and choose Delete Columns from the context menu, or choose Table ➤ Delete Columns.

To delete multiple columns, select the columns you want to delete, right-click, and choose Delete Columns from the context menu, or choose Table ➤ Delete Columns.

TIP   To delete an entire table, first select the table using Table ➤ Select Table and then choose Table ➤ Delete Rows.

Editing Text in a Table

Once the insertion point is inside a cell, you can enter and edit text (and other elements) as in any Word document, except for entering tabs, for which you need to press Ctrl+Tab.

Row height adjusts automatically as you add more text to a cell or as you increase the height of the text. You can also adjust it manually, as we'll see in a moment.

Formatting a Table

As with editing text in a table, you can use the regular Word formatting features—from the toolbars, the Font and Paragraph dialog boxes, and so on—to format your tables. However, there are a couple of exceptions worth mentioning: alignment and indents.

Setting Alignment in Tables

Alignment in tables is very straightforward once you know that not only can any row of the table be left-aligned, right-aligned, or centered (all relative to the margins set for the page), but also within those rows, the text in each cell can be left-aligned, right-aligned, centered, or justified, relative to the column it's in. If that's not enough, the contents of any cell can be aligned top or bottom or centered vertically.

For example, you could center your table horizontally on the page and have the first column left-aligned, the second centered, the third justified, and the fourth right-aligned (though the result would almost certainly look weird). Figure 9.7 shows a table that is more reasonably aligned: The first column is right-aligned to present the numbers in a logical fashion; the second column is right-aligned; and the third left-aligned with the space between the columns reduced to display each first name and last name together while retaining the ability to sort by last name. The Age column is centered (for aesthetics and this example), and the numbers in the Years of Service column are right-aligned. The table itself is centered on the page.

To set alignment within any cell, use the methods discussed in Chapter 6: the alignment buttons on the Formatting toolbar, the keyboard shortcuts, or the Paragraph dialog box.

Our four most trusted employees have been with the company for varying lengths of time, but have all demonstrated unswerving loyalty to our vision and mission. They are:

ID#	FIRST NAME	LAST NAME	AGE	YEARS OF SERVICE
4463	Mike	van Buhler	44	8
4460	Tomoko	Thenard	31	1
4401	Julianna	Thompson	59	33
4455	Karl	Soennichsen	22	2

How much, you might wonder, will they receive in salary increases and strategic

FIGURE 9.7: Use the different types of alignment to display your information clearly.

To set alignment for a row, choose Table ➤ Cell Height and Width and choose Left, Center, or Right in the Alignment group box on the Row tab of the Cell Height and Width dialog box (see Figure 9.8).

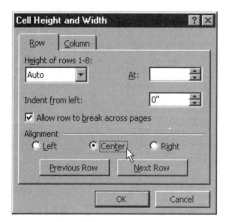 To set vertical alignment for a cell, click the Align Top, Center Vertically, or Align Bottom button on the Tables and Borders toolbar. Alternatively, right-click in the table, choose Alignment from the context menu, and select Align Top, Center Vertically, or Align Bottom from the Alignment submenu.

FIGURE 9.8
Set alignment for a row on the Row tab of the Cell Height and Width dialog box.

Setting Indents in Tables

As with alignment, you can indent the entire table or the contents within each cell. By understanding the difference, you can position your tables precisely where you want them on the page and lay out the table text using suitable indents.

To set indentation for the text in the current cell, use the methods you learned in Chapter 6—drag the indentation markers on the ruler or change the settings in the Indentation area on the Indents and Spacing tab of the Paragraph dialog box. For example, the numbers in the Years of Service column in the table shown in Figure 9.7 have been indented 0.4" from the right margin of the cell to display them more clearly.

To set indentation for a row, choose Table ➤ Cell Height and Width to display the Cell Height and Width dialog box. Enter a measurement in the Indent from Left box on the Row tab and click the OK button.

Adding Borders and Shading to Your Tables

Adding borders and shading to your tables is a little more complex than you might expect. Because Word lets you add borders and shading to the paragraphs inside the table, to any given cell, or to the whole table, you have to be careful about what you select.

TIP | **The quickest way to add borders and shading to a table is to use the Table AutoFormat command, discussed earlier in "Using Table Autoformatting." If you want more information, read on. You can also experiment by using the Border button and Shading button on the Tables and Borders toolbar.**

Adding Borders and Shading to the Whole Table

To add borders and shading to the whole table, click anywhere in it, but don't select anything, and then choose Format ➤ Borders and Shading. Word will display the Borders and Shading dialog box. Make sure the Apply To drop-down list shows Table. Choose the border options you want on the Borders tab and the shading options you want on the Shading tab; then click the OK button.

Adding Borders and Shading to Selected Cells

To add borders and shading to selected cells in a table, select the cells by dragging through them or by using the keyboard. (If you're selecting just one cell, make sure you select its end-of-cell mark as well, so the whole cell is highlighted, not just part of the text.) Then choose Format ➤ Borders and Shading to display the Borders and Shading dialog box. Make sure the Apply To drop-down list shows Cell rather than Table, Paragraph, or Text. Again, choose the border options you want on the Borders tab and the shading options you want on the Shading tab; then click the OK button.

Adding Borders and Shading to Paragraphs within Cells

To add borders and shading to paragraphs within a cell, select the text you want to format in the cell but don't select the end-of-cell mark. Then choose Format ➤ Borders and Shading to display the Borders and Shading dialog box. This time, make sure the Apply To drop-down list shows Text (for less than a paragraph) or Paragraph (for more than one paragraph). Choose the border and shading options you want.

If you want to adjust the placement of the borders from the text, click the Options button to display the Border and Shading Options dialog box, and then set the placement in the Top, Bottom, Left, and Right boxes in the From Text area and click OK.

Merging Cells

Once you've set up your table, you can create special layout effects by *merging* cells—converting two or more cells into a single cell. To merge cells, select the cells to merge; then either click the Merge Cells button on the Tables and Borders toolbar, or right-click and choose Merge Cells from the context menu, or choose Table ➤ Merge Cells. Word will combine the cells into one, putting the contents of each in a separate paragraph in the merged cell; you can then remove the paragraph marks to reduce them to one paragraph if necessary.

Merged cells are especially useful for effects such as table spanner heads. In the example shown here, the headings "Western Region Results" and "Eastern Seaboard Results" occupy merged cells that span the whole table.

1994	1995	1996	1997	1998	1999	2000
Western Region Results						
44	48	65	67	71	79	100
Eastern Seaboard Results						
11	12	15	22	23	26	43

Changing Column Width

The easiest way to change column width is to move the mouse pointer over a column's right-hand border, so the insertion point changes into a two-headed arrow pointing east and west. Then click and drag the column border to a suitable position. (You can also click in the column division mark in the horizontal ruler and drag that instead.)

TIP   **Hold down Shift while you drag the column border to affect only the column whose right border you're dragging. Otherwise, Word will change the width of the column to the right of the border you're moving as well.**

To change column width more precisely, position the insertion point in the column you want to change, and then choose Table ➤ Cell Height and Width. In the Cell Height and Width dialog box, click the Columns tab to bring it to the front if it isn't already there, and then set the column width in the Width of Column *n* box. Some of the other options you can set include the following:

- If you like, you can also change the amount of space separating columns by entering a different measurement in the Space between Columns box.
- Use the Previous Column and Next Column buttons to move to different columns and set their width.
- Click the AutoFit button to have Word automatically set a width for the column based on its contents.

When you're finished, click the OK button to close the Cell Height and Width dialog box.

TIP   To share available space evenly among columns, select the columns (or the whole table) and choose Table ➤ Distribute Columns Evenly.

Changing Row Height

Word sets row height automatically as you add text to (or remove text from) the cells in any row or adjust the height of the contents of the cells. But you can also set the height of a row manually by placing the insertion point in it and choosing Table ➤ Cell Height and Width. Word will display the Cell Height and Width dialog box. If the Row tab isn't foremost, click it.

TIP   To make a number of rows the same height as the one that contains the tallest cells, select the rows (or the whole table) and choose Table ➤ Distribute Rows Evenly.

From the Height of Rows *n* drop-down list, choose At Least to enter a minimum height for the row or Exactly to enter a precise height. Then enter the measurement in the At box.

- Use the Previous Row and Next Row buttons to move to the previous or next row and set its height.
- Check the Allow Row to Break across Pages box if you're working with long cells that you can allow to break over pages.

Click the OK button to close the Cell Height and Width dialog box when you're finished.

TIP You can also change row height in Page Layout view by clicking and dragging a row-break mark (a double horizontal line) on the vertical ruler or clicking and dragging any horizontal border except the top one in a table.

Table Headings

If you're working with tables too long to fit on a single page, you'll probably want to set table headings that repeat automatically on the second and subsequent pages. To do so, select the row or rows that form the headings, and then choose Table ➤ Headings. Word will place a check mark by the Headings item in the Table menu.

Word will repeat these headings automatically if the table is broken with an automatic page break, but not if you insert a manual page break. Word displays the repeated headings only in Page Layout view and Print Preview, so don't expect to see them in Normal view.

To remove table headings, choose Table ➤ Headings again. Word will remove the check mark from the Headings item in the Table menu.

Table Formulas

If you're using tables for numbers—sales targets, net profits, expense reports, or whatever—you may want to use Word's table formula. These include a variety of mathematical functions, including rounding and averaging, that you may want to get into on your own but which go beyond the scope of this book. To work with formulas, select the Table ➤ Formula command to display the Formula dialog box.

 The most useful formula for everyday purposes is the SUM formula. To add the numbers in a row or column of cells, click the AutoSum button on the Tables and Borders toolbar.

TIP Using table formulas is a bit like building a mini-spreadsheet in Word. If table formulas aren't enough to satisfy you and you need to create a full-fledged spreadsheet in Word, look back to Chapter 2 and the discussion of how you can embed an Excel spreadsheet (and worse) in a Word document.

Copying and Moving within Tables

To copy or move material within a table, either use the mouse and drag to move the selection (or Ctrl-drag to copy it), or use the Cut, Copy, and Paste commands via the Standard toolbar, the Edit menu, or their keyboard shortcuts.

Converting a Table to Text

Sooner or later you're going to need to convert a table back to text. To do so, simply select the table by choosing Table ➤ Select Table or by Alt+double-clicking inside it, and then choose Table ➤ Convert Table to Text. Word will display the Convert Table to Text dialog box with its best guess (based on the contents of the table) at how it should divide the cells when it converts it: with paragraphs, with tabs, with commas, or with another character of your choice. Correct the Separate Text With setting if it's inappropriate, and then click the OK button.

Sorting Information

Once you've created tables of information (or even multicolumn lists formatted using tabs), you'll probably need to sort the information.

Word's sorting feature lets you sort data by up to three types of information at once, such as last name, street name, and zip code. If that doesn't produce fine enough results, you can then sort the same data again using different types of information, such as first name and age—and again, if need be.

How Word Sorts

To make full use of sorting, you need to know *how* Word sorts information. Word sorts by *records* and *fields*, two familiar words that carry quite different meanings in computing. A *record* will typically make up one of the items you want to sort and will consist of a number of *fields*, each of which contain one piece of the information that makes up a record. For example, in a mailing database containing name and address information, each customer and the customer's associated set of data would form a record; that record would consist of a number of fields, such as the customer's first name, middle initial, last name, street address, city, state, zip code, area code, phone number, and so on. In Word, this record could be entered in a table, with one field per cell, or as a paragraph, with the fields separated by tabs, commas, or a character of your choice.

Next, you need to know what order Word sorts things in. Here are the details:

- Word can sort alphabetically, numerically, or chronologically (in a variety of date formats).
- Word can sort in ascending order—from A to Z, from 0 to 9, from early dates to later dates—or in descending order (the opposite).
- Word sorts punctuation marks and symbols (such as **&** and **!**) first, and then numbers, and finally letters. If two items start with the same letter, Word goes on to the next letter and sorts them by that, and so on; if two fields are the same, Word sorts using the next field, and so on.

Arranging Your Data for Sorting

If you've already entered all the data in your document or table and are raring to go ahead and sort it, skip to the next section, "Performing a Multilevel Sort." If you're still in the process of entering your data, or haven't yet started, read on.

The first key to successful sorting is to divide your records into as many fields as you might possibly want to sort by. Put first names and last names in separate fields, so you can sort by either; likewise, break addresses down into street, city, state, and zip code, so you can sort your data by any one of them. To target customers street by street, break up the street address into the number and the street name, so you can produce a list of customers on Green Street, say, or Hesperian Avenue.

Use a table for complex data or for data that won't all fit on one line of a tabbed document. (You can carry over tabs from the first line of a paragraph onto the second and subsequent lines, but it's visually confusing and rarely worth the effort when table cells can wrap text and keep it visually clear.)

WARNING Above all, before running any complex sorts, save your data and make a backup of it—or even run a practice sort on a spare copy of the data.

Performing a Multilevel Sort

You can perform either a multilevel sort or a single-level sort with paragraph text and with tables. Sorting text in paragraphs is very similar to sorting text in tables, so in this section, we'll look primarily at sorting text in tables, with notes on how to sort text in paragraphs.

Word sorts tables by rows, treating each row as a unit, unless you tell it otherwise. For example, if you select only cells in the first two columns of a four-column table and run a sort operation, Word will rearrange the third and fourth columns according to the sort criteria you chose for the first two columns as well. Likewise, when you sort text in paragraphs, Word treats each paragraph as a unit to be sorted unless you tell it to do otherwise.

NOTE **To sort table columns without sorting entire rows, or to sort only part of a number of paragraphs, see the section titled "Using Sort Options" later in this chapter.**

To perform a multilevel sort:

1. Select the part of the table you want to sort, or select the paragraphs. To sort a whole table, just click anywhere inside the table; Word will automatically select the whole table for you when you choose Table ➤ Sort.

2. Choose Table ➤ Sort to display the Sort dialog box (see Figure 9.9). When sorting paragraphs, you will see the Sort Text dialog box.

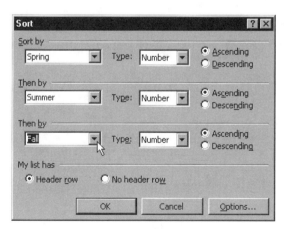

FIGURE 9.9
Choose options for sorting tables in the Sort dialog box.

3. Look at the My List Has area at the bottom of the dialog box and ensure that Word has correctly identified any header row (row of headings) at the top of the table or of the rows you're sorting. Word omits the header row from the

sort, figuring that you'll still want it at the top of the table. If the text has a header row, make sure the Header Row option button is selected— otherwise, Word will treat the header row as text and sort it along with everything else. You will need to select at least three rows to persuade Word that the rows have a header row.

- If you've set table headings using the Table ➤ Headings command, you don't need to worry about the My List Has area—Word knows that the table has headings and dims the My List Has options.
- When you're sorting paragraphs, Word identifies a header row by the differences in formatting from the rest of the text—a different style, font, font size, bold, italic, and so on. (The header row doesn't have to be a bigger font size or boldfaced—it can be smaller than the other text or have no bold to the other text's bold—just so long as Word can recognize it as being different.) Be warned that Word may miss your header row if several paragraphs—not just the first paragraph—have different formatting; it may also miss the header row for reasons known only to itself.

4. In the Sort By group box, choose the column (the field) by which to sort the rows of cells first.

- If your table (or your selected rows) has a header row, Word will display the names of the headings (abbreviated if necessary) in the drop-down list to help you identify the sort key you want. If your text has no header row, Word will display Column 1, Column 2… for tables, and Field 1, Field 2… for paragraph text.
- If your text consists of paragraphs with no fields that Word can identify, Word will display Paragraphs in the Sort By box.

5. In the Type box, make sure that Word has chosen the appropriate option: Text, Number, or Date.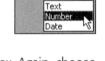

6. Choose Ascending or Descending for the order in which to sort the rows.

7. If necessary, specify a second sort key in the first Then By box. Again, choose the field by which to sort, verify the Type, and choose Ascending or Descending.

8. To sort by a third sort key, repeat step 7 for the second Then By box.

9. Click the OK button to perform the sort and close the Sort dialog box.

Word will leave the table (or the selection of rows or paragraphs) highlighted, so if you want to run another sort to get your data into a more precise order, simply repeat steps 2–9.

Using Sort Options

To allow you to direct its sorting capabilities even more precisely, Word offers five sort options in the Sort Options dialog box (see Figure 9.10). Some of these options are available only for particular types of sorts.

FIGURE 9.10
The Sort Options dialog box provides ways of refining your sorting.

To choose sort options, click the Options button in the Sort Text dialog box or the Sort dialog box. The Sort Options group box in the Sort Options dialog box offers the following options:

> **Sort Column Only** Sorts only the selected columns of a table or the selected columns of characters in regular text or in a tabbed list (selected by Alt-dragging). This option is not available if you've selected entire paragraphs or columns.
>
> **Case Sensitive** Sorts uppercase before lowercase, all uppercase before initial capitals, initial capitals before sentence case, and sentence case before all lowercase.

The Separate Fields At group box lets you specify which character separates the different fields of text when sorting paragraphs: Tabs, Commas, or Other. Word can usually identify fields separated by tabs or commas, or even with conventional separators such as hyphens, but if your boss has used something bizarre like em dashes as separators, you'll need to specify that in the Other box.

The Sorting Language group box allows you to specify that your text be sorted in a different language. This will change the sort order to follow the alphabet and sorting rules of that language.

Once you've made your choices in the Sort Options dialog box, click the OK button to return to the Sort Text dialog box or Sort dialog box.

Chapter 10

Chapter 10

MAIL MERGE

FEATURING

- **Creating the main document**
- **Creating the data source**
- **Choosing merge options**
- **Merging the data**
- **Using non–Word documents as data sources**

At the dawn of word processing, mail merge was a tangled and feared procedure that people avoided for good reasons. Mail merge in today's word-processing applications is comparatively friendly and fun. With just a little attention to the details of what you're doing, you can whip together merged letters, forms, envelopes, labels, or catalogs. Word's Mail Merge Helper smoothes out many of the potential speed bumps in the process.

TIP

You can easily use data sources from other applications—
ple, data from Excel spreadsheets or contact names fr
Outlook address book—with zero complications.

While Word's Mail Merge Helper lets you carry out merges in a variety of differe
orders, in this chapter we'll look at the most conventional order of proceeding. Once
you see what's what, you can mix and match to produce the variations that suit you
best. You'll also find that mail merge has a number of different areas, and in some of
them, the water gets deep fast—hit a couple of buttons and Word will be expecting
you to put together some SQL statements for MS Query to use in hacking a FoxPro
database (or worse). In the spirit of cooperation so far sadly lacking in the 1990s, I'll
show you how to avoid such predicaments and to steer a path through the pitfalls of
mail merge.

Enough mixed metaphors. Let's look first at creating the main document for the
merge.

Creating the Main Document

The *main document* is the file that contains the skeleton into which you fit the variable information from the *data file*. The skeleton consists of the text that stays the
same in each of the letters, catalogs, or whatever, and the *merge fields* that receive
the information from the data file. The data file is typically a Word table that contains
information about the recipients of the form letters or the products you're trying to sell
them.

First, if you've got a main document that you want to use, open it and make it the
active window.

Choose Tools ➤ Mail Merge to start the merging process. Word will respond by displaying the Mail Merge Helper dialog box (see Figure 10.1).

Click the Create button in the Main Document
area and choose the type of document you want to
create: Form Letters, Mailing Labels, Envelopes, or
Catalogs. (For the example, I chose Form Letters
because that still seems to be the most popular type
of mail merge.)

Using Sort Options

To allow you to direct its sorting capabilities even more precisely, Word offers five
sort options in the Sort Options dialog box (see Figure 9.10). Some of these options
are available only for particular types of sorts.

FIGURE 9.10
The Sort Options dialog
box provides ways of
refining your sorting.

To choose sort options, click the Options button in the Sort Text dialog box or the
Sort dialog box. The Sort Options group box in the Sort Options dialog box offers
the following options:

Sort Column Only Sorts only the selected columns of a table or the selected
columns of characters in regular text or in a tabbed list (selected by Alt-dragging).
This option is not available if you've selected entire paragraphs or columns.

Case Sensitive Sorts uppercase before lowercase, all uppercase before initial
capitals, initial capitals before sentence case, and sentence case before all
lowercase.

The Separate Fields At group box lets you specify which character separates the different fields of text when sorting paragraphs: Tabs, Commas, or Other. Word can usually identify fields separated by tabs or commas, or even with conventional separators
such as hyphens, but if your boss has used something bizarre like em dashes as separators, you'll need to specify that in the Other box.

The Sorting Language group box allows you to specify that your text be sorted in a
different language. This will change the sort order to follow the alphabet and sorting
rules of that language.

Once you've made your choices in the Sort Options dialog box, click the OK button
to return to the Sort Text dialog box or Sort dialog box.

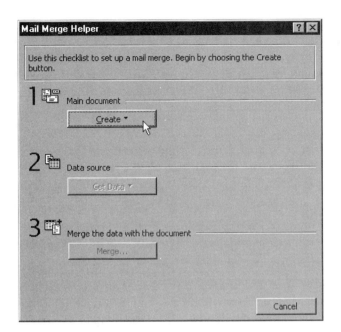

FIGURE 10.1:
The first of many appearances for the Mail Merge Helper dialog box. Click the Create button in the Main Document area to get started.

TIP   The Mail Merge Helper dialog box displays increasing amounts of information and instructions about the merge as you go through the process. If you get confused about which stage you've reached, and you don't have the Mail Merge Helper dialog box on screen to help you, choose Tools ➤ Mail Merge to display the Mail Merge Helper, and scan the information and instructions it's currently displaying.

In the message box that appears, choose whether to use the document in the active document window—the document that was open when you started the Mail Merge Helper—or to create a new main document.

- If you choose to use the active document, Word records its name and path underneath the Create button in the Mail Merge Helper dialog box.
- If you choose to create a new main document, Word opens a new document for you and records its name under the Create button: *Document2* or a similar name. Leave the document there for the time being while we specify the data source.

Specifying the Data Source

Next you need to specify the data source for the mail merge. Click the Get Data button and choose an option from the drop-down list:

- Create Data Source lets you create a new mail merge data source for this merge project.
- Open Data Source lets you open an existing data source (for example, the one from your last successful mail merge).
- Use Address Book lets you use an existing electronic address book, such as your Outlook address book or your Personal Address Book, as data for the merge.
- Header Options is a little more esoteric. We won't get into it in detail here, but this option lets you run a merge in which the data comes from one source and the header information that controls the data comes from another source. This can be useful if you already have a main document with fields defined and a data source with headers that don't match the fields: Instead of changing the headers in the data source (and perhaps thereby rendering it unsuitable for its regular uses), you can choose Header Options, click the Create button, and set up a new set of headers that will bridge the gap between the main document and the data source.

Creating a New Data Source

To create a new data source, click the Get Data button and choose Create Data Source from the drop-down list. Word will display the Create Data Source dialog box (see Figure 10.2).

First, you create the *header row* for the data source—the field names that will head the columns of data and that you will enter into your main document to tell Word where to put the variable information.

Word provides a list of commonly used field names for you to customize: Title, FirstName, LastName, JobTitle, and so on. You'll find these more suitable for some projects than others—for example, for a parts catalog, you'll probably want to customize the list extensively, whereas the list is pretty much on target for a business mailing.

Here's how to work in the Create Data Source dialog box:

- To add a field name to the list, type it in the Field Name box, and then click the Add Field Name button. (The most fields you can have is 31, at which point Word will stop you from adding more.)

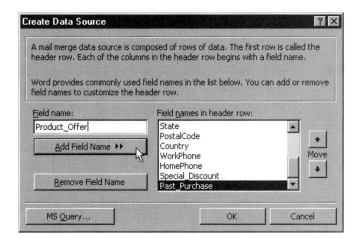

FIGURE 10.2:
Creating a new data source in the Create Data Source dialog box

---

TIP   **Field names can be up to 40 characters long, but you'll usually do better to keep them as short as possible while making them descriptive—ultra-cryptic names can cause confusion later in the merge process. Names can use both letters and numbers (no symbols or punctuation), but each name must start with a letter. You can't include spaces in the names, but you can add underscores instead—Career_Prospects, for example—which helps make them readable.**

- To remove a field name from the list, select it in the Field Names in Header Row list box and click the Remove Field Name button.
- To rearrange the field names in the list, click a field name and then click the Move buttons to move it up or down the list.

TIP   **The list of field names in the Field Names in Header Row list box forms a loop, so you can move the bottom field to the top of the list by clicking the down button.**

When you've got the list of field names to your liking, click the OK button to close the Create Data Source dialog box and save the data source you're creating.

WARNING Clicking the MS Query button in the Create Data Source dialog box takes you off into the Twilight Zone of Structured Query Language (SQL, pronounced "sequel" by aficionados, in case you're wondering). I suggest not clicking it unless you're experienced in SQL queries and are happy playing with databases.

Word will now display the Save As dialog box for you to save the data source. Save your document in the usual way.

Once the document is saved, Word will display a message box telling you that the document contains no data—no surprise, since you've just created it—and inviting you to edit it or to edit the main document. For now, choose the Edit Data Source button.

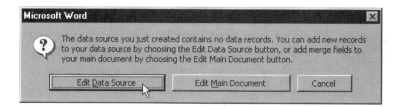

Word will display the Data Form dialog box (see Figure 10.3), which is a custom dialog box built from the field names you entered in the Create Data Source dialog box.

Add data to the data source: Type information into the fields in the dialog box. Press Enter or Tab to move between fields. The Data Form dialog box offers you the following options:

- Click the Add New button to begin a new record after entering the first one.
- Click the Delete button to delete the current record.

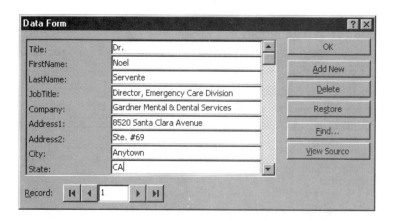

FIGURE 10.3:
In the Data Form dialog box, enter records for the data source you just created.

- Click the Restore button to restore the record to its previous condition (the information it contained before any changes you just made on screen).
- Click the View Source button to see the kind of data source you're working with in Word. (Usually this means Word will display a table containing the records you've entered.) To return to the data form, click the Data Form button (the leftmost button) on the database toolbar that Word displays.
- Click the Record buttons at the bottom of the Data Form dialog box to see your records: the four buttons call up the first record, previous record, next record, and last record, respectively, and the Record box lets you type in the record number that you want to move to.

Click the OK button when you've finished adding records to your data source. Word will close the Data Form dialog box and take you to your main document with the Mail Merge toolbar displayed. If you're working through this (rather than just reading), skip ahead to "Adding Merge Fields to the Main Document" for the next step.

Using an Existing Data File

To use an existing data file for your mail merge, click the Get Data button in the Mail Merge Helper dialog box and choose Open Data Source. Word will display the Open Data Source dialog box (shown in Figure 10.4), which you'll recognize as the Open dialog box in disguise. Navigate to the data source document the usual way, select it, and open it by clicking the Open button.

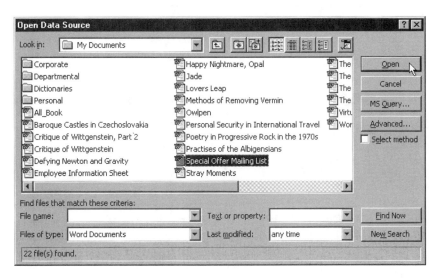

FIGURE 10.4: Open your existing data source from the Open Data Source dialog box.

Word will now check your purported data source for fields. If it doesn't contain any fields that Word can recognize, Word will display the Header Record Delimiters dialog box for you to indicate how the fields and records are divided (*delimited*), as shown in Figure 10.5. Pick the delimiter characters in the Field Delimiter and Record Delimiter drop-down lists (you get to choose from paragraphs, tabs, commas, periods, exclamation points, and anything else Word thinks might be a delimiter character in this document), and then click the OK button. (If you opened the wrong file, click the Cancel button to close the Header Record Delimiters dialog box, and then click the Get Data button again to reopen the Create Data Source dialog box.)

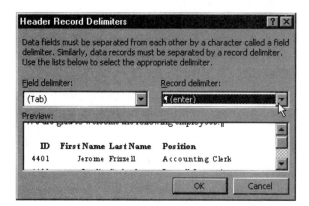

FIGURE 10.5:
If Word displays the Header Record Delimiters dialog box, you may have picked the wrong file by mistake. If not, indicate to Word how the fields and records are divided.

Once Word has established that your data source contains fields, it will check your main document for merge fields. If it finds none—most likely if you're creating a new main document for the merge—it will display a message box inviting you to insert them:

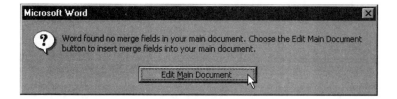

Click the Edit Main Document button, and Word will return you to your main document. Now it's time to add merge fields to it. Skip ahead to "Adding Merge Fields to the Main Document."

Using Excel as a Data Source

To use Excel as a data source for a mail merge, click the Get Data button and choose Open Data Source. In the Open Data Source dialog box, choose MS Excel Worksheets (*.xls) from the Files of Type drop-down list in the lower-left corner of the dialog box, navigate to the workbook, and open it in the usual way.

Unless Excel is already open, Word will fire up a copy of it in the background (you'll still see Word on screen) and will open the designated workbook. Word will then display a dialog box in which you select the range of cells to use for the merge (see Figure 10.6).

FIGURE 10.6:
When using an Excel spreadsheet as a data source, select a named range or cell range from the Named or Cell Range box to use for the merge.

Once you've done that, Word will put you back into the regular mail-merge loop of editing your main document. When you choose to edit your main document (which we'll look at in a moment), you'll be able to insert any or all of the fields in the workbook by using the Insert Merge Field button.

When the merge is finished, Word will close Excel (unless it was already open, in which case Word will close only the workbook it opened).

Using Outlook as a Data Source

Your contact database in Outlook can be a gold mine for mail merges. To use it, click the Get Data button in the Mail Merge Helper dialog box and choose Use Address Book to display the Use Address Book dialog box (see Figure 10.7). Select Outlook Address Book and click OK.

If you see the Confirm Data Source dialog box, click on OK to have Word import your Outlook contact data (you can also select the Show All check box to view all data source types you can open).

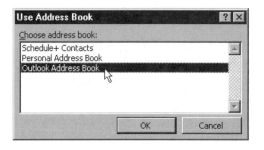

FIGURE 10.7:
Choose your Outlook
Address Book in the
Use Address Book
dialog box.

When you choose to edit your main document, you'll be able to insert any or all of the Outlook fields by using the Insert Merge Field button.

When the merge is finished, Word will close Outlook (unless it was already open, in which case Word will close only the address book you chose).

Using Access as a Data Source

If you have Access, you'll probably also want to use Access databases for mail merges from time to time.

To use an Access database as a mail-merge data source:

1. Click the Get Data button and choose Open Data Source from the drop-down list.

2. In the Open Data Source dialog box, choose MS Access Databases in the Files of Type drop-down list to display Access databases in the Look In box. (Navigate to another folder if necessary.)

3. Select the database to open and then click the Open button.

4. The Mail Merge Helper will display the Microsoft Access dialog box (see Figure 10.8) for you to pick the table or query to use for the merge.

5. Choose the table on the Tables tab or the query on the Queries tab; then click the OK button.

Word will then invite you to insert merge fields into your main document, where you'll be able to insert any or all of the fields in the database by using the Insert Merge Field button.

When the merge is finished, Word will close Access (unless it was already open, in which case Word will close only the database you chose).

FIGURE 10.8:
In the Microsoft Access dialog box, choose the table or query you want to use for the mail merge.

Adding Merge Fields to the Main Document

Back in the main document, you'll see that Word has opened a Mail Merge toolbar that provides buttons for inserting merge fields and Word fields into the main document. Figure 10.9 shows the Mail Merge toolbar.

If you're starting a main document from scratch, add the merge fields as you write it. If you started off with the basis of your merge document already written, you just need to add the merge fields to it.

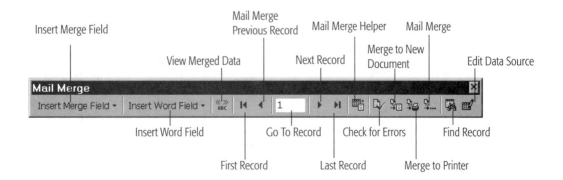

FIGURE 10.9: The Mail Merge toolbar

To insert a merge field, click the Insert Merge Field button and choose the merge field from the drop-down

> Insert Merge Field ▾

list of merge fields in the data source you created or chose. For example, to enter an address, choose the Title field; Word will insert the field name within angle brackets, ≪Title≫, in the document. Follow that with a space, insert the FirstName field and another space, and then insert the LastName field. Press ↵ and start entering the address fields. Remember the spaces and punctuation that the words will need—they're easy to forget when you're faced with a large number of fields.

> ≪Title≫ ≪FirstName≫ ≪LastName≫
> ≪JobTitle≫
> ≪Company≫
> ≪Address1≫, ≪Address2≫
> ≪City≫, ≪State≫ ≪PostalCode≫

TIP **The Insert Word Field button produces a drop-down list of special fields for use in complex merges, such as Ask, Fill-in, If... Then... Else.... These fields provide you with a way to customize your merge documents, so the documents prompt the user for keyboard input, act in different ways depending on what kind of data they find in merge fields, and so on. They're beyond the scope of this book, but if you do a lot of complex mail merges, you'll no doubt want to learn how to use them.**

At this point, you've got the components of the merge in place—a data source with records and a main document with field codes that match the header names in the data source. Next, you can specify options for the merge—filtering and sorting, error checking, and more—or just damn the torpedoes and merge the documents.

 If you need to make adjustments to your data source, click the Edit Data Source button on the Mail Merge toolbar—the rightmost button on the toolbar.

 If you suddenly realize you've selected the wrong data source, click the Mail Merge Helper button on the Mail Merge toolbar, click the Get Data button in the Mail Merge Helper dialog box, and choose the correct data source.

Setting Merge Options

In this section, we'll look quickly at how you can sort and filter merge documents, so you can perform a merge without producing documents for every single record in your database. If you don't want to try sorting or filtering, go straight on to the section titled "Merging Your Data."

Sorting the Records to Be Merged

By filtering your records, you can restrict the scope of your mail merges to just the appropriate part of your data source rather than creating a label, catalog, or form letter for every single record. For example, you can filter your records so that you print labels of only your customers in California and Arizona, or you send a letter extolling your pine-colored leatherette goblins only to people called Green (first name or last).

You can use sorting to restrict mail merges, too. Instead of having Word print out your merge documents in the order in which you entered the records on which they're based in the data source, you can sort them by state and by city to placate the mail room.

To sort your records:

1. Click the Mail Merge Helper button to display the Mail Merge Helper dialog box.

2. Click the Query Options button to open the Query Options dialog box (see Figure 10.10). Click the Sort Records tab to bring it to the front if it isn't already there. (You can also get to the Query Options dialog box by clicking the Query Options button in the Merge dialog box.)

3. In the Sort By box, choose the first field you want to sort by from the drop-down list, and then choose Ascending or Descending sort order.

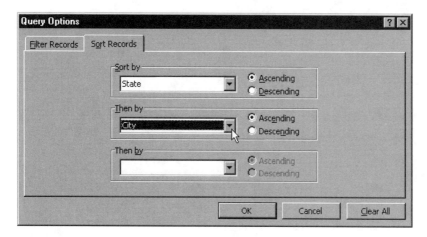

FIGURE 10.10:   On the Sort Records tab of the Query Options dialog box, choose how to sort your records.

4. To sort more precisely, choose the second field in the first Then By box. (For example, to sort by city within state, choose State in the Sort By box and City in the first Then By box.) Again, choose Ascending or Descending order.

5. Specify another sort field in the second Then By box if necessary, and choose the order.

6. Click the OK button to close the Query Options dialog box.
   - If you want to filter your sorted data, click the Filter Records tab instead and skip to step 3 in the next section.
   - If you choose the wrong sort fields, click the Clear All button to reset the drop-down lists to no field.

Filtering the Records to Be Merged

To filter the records you'll be merging:

1. Click the Mail Merge Helper button to display the Mail Merge Helper dialog box.

2. Click the Query Options button to open the Query Options dialog box (see Figure 10.11). Click the Filter Records tab to bring it to the front if it isn't already displayed.

3. In the Field drop-down list in the top row, choose the field you want to use as the first filter.

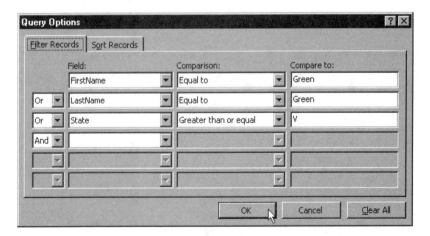

FIGURE 10.11: On the Filter Records tab of the Query Options dialog box, choose how to filter the records you'll be merging.

4. In the Comparison drop-down list in the top row, choose the filtering operator to specify how the contents of the field must relate to the contents of the Compare To box:

    Equal to (match)

    Not Equal to (not match)

    Less Than

    Greater Than

    Less than or Equal

    Greater than or Equal

    Is Blank (the merge field must be empty)

    Is Not Blank (the merge field must not be empty)

TIP   For these mathematically inclined comparisons, Word evaluates numbers using the conventional manner (1 is less than 11, and so on) and text using the American National Standards Institute (ANSI) sort order: *ax* comes before *blade* alphabetically, so *ax* is "less than" *blade*. You could also use State is Greater than or Equal to V to filter records for Vermont, Virginia, Washington, and Wyoming. For fields that mix text and numbers, Word treats the numbers as text characters, which means that 11 will be sorted between 1 and 2 (and so on).

5. In the first Compare To box, enter the value against which you're comparing the field.

6. In the second and subsequent rows, choose And or Or in the unnamed first column before the Field column to add a finer filter to the filter in the previous row or to apply another filter. For example, you could choose And LastName is Equal to Green to restrict your merge to Greens in Vermont.

TIP   Click the Clear All button if you need to reset all the filtering fields.

7. Click the OK button when you've finished defining your filtering criteria. Word will return to the Mail Merge Helper dialog box (unless you got to the Query Options dialog box by clicking the Query Options button in the Merge dialog box, in which case Word will take you there).

Merging Your Data

Now you're all set to merge your data source with your main document. In the Mail Merge Helper dialog box, click the Merge button. Word will display the Merge dialog box (see Figure 10.12).

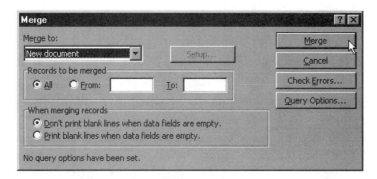

FIGURE 10.12: In the Merge dialog box, choose whether to merge to a new document, to a printer, or to e-mail.

To merge your data:

1. Choose whether to merge to a new document, to your printer, or to e-mail or fax (if you have Outlook installed and correctly configured):

- If you merge to a new document, Word will divide the resulting documents as it thinks best. For example, it will put page breaks between form letters so that they're ready for printing, whereas mailing labels will share a page with each other.

| **TIP** | By merging to a new document, you give yourself a chance to check the merged documents for errors—and, if you want, to add to partic- ular documents a personalized note that you didn't want to put into your data source. |

- If you merge to your printer, Word simply prints all the documents and doesn't produce an on-screen copy.

- If you merge to e-mail or to fax, click the Setup button to display the strangely named Merge To Setup dialog box (see Figure 10.13). For e-mail, specify the field that contains the e-mail address in the Data Field with Mail/Fax Address text box, add a subject line for the message in the Mail Message Subject Line text box, and select the Send Document as an Attachment check box if the document contains formatting that will not survive transmission as an e-mail message. (This depends on the sophistication of your e-mail package and of the service provider you're using; with basic e-mail, not even bold or italic will make it through unscathed.) For fax, specify the fax phone number in the Data Field with Mail/Fax Address.

Then click the OK button to close the Merge To Setup dialog box and return to the Merge dialog box.

FIGURE 10.13:
In the Merge To Setup dialog box, specify the merge field that contains the e-mail address and add a subject line for the message.

2. Choose which records to merge in the Records to Be Merged group box. Either accept the default setting of All, or enter record numbers in the From and To boxes.
   - If you're using sorting or filtering, the records will be in a different order from that in which they were entered in the data source.
   - To merge from a specific record to the end of the record set, enter the starting number in the From box and leave the To box blank.
3. In the When Merging Records group box, select the Print Blank Lines When Data Fields Are Empty option button if you need to track gaps in your data. Usually, though, you'll want to leave the Don't Print Blank Lines When Data Fields Are Empty option button selected to produce a better-looking result.
4. Click the Check Errors button and verify which option button has been selected in the Checking and Reporting Errors dialog box. The default choice is "Complete the Merge, Pausing to Report Each Error As It Occurs"; you can also choose "Simulate the Merge and Report Errors in a New Document" if you consider the merge potentially problematic; or you can choose

"Complete the Merge without Pausing. Report Errors in a New Document."
Click the OK button when you've made your choice.

5. Click the Merge button to run the mail merge.
   - If you're merging to a new document, Word will display it on screen. You can then check the merged documents for errors before printing, and you can save it if you want to keep it for future use.
   - If you're merging to a printer, Word will display the Print dialog box. Choose the page range and number of copies, if necessary, and then click the OK button to print the documents. When Word has finished printing, it will return you to your main document. Word doesn't create the merged documents on disk, so you can't save them.
   - If you're merging to e-mail, Word will check your Exchange settings, and then mail the messages and documents (if you're currently online or connected to the network that handles your e-mail) or place them in your Outbox (if you're not currently online or connected to the network).
   - If you're merging to fax, Word will crank up Exchange to fax the documents.

Merging Labels and Envelopes

In Chapter 8, we looked at how you can print labels and envelopes with Word. In this section, we won't grind through *all* that information again—we'll just look at the parts that are different when you're running a mail merge to print labels and envelopes.

Merge-Printing Labels

To create labels for a merge-print:

1. Choose Tools ➤ Mail Merge, select Mailing Labels from the Create drop-down list, and then follow the procedures described earlier in this chapter until you've created or selected your data source. Then Word will display a

message box telling you it needs to set up your main document; accept by clicking the Set Up Main Document button.

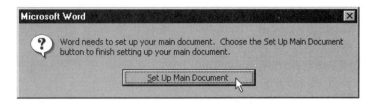

2. Word will then display the Label Options dialog box. Choose your labels as discussed in Chapter 8 and click the OK button.

3. Word will then display the Create Labels dialog box (see Figure 10.14), so you can set up a label format. Click the Insert Merge Field button, and choose the fields for the labels from the drop-down list. Word will insert them in the Sample Label box. Include punctuation and spaces, and start new lines as appropriate.

TIP You can apply formatting to the merge field codes by selecting them and either using keyboard shortcuts (such as Ctrl+B for boldface and Ctrl+I for italic) or right-clicking and choosing Font from the context menu to display the Font dialog box. You can adjust the paragraph layout by right-clicking and choosing Paragraph from the context menu.

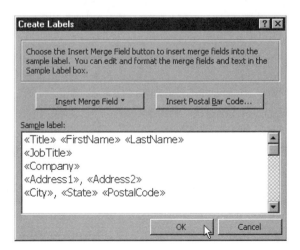

FIGURE 10.14:
In the Create Labels dialog box, set up your labels for merge-printing.

4. If you want to include a postal bar code for the address, click the Insert Postal Bar Code button, and select the fields from the Merge Field with ZIP Code and Merge Field with Street Address drop-down lists.

5. Click the OK button to close the Insert Postal Bar Code dialog box. Word will insert a boldfaced line saying, **Delivery point bar code will print here!** at the top of the Sample Label box in the Create Labels dialog box.

6. Click the OK button to close the Create Labels dialog box.

Word will create the main document for the labels from the contents of the Sample Label box and will return you to the Mail Merge Helper dialog box. From there, follow the instructions in the section titled "Merging Your Data" to complete the merge.

Merge-Printing Envelopes

To set up envelopes for a merge-print:

1. Choose Tools ➤ Mail Merge, select Envelopes from the Create drop-down list, and then follow the procedures described earlier in this chapter (in "Creating the Main Document" and "Specifying the Data Source") until you've created or selected your data source. As with labels, Word will display a message box asking you to click the Set Up Main Document button to finish setting up your main document.

2. Click the Set Up Main Document button and Word will display the Envelope Options dialog box that we investigated in Chapter 8.

3. Make your choices in the Envelope Options dialog box, and then click the OK button to display the Envelope Address dialog box. This dialog box is almost identical to the Create Labels dialog box shown in Figure 10.14 and works the same way.

4. Click the Insert Merge Field button and choose the fields for the envelopes from the drop-down list. Word will insert them in the Sample Envelope Address box.
   - Include punctuation and spaces, start new paragraphs where you want them to be, and add any text that you want on each envelope.
   - You can apply formatting to the merge field codes by either using keyboard shortcuts or by right-clicking and choosing Font from the context menu to display the Font dialog box.

- You can change the paragraph layout by right-clicking and choosing Paragraph from the context menu.

5. To include a postal bar code for the address, click the Insert Postal Bar Code button to display the Insert Postal Bar Code dialog box for envelopes, and then select the fields from the Merge Field with ZIP Code and the Merge Field with Street Address drop-down lists. The Insert Postal Bar Code dialog box for envelopes includes an FIM-A Courtesy Reply Mail check box that you can select if you want to print a Facing Identification Mark on courtesy reply envelopes.

6. Click the OK button to close the Insert Postal Bar Code dialog box. Word will insert a boldfaced line saying, **Delivery point bar code will print here!** at the top of the Sample Label box.

7. Click the OK button to close the Envelope Address dialog box.

Word will create the main document for the envelopes from the contents of the Sample Envelope Address box and will return you to the Mail Merge Helper dialog box. From there, follow the instructions in the section titled "Merging Your Data" to complete the merge. If you choose to merge to a printer, line up the envelopes so they are ready for printing.

Restoring a Main Document to a Regular Document

If you know you won't need to use your main document again for a mail merge, be reassured that it isn't merged forever—you can easily restore it to a regular Word document.

To restore a main document to a regular document:

1. Open the main document.

2. Choose Tools ➤ Mail Merge to display the Mail Merge Helper dialog box.

3. Click the Create button and choose Restore to Normal Word Document from the drop-down list; then choose the Yes button in the confirmation dialog box that Word displays. Word will break the main document's attachment to its data file and restore it to normal document status.

Chapter 11

OUTLINES, FIND, AND AUTOMATIC FEATURES

- **Working with outlines**
- **Using advanced Find and Replace**
- **Using the AutoText feature**
- **Using automatic bullets and numbering**

In addition to the Office-wide spelling checker and AutoCorrect features that we looked at in Chapter 2, Word offers several automation features that can greatly increase the speed at which you work with documents. Outlines let you collapse a document to different heading levels and then reshuffle the headings and their associated text; AutoText lets you create abbreviations for boilerplate text you enter frequently in documents; and automatic bullets and numbering (including heading numbering) lets you format and identify your documents effortlessly. We'll look at each of these features in turn in this chapter.

Outlines

Outline view is one of Word's most useful features if you're writing anything longer than a couple of pages. Using Outline view and Word's heading styles, you can collapse a document to an outline showing any number of heading levels from one to seven. For example, you can collapse a document to show three levels of headings, hiding any subheadings and body text between the headings. You can then zero in on a crucial heading and expand the text underneath it, so you can make a strategic addition or two before collapsing that text again to move quickly to another heading. You can also move blocks of text around your document quickly or promote or demote a whole series of headings in one move.

Outline numbered lists offer similar capabilities to Outline view. We'll look at how to create and use outline numbered lists at the end of this section.

How Outlines Work

Outlines work by using Word's nine heading styles, Heading 1 to Heading 9. These styles are predefined, so you can't delete them, no matter how hard you try, though you can format them however you like. (These styles are also used for tables of contents, which are remarkably similar to outlines.)

To recap Chapters 6 and 7 quickly, Word offers paragraph styles for formatting paragraphs and character styles for formatting characters. By using paragraph styles, you can quickly apply consistent formatting to all the instances of any element in a document. For example, by setting Heading 1 to be 24-point Gill Sans Ultra with 18 points of space above it and 12 points below (and also using indentation, borders, shading, and worse to your liking) and then applying the Heading 1 style to each heading, you can make sure they all look the same on the page. (For more details, see the section titled "Style Formatting" in Chapter 7.)

Creating an Outline

Creating an outline in Word could hardly be simpler. You can start with either the blank slate of a new document and build an outline from scratch, or you can start with an existing document.

TIP   Even if you're creating a short document, Outline view can save you time. As discussed in the section titled "Creating a New Style" in Chapter 7, most Heading styles are typically followed by a different paragraph style on the assumption that you won't want to type several headings in a row—for example, you might want a Heading 1 paragraph to be followed by Body Text or by some special graphical element that would offset the heading and draw the reader's attention. In Outline view, however, pressing Enter creates another paragraph with the same paragraph style, so you can quickly crank out a full chapter's worth of Heading 1 paragraphs, Heading 2 paragraphs, or whatever.

Creating a New Outline

To create an outline in a new document:

1.   Start a new document by choosing File ➤ New and choosing the template you want in the New dialog box.

2.   Choose View ➤ Outline to switch to Outline view. Word will display the Outlining toolbar (see Figure 11.1).

3.   Make sure the paragraph style in the Style drop-down list on the Formatting toolbar is set to Heading 1 style. (Word will usually start the new document with a paragraph in Heading 1 style, depending on which template you chose in step 1.

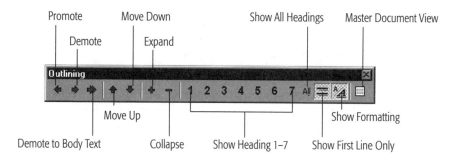

FIGURE 11.1:   The Outlining toolbar provides quick access to the main features at Outline view.

4. Enter the first-level headings, pressing Enter after each one. Word will start each new paragraph in Heading 1 style, no matter what the Style for Following Paragraph is set to.

5. To enter a second-level heading, press Tab to switch to Heading 2 style. Type the text for the heading and press Enter; Word will start a new paragraph also based on the Heading 2 style.
   - To enter third-level headings, fourth-level headings, and so on, press Tab to move down through the Heading styles.
   - To move back up through the heading styles, press Shift+Tab once for each level.

6. Save the outline as usual.

Outlining an Existing Document

To outline an existing document:

1. Open the document.

2. If the document isn't already formatted with styles, apply Heading styles to the headings by using the Formatting toolbar or the Format ➤ Style command (described in the section titled "Applying Styles" in Chapter 7).

3. Switch the document to Outline view as described in the next section, "Viewing an Outline."

Viewing an Outline

To switch a document to Outline view, choose View ➤ Outline or click the Outline View button on the horizontal scroll bar (if you have it displayed). Word will shuffle your document into Outline view.

When you choose Outline view, Word displays the Outlining toolbar and an outline symbol to the left of the first line in each paragraph, as shown in Figure 11.2. A fat plus sign appearing next to a heading indicates that the heading has subheadings or text (or both) underneath it; a fat minus sign means the heading has nothing between it and the next heading. A small empty square indicates a paragraph of non-heading text.

To collapse or expand the outline to different levels, use the Expand and Collapse buttons and the seven numbered buttons on the Outlining toolbar. The Expand button reveals the subtext for the selected heading— for example, if you position the insertion point in a Heading 2 paragraph and click the Expand button, Word will display any Heading 3 paragraphs beneath the Heading 2 paragraph. If there are no Heading 3 paragraphs, Word will display paragraphs with the next Heading level style (Heading 4, then Heading 5, then Heading 6,

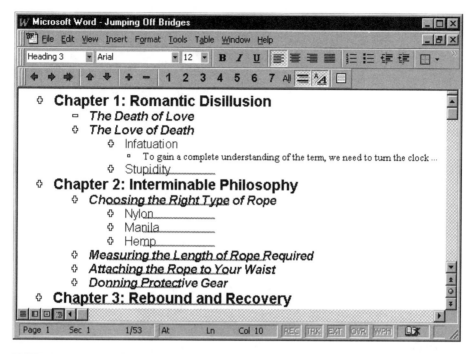

FIGURE 11.2:   In Outline view, Word displays a hierarchy of headings that you can collapse to different levels.

and so on); if there are no headings at all between the selected Heading paragraph and the end of the document, Word will display body text. The Collapse button reverses the process, collapsing the outline one available level at a time.

TIP   If you've defined Word's Heading styles with large font sizes, you won't be able to see many headings on screen at once in Outline view with formatting displayed. Either zoom the view to a smaller percentage—perhaps 75% or 50%—to display more headings on screen, or click the Show Formatting button to toggle off the formatting.

The seven Show Heading *n* buttons on the Outlining toolbar expand or collapse the whole outline to that level of heading, while the All button toggles the display of all heading levels and body text.

You can also collapse (or expand) all the headings under a heading by double-clicking the fat plus sign next to it or by holding down Shift and rolling the IntelliMouse roller back (or forward).

The Show First Line Only button on the Outlining toolbar toggles the display between only the first line of non-heading paragraphs and all lines of non-heading paragraphs. This option can be a great help in getting an overview of a large part of your document.

Promoting and Demoting Items

Two of the most useful buttons on the Outlining toolbar are the Promote and Demote buttons, which you can use to reorganize the headings in a document quickly. Click these once to promote or demote the current heading or selected headings one level at a time.

When you select a heading using its outline symbol (the fat plus sign or fat minus sign), you select all its subheadings as well (whether or not they're displayed). When you promote or demote a heading with its subheadings selected, you promote or demote the subheadings as well. For example, if I demote the Chapter 2 heading, shown here, from Heading 1 to Heading 2, the Heading 2 paragraphs will be demoted to Heading 3, the Heading 3 paragraphs to Heading 4, and so on.

Heading 1	⬦ **Chapter 2: Interminable Philosophy**
Heading 2	⬦ *Choosing the Right Type of Rope*
Heading 3	⬦ Nylon
Heading 3	⬦ Manila
Heading 3	⬦ Hemp
Heading 2	⬦ *Measuring the Length of Rope Required*
Heading 2	⬦ *Donning Protective Gear*
Heading 2	⬦ *Attaching the Rope to Your Waist*

To promote (or demote) a heading without promoting (or demoting) all its subheadings, first expand the outline to display the subheadings. Then click *in* the heading and click the Promote (or Demote) button until the heading has reached the level you want it to be.

To select a heading without selecting its subheadings, click in the selection bar next to the heading. To select several headings, click and drag in the selection bar.

 To demote a heading to text, click the Demote to Body Text button. Word will apply the Normal style to it.

> **TIP** You can also demote the paragraph you're working in by pressing Tab and promote it by pressing Shift+Tab. To type a tab in Outline view, press Ctrl+Tab.

Moving Items Up and Down the Outline

Outline view makes reordering the items in an outline speedy and simple. To move a heading up and down the outline, simply expand or collapse the outline so the heading is displayed, and then click the symbol next to the heading and drag it up or down the outline. (Again, you'll be moving any subheadings and text along with the heading.) You'll see a line move up or down the screen indicating where the paragraph will end up when you let go of it.

> ⊕ *Measuring the Length of Rope Required*
> ↕⊕ *Donning Protective Gear*
> ⊕ *Attaching the Rope to Your Waist*

 Alternatively, select the heading (and any subheadings you want to move with it) and click the Move Up or Move Down button to move it up or down the outline one displayed paragraph at a time.

Using Heading Numbering

Heading numbering can be a great asset in Outline view. Instead of your needing to renumber your chapters as you drag them about the outline, you can let Word take care of the numbering automatically.

To apply heading numbering to a document:

1. Right-click in a heading and choose Bullets and Numbering from the context menu, or choose Format ➤ Bullets and Numbering, to display the Bullets and Numbering dialog box.
2. If the Outline Numbered tab is not displayed, click it to bring it to the front of the dialog box (see Figure 11.3).
3. Choose one of the numbering styles that includes the word *Heading,* and then click the Customize button to display the Customize Outline Numbered List dialog box (see Figure 11.4). If you see a smaller dialog box than this one, click the More button to display the bottom section (and—you've guessed it—change the More button to a Less button).
4. In the Level list box, choose the heading level on which to work.

5. In the Number Format text box, choose how you want the heading numbering to appear. For example, you could enter a word in front of the number to produce numbering like *Part 1*, or you could enter a colon or other separator character after the number. The Preview box will show the effects of the change.

6. In the Number Style drop-down list, choose the style of numbering: 1, 2, 3; I, II, III; A, B, C; and so on.

7. In the Start At box, adjust the starting number (or letter) if necessary.

8. In the Previous Level Number drop-down list, choose the number for the previous level if you want to produce a multipart number (such as 3.2.4). This works only for levels below Level 1.

9. To change the font formatting of the numbering, click the Font button to display the Font dialog box. Choose font formatting as usual; then click OK to apply the formatting and close the Font dialog box.

10. In the Number Position group box, change the alignment and positioning of the number as needed.

11. In the Text Position box, adjust the indent of the text if necessary.

12. In the Link Level to Style drop-down list, make sure the level is associated with the appropriate paragraph style.

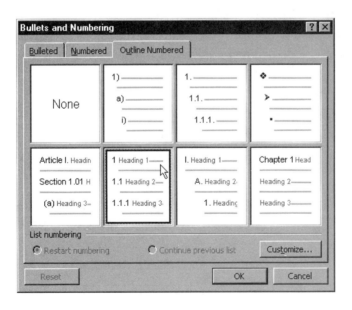

FIGURE 11.3:
Choose heading numbering on the Outline Numbered tab of the Bullets and Numbering dialog box.

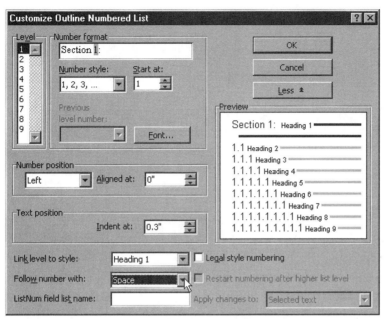

FIGURE 11.4:   In the Customize Outline Numbered List dialog box, choose how you want the heading numbering to appear.

13. In the Follow Number With drop-down list, choose whether to follow the number with a tab, a space, or nothing.

14. Repeat steps 4 through 13 if necessary for other heading levels.

15. In the Apply Changes To drop-down list, make sure Whole List is selected.

16. Click the OK button to apply the outline numbering to the document.

Formatting in Outline View

As we saw in "Viewing an Outline" earlier in the chapter, you can click the Show Formatting button on the Outlining toolbar to stop Word from displaying character formatting in Outline view. This feature can help you get more headings on-screen in a readable format.

You can apply character formatting and style formatting as usual in Outline view, but you can't apply paragraph formatting. Bear in mind when applying style formatting to headings that you may not see the effect of the changes you're making. Consider splitting the window (by double-clicking or dragging the Split bar at the top of the vertical scroll bar) and switching one of the resulting panes to Normal view or Page Layout view—or simply switch to another view altogether when you need to apply formatting.

Printing an Outline

When you print from Outline view, Word prints only the information displayed on screen—for example, to print only the first three heading levels, click the Show Heading 3 button and choose File ➤ Print.

Creating an Outline Numbered List

You can also create an outline numbered list using styles other than the Heading styles. For example, you might want to create an outline numbered list as part of a document without disturbing the headings.

To create an outline numbered list:

1. Right-click and choose Bullets and Numbering from the context menu, or choose Format ➤ Bullets and Numbering, to display the Bullets and Numbering dialog box.
2. If the Outline Numbered tab is not displayed, click it to bring it to the front of the dialog box.
3. Choose a style with appropriate numbering (but not one with *Heading* in it), and then click the OK button.

TIP   **You can customize the style by selecting it on the Outline Numbered tab, and then clicking the Customize button to display the Customize Outline Numbered List dialog box. Customize the style as described in steps 4 through 13 of the previous section, but leave the Link Level to Style drop-down list set to (*no style*).**

---

4. Enter the text for the list:
    - Press Enter to create another paragraph at the same numbering level as the previous one.
     - To demote the current paragraph by one level, click the Increase Indent button, or press Tab with the insertion point at the beginning of the paragraph.
     - To promote the current paragraph by one level, click the Decrease Indent button, or press Shift+Tab with the insertion point at the beginning of the paragraph.

To remove outline numbering from a list, click the Numbering button on the Formatting toolbar.

Find and Replace

Word's Find and Replace features go far beyond the standard Office Find and Replace features that we looked at in Chapter 2. You can also search for special characters (such as tabs or paragraph marks), for *wildcard characters* (such as any digit or any character or range of characters), for particular formatting (such as double-underline, bold, and italic in Engravers Gothic font), or for a particular style. You can search for text in a particular language, for paragraphs with particular tab formatting, or for text that sounds like other text. You can even combine many of these elements to conduct searches of truly fiendish complexity that will confound your colleagues and impress your friends.

Finding Text

Word offers a large number of features for finding text. You can search for text without worrying about its formatting; you can search for text with particular formatting, such as bold, double underline, or 44-point Allegro font; or you can search for a particular style.

NOTE   **You can also combine these Find operations with Replace operations; we'll get to this a little later in the chapter in the sections titled "Finding and Replacing Text," "Finding and Replacing Formatting," and "Finding and Replacing Styles."**

To find text:

1. Choose Edit ➤ Find to display the Find and Replace dialog box (see Figure 11.5). If you see only the top half of the dialog box shown here, click the More button to display the rest of it. (The More button will be replaced by a Less button.)

2. In the Find What box, enter the text you're looking for.
   - You can use wildcard characters to find a variety of characters. We'll get into this in "Finding Special Characters and Using Wildcards."

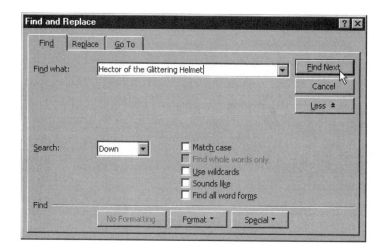

FIGURE 11.5:
The Find and Replace dialog box gives you a quick way to access any combination of characters or formatting in your document. If you're seeing a smaller version of the Find and Replace dialog box, click the More button to expand it.

- Word stores the Find operations from the current session in a drop-down list that you can access by clicking the arrow at the right-hand end of the Find What box.

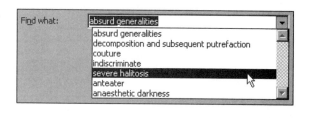

3. Choose the direction to search from the Search drop-down list: Down, Up, or All. If you choose Down or Up, Word will prompt you to continue when it reaches the end or beginning of the document (unless you started Find at the beginning or end of the document).

4. Choose the options you want from the column of check boxes. Each option you choose will be listed under the Find What box.

Match Case   Makes Word pay attention to the capitalization of the word in the Find What box. For example, with Match Case selected and **laziness** entered in the Find What box, Word will ignore instances of *Laziness* in the document and find only *laziness*.

Find Whole Words Only   Makes Word look only for the exact word entered in the Find What box and not for the word when it is part of another word. For example, by selecting the Find Whole Words Only check box, you could find *and* without finding *land*, *random*, *mandible*, and so on. Find Whole Words Only is not available if you type a space in the Find What box.

Use Wildcards   Provides special search options that we'll look at in "Finding Special Characters and Using Wildcards," later in this chapter.

Sounds Like   Finds words that Word thinks sound like those in the Find What box. Your mileage may vary depending on your own pronunciation. For example, if you check the Sounds Like check box and enter **meddle** in the Find What box, Word will find both *middle* and *muddle*, but it won't find rhyming words, such as *peddle* and *pedal*.

Find All Word Forms   Attempts to find all forms of the verb or noun in the Find What box. This is particularly useful with Replace operations: Word can change *break*, *broken*, *breaking*, and *breaks* to *fix*, *fixed*, *fixing*, and *fixes*. Enter the basic form of the word in the Find What and Replace With boxes—in this example, use **break** and **fix**.

WARNING   **Find All Word Forms is an ambitious feature prone to random behavior if you use it unwisely. To give Microsoft credit, Word will warn you that choosing Replace All with Find All Word Forms selected may not be advisable—it's likely to find (and change) more than you bargained for. If you use it, use it carefully, and be especially careful with words such as *lead* because the metal *lead* will likely be considered the verb to *lead*.**

5. Make sure no formatting information appears in the box under the Find What text box. If the No Formatting button at the bottom of the dialog box is active (not dimmed), that means Word will look for words only with the selected formatting; click the button to remove the formatting.

6. Click the Find Next button to find the next instance of your chosen text. If Word finds the text, it will stop; otherwise, it will tell you that it was unable to find the text.

7. Click the Find Next button again to keep searching, or click the Cancel button to close the Find dialog box.

TIP   **Word's Find feature is particularly useful in macros, which we'll look at in Chapter 12. With Find, you can seek out specific parts of form documents, and once you've located them, you can format them, eviscerate them, or even create new documents from them.**

Once you perform a Find operation (or a Find and Replace operation), Word sets the Object Browser to browse by the item you last found. You'll see that the Next Page and Previous Page buttons at the foot of the vertical scroll bar turn from black to blue, and if you move the mouse pointer over them, you'll see that the ScreenTips identify them as Next Find/Go To and Previous Find/Go To, respectively. You can then click these buttons to move to the next or previous instance of the item you last found; you can also press Ctrl+PageDown or Ctrl+PageUp for the same effect.

To reset the Object Browser to browse by page, click the Select Browse Object button and choose the Browse by Page icon from the pop-up panel, as shown here. (To switch back to Browse by Find after that, you can click the Select Browse Object button again and choose the Browse by Find icon—the binoculars—from the pop-up panel.)

Finding Special Characters and Using Wildcards

Often, you'll want to search for something more complex than plain text—perhaps you'll need to search for an em dash (—), or a paragraph mark, or any number—or you may want to search for words beginning with one character but not another, or for words that begin with a certain range of letters. For the first three of these, you'll need to use Word's special characters; for the last two, Word's wildcard characters will do the trick.

Special Characters

To find a special character, such as a paragraph mark, a tab character, or a graphic, click the Special button on the Find dialog box and choose the character from the drop-down list that appears (see Figure 11.6).

You can combine special characters with regular text to make your Find operations more effective. For example, the special character for a paragraph mark is ^p; to find every instance where *Joanne* appears at the beginning of a paragraph, you could search for **^pJoanne**.

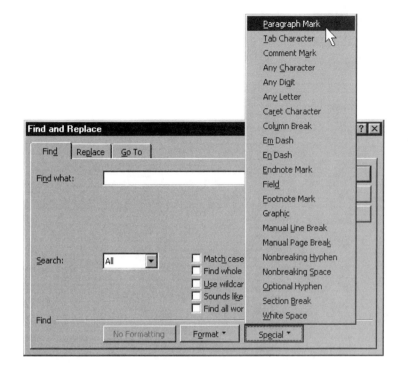

FIGURE 11.6:
You can find special characters, such as page breaks or endnote marks, by using the Special drop-down list in the Find dialog box.

It's usually easiest to enter special characters from the Special drop-down list, but you can also enter them manually for speed. Here's the full list of characters and what they find:

Character	Finds
^?	Any one character
*	A string of characters. Select the Use Wildcards check box when you use this (it's actually a wildcard rather than a special character, but it's simpler to use than the other wildcards)
^p	A paragraph mark
^t	A tab
^a	A comment mark
^#	Any digit

Character	Finds
^$	Any letter
^^	A caret (^)
^n	A column break
^+	An em dash (—)
^=	An en dash (–)
^e	An endnote mark
^d	A field
^f	A footnote mark
^g	A graphic
^l	A manual line break
^m	A manual page break
^~	A nonbreaking hyphen
^s	A nonbreaking space
^-	An optional hyphen
^b	A section break
^w	A white space

Of these, you'll probably find yourself using ^? and * the most. For example , you could use **sh^?p** to find *ship, shop,* etc., and **f*d** to find *fad, fatherhood,* and *flustered*—not to mention."*after the tragic d*eath of Don Quixote."

WARNING   **As you can see from the Don Quixote example, you need to be a little careful when using the * special character, particularly with only one identifying letter on either side of it.**

Using Wildcards

Word's wildcards go one stage beyond the special characters. You can search for one character out of several specified, any character in a range, any character *except* the given one, and even a string of characters at the beginning or end of a word only. To enter wildcards, select the Use Wildcards check box, and then click the Special button to display the drop-down list (see Figure 11.7).

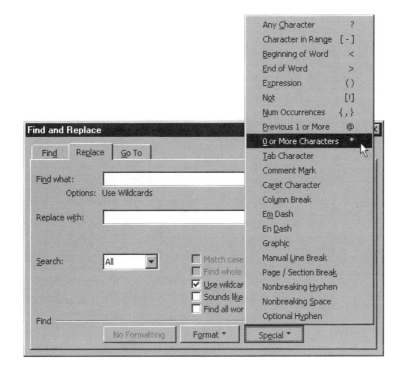

FIGURE 11.7:
To search for
wildcards,
select the
Use Wildcards
check box, and
then choose the
wildcards from
the Special drop-
down list.

Here is the list of wildcards and what they find:

Wildcard	Finds	Examples
[]	Any one of the given characters	**s[iou]n** finds *sin, son,* and *sun.*
[-]	Any one character in the range	**[g-x]ote** finds *note, mote, rote,* and *tote.* Enter the ranges in alphabetical order.
[!]	Any one character except the characters inside the brackets	**[!f][!a]therhood** finds *motherhood,* but not *fatherhood.*
[!x-z]	Any one character except characters in the range inside the brackets	**a[!b-l]e** finds *ape, are,* and *ate,* but not *ace, age,* or *ale.*
{x}	Exactly *x* number of occurrences of the previous character or expression	**we{2}d** finds *weed* but not *wed* because *weed* has two *e*s.

Wildcard	Finds	Examples
{x,}	At least *x* occurrences of the previous character or expression	**we{1,}d** finds *weed* and wed because both words have at least one *e*.
{x,y}	From *x* to *y* occurrences of the previous character or expression	**40{2,4}** finds *400, 4000,* and *40000* because each has between two and four zeros; it won't find *40* because it has only one zero.
@	One or more occurrences of the previous character or expression	**o@h!** finds *oh!* and *ooh!,* which both contain one or more *o*s and then an *h*.
<	The following search string (in parentheses) at the beginning of a word	**<(work)** finds *working* and *workaholic,* but not *groundwork.*
>	The preceding search string (in parentheses) at the end of a word	**(sin)>** finds *basin* and *moccasin,* but not *sinful.*

Finding and Replacing Text

To find and replace text:

1. Choose Edit ➤ Replace to display the Replace tab of the Find and Replace dialog box (see Figure 11.8). If you're already working on the Find tab of the Find and Replace dialog box, click the Replace tab.
2. In the Find What box, enter the text to find. To find text you've searched for before in the current session, click the arrow at the right-hand end of the Find What box and choose the text from the drop-down list.
3. In the Replace With box, enter the text you want to replace the found text with. To reuse replacement text from the current session, click the arrow at the right-hand end of the Replace With box and choose the text from the drop-down list.
4. Choose a search direction from the Search drop-down list: All, Down, or Up.
5. Choose Replace options such as Match Case and Find Whole Word Only as appropriate (see the section "Finding Text" earlier in this chapter for an explanation of these options).

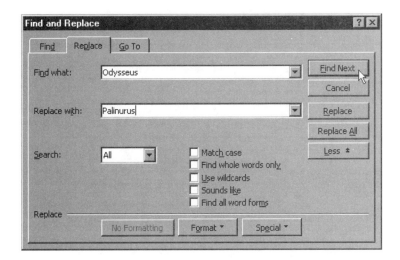

FIGURE 11.8:
The Replace
tab of the Find
and replace
dialog box

6. Start the Replace operation by clicking the Find Next button, the Replace button, or the Replace All button:

   • The Find Next button and Replace button will find the next instance of the text in the Find What box. Once you've found it, click the Find Next button to skip to the next occurrence of the text without replacing it with the contents of the Replace With box, or click the Replace button to replace the text with the contents of the Replace With box and have Word find the next instance of the Find What text.

   • The Replace All button will replace all instances of the text in the Find What box with the text in the Replace With box.

   If you've chosen Up or Down in the Search drop-down list and start the search anywhere other than the opposite end of the document, Word will prompt you to continue when it reaches the beginning or end of the document.

7. When you've finished your Replace operation, click the Cancel button to close the Replace dialog box.

WARNING   When replacing simple text, make sure Word is displaying no formatting information below the Find What box and Replace With boxes—otherwise Word will find only instances of the text that have the appropriate formatting information (bold, italic, Book Antiqua font, or Heading 4 style, and so on), or it will replace the text in the Find What box with inappropriately formatted text from the Replace With box. To remove formatting information from the areas below the Find What box and Replace With box, click in the appropriate box, and then click the No Formatting button.

Finding and Replacing Formatting

There's no need to use text for Replace operations in Word—you can simply find one kind of formatting and replace it with another. For example, say you received an article for your newsletter in which the author had used boldface rather than italic for emphasizing words she intended to explain. To convert these words from bold to italic, you could replace all text with Bold formatting with text with No Bold, Italic formatting.

Such replacing sounds suspiciously utopian, but it works well. Alternatively, you can replace particular strings of text that have one kind of formatting with the same strings of text that have different kinds of formatting; or you can replace formatted strings of text with other formatted strings of text.

To replace one kind of formatting with another kind of formatting:

1. Choose Edit ➤ Replace to display the Find and Replace dialog box.
2. With the insertion point in the Find What box, click the Format button and choose Font, Paragraph, Tabs, or Language from the drop-down list. Word will display the Find Font, Find Paragraph, Find Tabs, or Find Language dialog box. These are versions of the Font, Paragraph, Tabs, and Language dialog boxes discussed in Chapters 6 and 7.
3. Choose the formatting you want Word to find, and then click the OK button to return to the Find and Replace dialog box. Word will display the formatting you chose in the Format box under- `Format:  Font: Haettenschweiler, 18 pt, Not Bold, Not It...` neath the Find What box.
4. Add formatting to the mix by repeating steps 2 and 3 with font, paragraph, tab, or language formatting.
5. With the insertion point in the Replace With box, click the Format button and choose Font, Paragraph, Tabs, or Language from the drop-down list. Word will display the Replace Font, Replace Paragraph, Replace Tabs, or Replace Language dialog box. Again, these are versions of the regular Font, Paragraph, Tabs, and Language dialog boxes discussed in Chapters 6 and 7.
6. Choose the replacement formatting, and then click the OK button to return to the Find and Replace dialog box. Word will display this formatting in the Format box under the Replace With box.
7. Again, add font, paragraph, or tab formatting, this time by repeating steps 5 and 6.
8. Start the search by clicking the Find Next, Replace, or Replace All button.

TIP   **Without any text entered in the Find What box and Replace With box, Word will replace all instances of the formatting you chose: For example, you could replace all boldface with italic, no boldface. You can also enter text in the Find What box and nothing in the Replace With box to have Word remove that text and put different formatting where it was—or vice versa, entering formatting in the Find What box and replacement text in the Replace With box. (This seems a bizarre concept until you find out how useful it is.) Or you can enter replacement text in both the Find What box and in the Replace With box and replace both the text and the formatting at once. For example, you could replace all boldfaced instances of the word break with italicized (without boldface) instances of the word fix.**

Finding and Replacing Styles

To replace one style with another:

1. Choose Edit ➤ Replace to display the Find and Replace dialog box.
2. Make sure that the Format boxes under the Find What box and the Replace With box don't contain any formatting information. To clear formatting information from the boxes, click in the appropriate box, and then click the No Formatting button.
3. With the insertion point in the Find What box, click the Format button and choose Style from the drop-down list Word will display the Find Style dialog box (see Figure 11.9).

4. Choose the style you want to find from the Find What Style list, and then click the OK button to return to the Find and Replace dialog box. The area underneath the Find What box will display the style you chose.
5. Click in the Replace With box (or press Tab to move the insertion point there), and then click the Format button and choose Style once more. Word will display the Replace Style dialog box, which is almost identical to the Find Style dialog box.
6. Choose the replacement style from the Replace With Style list, and then click the OK button to return to the Find and Replace dialog box. The area underneath the Replace With box will display the style you chose.

7. Choose a search direction from the Search drop-down list if necessary.
8. Start the search by clicking the Find Next, Replace, or Replace All button.

TIP

To replace words or characters in one style with words or characters in another style, choose the styles as described above, and then enter the appropriate text in the Find What box and Replace With box.

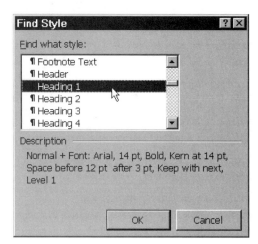

FIGURE 11.9:
In the Find Style dialog box, choose the style you want Word to find.

AutoText

Word's AutoText feature provides another way of inserting frequently used text and graphics in your documents. AutoText has several components that we'll look at in the following sections.

Creating an AutoText Entry

To create an AutoText entry:

1. Select the text (and/or graphics, etc.) from your document for the AutoText entry. Make sure that it contains all the formatting it needs.

2. Click the Create AutoText button on the AutoText toolbar or press Alt+F3 to display the Create AutoText dialog box (see Figure 11.10). (If the AutoText toolbar isn't displayed, right-click on the menu bar or on any displayed toolbar and choose AutoText from the drop-down list of toolbars to display it.)

3. In the Please Name Your AutoText Entry text box, enter the name you'll use to identify the AutoText entry.

    • If you chose text for the AutoText entry, Word will automatically display the first couple of words from your selection in the Please Name Your AutoText Entry box. Often you'll want to change this and use something catchy that you won't forget in a hurry.

    • Unlike AutoCorrect entries, AutoText entries can have plain-English names that you type all the time because AutoText does not automatically replace your typing.

4. Click the OK button to add the AutoText entry to Word's list and close the Create AutoText dialog box. If an AutoText entry with the same name already exists, Word will ask if you want to redefine it. Choose Yes or No; if you choose No, Word will let you choose another name for the AutoText entry; if you choose Yes, Word will replace the existing AutoText entry with the new one.

FIGURE 11.10:
In the Create AutoText dialog box, select a name for your AutoText entry, and then click the OK button.

Inserting an AutoText Entry

You can insert an AutoText entry in several ways:

• Using the AutoText toolbar
• Typing and using the AutoComplete feature
• Typing and choosing the entry manually
• Using the Insert ➤ AutoText menu item

Inserting an AutoText Entry from the AutoText Toolbar

To insert an AutoText entry from the AutoText toolbar, you use the Insert AutoText button. This button will bear the name of the style of the current paragraph, such as *Heading 1* or *Body Text.* Click the button to display a list of the AutoText entries associated with the current style as shown here.

To insert an entry associated with another style, or one of Word's predefined entries, hold down Shift as you click the Insert AutoText button. Word will display a menu of all the AutoText categories that it contains, including its predefined categories (Attention Line, Closing, Header/ Footer, and so on) and all the styles that have AutoText entries defined. Select the category you want; then choose the item from the sub-menu that appears as shown in the second illustration here.

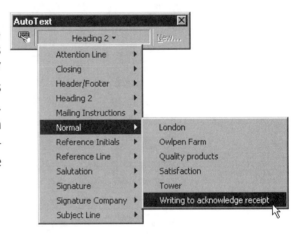

Inserting an AutoText Entry Using the AutoComplete Feature

To insert an AutoText entry quickly using the AutoComplete feature, start typing the name of the entry. As soon as you've typed four letters, or enough of it to distinguish it from any other AutoText entry that starts with the same four letters, AutoComplete will pop up a suggestion box, as shown here. Press Enter or F3 to replace the name of the entry with the full text of the entry; keep typing to ignore the suggestion.

You can turn off the AutoComplete feature as follows:

1. Click the AutoText button, or choose Insert ➤ AutoText ➤ AutoText to display the AutoText tab of the AutoCorrect dialog box.
2. Clear the Show AutoComplete Tip for AutoText and Dates check box.
3. Click the OK button to close the AutoCorrect dialog box.

Inserting an AutoText Entry Manually

When you've turned off AutoComplete, you can insert an AutoText entry by typing the first three letters of its name (or enough letters to distinguish it from any other AutoText entry) and then pressing F3 to insert the entry.

Inserting an AutoText Entry from the Insert Menu

You can also insert an AutoText entry from the Insert menu:

- To display the AutoText submenu of AutoText entries associated with the current style, choose Insert ➤ AutoText.
- To display the AutoText submenu of all AutoText categories, pull down the Insert menu, hold down Shift, and select AutoText.

Choose the entry you want either from the AutoText submenu or from one of the categories on the AutoText submenu, as shown in Figure 11.11.

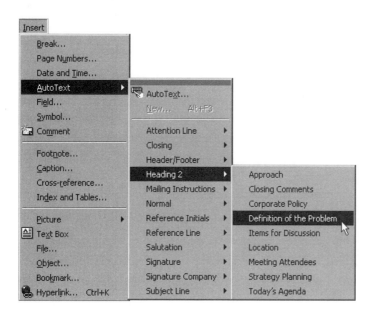

FIGURE 11.11:
You can also insert AutoText entries from the Insert ➤ AutoText submenu.

Changing an AutoText Entry

You can't edit an AutoText entry on the AutoText tab of the AutoCorrect dialog box. Instead, to change an AutoText entry, simply insert it in text (as described in the previous section), and then edit it using regular Word editing techniques. Once you've got the material for the entry to your satisfaction, select it, choose Insert ➤ AutoText to display the AutoText dialog box, and click the New button.

Deleting an AutoText Entry

To delete an AutoText entry:

1. Click the AutoText button or choose Edit ➤ AutoText ➤ AutoText to display the AutoText tab of the AutoCorrect dialog box.
2. Select the entry in the list box.
3. Click the Delete button to delete the entry.
4. Either delete more AutoText entries while you're at it, or click the Close button to close the AutoCorrect dialog box.

Automatic Bullets and Numbering

In this section, we'll look at the options Word offers for adding automatic bullets and numbering to your documents.

The bullets and numbering that Word applies automatically are paragraph formatting rather than actual characters on the page. This means that once you've added a bullet to a list, you can't just select the bullet and delete it as you might delete a character—you have to remove it from the paragraph's formatting. We'll look at this process later in "Removing Bullets and Numbering."

Adding Bullets and Numbering

You can add straightforward bullets and numbering to existing text by using the buttons on the Formatting toolbar.

To add bullets, first select the paragraphs you want to add bullets to, and then click the Bullets button on the Formatting toolbar. Word will add the bullets and apply a hanging indent to each of the paragraphs, but will leave them in their current style.

TIP   **To continue a numbered or bulleted list, press ↵ at the end of the list. To discontinue the list, press ↵ twice at the end of the list.**

To add numbers, select the paragraphs you want to number, and then click the Numbering button on the Formatting toolbar.

To create your own styles of bullets and numbering:

1. Select the paragraphs you want to add bullets or numbers (or both) to.

2. Choose Format ➤ Bullets and Numbering to display the Bullets and Numbering dialog box.

3. Select the appropriate tab and the format that suits you best, and then click the Customize button. Word will display the Customize Bulleted List dialog box, the Customize Numbered List dialog box, or the Customize Outline Numbered List dialog box as appropriate. Figure 11.13 shows the Customize Bulleted List dialog box, and the steps that follow discuss the options available in this dialog box; the Customize Numbered List dialog box and Customize Outline Numbered List dialog box look a little different, but the options work in similar ways.

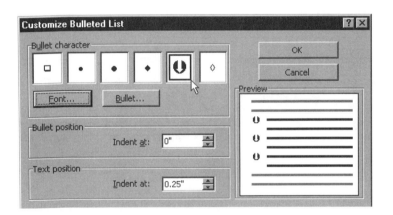

FIGURE 11.13:
In the Customize bulleted List dialog box, you can choose almost any bullet character that your computer can produce.

4. In the Bullet Character group box, choose one of the six bullets displayed; or click the Bullet button to open the Symbol dialog box, choose a character, and then click OK to return to the Customize Bulleted List dialog box. Click the Font button to display the Font dialog box, and choose a suitable font, font size, and other formatting for the bullet; click the OK button to close the Font dialog box and return to the Customize Bulleted List dialog box.

5. In the Bullet Position group box, use the Indent At measurement to specify any indent the bullet should receive.

6. In the Text Position group box, use the Indent At measurement to specify the indent of the text. Usually, you'll want this to be more than the indent for the bullet.

7. Click the OK button to apply the formatting to your list.

For a variety of styles of bullets and numbering, select the paragraphs, and then either right-click in the selection and choose Bullets and Numbering from the context menu or choose Format ➤ Bullets and Numbering to open the Bullets and Numbering dialog box (see Figure 11.12).

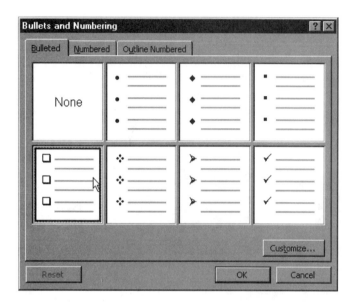

FIGURE 11.12:
The Bullets and Numbering dialog box gives you plenty of choices for formatting bulleted and numbered lists.

Choose the tab that corresponds to the type of list you want to create: Bulleted, Numbered, or Outline Numbered, and then click the style that suits you best. Click the OK button to apply the bullets or numbers and to close the Bullets and Numbering dialog box.

Removing Bullets and Numbering

To remove bullets or numbering from selected paragraphs:
- Click the Bullets button or the Numbering button.
- Choose Format ➤ Bullets and Numbering to display the Bullets and Numbering dialog box, select the None option, and click the OK button.

Modifying the Bullets and Numbering Styles

If you find the choices offered in the Bullets and Numbering dialog box inadequate for your needs, you can create your own bullets or numbers to adorn your text.

Captioning

Word's captioning features offer relief for those needing to ensure that the figures, graphics, tables, slides, video clips, equations, and so on, throughout their long documents are numbered consistently and sequentially. You can forget about laboriously renumbering all subsequent figures when you delete one at the beginning of a chapter—Word will handle it for you in seconds.

You can add either automatic numbering to captions of your own devising, or you can designate boilerplate captions that Word will add automatically to every table or equation or video clip or whatever you insert in your document.

Inserting a Caption

To insert a caption:

1. Select the item that you want to caption. For example, select a picture or a table.

2. Choose Insert ➤ Caption. Word will display the Caption dialog box (see Figure 11.14).

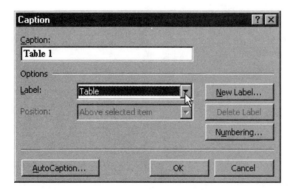

FIGURE 11.14:
The Caption dialog box lets you add captions to items in your document

3. From the Label drop-down list, choose Figure, Equation, or Table. Word will display it in the Caption text box. To add a new label to the list (and to the Caption text box), click the New Label button. In the New Label dialog box that Word displays, enter the text for the new label in the Label box and click the OK button. Word will insert the new label in the Caption box with its regular numbering.

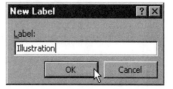

TIP

To delete a caption you've created, select the caption in the Label drop-down list and click the Delete Label button. You can tell which captions are Word's and which are yours because Word won't let you delete any of its captions (the Delete Label button will be dimmed).

4. Adjust the numbering of the caption if necessary: Click the Numbering button to display the Caption Numbering dialog box (see Figure 11.15). Click the OK button when you've finished.

- From the Format drop-down list, choose the numbering format you want: 1, 2, 3; a, b, c; A, B, C; i, ii, iii; or I, II, III.

- To include the chapter number with the illustration (for example, to produce *Figure 11.16*), select the Include Chapter Number check box. Specify the style at the beginning of each chapter from the Chapter Starts with Style drop-down list, and then choose a separator character from the Use Separator drop-down list. As you can see from this book, periods are the classiest separator characters, but Word also offers hyphens, colons, and em and en dashes.

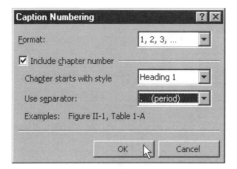

FIGURE 11.15:
Specify different numbering for your caption in the Caption Numbering dialog box.

5. In the Position drop-down list, choose whether you want the caption to appear above or below the selected item.

6. Click the OK button in the Caption dialog box to apply the caption numbering and return to your document. Add your specific caption to the generic caption that Word has inserted.

Using AutoCaption for Truly Automatic Captions

You can also choose to add automatic captions to recurring elements in a Word document. For example, if you're adding a number of tables to a document, you could have Word automatically add captions to each as you insert it to prevent you from accidentally missing one or using a wrong or inconsistent caption.

To add automatic captions to an element:

1. Choose Insert ➤ Caption to display the Caption dialog box.

2. Click the AutoCaption button to display the AutoCaption dialog box (see Figure 11.16).

3. In the Add Caption When Inserting list box, select the check box for the element you want to have captioned automatically. If you want several elements to have the same caption, select each one.

4. In the Options area, specify what the label should be and whether Word should position it above or below the element.

    • The Use Label drop-down list offers standard choices: Equation, Figure, or Table. If you chose Microsoft Equation or Microsoft Word Table in the Add Caption When Inserting box, Word will offer you Equation and Table, respectively. Otherwise, it will offer you Figure as a generic title.

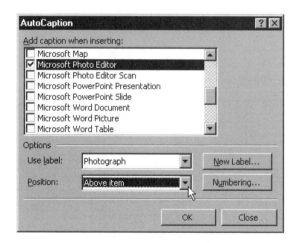

FIGURE 11.16:
In the AutoCaption dialog box, choose the element or elements to which you want to add automatic captions, and then customize the captions and numbering.

    • To change the label, click the New Label button and insert the text of the new label in the New Label dialog box.

    • To specify the numbering for the element, click the Numbering button and make your choices in the Caption Numbering dialog box. (For details, see step 4 in the previous section, "Modifying the Caption Style.") Click OK when you've finished.

    • Use the Position drop-down list to specify the position of the caption: Above Item or Below Item.

5. To add a different AutoCaption to another item, repeat steps 3 and 4.

6. Click the OK button to close the AutoCaption dialog box and return to your document.

Updating Captions

Word renumbers captions whenever you insert a new caption. If you move a caption to a different position in the document or delete a caption, you'll need to tell Word to update the captions. To do so, select the whole document (Edit ➤ Select All, or Ctrl+click in the selection bar) and press the F9 key.

TIP	If you want to update only one caption or to update captions one-by-one without updating other fields in the document, select that caption and press F9.

Using Bookmarks

Word's electronic bookmarks provide a way of assigning names to parts of your documents, so you can access them swiftly. A bookmark can mark a single point in the text, one or more characters, a graphic—pretty much any item in a document.

Adding a Bookmark

To add a bookmark:

1. Position the insertion point where you want to insert the bookmark. If you want the bookmark to mark a particular section of text, a graphic, a frame, a table, or another element, select that item.
2. Choose Insert ➤ Bookmark to display the Bookmark dialog box (see Figure 11.17).
3. Enter the name for the bookmark in the Bookmark Name text box.
   - Bookmark names can be up to 40 characters long and can contain letters, numbers, and underscores, but no spaces or symbols. The names must start with a letter; after that, you can mix letters, numbers, and underscores to your heart's desire.
   - To reuse an existing bookmark name, select it in the Bookmark Name list box.
4. Click the Add button to add the bookmark and close the Bookmark dialog box.

FIGURE 11.17:
In the Bookmark dialog box, enter the name for the bookmark and click the Add button.

Going to a Bookmark

Once you've added bookmarks to a document, you can quickly move to them by using either the Bookmark dialog box or the Go To dialog box.

To move to a bookmark using the Bookmark dialog box:

1. Choose Insert ➤ Bookmark to display the Bookmark dialog box.
2. In the Bookmark Name list box, select the bookmark to move to.
   - To sort the bookmarks alphabetically by Name, select the Name option button in the Sort By area; to sort them by their location in the document (from first to last), select the Location option button.
   - To display hidden bookmarks, such as those that Word uses to mark cross references, select the Hidden Bookmarks check box.
3. Click the Go To button to move to the bookmark, and then click the Close button (into which the Cancel button will have changed) to close the Bookmark dialog box.

To move to a bookmark using the Go To dialog box:

1. Double-click in open space in the status bar, press F5, or choose Edit ➤ Go To to display the Go To tab of the Find and Replace dialog box (see Figure 11.18).
2. Choose Bookmark in the Go to What list box.
3. Select the bookmark from the Enter Bookmark Name drop-down list, and then click the Go To button.
4. Click the Close button to close the Go To dialog box.

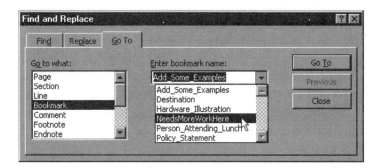

FIGURE 11.18:
Choose the bookmark to move to on the Go To tab of the Find and Replace dialog box, and then click the Go To button.

Viewing Bookmarks

Word doesn't normally display bookmarks, which makes it easier to read your documents. But when you do need to see where your bookmarks are, you can display them by choosing Tools ➤ Options to display the Options dialog box and selecting the Bookmarks check box in the Show area on the View tab; then click OK.

Empty bookmarks appear as a heavy I-beam disconcertingly similar to a mouse pointer on steroids, while bookmarks that contain text or another item enclose it within square brackets. The example here shows both types of bookmarks.

> The [Vice President of Communication] will meet you at I for lunch.

Deleting a Bookmark

To delete a bookmark:

1. Choose Insert ➤ Bookmark to display the Bookmark dialog box.
2. In the Bookmark Name list box, select the bookmark you want to delete.
3. Click the Delete button to delete the bookmark. The bookmark's contents will not be affected.
4. Repeat steps 2 and 3 as needed, and then click the Close button to close the Bookmark dialog box.

You can also delete a bookmark by selecting it and pressing the Delete key. Using this method will delete the bookmark's contents as well.

Chapter 12

CREATING MACROS AND CUSTOMIZING WORD

FEATURING

- **Creating macros to speed repetitive tasks**
- **Customizing toolbars, menus, and keyboard shortcuts**
- **Setting environment options**
- **Working with templates**

In this chapter, we'll look at three of Word's most appealing features—easy macro recording in a powerful macro language; a user interface (screens, menus, and keyboard shortcuts) customizable to the *n*th degree; and templates that you can pack with special styles, AutoText entries, toolbars, and macros.

By recording macros, you can automate routine tasks (such as creating or formatting documents) so you can run them with one keystroke or click, thus saving significant amounts of time and effort.

By customizing the Word user interface, you can ensure that the menus and tool-bars you or your colleagues use contain the commands most useful to you or them—or you can take commands that might cause problems out of temptation's way. You can also set Word's environment options—such as the Edit and File Locations options—to further simplify your working life.

By using templates, you can use boilerplate text and formatting to greatly speed the creation of documents.

Macros

A macro is a sequence of commands that you can assign to a single key, toolbar button, or menu item, and then repeat at will. For example, you might create a macro to automate basic formatting tasks on a type of document you receive regularly in an inappropriate format and which requires a clearly defined sequence of steps to refor-mat it.

In Word, you can swiftly create macros by turning on Word's macro recorder and performing the sequence of actions you want the macro to contain. (If you're feeling ambitious, you can then open the macro in the Visual Basic Editor and change it by deleting parts of what you've recorded or by typing in extra commands, or you can write a macro from scratch.)

Once you've created a macro, you can assign it to a menu item, a key combination, or a toolbar button and run it at any time.

Recording a Macro

First, start the macro recorder by double-clicking the REC indicator on the status bar. Word will display the Record Macro dialog box (see Figure 12.1).

Enter a name for the new macro in the Macro Name text box. The macro name can be up to 80 characters long and can contain both letters and numbers, but it must start with a letter. It cannot contain spaces, punctuation, or special characters (such as ! or *), though it can contain underscores.

TIP   If you type a space or a forbidden character in the Macro Name text box, Word will complain with an "Invalid Procedure Name" message box when you click the OK button.

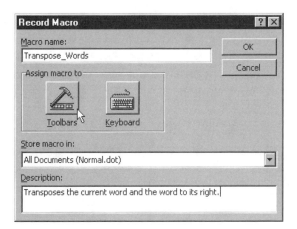

FIGURE 12.1:
In the Record Macro dialog box, enter a name for the macro you're about to record, and give it an illuminating write-up in the Description box.

Enter a description for the macro in the Description box. This description is to help you (and anyone you share the macro with) identify the macro; it can be up to 255 characters long.

If you want to restrict the macro to just the current template, choose the template from the Store Macro In drop-down list. If you want the macro to be available no matter which template you're working in, make sure the default setting, All Documents (Normal.dot), appears in the Store Macro In drop-down list box.

Next, click the Toolbars button or the Keyboard button in the Assign Macro To group box.

- If you chose Toolbars, Word will display the Customize dialog box (see Figure 12.2) with the Commands tab displayed and Macros selected in the Categories list box. Click the macro name in the Commands list box and drag it to any convenient toolbar or menu bar. Word will add a button or menu item for the macro, giving it the macro's full and unappealing name, such as NORMAL.NEWMACROS.TRANSPOSEWORDS. You can now rename the button or menu item by right-clicking it and entering a more attractive and descriptive name in the Name box. For a menu item, put an ampersand (**&**) before the character you want to use as an access key for the item. Click the Close button to close the Customize dialog box.

TIP

Two quick things here: First, the menu item name or button name for a macro doesn't have to bear any relation to the macro's name. Second, you can also create new toolbars and new menus as you need them, as we saw in Chapter 2, "Using Shared Tools in the Office Applications."

- If you chose Keyboard, Word will display the Customize Keyboard dialog box. With the insertion point in the Press New Shortcut Key box, press the key combination you want to use (see the section "Assigning a Keyboard Shortcut" later in this chapter for details about what key combinations can be), and then click the Assign button. Click the Close button to close the Customize Keyboard dialog box.

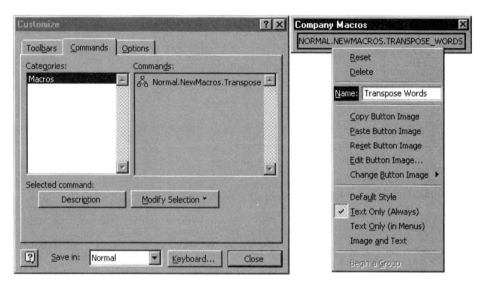

FIGURE 12.2: Choose a way to run the macro in the Customize dialog box. As you can see here, I've dragged the Normal.NewMacros.Transpose_Words macro to the Company Macros toolbar (where it became a button named NORMAL.NEWMACROS.TRANSPOSE_WORDS) and right-clicked to display the context menu so I could change its name to something more sensible.

   Word will then display the Stop Recording toolbar and will add a cassette-tape icon to the mouse pointer to remind you that you're recording. The REC indicator in the status bar will be black, too.

   Now record the sequence of actions you want to immortalize. You can use the mouse to select items from menus and toolbars and to make choices in dialog boxes, but not to select items on screen—for that, you must use the keyboard.

When you make choices in a dialog box—for example, the Paragraph dialog box—Word records the current settings for all the options on that tab of the dialog box when you click on OK. So when you make a change to, say, the left indentation of a paragraph, Word will record all the other settings on the Indents and Spacing tab as well (Alignment, Before and After spacing, and so forth). You can, however, edit these out later if you don't want them.

 To perform any actions you don't want recorded, you can pause the macro recorder at any time by clicking the Pause Recording button on the Stop Recording toolbar. Click the Pause Recording button again to resume recording.

 To stop recording, click the Stop Recording button on the Stop Recording toolbar. (You can also double-click the REC indicator on the status bar or choose Tools ➤ Macro ➤ Stop Recording.) Word has now recorded your macro and assigned it to the control you chose.

Running a Macro

To run a macro, simply click the toolbar button or choose the menu item or press the key combination you assigned to it.

If you chose not to assign a button, menu item, or key combination (perhaps you have too many macros, as I do), you can run a macro by choosing Tools ➤ Macro ➤ Macros to display the Macro dialog box, selecting the macro from the Macro Name list, and clicking the Run button.

To stop a macro you've started running, press Ctrl+Break (Break is usually written on the front face of the Pause key). Visual Basic will display an angry dialog box telling you that "Code execution has been interrupted." Click the End button to dismiss this dialog box.

If you make a mistake while recording a macro, you can choose to re-record it, but often a better option is to edit the mistakes out of it. If you're prepared to spend a few minutes looking at the Visual Basic for Applications programming language (VBA for short), you can usually figure out which the offending line is and simply remove it. You can also add further commands at this stage.

To edit a macro:

1. Choose Tools ➤ Macro ➤ Macros to display the Macros dialog box.
2. Select the macro you want to edit, and click the Edit button to display the macro ready for editing in the Visual Basic Editor (see Figure 12.3).
3. Make such changes as necessary in the macro by adding, deleting, and editing actions.
4. Choose File ➤ Save *templatename* to save the template and the changes you've made to it.
5. Choose File ➤ Close and Return to Microsoft Word to close the Visual Basic Editor and return to Word.

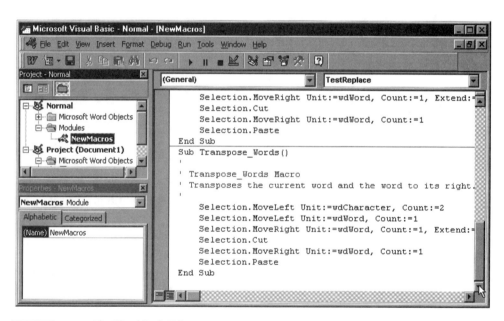

FIGURE 12.3: The Visual Basic Editor

NOTE   **For information about working with macros in Word 97, see the *Word 97 Macro & VBA Handbook*, also from Sybex.**

Getting Help on Visual Basic for Applications

The Visual Basic Editor offers comprehensive help on the Visual Basic for Applications programming language. To view it in the Visual Basic Editor, choose Help ➤ Microsoft Visual Basic Help or Help ➤ Contents and Index. Most of the statements and functions have examples, which can be particularly helpful when creating and troubleshooting your macros.

TIP If your computer doesn't offer you any help on VBA, whoever installed Office on your computer may not have installed the relevant files (perhaps to save space). If that's the case, you'll need to dig out your CD of Office and run the Setup program again. See the Appendix for details on running this program.

Deleting a Macro

To delete a macro that you no longer need, display the Macro dialog box by choosing Tools ➤ Macro ➤ Macros. Choose the macro in the Macro Name list box, and click the Delete button. Choose Yes in the warning message box.

Customizing Word

In Word, you can customize the toolbars, the menus, and the menu bar; the keyboard shortcuts; and certain environment options that control where Word stores files of different types and so on. The first of these—customizing toolbars, menus, and the menu bar—we looked at in Chapter 2; the rest we'll look at here.

Customizing Keyboard Shortcuts

Even if you're not a die-hard WordStar user who's finally upgraded to Word, you can speed and simplify your work by customizing the keyboard to suit your needs. While Word comes with an impressive array of preprogrammed keyboard shortcuts, you're likely to find other items that you need to have at hand instead. (If you *are* a former WordStar user, you can remap most of the keyboard….)

Assigning a Keyboard Shortcut

To set a keyboard shortcut:

1. Choose Tools ➤ Customize to display the Customize dialog box.
2. Click the Keyboard button to display the Customize Keyboard dialog box (see Figure 12.4).

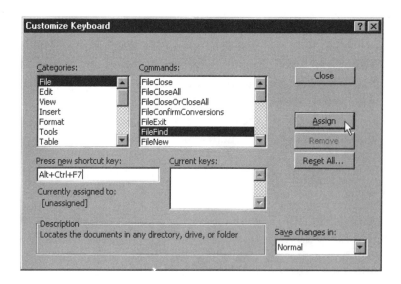

FIGURE 12.4:
Set keyboard shortcuts in the Customize Keyboard dialog box.

3. Specify the template to change in the Save Changes In drop-down list if necessary. (Leave Normal selected if you want the changes to apply to all templates that don't have this keyboard combination set to another command.)
4. In the Categories list, select the category of item for the new keyboard shortcut.
5. Choose the item to add in the Commands list box. (If you chose Macro Fonts, AutoText, Styles, or Common Symbols in the Categories list, the box will change its name to match your choice—Macros, Fonts, and so o
6. Click in the Press New Shortcut Key text box and press the key combina you want; Word will display it in the Press New Shortcut Key box. A key combination can be any of the following:
   - Alt plus a regular key not used for a menu access key
   - Alt plus a function key
   - Ctrl plus a regular key or function key
   - Ctrl+Alt plus a regular key or function key

- Shift plus a function key
- Ctrl+Shift plus a regular key or function key
- Alt+Shift plus a regular key or function key
- Ctrl+Alt+Shift plus a regular key or function key

Because this last option involves severe contortions of the hands for most people, it's not great for keyboard combinations you expect to use frequently.

NOTE   **You can set up shortcut keys that have two steps—for example, Ctrl+Alt+F, 1 and Ctrl+Alt+F, 2—by pressing the second key after pressing the key combination. These tend to be more trouble than they're worth unless you're assigning literally hundreds of extra shortcut keys.**

---

7. Check the Current Keys box to see if that key combination is already assigned. (If it is and you don't want to overwrite it, press Backspace to clear the Press New Shortcut Key text box, and then choose another combination.)

8. Click the Assign button to assign the shortcut.

9. Repeat steps 3–8 to assign more keyboard shortcuts; when you're finished, click the Close button to close the Customize Keyboard dialog box.

10. Click the Close button to close the Customize dialog box.

If Word prompts you to save changes to the Normal template the next time you close Word, choose Yes.

Removing a Keyboard Shortcut

Usually you remove a keyboard shortcut by assigning that shortcut to another item—for example, if you assign Ctrl+P to a Photograph style you've created, Word will overwrite Ctrl+P as the shortcut for the Print command. But sometimes you may need to remove a shortcut without assigning it to another item—for example, if you want to prevent another person from performing certain actions.

To remove a keyboard shortcut:

1. Choose Tools ➤ Customize to display the Customize dialog box.

2. Click the Keyboard button to display the Customize Keyboard dialog box.

3. Specify the template to change in the Save Changes In drop-down list if necessary. (Leave Normal selected if you want the changes to apply to all templates that don't have this keyboard combination set to another command.)

4. In the Categories list, select the category of the item that currently has the keyboard shortcut you want to remove.

5. Choose the item in the Commands list box. (If you chose Macros, Fonts, AutoText, Styles, or Common Symbols in the Categories list, the list box will change its name to suit your choice—Macros, Fonts, and so on.)

6. In the Current Keys list box, select the key combination to remove (there may be several for some commands).

7. Click the Remove button.

8. Remove more keyboard shortcuts if necessary, and then click the Close button to close the Customize Keyboard dialog box.

9. Click the Close button to close the Customize dialog box.

Resetting All Keyboard Shortcuts

You can quickly reset all keyboard shortcuts for the template specified in the Save Changes In drop-down list by clicking the Reset All button in the Customize Keyboard dialog box. Word will display a confirmation message box to make sure you want to take this drastic step:

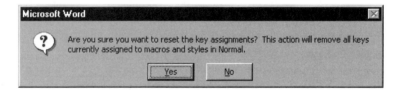

Choose Yes to reset the keyboard shortcuts, and then click Close to exit the Customize Keyboard dialog box and Close again to close the Customize dialog box.

Choosing Environment Options

As we've seen in earlier chapters, Word offers any number of options for editing, printing, spelling and grammar, and the like, on the ten tabs of the Options dialog box (Tools ➤ Options). In this section, we'll look at the different categories of options and discuss those not touched on in other sections of this book. We won't grind through all the details for every single option, but I'll try to indicate the most useful options for conventional uses of Word.

View Options

The options on the View tab let you specify which tools and elements you see on screen.

NOTE | **Word's different views offer some different view options—for example, Page Layout view does not offer the Wrap to Window and Draft Font options, but it does offer Text Boundaries (dotted lines around page elements), Drawings (for displaying drawing objects created in Word), and Object Anchors (the anchor symbols that indicate an item is attached to a particular paragraph). Online Layout view offers an Enlarge Fonts Less Than option instead of Style Area Width.**

Show Options Select the Picture Placeholders check box to have Word display empty boxes instead of graphics. This will let you scroll through your documents faster, particularly when using a slower computer.

Select the Field Codes check box to have field codes rather than results displayed in text. Select the Bookmarks check box to have bookmark markers appear in text.

Clear the Animated Text check box if you want to suppress the display of animated font formatting.

Nonprinting Characters Choose which characters and items you want to see on screen: tabs, spaces, paragraph marks, optional hyphens, hidden text, or all of the above.

Window Options Choose whether to have the status bar, horizontal scroll bar, and vertical scroll bar displayed.

Select the Wrap to Window check box to have Word adjust the line length to fit the window and make the text more readable.

In the Style Area Width box, enter a measurement other than 0" if you want to display the style area, a pane on the left side of the Word window which displays the style for each paragraph.

In Online Layout view, choose the smallest font size you want to see by setting the font size in the Enlarge Fonts Less Than box.

General Options

The options on the General tab of the Options dialog box offer a mishmash of choices.

Background Repagination repaginates your documents in the background as you work. On long documents, this may slow down your computer.

NOTE   **Background Repagination isn't available in Page Layout view because this view is always up-to-date with its pagination.**

Help for WordPerfect Users performs equivalent Word commands when you press a WordPerfect key combination. For example, if you press Home Home ↑ with Help for WordPerfect Users on, Word will move to the beginning of the document; if you press Home Home ↑ without Help for WordPerfect Users on, Word will move to the beginning of the line, beep, and then move up one line. When this option is on, WPH appears on the status bar.

Navigation Keys for WordPerfect Users makes the PageUp, PageDown, Home, End, and Esc keys behave in Word as they do in WordPerfect. When this option is on, WPN appears on the status bar. (If both Help for WordPerfect Users and Navigation Keys for WordPerfect Users are on, WP appears on the status bar.)

Blue Background, White Text displays white text on a blue background, which can be visually restful. If you also choose View ➤ Full Screen and the two WordPerfect options, you can pretend you're using WordPerfect 5.1 for DOS....

Provide Feedback with Sound controls whether Word plays sounds when something goes wrong or when Word completes an action (such as saving a file). If an irregular stream of cutesy sounds annoys you, clear this check box.

Provide Feedback with Animation animates the mouse cursor when Word is performing an action and animates Word actions, such as closing dialog boxes. It also controls whether the ruler pops up when you move the mouse pointer over the gray bar at the top or left side of the Word window.

Confirm Conversion at Open displays a Convert File dialog box when you open a file in a format other than Word. Select this check box if Word is misconverting your files and you want to try a different conversion.

Update Automatic Links at Open updates any automatic links in a document when you open it. (See Chapter 2 for information on linking.)

Mail as Attachment lets you e-mail a document as an attachment.

Recently Used File List controls the number of most recently used files that appear at the foot of the File menu. Increase or decrease the number in the Entries box to list more or fewer files (from one to nine); clear the check box to have none appear at all (for example, for security reasons).

Macro Virus Protection scans documents you open and warns you if they might contain a macro virus. Keep this check box selected, but be prepared for Word to give you false alarms.

Measurement Units controls the units in which the rulers, Paragraph dialog box, and so on display measurements: choose Inches, Centimeters, Points, or Picas.

Edit Options

Because the options on the Edit tab of the Options dialog box can make a great deal of difference to your daily maneuverings, they bear further investigation.

Typing Replaces Selection causes Word to overwrite selected text when you start typing. If this disconcerts you, clear the check box, and Word will move the insertion point to the beginning of a selection when you start typing.

Drag-and-Drop Text Editing controls whether you can use drag-and-drop, which we looked at in Chapter 2. If you don't use drag-and-drop, turning this off may speed up Word a bit.

When Selecting, Automatically Select Entire Word lets you quickly select multiple words. (See "Selecting Text" in Chapter 5 for details.)

Use the INS Key for Paste makes the Insert (or Ins, depending on your keyboard) key perform the Paste command.

Overtype Mode turns on Overtype mode, discussed in "Insert and Overtype Modes" in Chapter 5.

Use Smart Cut and Paste adds and removes spaces as needed when you cut, paste, and drag-and-drop text. You'll usually want to keep this check box selected.

Use Tab and Backspace Keys to Set Left Indent lets you indent and outdent the left margin by pressing Tab (after you've entered one tab stop) and Backspace, respectively.

Allow Accented Uppercase in French does just that.

Print Options

The Print tab of the Options dialog box lets you select the default tray of paper for the printer and specify whether to print just the data when printing a form. Then there are seven Printing Options and five Include with Document options.

Printing Options The Printing Options area on the Print tab offers the following:
- Draft Output lets you print a stripped-down version of your document on some printers. Your mileage may vary.
- Update Fields updates all unlocked fields whenever you print.
- Update Links updates all unlocked links whenever you print.
- Allow A4/Letter Paper Resizing allows Word to resize documents formatted for A4 to print them on letter-size paper (which is proportioned a little differently) and vice versa. Word adjusts the printout, not the formatting of the document. If you work with documents from, say, a European firm, this capability can be a lifesaver.
- Background Printing lets you keep working (albeit a bit more slowly) while Word is printing your documents.
- Print PostScript over Text is primarily useful if you need to print a document created in Word for the Macintosh containing PostScript code for special printing effects.
- Reverse Print Order prints documents from last page to first.

Include with Document Choose whether to print document properties, field codes, comments, hidden text, and *drawing objects* (objects created in Word, including lines) when printing your document. Document properties and comments will each print on a separate page at the end of the document; field codes, hidden text, and drawing objects will print where they occur in the document.

WARNING **Printing hidden text will alter the layout of your pages. Use Print Preview to check the effect of including hidden text before actually printing.**

Save Options

The options on the Save tab of the Options dialog box can help keep your work safe when all around you are losing theirs (and blaming it on you). Always Create Backup Copy creates a backup copy each time you save a document by renaming the previously saved version of that document to Backup of *filename* and giving it the extension .wbk. This is a valuable option—with two caveats: First, it will slow down your save operations a little, though usually not enough to worry about; and second, you need to understand that the backup "copy" is *not* the same as the currently saved version of the file—if you destroy the latest saved version, the backup will provide you with the previous version.

TIP

To make the backups of your documents virtually identical to the currently saved copies, always save twice in immediate succession. (You could write a macro to do this.) In any case, always save your documents when you've made changes that you wouldn't want to lose (or have to make again) if your computer suffered a power problem or a software or hardware error. Depending on your work habits, this could mean anything from saving your work every couple of minutes to every couple of hours.

Allow Fast Saves speeds up save operations by saving only the changes to a file, not actually saving the file itself. This option can create bizarre results—if you delete most of a large file (or most of a file containing graphics) and then fast-save it, the file size will still be large; and fast-saved documents will always be somewhat larger than regularly saved documents. Bear this in mind if disk space is at a premium or you're often transferring documents by modem without compressing them first.

NOTE

You can't choose Always Create Backup Copy and Allow Fast Saves at the same time—it's one or the other. Allow Fast Saves saves you only a little time unless you have a very slow computer or you're working with huge documents (or both).

Prompt for Document Properties displays the Properties dialog box automatically the first time you save a document. This is useful if you use the document properties information to identify your documents; if you don't, it rapidly proves tedious.

Prompt to Save Normal Template makes Word check with you before it saves changes to Normal.dot, the global template. Select this option if you spend time mucking about with Normal.dot and want to be able to escape any embarrassing changes you make by mistake. Otherwise, leave this check box selected to have Word save changes to Normal.dot automatically.

Embed TrueType Fonts lets you save the fonts used in a document with the document, so the document appears the same on a computer that doesn't have those particular fonts installed.

WARNING Using Embed TrueType Fonts can greatly increase the size of document files. Use it only if you're sharing files and need to ensure they look exactly the same on other computers. If you do use this option, select the Embed Characters in the Use Only check box to let Word keep the file size down as much as possible.

Allow Background Saves notionally allows you to keep working while Word saves a file to disk. In my experience, it seems to help neither on fast computers nor on slow ones.

Save AutoRecover Info Every *nn* Minutes causes Word to save an automatic backup of documents at a specified interval (from one minute to 120 minutes). You can use these AutoRecover files to recover documents if Word or your computer crashes. When you exit Word successfully, it deletes any AutoRecover files made in that session. These backups are stored in the AutoRecover Files location specified on the File Locations tab of the Options dialog box (which we'll discuss in a page or two). When you restart Word after a crash, it should open any AutoRecovered files that haven't been deleted and display them to you as Recovered. Check them carefully and save them under new names if they're still of any use.

WARNING Don't rely too heavily on the AutoRecover feature to save your bacon when your computer runs into problems. Save your work regularly, and preferably keep backup copies of your most important files as well.

The Save Word Files As drop-down list lets you choose to save files by default as a different type of document than Word 97 format. For example, you might choose Word 6.0/95 (*.doc) to save your files in the Word 6/Word 95 format if you or your colleagues are still working with those versions of Word on some computers. The File-Sharing options are for protecting your documents from intrusion, alteration, and damage. Consult the Help files for details.

Spelling & Grammar Options

The options on the Spelling & Grammar tab of the Options dialog box—for controlling Word's automatic spell-checking and grammar-checking, working with dictionaries, and so on—are discussed in Chapter 2.

User Information Options

Make sure your name, initials, and mailing address are entered correctly on the User Information tab of the Options dialog box. Among other things, Word uses this name for document properties information, the initials for annotations, and the mailing address for envelopes.

File Locations Options

The options on the File Locations tab of the Options dialog box let you specify where Word should locate documents, clip-art pictures, templates, AutoRecover files, and other files it maintains.

Documents is the category that can save you the most time: If you want Word to suggest saving documents somewhere other than the My Documents folder (or the Personal folder in NT 4), change Documents straight away.

To change a file location:

1. Choose the item to change in the File Types list box.
2. Click the Modify button to display the Modify Location dialog box.
3. Choose the new folder for the file location using standard Windows techniques.
4. Click the OK button to close the Modify Location dialog box.

Templates

As discussed in Chapter 2, Word offers a number of different templates that provide you with shortcuts to creating specific types of documents. You can also create your own

templates by choosing File ➤ New, selecting Template in the Create New group box in the New dialog box, and then customizing and saving the file.

Any template can contain its own styles (for formatting text), AutoText entries (for inserting text and other elements quickly), toolbars (for quick access to the commands you need), and macro modules (for performing repetitive actions). You can also copy any of these four types of items between any two templates.

Copying Styles, AutoText, Toolbars, or Macro Modules from One Template to Another

To copy one or more styles, toolbars, AutoText entries, or macro modules from one template to another, open the Organizer dialog box by choosing Tools ➤ Templates and Add-Ins to display the Templates and Add-Ins dialog box; then click the Organizer button in the Templates and Add-ins dialog box. Select the appropriate tab (Styles, AutoText, Toolbars, or Macro Project Items) to bring it to the front of the Organizer dialog box. Figure 12.5 shows the Organizer dialog box with the Toolbars tab displayed, and the paragraphs below discuss transferring toolbars; however, the procedure is the same for styles, AutoText entries, and macro project items.

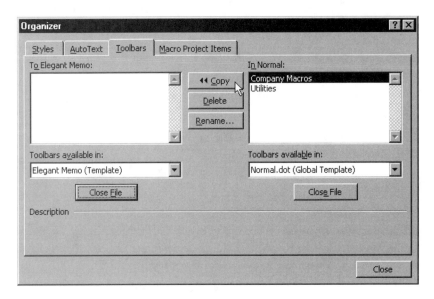

FIGURE 12.5:   The Organizer box lets you copy styles, AutoText entries, toolbars, or macro modules from one template to another.

Word displays the toolbars you've created in Normal.dot in the right-hand panel and the toolbars for the current document in the left-hand panel.

To work with the template for the current document, select it from the Toolbars Available In drop-down list in the panel listing the current document. Otherwise, open the templates you want: Click the Close File button on one side to close the currently open file and then click the Open File button (into which the Close File button will have changed) to open the other file. Choose the template from the Open dialog box that Word then displays.

Copy the toolbar by selecting it in the left-hand or right-hand box and clicking the Copy button. When you click the Close button to exit the Organizer dialog box, Word will invite you to save any changes to affected templates; choose Yes.

Deleting and Renaming Items in the Organizer Dialog Box

You can also use the Organizer dialog box to delete or rename styles, AutoText entries, toolbars, or macro modules. Open the Organizer dialog box, open the appropriate template as described in the previous section, and select the tab for the item you want to change.

Renaming an Item

Choose the item to rename, and then click the Rename button. Enter the new name for the item in the Rename dialog box and click OK.

Deleting an Item

Choose the item to delete, and click the Delete button. Choose Yes in the confirmation message box that Word displays. (To delete more than one item at a time, you can select a range of items by selecting the first one, holding down Shift, and clicking the last; or you can select noncontiguous multiple items by selecting the first one and then holding down Ctrl as you click on the others.)

When you've finished deleting or renaming items, click the Close button to close the Organizer dialog box.

Part 4

Excel

Chapter 13

CREATING WORKSHEETS AND ENTERING DATA

FEATURING

- **Understanding what Excel is and what it does**
- **Creating a spreadsheet**
- **Entering data**

Excel is a spreadsheet program that you can use to enter, manipulate, and crunch data to your heart's content. This data can be pretty much anything—deposits in your daughter's bank account and putative interest accrued by the year 2015, employee hiring and firing information by department, or detailed data on the mating habits of frogs in Borneo.

In this chapter, we'll look briefly at what Excel is and what it does. Once we've set the scene, we'll look at how to create a spreadsheet and enter data in it. In the next chapter, we'll look at how to work with that data, change it, and format it as appropriate.

Spreadsheets, Worksheets, and Workbooks

First, we need to spend a moment with the terms we'll be using. Excel is a *spreadsheet* program—a program designed to work with numbers (as opposed to a word processor, such as Word, which is designed to work with words). You enter your data in *cells* arrayed into horizontal rows and vertical columns on a *worksheet*, an arrangement somewhat reminiscent of an accountant's ledger but far more flexible.

Excel organizes worksheets by workbook, on the basis that you may need more than one worksheet for any given project. Each new workbook you open contains three worksheets by default, but you can add worksheets up to a maximum of 255. (You can also remove one or two worksheets from the original three if you need fewer.)

Each worksheet contains 65,536 rows (numbered from 1 to 65536) and 256 columns (numbered from A to IV—the first 26 columns are numbered A to Z, the next 26 AA to AZ, the next 26 BA to BZ, and so on.). The worksheets are numbered automatically from Sheet 1 to Sheet 256, but you can change their names to anything that suits you, provided the name contains fewer than 32 characters and doesn't contain any of these characters: / \ ? : *

Because this is happening on a computer, the whole thing is virtual as opposed to physical, but imagine these virtual worksheets as being stacked on top of each other, with the first at the top. As a result, you can work with cells in three dimensions—across in the rows, down in the columns, and down *through* the stack of worksheets in the workbook. You can include formulas to automatically perform calculations on the data contained in the workbook; we'll look at formulas in Chapter 16.

For example, consider the worksheet, 1996, shown in Figure 13.1. As you can see from the worksheet tabs at the bottom of the screen, this is the thirteenth worksheet in the workbook, following the first twelve worksheets named January through December, each of which tracks one month's sales of the various products foisted on a gullible public by Text Butcher Communications, Inc.

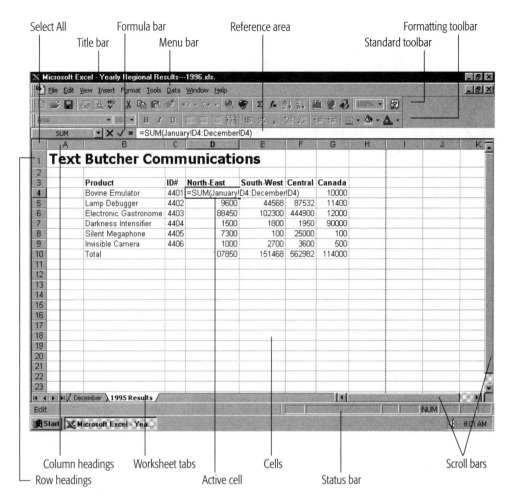

FIGURE 13.1:   The parts of the Excel window, featuring a sample spreadsheet that performs calculations down through the stack of worksheets.

Parts of the Excel Screen

As you can see in Figure 13.1, the Excel screen has standard Windows application items: a title bar, a menu bar, a status bar, toolbars, scroll bars, and more. To these Excel adds the following:

• The *reference area* displays the location of the active cell.

• The *formula bar* is where you enter and edit data and formulas.

- *Cells* are where you enter data and formulas.
- *Row headings* and *column headings* let you quickly select a row or a column.
- *Worksheet tabs* let you quickly move between worksheets (by clicking on the tab of the worksheet you want).

Working with Worksheets

In this section, we'll look at the basics of working with worksheets in Excel: how to move to different parts of a worksheet; how to select a worksheet; how to add, delete, and rename worksheets; and how to rearrange the worksheets in a workbook. Once we've done that, we'll move on to entering data in the cells of a worksheet.

Moving about the Worksheet

You can move from cell to cell using the mouse or navigation keys (←, →, ↑, ↓). To move with the mouse, click in the cell you want to make active; use the scroll bars to scroll to other areas of the worksheet.

Here's how you move using the navigation keys:

- The Home key moves the active cell to column A in the current row.
- Ctrl+Home moves the active cell to cell A1 in the current worksheet.
- Ctrl plus an arrow key moves the active cell to the end of the worksheet in that direction—Ctrl+↓ moves the active cell to the last row, Ctrl+← moves the active cell to the first column, and so on.
- PageUp and PageDown move the active cell up and down one screen's worth of rows.
- Alt+PageUp and Alt+PageDown move the active cell left and right one screen's worth of columns, respectively.
- End+Home moves the active cell to the last cell in the worksheet that contains data.
- End plus an arrow key (for example., End+→) moves the active cell to the first cell in that direction that contains data and is next to an empty cell.

Moving among Worksheets

The easiest way to move from one worksheet to another is to click the worksheet tab of the worksheet you want to move to.

To move to the first worksheet in the workbook, click the Move to First button at the bottom of the Excel window next to the worksheet tabs.

 To move to the last worksheet in the workbook, click the Move to Last button.

 To move to the next worksheet in the workbook, click the Next button.

 To move to the previous worksheet in the workbook, click the Previous button.

TIP   **Ctrl+PageUp moves the active cell to the previous worksheet; Ctrl+PageDown moves the active cell to the next sheet.**

Selecting Worksheets

Use the mouse to select worksheets as follows:
- To select a worksheet, click on its tab at the bottom of the Excel window.
- To select a range of worksheets, click on the tab for the first worksheet in the range, hold down Shift, and click on the tab for the last one.
- To select multiple noncontiguous worksheets, click on the tab for the first worksheet; then hold down Ctrl and click on the tabs for the other worksheets in turn.
- To select all the worksheets in a workbook, right-click on a worksheet tab and choose Select All Sheets from the context menu.

Adding a Worksheet

To add a worksheet before the worksheet currently selected, choose Insert ➤ Worksheet.

To add more than one worksheet at a time, select the same number of worksheet tabs as you want to insert new worksheets, and then choose Insert ➤ Worksheet. Excel will add the new worksheets to the left of the leftmost worksheet tab you selected.

Deleting a Worksheet

To delete a worksheet from the workbook, right-click on its tab and choose Delete from the context menu. Choose OK in the confirmation message box.

WARNING   **When you delete a worksheet, you delete all the data on it too. You cannot undo this deletion except by closing the file immediately without saving changes and then reopening it. (You'll also lose any other unsaved changes in the workbook, so consider saving the workbook before deleting a worksheet.)**

To delete multiple worksheets at once, select their tabs, right-click on one of them, choose Delete from the context menu, and choose OK in the confirmation message box.

Renaming a Worksheet

Sheet1, Sheet2, and so on, are not particularly catchy names (though superbly logical and orderly), so you'll probably want to assign the worksheets you use more informative names. To rename a worksheet, right-click on its tab and choose Rename  from the context menu. Excel will select the worksheet's name on the worksheet tab; enter the new name, and then press Enter or click elsewhere to make the change. Worksheet names can be up to 31 characters long; the longer the names, the fewer tabs you'll see at once on-screen.

Rearranging the Worksheets in a Workbook

To quickly rearrange the worksheets in a workbook, click on a worksheet tab and drag-and-drop it where you want it. An inverted black triangle will indicate the position where it will be dropped between the other tabs.

To copy a worksheet to a different location in a workbook, hold down Ctrl and drag the worksheet tab to the new location. Excel will identify the copy by appending (2) to the name of the original—or a higher number if you make more copies.

To move or copy a worksheet between open workbooks:

1. Right-click on the worksheet tab, and choose Move or Copy from the context menu to display the Move or Copy dialog box.

2. In the To Book drop-down list, choose the workbook to which you want to move the worksheet.

3. In the Before Sheet list box, select the worksheet before which you want the other worksheet to appear. Select the (move to end) choice if you want the worksheet you're moving or copying to appear after all the others.

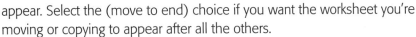

4. To copy the worksheet, select the Create a Copy check box.

5. Click the OK button to close the Move or Copy dialog box and move or copy the worksheet.

NOTE **To move or copy multiple worksheets at once, select them first.**

Creating a Spreadsheet

In this section, we'll look briefly at starting a new spreadsheet and entering some data in it. Along the way, we'll discuss the different types of data that Excel recognizes, because this affects the data you enter in the cells of any worksheet.

Starting a New Workbook

When you start Excel, it will open a fresh workbook for you with the default three blank worksheets.

To start a new workbook based on the default workbook template, click the New button on the Standard toolbar. To start a workbook based on a spreadsheet template, choose File ➤ New to display the New dialog box, click the Spreadsheet Solutions tab, choose one of the templates shown there (look at the Preview box to see how the first worksheet in the template will look), and click the OK button.

Types of Data in Excel

Before you enter data, you need to know how Excel handles it. Excel recognizes five different types of data: numbers, dates, times, text, and formulas.

Numbers

Numbers are values that can be calculated. They can consist of the numerals 0 through 9, with a decimal point (a period) as a separator for decimal places and with commas as separators for thousands.

Numbers can start with a dollar sign ($) or other currency symbol, or with a + or – sign. They can end with a % sign; they can also be enclosed in parentheses (as an alternative to the – sign, for indicating negative numbers).

You control the display of numbers by formatting the cells that contain them—for example, you could format a cell to display currency amounts with two decimal places. We'll look at cell formatting in Chapter 14.

Dates

Excel handles dates as *serial numbers*, which represent the number of days elapsed since 1/1/1900, which is serial number 1 (for example., 1/31/1900 is serial number 31). With serial numbers, Excel can perform calculations easily—to sort 1/1/97, 3/3/97, and 2/2/97 into reverse order, Excel simply works with the dates 35431, 35492, and 35463 (respectively). The good news is in two parts: First, Excel handles the serial numbers in the background, so you don't need to worry about them; and second, if you enter a date in one of the four formats shown here, Excel will automatically identify it as a date, store it as a serial number, and represent it to you as a date formatted in the way you choose.

Date Format	Example
MM/DD/YY	9/3/96 or 09/03/96
MMM-YY	Sep-96
DD-MMM-YY	03-Sep-96
DD-MMM	03-Sep

Excel uses slashes when displaying dates that need them, but you can use hyphens when entering dates—for example, both **11/28/64** and **11-28-64** will be stored correctly.

Times

Excel uses serial numbers for times as well, representing the 24 hours of the day as values between 0 and 1. For example, 6 AM is 0.25, noon is 0.5, 6 PM is 0.75, and so on. You can enter time in the formats listed below; specify AM or PM if you don't want Excel to use the 24-hour format.

Time Format	Example
HH:MM	10:15
HH:MM:SS	22:15:17
HH:MM AM/PM	10:15 PM
HH:MM:SS AM/PM	10:15:17 PM

You can combine the date and time values to refer to a given time on a given day: For example, 6 PM on December 25, 1996, would be 35424.75. Enter these date and time values in the following formats:

Date and Time Format	Example
MM/DD/YY HH:MM	9/3/96 10:15 (AM/PM optional)
HH:MM MM/DD/YY	22:15 9-3-96

Formulas

Formulas are mathematical formulas telling Excel to perform calculations on data in cells. For example, to add the data in the cells A1, B2, and C3 and display the result in cell D4, you would enter the formula **+A1+B2+C3** in cell D4. We'll look at formulas in detail in Chapter 16.

Text

Excel considers any data that it does not recognize as a number, date, time, or formula to be text. This is a wide brief; in practice, it means that data containing letters (other than cell addresses, AM or PM, and so on) will be treated as text. For example, if you enter a list of employees' names, positions, and work histories, Excel will treat them as text.

Excel will also treat as text any numeric entries that are formatted outside of its accepted number, date, and time formats—for example, if you type **10%8**, **510,99**, or **11:59AM**, Excel will treat the entry as text because it's not correctly formatted as a percentage, a number, or a time (which needs a space before the **AM**).

Text too long for the cell it's in will be displayed in the cell or cells to the right if they're empty; otherwise, only the part that fits in the cell will be displayed, though all of the text is stored. (To see the whole contents of a cell, make it active by clicking on it; Excel will display the contents in the reference area.)

Entering Data

To enter data in the active cell, type it in; alternatively, cut or copy the information from elsewhere, and then paste it into the active cell. As you type the first character, it will appear in both the cell and in the reference area, which will display a Cancel button, an Enter button, and an Edit Formula button, as shown here from left to right.

After you finish typing the entry, you can either press Enter, press one of the arrow keys ($\leftarrow$, $\rightarrow$, $\uparrow$, $\downarrow$), click the Enter button, or click in another cell with the mouse to enter the entry in the cell. Excel will enter the data and will hide the Cancel and Enter buttons that were in the reference area. (Alternatively, click the Cancel button to cancel the entry.) If you pressed one of the arrow keys to enter the information, Excel will move the active cell to the cell in the direction of the arrow key.

TIP   **Sometimes you may need to persuade Excel to treat a number as text—for example, you may need a zip code to retain a leading zero rather than being truncated to what Excel considers to be its "true" value. You can do this by entering the label prefix for text—an apostrophe (')—in front of the number.**

Now move to the next cell and enter information as appropriate. Two features you can use to speed this process are AutoFill and AutoComplete, which we'll discuss briefly in the next sections.

You can also enter the same text quickly in multiple cells by selecting them, typing the text into the last cell, and pressing Ctrl+Enter. To select multiple cells, either click and drag through the range or Ctrl+click to select noncontiguous cells.

Using AutoFill

Excel's AutoFill feature lets you quickly enter predefined series of data, such as dates, text, or numbers, in your worksheets. After you've entered just enough information to let Excel know what you're trying to enter in the cells, drag the AutoFill handle to tell Excel which cells you want to affect.

1. Start the series in the first cell of the range that will contain the information.
    *   For a series of numbers that increase by a given amount, enter the first two numbers in the first two cells. For example, you might enter **1996** in cell A5 and **1997** in cell A6.
    *   For a known text series such as the months of the year, enter the first text label. For example, enter **January** in cell A5.
2. Select the cell or cells containing the information.
3. Click the AutoFill handle in the lower-right corner of the rightmost or lower cell and drag the resulting border across or down through the cells that will contain the information. (The AutoFill handle is the small black square in the lower-right corner of the cell; when you move the mouse pointer over it, the pointer changes to the black cross you see in the graphic here.) Excel will fill the series with the data given:
    *   In the first example in step 1, if you drag from the lower-right corner of cell A6 through cell A16, Excel will input the years 1998–2007 in cells A7 through A16.
    *   In the second example, if you drag from the lower-right corner of cell A5 through cell L5, Excel will input the months February through December in cells B5 through L5.

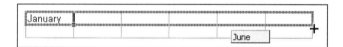

Using AutoComplete

Many times you'll find yourself repeating information in different cells in the same column; here Excel's AutoComplete feature can help you enter data speedily. Auto-Complete monitors the items you've entered in the current block of cells containing entries in a column and suggests a previous item when it thinks you're starting to enter it in another cell. For example, if you enter the months January through December in cells A2 to A13 and then type **F** in cell A1 or A14, AutoComplete will suggest **February**, which you can accept by pressing Enter or one of the arrow keys (or by clicking the Enter button or another cell). If you type **J** as the first letter of cell A14, AutoComplete will not be able to decide between January, June, and July, and will wait for the second letter. If the second letter is **a**, it will suggest **January**; if not, it will wait for the third letter, whereupon it will suggest **June** or **July** if the third letter matches either.

You can also use AutoComplete to add entries with the mouse by right-clicking in the previous or next adjacent cell to a column entry (or in one of the cells already containing an entry), choosing Pick from List from the context menu, and selecting the entry from the resulting drop-down list.

AutoComplete is generally quite helpful—you can ignore any suggestions by typing resolutely through them—but you can turn it on and off as necessary:

1. Choose Tools ➤ Options to display the Options dialog box.
2. On the Edit tab, select or clear the Enable AutoComplete for Cell Values check box.
3. Click the OK button to close the Options dialog box.

Saving and Closing a Workbook

In the next chapter, we'll look at editing and formatting information. For the time being, save and close the workbook:

- To save a workbook, choose File ➤ Save or click the Save button and save the file as described in Chapter 2.
- To close a workbook so you can work with another workbook, choose File ➤ Close. If the current workbook contains unsaved changes, Excel (or the Office Assistant) will prompt you to save the changes before closing the workbook.
- To close all open workbooks, hold down Shift as you click on the File menu, and then choose Close All.
- To exit Excel, choose File ➤ Exit. Excel will prompt you to save unsaved changes to any workbooks before it shuts down.

Chapter 14

EDITING AND FORMATTING A WORKBOOK

FEATURING

- **Editing data in a workbook**
- **Working with ranges**
- **Formatting cells and worksheets**
- **Sorting data**
- **Entering series**

In the previous chapter, we saw how you can quickly create a workbook and enter data in its worksheets. In this chapter, we'll look at working with the data you've entered in the worksheets: viewing the worksheet, editing the data, formatting it, and sorting it as appropriate. We'll also look at how you can speed up your work in Excel by working with ranges.

Viewing the Worksheet

First, we'll discuss four features that Excel offers for viewing your spreadsheets: zooming the view, splitting a window, freezing panes of a window, and full-screen view.

Zoom

As in Word and PowerPoint, you can zoom the view in Excel by choosing a zoom percentage in the Zoom Control drop-down list on the Standard toolbar (as shown here). The drop-down list offers set zoom percentages from 25 to 200, but you can set a percentage of your choosing by typing in any value from 10 to 400 and pressing Enter. The Selection choice on the Zoom Control drop-down list will zoom the view to the largest percentage that will display the currently selected cells in the Excel window (up to a maximum of 400%).

Alternatively, you can set a zoom percentage by choosing View ➤ Zoom to display the Zoom dialog box, making a choice in the Magnification group box, and clicking OK.

You can also zoom the view by holding down Ctrl and rolling the IntelliMouse wheel. Roll it forwards (away from you) to zoom out and backwards (towards you) to zoom in.

Split

You can split the Excel window so you can see nonadjacent parts of one worksheet at once, which makes it easier to compare data spread out over a number of rows or columns.

To split the window, select the cell above which and to the right of which you want to split the window, and then choose Window ➤ Split. You can then scroll around each window using its scroll bars.

To adjust the split of the windows, move the mouse pointer over the horizontal or vertical split bar (or over the intersection of the two), click, and drag the split bars to where you want them.

To unsplit a window, choose Window ➤ Remove Split.

Freezing Panes

You may also want to freeze the rows at the top of the screen and the columns on the left of the screen, so they do not move when you scroll. By doing this, you can keep row and column headings visible while you scroll to far-flung regions of your worksheets.

To freeze the panes, select the cell to the left of which and above which you want to freeze the panes, and then choose Window ➤ Freeze Panes. Excel will display lines indicating the division. For example, if you freeze the panes with cell C5 active, Excel will freeze the panes above row 5 and to the left of column C.

To unfreeze the panes, choose Window ➤ Unfreeze Panes.

Full-Screen View

To display the maximum amount of spreadsheet on screen, use Excel's full-screen view by choosing View ➤ Full Screen. Excel will maximize its window if it isn't maximized already, maximize the current worksheet if it isn't maximized already, hide all displayed toolbars (but not the menu bar), and display the Full Screen toolbar.

To close full-screen view and return to the view you were in previously, click the Close Full Screen button on the Full Screen toolbar or choose View ➤ Full Screen again.

Working with Ranges

A *range* is one or more cells. Ranges can be *contiguous* (rectangular blocks of cells, referred to by the cells at their upper-left and lower-right corners) or *noncontiguous* (irregular blocks of cells or cells that are not adjacent to each other).

Ranges give you a way to work with a number of cells at once, for example, when formatting cells or entering data in them. You can also name ranges, so you can easily identify them and move to them. To quickly go to and select a named range, select the range name from the Name Box drop-down list.

The Name Box at the left end of the formula bar displays the name of the currently selected range.

Selecting a Range

To select a contiguous range of cells:

- Click in the upper-left cell of the range, hold down Shift, and then click in the lower-right cell of the range.

- Click in the upper-left cell of the range and drag to the lower-right cell of the range.
- Click in the upper-left cell of the range, hold down Shift, and use the arrow keys to move to the lower-right cell of the range.

NOTE   **You don't have to work from upper left to lower right—you can work from upper right to lower left if you prefer, or from either lower corner of a range to the opposite upper corner.**

To select a noncontiguous range of cells, click in the first cell, and then hold down Ctrl and click in the other cells in the range (scroll to them if necessary).

You can quickly select a row by clicking the row heading, a column by clicking the column heading, and the whole worksheet by clicking the Select All button. To select the current row quickly using the keyboard, press Shift+spacebar; to select the current column quickly, press Ctrl+spacebar.

Naming a Cell or Range

To name a cell or a range quickly:

1. Select the cell or range.
2. Click in the Name drop-down list box at the left end of the formula bar.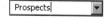
3. Enter the name for the range; it can be up to 255 characters with no spaces, and it must begin with a letter, a backslash, or an underscore; however, capitalization does not matter for naming.
4. Press Enter.

Changing and Deleting Range Names

Using the Name box is the easiest way to define range names, but the Define Name dialog box also lets you change and delete range names:

1. Select the cell or range.
2. Choose Insert ➤ Name ➤ Define to display the Define Name dialog box (see Figure 14.1). You'll see the names of currently named ranges in the Names in Workbook list box. If the upper-left anchor cell of the range contains a text label, Excel will suggest that label as a range name, replacing any spaces and other unusable characters with underscores.

3. Add, change, or delete the range name:
   - Type a new name for the range into the Names in Workbook text box and click Add.
   - Reuse an existing range name by choosing it in the Names in Workbook list box and clicking on Add.
   - Select the range name in the Names in Workbook list and click Delete.
4. Add, change, or delete further range names if necessary, and click OK.

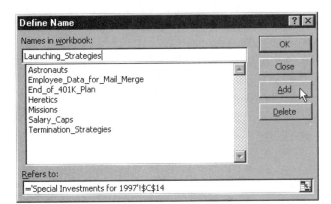

FIGURE 14.1:
Enter the name for the cell or range in the Define Name dialog box.

Editing Data in a Worksheet

Editing data in a worksheet is fast and straightforward. First, make the cell you want to edit active by clicking on it or moving the active cell indicator to it using the arrow keys. Then press F2 or double-click in the cell to enter Edit mode, which Excel will indicate by displaying *Edit* at the left end of the status bar. Excel will display the data from the cell in the reference area and will display a blinking insertion point in the cell at the point where the edits will take effect. If you prefer to edit in the reference area, click once in the cell you want to edit, and then click once in the reference area to place the insertion point in it.

Edit the data in the cell (or in the reference area) as needed. You can double-click on a word to select it, and you can use ← to move left, → to move right, Home to move to the beginning of a cell, and End to move to the end of a cell. Alternatively, use the mouse to position the insertion point where you want to edit or to select words you want to enhance or delete.

To delete the contents of a cell or a range, select the cell or range and press Delete, or right-click and choose Clear Contents from the context menu.

Copying and Moving Data

You can copy and move data in Excel by using Cut, Copy, and Paste (as discussed in Chapter 2) or drag-and-drop. There are two quick points to note here:

- When pasting a range of data, you need only select the upper-left anchor cell of the destination, but be sure Excel won't overwrite any important data in the other cells that the range will cover.

- To use drag-and-drop, select the cell or range to move or copy, and then move the mouse pointer to one of its borders, where the pointer changes from a fat cross to an arrow. You can then drag  and drop as usual. Watch the information box identifying the range in which the selection will land.

Formatting Your Data

You can apply formatting to cells using either the Formatting toolbar or the Format Cells dialog box. In this section, we'll look at the easiest ways to apply the most useful types of formatting to your data.

Number Formatting

Because Excel is set up for number crunching, it provides many different number formats for use with different kinds of data. You can quickly apply number formatting using the Currency Style, Percent Style, and Comma Style buttons on the Formatting toolbar.

Alignment

As we discussed in the previous chapter, Excel identifies any data item as a number, date, time, formula, or text. By default, Excel applies the appropriate horizontal alignment to each of these: For example, Excel right-aligns numbers and left-aligns text. You can overwrite this by applying alignment to the cells as described in the following section; you can also apply vertical alignment to cells for special display effects.

Setting Horizontal Alignment

To apply horizontal alignment, use the four alignment buttons—Align Left, Center, Align Right, and Merge and Center—on the Formatting toolbar (see Figure 14.2).

Merge and Center lets you center the contents of a cell across a number of columns. Enter the text in one of the cells; then select the horizontal range of cells across which you want to center the text, and click the Merge and Center button The effect is shown to the right.

	Text using Merge and Center			

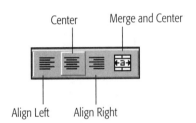

Center   Merge and Center

Align Left   Align Right

FIGURE 14.2:
Use the four alignment buttons on the Formatting toolbar to quickly apply alignment to cells.

Setting Horizontal and Vertical Alignment

To apply more sophisticated alignment options than those mentioned above:

1. Choose Format ➤ Cells to display the Format Cells dialog box.
2. Click the Alignment tab to bring it to the front (see Figure 14.3).
3. In the Horizontal group box, choose the horizontal alignment option you want:
    - General applies Excel's default alignment option for the contents of the cell, such as left alignment for text and right alignment for numbers.
    - Left, Center, and Right, we've looked at already.
    - Fill repeats the contents of the cell until it is full.
    - Justify aligns selected text to both the left and the right margins. You'll need to have more than one line of wrapped text (with the Wrap Text check box selected)—anything less than one cell-width's worth of text will not be justified because it's not long enough—and unless your columns are unusually wide, this is apt to look bad.
    - Center across Selection centers the text across the selected columns.

4. In the Vertical group box, specify the vertical alignment for the selected cells by choosing Top, Center, Bottom, or Justify.

5. If necessary, choose a different orientation for text in the Orientation group box. (The orientation options will be unavailable if you choose Fill or Center across Selection in the Horizontal group box.) Click on one of the points of the half-compass to set an angle quickly, or specify a precise number of degrees in the Degrees box.

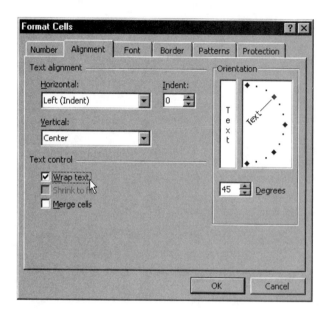

FIGURE 14.3:
Choose alignment options on the Alignment tab of the Format Cells dialog box.

6. Click the OK button to apply your choices to the selected cells, or click one of the other tabs in the Format Cells dialog box to make further changes.

Font Formatting

Excel supports a wide range of font formatting that you can use to beautify your worksheets or make the most important information stand out.

To apply font formatting quickly to the selected cells (or selected text within a cell), use the Font drop-down list box, the Font Size drop-down list box, and the Bold, Italic, and Underline buttons, shown here from left to right.

For more complex font formatting, choose Format ➤ Cells to display the Format Cells dialog box, click on the Font tab if it isn't already at the front of the dialog box, make your choices on it, and then click the OK button.

Border Formatting

As well as font formatting, Excel provides a full complement of borders that you can apply to the selected cell or range of cells by clicking the Borders button on the Formatting toolbar. You can then select from twelve border styles by clicking the drop-down list button on the Borders button and choosing the style of border you want; this style will stick until you change it, so once you've chosen the style, you can quickly apply it to selected cells by clicking the Borders button.

You can also apply borders to the active cell or selected cells by choosing Format ➤ Cells to display the Format Cells dialog box, clicking the Border tab, making choices in the Border and Style group boxes, and clicking the OK button.

Using Patterns and Colors

Excel also offers patterns and colors that you can use to make the display of your worksheets more vibrant and appealing. Unless you're using a color printer, you will probably find colors most useful for on-screen viewing, but patterns can greatly enhance even black-and-white printouts. You can change both the font color, in which the text will display, and the background color of cells, which can make vital information really pop out.

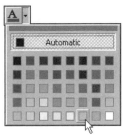

To change the color of the font in selected cells, click the Font Color drop-down list button on the Formatting toolbar and select the color from the drop-down list. This color will stick until you change it, so you can quickly apply it to selected cells by clicking the Font Color button.

You can also change the background color of selected cells by clicking the Fill Color drop-down list button on the Formatting toolbar and choosing the new background color. This color will also stick until you change it.

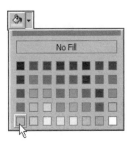

To change the pattern of selected cells, choose Format ➤ Cells to display the Format Cells dialog box, and then click the Patterns tab. Select a pattern from the Pattern drop-down list, and use the Sample box to see how the pattern will work with the currently selected color. Click the OK button to close the Format Cells dialog box when you're satisfied.

Protection

Excel's protection is an invisible form of cell formatting. You can format selected cells as either locked (so their contents cannot be changed) or hidden (so their contents are not visible). Then, when you enable protection on the workbook or worksheet, Excel will treat the cells as locked or hidden.

1. Choose Format ➤ Cells to display the Format Cells dialog box.
2. Click the Protection tab.
3. Select the Locked check box or the Hidden check box (or both).
4. Click the OK button to close the Format Cells dialog box.
5. Choose Tools ➤ Protection ➤ Protect Sheet to display the Protect Sheet dialog box (see Figure 14.4), Tools ➤ Protection ➤ Protect Workbook to display the Protect Workbook dialog box, or Tools ➤ Protection ➤ Protect and Share Workbook to display the Protect Shared Workbook dialog box. These three dialog boxes offer different options: follow step 6 for protecting a worksheet, step 7 for protecting a workbook, and step 8 for protecting a workbook for sharing.

FIGURE 14.4:
Set protection for the active worksheet in the Protect Sheet dialog box.

6. Choose options for protecting the worksheet in the Protect Sheet dialog box:

    Contents Prevents the user from changing locked cells or charts.

    Objects Prevents the user from changing graphic objects.

    Scenarios Prevents the user from changing scenarios (an advanced Excel feature for projecting the outcome of a model created in a worksheet).

7. Choose options for protecting the workbook in the Protect Workbook dialog box:

    Structure Prevents the user from moving, deleting, hiding, inserting, or renaming worksheets in the workbook.

Windows   Prevents the user from moving, resizing, hiding, or closing the windows in the workbook.

8.   In the Protect Shared Workbook dialog box, select the Sharing with Track Changes check box if you want to use Excel's change-tracking capabilities for marking changes made to the workbook by the colleagues with whom you share it.

9.   Enter a password in the Password text box if you want to password-protect the worksheet or workbook. This password can be up to 255 characters long and can contain letters, numbers, and symbols; it is also case sensitive, so use uppercase and lowercase as appropriate.

10.   Click the OK button to close the dialog box and enable protection. If you entered a password in step 9, Excel will display the Confirm Password dialog box; enter the password again and click the OK button. If you chose to protect an unnamed workbook for sharing, Excel will display the Save As dialog box so that you can save it.

To remove protection, choose Tools ‰ Protection ➤ Unprotect Sheet, Tools ➤ Protection ➤ Unprotect Workbook, or Tools ➤ Protection ➤ Unprotect Shared Workbook. If the worksheet or workbook had a password assigned, Excel will display the Unprotect Sheet, Unprotect Workbook, or Unprotect Sharing dialog box. Enter the password in the Password text box and click the OK button.

AutoFormatting Worksheets

For formatting tables quickly, try Excel's AutoFormat feature—which, like Word's Table AutoFormat feature that we looked at in Chapter 9, offers sundry predefined table formats encompassing all formatting from fonts through borders and shading. To use AutoFormat on selected cells or on a range of cells surrounded by blank cells:

1.   Choose Format ➤ AutoFormat to display the AutoFormat dialog box (see Figure 14.5).

2.   Choose a format from the Table Format list box. Watch the Sample box for a preview of how your table will look.

3.   If you want to apply only some of the formatting characteristics, click the Options button to display the six options in the Formats to Apply group box at the bottom of the AutoFormat dialog box. Clear the check boxes for the options you do not want to apply.

4.   Click the OK button to close the AutoFormat dialog box and apply the autoformatting you chose.

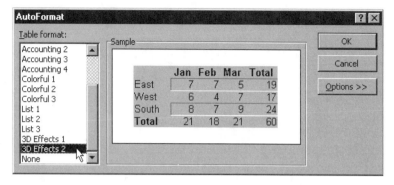

FIGURE 14.5: In the AutoFormat dialog box, choose the look you want for the selected cells.

NOTE   **Once you've applied it, you can change autoformatting using the normal formatting commands discussed earlier in this chapter.**

Using Styles

In Chapter 7, we looked at the styles that Word provides for quickly formatting your documents consistently. Excel's styles are similar to Word's in that they provide quick access to specific cell formatting, including font, number formatting, color, background color, alignment, patterns, borders, and protection. Like Word, Excel provides a number of predefined styles, and you can add to these any custom formats that you use often and want to keep handy. Also like paragraphs in Word, cells in Excel receive a Normal style by default until you apply another style to them, and you can apply further formatting on top of a style if necessary.

Creating a New Style

You can quickly create a new style from the formatting applied to the active cell:

1. Choose Format ➤ Style to display the Style dialog box (see Figure 14.6).
2. Enter the name for the style in the Style Name drop-down list box.
3. In the Style Includes (By Example) group box, clear the check boxes for any aspects of the active cell's formatting that you do not want to include in the style.

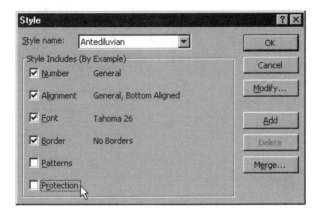

FIGURE 14.6:
To create a new style from the formatting of the active cell, enter the name for the new style in the Style Name drop-down list box on the Style dialog box.

4. Click the Add button to create the new style.

5. Click the OK button to close the Style dialog box.

Applying a Style

To apply a style to selected cells:

1. Choose Format ➤ Style to display the Style dialog box.

2. In the Style Name drop-down list box, choose the style to apply.

3. In the Style Includes group box, clear the check boxes for any formatting included in the style that you do not want to apply to the selected cells; for example, you could clear the Number and Alignment check boxes if you wanted the data in the selected cells to retain their original formatting characteristics.

4. Click the OK button to close the Style dialog box and apply the style.

Modifying a Style

By modifying an existing style, you can instantly change all the cells assigned that style:

1. Choose Format ➤ Style to display the Style dialog box with the name of the style in the active cell displayed. (You can also choose the style to modify from the Style Name drop-down list on the Formatting toolbar.)

2. Click the Modify button to display the Format Cells dialog box.

3. Use the options on the six tabs of the Format Cells dialog box to change the style.

4. Click the OK button in the Format Cells dialog box to return to the Style dialog box.
5. Click the OK button in the Style dialog box to save the changes to the style and apply them to all the cells in the worksheet that have that style.

Deleting a Style

You can quickly delete a style you've created by choosing Format ➤ Style, selecting the style name in the Style Name drop-down list, and clicking Delete. Excel will remove all instances of that formatting from the workbook. Click the OK button to close the Style dialog box when you've finished deleting styles.

Merging Styles between Workbooks

You can quickly copy styles between open workbooks using the Merge command:

1. Activate the workbook that will receive the style or styles from the other workbook.
2. Choose Format ➤ Style to display the Style dialog box.
3. Click the Merge button to display the Merge Styles dialog box (see Figure 14.7).

FIGURE 14.7:
Use the Merge Styles dialog box to copy styles from one workbook to another.

4. In the Merge Styles From list box, select the workbook containing the styles you want to copy to the current workbook.
5. Click the OK button to close the Merge Styles dialog box and copy the styles to the current workbook, so they are available for use. Excel will return to the Style dialog box so you can apply the styles.
6. In the Style dialog box in the first workbook, apply a style from the Style Name drop-down list, or click the Close button to close the Style dialog box.

Restructuring the Worksheet

You can quickly insert (or delete) rows and columns in your worksheet as you need them; you can even delete blocks of cells without deleting entire rows.

WARNING   **When you delete a cell, a row, or a column, you delete all the data it contains at the same time.**

Inserting and Deleting Rows or Columns

To insert complete rows or columns:

1.   For rows: Drag through the headings of the rows above which you want to add the new rows. For columns: Drag through the headings of the columns to the left of which you want to add the new columns. Select the same number of row or column headings as you want to insert.
2.   Right-click anywhere in the selected rows or columns, and choose Insert from the context menu. Alternatively, press Ctrl+Shift+= (i.e., Ctrl++).

To delete complete rows or columns:

1.   Drag through the headings of the rows or columns you want to delete.
2.   Right-click anywhere in the selected rows or columns, and choose Delete from the context menu. (Alternatively, press Ctrl+−.) Excel moves the remaining rows and columns to fill the space.

Inserting and Deleting Blocks of Cells

When you don't want to insert a whole row or column, you can insert a block of cells and choose to move the existing cells to the right or down:

1.   Select the range of cells where you want to insert the block.
2.   Right-click in the selection and choose Insert from the context menu to display the Insert dialog box.
3.   Make sure Excel has chosen the most appropriate option in the Insert group box: Shift Cells Right or Shift Cells Down. Select the other option if necessary.
4.   Click the OK button to insert the cells.

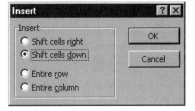

When you delete a block of cells, you can choose whether to fill the gap with the cells to the right of or beneath where the block was:

1. Select the range of cells you want to delete.
2. Right-click in the selection, and choose Delete from the context menu to display the Delete dialog box.
3. Check whether Excel has chosen Shift Cells Left or Shift Cells Up; change this if necessary.
4. Click the OK button to delete the cells.

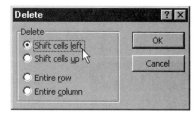

NOTE   You can also choose to insert or delete complete rows or columns in the Insert dialog box and Delete dialog box, but working with the row and column headings is faster.

Formatting Rows and Columns

The cells in Excel's worksheets come with a default column width of 8.43 characters and a height of 12.75 points (where one point is ½ inch). Excel automatically adjusts row height if you enter taller characters (or graphics) in a cell; you can also adjust both row height and column width manually.

Changing Row Height

To change row height for one row quickly, click on the bottom border of a row heading and drag it up or down until the row is the height you want.

To change row height for several rows at once:

1. Select the rows by dragging through the row headings or through cells in the rows.
2. Choose Format ➤ Row ➤ Height to display the Row Height dialog box.
3. Enter the new height in points for the rows in the Row Height text box.
4. Click the OK button to close the Row Height dialog box.

Changing Column Width

To change column width for one column quickly, click on the right-hand border of a column heading and drag it left or right until the column is the width you want.

To change column width for several columns at once:

1. Select the columns by dragging through the column headings or through cells in the columns.

2. Choose Format ➤ Column ➤ Width to display the Column Width dialog box.

3. Enter the new column width in the Column Width text box.

4. Click the OK button to close the Column Width dialog box.

You can also set a different default column width in a worksheet by choosing Format ➤ Column ➤ Standard Width and setting a default column width in the Standard Column Width text box in the Standard Width dialog box.

Autofitting

Excel's AutoFit feature automatically adjusts column width to fit the widest entry in any selected column. To use AutoFit, select the columns you want to adjust (select the whole worksheet if necessary) and choose Format ➤ Column ➤ AutoFit Selection.

> **TIP** **Wait until you've nearly finished formatting your worksheet before using AutoFit: If you change the data in a column on which you've used AutoFit, you will need to run AutoFit again to change its width—it won't adjust automatically.**

Excel automatically autofits row height, but if you override autofitting by setting a row height manually, you can reapply it by choosing Format ➤ Row ➤ AutoFit.

Sorting Data

One of the great advantages of a spreadsheet is that you can manipulate your data easily. Excel offers simple sorting for swiftly arranging the contents of a column and complex sorting for arranging the contents of a table using several sort keys.

Simple Sorting

To sort data in a column or in selected cells quickly, click the Sort Ascending or Sort Descending button on the Standard toolbar. Sort Ascending sorts the cells in the column alphabetically or from lowest to highest value; Sort Descending sorts the cells into reverse alphabetical order or from highest to lowest value. Selected cells are sorted by their first column; for example, if you sort the range A1:E5, the cells will be sorted by the data in column A rather than column B, C, D, or E.

Complex Sorting

To perform a complex sort on selected cells:

1. Choose Data ➤ Sort to display the Sort dialog box (see Figure 14.8). If Excel finds data in the cells next to your selection, it will display the Sort Warning dialog box to find out if you intended to include those cells in the sort. In the What Do You Want to Do group box, choose either the Expand the Selection option button or the Continue with the Current Selection option button, and then click the OK button. Excel will then display the Sort dialog box.

FIGURE 14.8:
In the Sort dialog box, choose up to three sort keys for your data.

2. If your data has a header row, make sure the Header Row option button is selected in the My List Has group box. This will prevent Excel from sorting the headers into their logical alphabetical or numerical position in the data.
3. Choose the first sort key in the Sort By group box, and then specify Ascending or Descending order.
4. Choose the second sort key in the first Then By group box. Again, specify Ascending or Descending order.
5. Choose the third sort key in the second Then By group box. Once again, specify Ascending or Descending order.

6. If necessary, choose sort options by clicking the Options button to display the Sort Options dialog box, in which you can choose a special First Key Sort Order (for example, by months), whether to use case-sensitive sorting, and whether to sort top to bottom (the conventional way) or left to right. When you've selected sort options, click the OK button to close the Sort Options dialog box and return to the Sort dialog box.

7. Click the OK button to close the Sort dialog box and perform the sort according to the sort keys and orders you chose.

Adding Comments

Excel's *comments* let you add text notes to any cell to provide extra information for you or your co-workers. Cell notes do not appear in the worksheet; they are indicated by a small red triangle in the upper-right corner of the cell to which they are attached.

To add a note to the active cell:

1. Choose Insert ➤ Comment to display a comment box attached to the cell.

2. Type your note into the comment box.

3. Click in another cell to continue working.

To read a comment, move the mouse pointer over the cell that contains it. Excel will display the comment box.

To edit a comment, right-click in the cell that contains it, and choose Edit Comment to display the comment box with the text ready for editing. You can then resize or move the comment.

- To resize a comment, move the insertion point over one of its sizing handles and drag inwards or outwards.
- To move a comment so you can see both it and the cells it was covering, move the insertion point into one of its borders so it turns into a four-headed arrow; then click and drag the comment to where you want it to appear.

To delete a comment, right-click in the cell that contains it, and choose Delete Comment from the context menu.

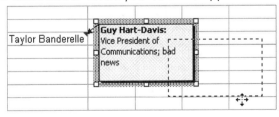

Adding Headers and Footers

To identify the work you print out, you will probably want to add a header or footer.

1. Choose View ➤ Header and Footer to display the Header/Footer tab of the Page Setup dialog box (see Figure 14.9). This tab shows previews of both the header and the footer and offers a number of automatic header and footer variants generated from the user information entered when Office was installed on your computer.

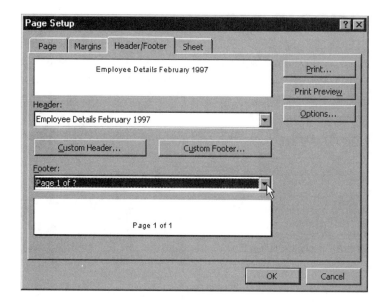

FIGURE 14.9: Set the header and footer on the Header/Footer tab of the Page Setup dialog box.

2. To use one of the automatically generated headers or footers, choose it from the Header drop-down list or Footer drop-down list. Choose (None) at the top of the list to remove the current header or footer.

3. To create a custom header or footer, click the Custom Header or Custom Footer button to display the Header dialog box (see Figure 14.10) or Footer dialog box, each of which offers Left Section, Center Section, and Right Section boxes.

4. To change a section, click in it and edit the contents using regular editing techniques. To apply font formatting to selected text, click the Font button, choose the formatting as usual in the Font dialog box, and then click the OK button.

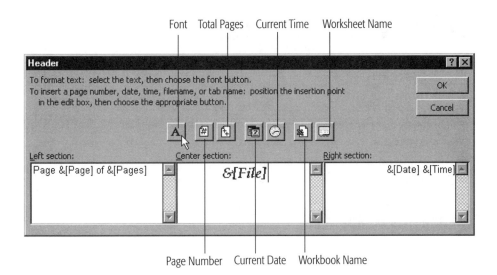

FIGURE 14.10: Creating a custom header in the Header dialog box

5. To insert the page number, number of pages, current date or time, workbook name or worksheet name, position the insertion point in one of the section boxes, and click the appropriate button to enter the code for the information:

Button	Information Code
Page Number	&[Page]
Number of Pages	&[Pages]
Current Date	&[Date]
Current Time	&[Time]
Workbook Name	&[File]
Worksheet Name	&[Tab]

6. Click the OK button to return to the Page Setup dialog box.

7. Click the OK button to close the Page Setup dialog box and return to your worksheet. (Alternatively, you can choose Print Preview to see how your header and footer mesh with the worksheet, or you can choose Print to go ahead and print it.)

Printing from Excel

In this section, we'll look quickly at the most important of the many printing options that Excel offers, from straightforward printing of the information in the current worksheet, to carefully laid-out pages containing a selected range of data.

First, though, you can print quickly and simply from Excel:

- To print the currently active worksheet with Excel's default settings, click the Print button on the Standard toolbar.
- To print only a range of data, select that range before clicking the Print button.

Choosing a Paper Type

For more complex printing, first make sure you and Excel agree on the size and layout of the paper you're using:

1. Choose File ➤ Page Setup to display the Page Setup dialog box.
2. If the Page tab isn't displayed, click it to bring it to the front (see Figure 14.11).
3. In the Orientation area, choose Portrait or Landscape.
4. Use the options in the Scaling area to adjust the size of what you're printing if necessary: either select the Adjust To option button and enter a percentage of normal size (100% is selected by default), or select the Fit To option button and specify the number of pages wide by the number of pages tall.

TIP   **If you adjust the scaling to a low percentage or select Fit To and specify a small number of pages, click the Print Preview button before printing to make sure the output will be legible.**

---

5. Choose the paper size from the Paper Size drop-down list.
6. If necessary, change the resolution in the Print Quality drop-down list.
7. To have page numbering start at a number other than 1, enter that number in the First Page Number text box. Otherwise, leave the setting at Auto.
8. Click the OK button to apply the settings you've chosen, or click one of the other tabs in the Page Setup dialog box to change the margins, header and footer, or worksheet options.

Setting Margins

Next, set margins and header positioning:

1. Choose File ➤ Page Setup to display the Page Setup dialog box.

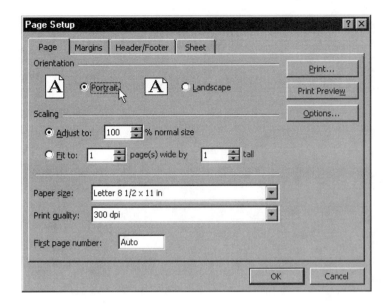

FIGURE 14.11:
On the Page tab
of the Page Setup
dialog box,
choose the type
of paper you'll
be using.

2. Click the Margins tab to bring it to the front (see Figure 14.12).
3. In the Top, Bottom, Left, and Right boxes, enter the margin measurements. The Preview box will reflect the effects your settings will produce.
4. In the Header and Footer boxes, enter the distance that the header and footer should appear from their respective edges of the page.
5. In the Center on Page area, select or leave cleared the Horizontally check box and the Vertically check box, depending on the visual effect you want your printout to deliver.
6. Click the OK button to close the Page Setup dialog box and apply your choices, or click one of the other tabs in the Page Setup dialog box to choose other page setup options.

Setting Worksheet Printing Options

Third, you can also set a number of options for printing worksheets:

1. Choose File ➤ Page Setup to display the Page Setup dialog box.
2. If the Sheet tab isn't displayed, click it to bring it to the front.
3. If you will always be printing the same range of cells, set the print area for the worksheet: Click in the Print Area box, and then drag in the worksheet to enter the range to print. While you're dragging, the Page Setup dialog box will obligingly reduce itself to a title bar and range box so you can see what you're doing.

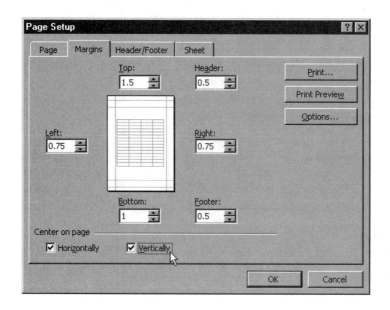

FIGURE 14.12:
Set margin and
header placement
on the Margins
tab of the Page
Setup dialog box.

4. If you're printing a worksheet that will break onto multiple pages, use the Rows to Repeat at Top and Columns to Repeat at Left boxes in the Print Titles area to specify which rows and columns to repeat on all pages. Again, click in a box, and then click and drag in the worksheet to enter the range; the Page Setup dialog box will again reduce itself to give you room to drag.

5. In the Print group box, choose options for printing:
   - Gridlines prints the lines that divide the cells.
   - Black and White prints colors as black and white (rather than gray), making for crisper black-and-white output.
   - Draft Quality prints lower-quality output at higher speed (and uses less ink).
   - Row and Column Headings prints the row numbers and column letters.
   - The Comments drop-down list lets you choose whether to include comments at the end of the worksheet or as displayed on the sheet, or not to include them.

6. In the Page Order group box, specify how Excel should divide a spreadsheet onto multiple pages.

7. Click the OK button to close the Page Setup dialog box and apply your choices, or click another tab in the Page Setup dialog box to set further options.

Using Print Preview

Before printing any worksheet or workbook, use Print Preview to make sure your printout will look like you want it to: Choose File ➤ Print Preview, click the

Print Preview button on the Standard toolbar, or click the Print Preview button in the Page Setup dialog box.

Print Preview displays the current page of the worksheet or workbook:

- Zoom the view to and from full-page view by moving the mouse pointer over the page (where it will appear as a magnifying glass) and clicking, or by clicking the Zoom button.
- Click the Next and Previous buttons to move from page to page in a multiple page worksheet.
- Click the Margins button to display margin lines and handles and column boundary handles. Drag a margin handle or a column boundary handle to adjust it.
- Click the Setup button to access the Page Setup dialog box.
- Click the Close button to exit Print Preview, or click the Print button to display the Print dialog box.

Moving Page Breaks

If you don't like what you see in Print Preview, you can use Page Break Preview to view and move page breaks. To enter Page Break Preview, choose View ➤ Page Break Preview. Excel will display page breaks on the worksheet as heavy dashed lines. To move a page break, move the mouse pointer over one of these lines so it becomes a two-headed arrow; then click and drag the page break to where you want it. Excel will then display the page break as a heavy black line.

To leave Page Break Preview, choose View ➤ Normal.

Printing

After checking your prospective printout in Print Preview, print it as follows:

1. Choose File ➤ Print to display the Print dialog box.
2. Specify a printer in the Printer group box.
3. In the Print What group box, make sure Excel has identified what you want to print: Selection (the currently selected cells), Active Sheet(s), or Entire Workbook.
4. In the Print Range group box, choose whether to print all pages of the item identified in the Print What group box or just the pages you choose.
5. To print more than one copy, set the number in the Number of Copies text box in the Copies group box. Select the Collate check box if you want to collate each copy in order.
6. Click the OK button to close the Print dialog box and print the item.

Chapter 15

CHARTING

- **Understanding the elements of a chart**
- **Creating a chart**
- **Modifying a chart**
- **Creating custom chart types**

There's no simpler way to enliven tedious figures or to illustrate a trend in data than to use a chart. Excel provides so many different types of charts—and so many options for each of them—you'll feel your head spin.

In this chapter, we'll look at how to create and format charts in Excel to present your data to maximum advantage.

Chart Terms and Basics

Before we get into the specific types of charts that Excel offers, let's look quickly at the different parts that make up a chart. A typical chart, such as the one shown in Figure 15.1, includes the following elements:

Axes	Two-dimensional charts have an *X-axis* (the horizontal axis) and a *Y-axis* (the vertical axis); three-dimensional charts also have a *Z-axis* (the depth axis).
Titles	A chart will typically have a chart title and a title for each axis.
Legend	The *legend* identifies each data series (for example, by color or pattern).
Data series	A *data series* is one of the sets of data from which the chart is drawn. A pie chart has only one data series, but most types of charts can have two or more data series.
Gridlines	Lines drawn across the chart from the axes for visual reference.
Categories	The items by which the data series is separated. For example, if a chart showed the years 1992–1999, each year would be a category.

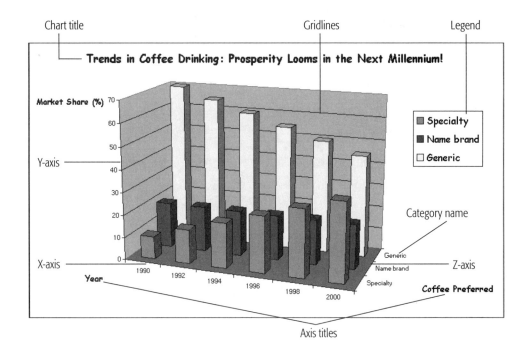

FIGURE 15.1: The elements of a typical chart

Choosing the Right Type of Chart

Excel offers many different types of charts, and choosing the right chart for your data can be a tough call. In this section, we'll look at the basic chart types and discuss what they're most useful for. The good news is that once you've created a chart in Excel, you can quickly modify it (by adding legends, titles, and so on) or even switch it to a different and more suitable chart type without losing any data.

Area charts are good for showing how much different data series contribute to a whole. These charts use connected points to map each series, and the space between the series is filled in with a color or pattern.

Bar charts are the type of chart typically used for showing performance against benchmarks. Each data point is marked by a horizontal bar that extends to the left or right of the baseline.

Column charts, which are similar to bar charts but use vertical bars instead of horizontal bars, are typically used for showing sales figures, rainfall, and the like.

Cylinder charts, *cone charts*, and *pyramid charts* use the shapes from which they take their names to present data in more interesting ways than bar and column charts.

Line charts are good for showing changes in data series over time; a typical use would be for charting temperature or changes in prices. The data points in each data series are connected by a line.

Pie charts are notorious enough from math class to need no introduction: a single data series is divided up into pie slices showing the relative contribution of the various data points. Pie charts are great for showing market share, survey results, and the like.

Doughnut charts are mutant pie charts that can show more than one data series. You might use a single doughnut chart instead of two pie charts to show changes in market share over two years.

Radar charts represent data points as symbols around a central point (the supposed radar scanner), with the value of each data point represented by its symbol's distance from the scanner. Radar charts can be confusing when misused; use them with care.

Surface charts are used to find the best combination between two sets of data.

XY or *scatter charts*, typically used for charting the results of surveys or experiments, plot a series of data pairs against XY coordinates. The result typically resembles a line chart that's lost its lines (some formats do have lines).

Stock charts are mutant scatter and column charts designed for tracking the movement of stock prices. For example, you can create a high-low-close chart to track a stock's high, low, and closing prices for each day.

Bubble charts are mutant scatter charts that use bubbles of different sizes to show one data series, whose relationship to the other two data series is indicated by placement against the axes. Bubble charts can bring more drama to mundane information than bar charts, but they tend to be harder to read.

Combination charts add a line chart to a column chart or bar chart, plotting one or more data series as lines and the others as bars or columns. You can use combination charts either to demonstrate two trends at once or to severely confuse your audience (or both).

3-D charts include 3-D area charts, 3-D bar charts, 3-D column charts, 3-D line charts, 3-D pie charts, and 3-D surface charts. Use them when the complexity of your data requires more than two dimensions.

Creating a Chart

Excel lets you create a chart either on a separate worksheet (a *chart sheet*) or embedded on the current worksheet. The easiest way to create a chart is to use the Chart Wizard:

1. First, select the range whose data you want to chart.
2. Click the Chart Wizard button on the Standard toolbar or choose Insert ➤ Chart to start the Chart Wizard and display the first Chart Wizard, the Chart Type dialog box (see Figure 15.2).
3. Choose the chart best suited to your data on either the Standard Types or Custom Types tab. The Standard Types tab offers the charts discussed in the previous section, and the Custom Types tab offers both Excel's built-in custom formats (which include amusing formats such as Blue Pie and Floating Bars) and any user-defined custom charts that you or your colleagues have set up. (We'll look at setting up custom chart types at the end of the chapter.)

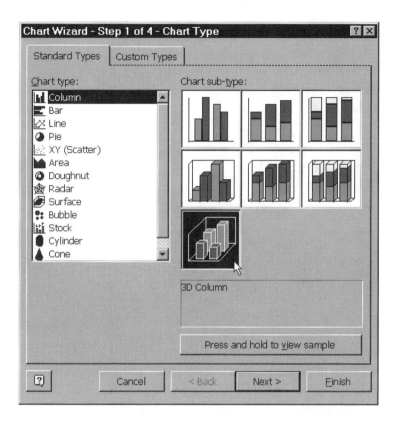

FIGURE 15.2:
In the Chart Type dialog box, choose the type of chart you want; then click the Next button.

- Choose the chart type in the Chart Type list box. For the chart types on the Standard Types tab, Excel will display the variety of available subtypes in the Chart Sub-Type box. Choose a subtype by clicking on it in the Chart Sub-Type box.
- To have Excel build a sample chart of that type from the data you selected in step 1, click on the Press and Hold to View Sample button and hold down the mouse button until the sample chart is displayed in the Sample box, into which the Chart Sub-Type box will change itself.

4. Click the Next button to display the second Chart Wizard, the Chart Source Data dialog box (see Figure 15.3).
- On the Data Range tab, make sure Excel is displaying the correct data range in the Data Range box. If not, click and drag through the worksheet to select the range of data. (The Chart Wizard will get out of your way as you do so by reducing itself to just the dialog box title bar and Data Range box, but if you want, you can click the Collapse Dialog Box button at the right end of the Data Range box to collapse the dialog box.) Then choose whether the data series are in rows or columns by selecting the Rows option button or the Columns option button.

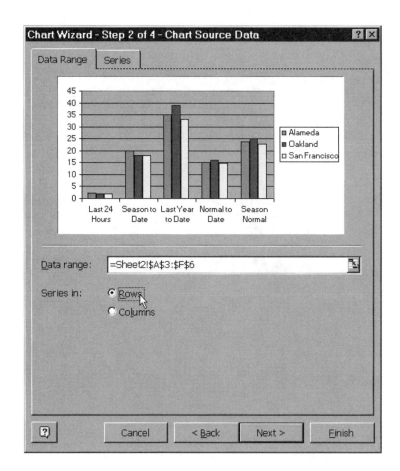

FIGURE 15.3:
In the Chart Source Data dialog box, choose the data range and series for the chart by clicking and dragging through the worksheet.

- On the Series tab, adjust the data series as necessary. These adjustments affect only the data in the chart—they do not affect the data in the worksheet. You can add and remove series by using the Add and Remove buttons, change the Name or Value of the series selected in the Series list box by clicking in the Name box or Value box and dragging in the worksheet, or change the X-axis labels by clicking in the Category (X) Axis Labels box and dragging in the worksheet.

5. Click the Next button to display the third Chart Wizard, the Chart Options dialog box (see Figure 15.4), which provides up to six tabs' worth of options for the chart (depending on the chart type you chose):
    - On the Titles tab, enter the chart title, X-axis title, Y-axis title, and Z-axis title (if the chart type has one) in the appropriate text boxes.
    - On the Axes tab, you can suppress the display of any of the axes as necessary. (Usually, you will not want to do this.)

Editing a Chart

You can edit many of the elements of a chart to change its appearance or highlight certain elements at the expense of others.

To edit an element in a chart, click the element so it displays handles and its name appears at the left end of the formula bar or in the Chart Objects box on the Chart toolbar (see Figure 15.6).

FIGURE 15.6: To edit a chart, click the element you want to edit, and then edit using normal Office editing techniques.

> **NOTE** You can also select elements in a chart by using ←, →, ↑, and ↓ to move from element to element. Press Esc to deselect a selection.

To edit the text of an element, such as an axis title you've selected, click in the element and use regular editing methods to change the text. Click elsewhere in the chart to enter the change.

To format an element that you've selected, right-click in it and choose the Format option from the context menu to display the Format dialog box for the element. (This will vary depending on the element you have selected: Format Chart Title, Format 3-D Area Group, Format Axis, and so on.) Choose options as appropriate, and click OK when you're satisfied.

To remove an element from a chart, right-click the element you want to delete and choose Clear from the context menu. (Alternatively, click in the element to select it, and then press the Delete key.)

You can insert a variety of elements in a chart, depending on what type of chart it is. For example, most charts (including radar charts and scatter charts) can have axes and

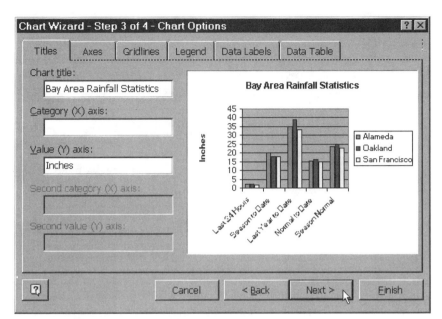

FIGURE 15.4: In the Chart Options dialog box, choose options for the chart.

- On the Gridlines tab, choose which gridlines to display on the chart by selecting or clearing the Major Gridlines and Minor Gridlines check boxes in the Category (X) Axis, Series (Y) Axis, and Value (Z) Axis check boxes. Major gridlines mark larger intervals in the data; minor gridlines mark smaller intervals within the major ones. Watch the sample box to see the effect the gridlines will produce on the chart.
- On the Legend tab, choose whether to show a legend by selecting or clearing the Show Legend check box. If you choose to show a legend, choose an option button in the Placement group box to indicate where it should appear relative to the chart: Bottom, Corner, Top, Right, or Left. Watch the sample box to see the effect.
- On the Data Labels tab, choose whether to show the data labels by clicking an option button in the Data Labels group box. For example, you can choose the Show Value option button to have the value of data points appear on the chart bars (columns, lines, or whatever) associated with them. If you choose to show data labels, you can select the Legend Key Next to Label check box to have a miniature legend box appear next to the data labels. (This can be useful for complex charts.)
- On the Data Table tab, you can select the Show Data Table check box to show the table of data from which the chart was drawn along with the chart. (This is primarily useful for chart sheets rather than embedded charts.) If you choose to show the data table, you can

select the Show Legend Keys check box to display legend keys in the data table for quick reference.

6. Click the Next button to display the fourth Chart Wizard, the Chart Location dialog box. In the Place Chart group box, choose whether to create the chart on a new sheet by selecting the As New Sheet option button and specifying a name in the text box, or as an embedded chart in an existing worksheet or chart sheet by selecting the As Object In option button and specifying the worksheet or chart sheet in the drop-down list.

7. Click the Finish button to have the Chart Wizard create the chart for you. Figure 15.5 shows a chart inserted as a worksheet object.

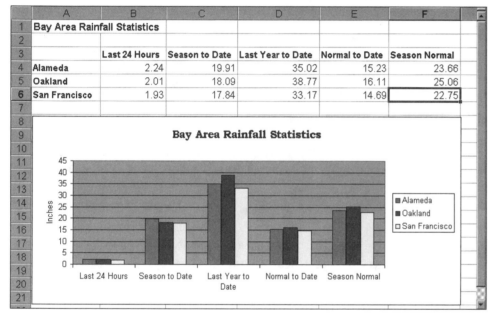

FIGURE 15.5: The chart embedded in the worksheet

Modifying a Chart

Once you've created a chart, you can easily modify it so it presents your data most effectively. In this section, we'll look at how you can resize and reposition a chart, edit its component parts, and even change it swiftly and painlessly to another chart type.

Moving a Chart

The easiest way to move an embedded chart to a different position on a worksheet is to click anywhere in it and drag it to the position you want it on the worksheet.

To move a chart from one worksheet to another, right-click in it and choose Cut from the context menu. Navigate to the worksheet on which you want to position the chart, right-click where you want the upper-left corner of the chart to appear, and choose Paste from the context menu.

You can also move a chart sheet to a different location in the workbook by clicking the chart sheet tab and dragging it to where you want it in the workbook.

To move a chart from a chart sheet to a worksheet, right-click in the chart, choose Location from the context menu to display the Chart Location dialog box, select the As Object In option button, choose the worksheet from the drop-down list, and click the OK button.

Resizing a Chart

To resize an embedded chart, click in any open space inside the chart to select it, and then move the mouse pointer over one of its handles to display a double-headed arrow. Click and drag until the dotted outline is the size you want:

- The side handles resize the chart in only one dimension, while the corner handles resize the chart in two dimensions.
- Hold down Shift as you drag a corner handle to resize the chart proportionally to how it was before.
- Hold down Ctrl as you drag to resize the chart around its midpoint rather than from a corner.
- Hold down Ctrl and Shift as you drag a corner handle to resize the chart proportionally around its midpoint.

Deleting a Chart

To delete an embedded chart, either click in it and press Delete, or right-click in open space inside it and choose Cut from the context menu.

To delete a chart sheet, right-click the sheet tab and choose Delete from the co menu, and then choose OK in the warning message box. You won't be able to this deletion.

gridlines, but pie charts and doughnut charts cannot. Excel handles such elements as options that can be set for the chart.

To insert elements in a chart, right-click in an open space inside the chart, and choose Chart Options from the context menu to display the Chart Options dialog box. This is the same Chart Options dialog box that the Chart Wizard displays when you are creating the chart. Set options as discussed in step 5 under "Creating a Chart," earlier in this chapter.

Excel lets you easily change a chart from one type to another, so when you're creating a chart from your data, you can feel free to mess around with different chart types until you find one that really suits your data and displays it to maximum advantage. You can change either an entire chart to a different type, or a selected data series to a different chart type to create a combination chart.

To change a chart from one type to another, right-click in any open space inside the chart, and choose Chart Type from the context menu to display the Chart Type dialog box. This is the same Chart Type dialog box as the Chart Wizard displays when you are creating the chart. Choose the chart type as discussed in steps 2 and 3 under "Creating a Chart," earlier in this chapter.

You can also change a chart quickly from one type to another by selecting the chart, clicking the Chart Type drop-down button on the Chart toolbar—as shown here—and selecting the type of chart you want from the drop-down list.

Using the Chart Toolbar

The Chart toolbar provides nine buttons for quick access to strategic parts of a chart (see Figure 15.7).

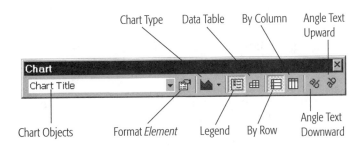

FIGURE 15.7:
Use the buttons on the Chart toolbar to speed up your work with charts.

- Use the Chart Objects drop-down list to pick the object you want to work with. The drop-down list box shows the item currently selected in the chart.
- Click the Format *Element* button to display the Format dialog box for the element selected in the Chart Objects drop-down list (or in the chart). For example, if you select an axis title in the Chart Objects drop-down list, this button will be named Format Axis Title, and clicking it will display the Format Axis Title dialog box.
- The Chart Type button applies the indicated chart type to the chart. Click the drop-down list button, and choose the chart type from the drop-down list.
- The Legend button toggles the display of the legend.
- The Data Table button toggles the display of the data table.
- By Row and By Column buttons switch the data series between the rows and the columns. These are available only for some types of charts.
- The Angle Text Downward and Angle Text Upward buttons tilt the selected text downward or upward at a 45-degree angle. Click these buttons again to toggle the text back to its previous angle.

Creating User-Defined Chart Types

As we saw in "Creating a Chart," Excel provides predefined custom chart types that you can use. It also allows you to define your own custom chart types for reuse or for sharing with your coworkers.

1. First, create a chart and apply to it all the formatting that you want the custom chart type to contain.
2. Right-click in the chart, and choose Chart Type from the context menu to display the Chart Type dialog box.
3. If the Custom Types tab is not displayed, click it to bring it to the front of the dialog box.
4. In the Select From group box, click the User-Defined option button.
5. Click the Add button to display the Add Custom Chart Type dialog box (see Figure 15.8).
6. Enter a name (of up to 31 characters) in the Name box and a description (of up to 250 characters) in the Description box.
7. Click the OK button to close the Add Custom Chart Type dialog box. Excel will add the chart type to the Custom Types tab of the Chart Type dialog box and include a preview of it culled from the chart you created.

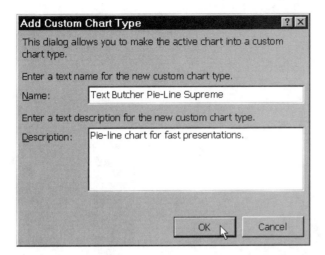

FIGURE 15.8:
In the Add Custom
Chart Type dialog
box, enter the name
and description for
the new custom chart
type, and then click
the OK button.

To delete a custom chart type, display the User-Defined list on the Chart Type dialog box's Custom Types tab, select the chart type in the Chart Type list, and click the Delete button. Excel will display a confirmation dialog box; click the OK button.

Chapter 16

WORKING WITH FORMULAS AND FUNCTIONS

F E A T U R I N G

- **Understanding formulas and functions**
- **Creating formulas**
- **Entering functions**
- **Dealing with error messages**

Excel was built to crunch numbers as you do granola, and formulas and functions are its raison d'être. As you might imagine, Excel provides enough calculating power to sink the proverbial battlecruiser. The good news is that formulas and functions can be extremely simple to use, and if you want to create a simple formula that, say, adds the contents of the cells in a column or divides the contents of one cell by the contents of another, it will take no more than a few clicks of your mouse.

In this chapter, we'll concentrate on the practical rather than the esoteric. We'll look at what formulas and functions actually are (and what the difference between the two is), what they consist of, and how you can enter them in your spreadsheets quickly and easily.

What Are Formulas and Functions?

A *formula*, as you'll remember from those blissful days in math class, is a recipe for performing calculations on numerical data. A formula can be anything from simple addition, such as the hours on an invoice, to complex calculations on how to build a bigger and faster Sojourner.

A *function* is a predefined formula built into Excel. Excel ships with enough functions to satisfy most computing needs—everything from a straightforward SUM to an ugly DSTDEVP for calculating standard deviation (don't ask) based on all the entries in a database. But for specialized projects, you can create your own powerful formulas swiftly and safely.

The Parts of a Formula

To create a formula in Excel, you need to indicate the data to be used in the computation and the operation or operations to be performed. Data can consist of constants (numbers) and references to cells, as we'll see in the next section. Operations use four categories of operators: arithmetic, logical, text, and reference.

Constants

A *constant* is a number entered directly in the formula—it uses a constant value in every calculation (unless you change the formula). For example, you could enter the following formula in a cell to subtract 31 from 33:

=33-31

When you press Enter, the cell will display 2. The initial **=** sign tells Excel that you're entering a formula in the cell; 33 and 31 are constants, and the minus sign is the operator for subtraction.

This example probably seems pretty pointless: You could do better to enter **2** in the cell and be done with it. And as you can imagine, using constants for all the values of a calculation in Excel is about as slow (and accurate) as punching them into a calculator. Usually you will want to use references in your formulas instead of constants.

References

A *reference* indicates to Excel the location of the information you want to use in a formula. By using references instead of constants, you can build formulas that you don't need to change when the data in your worksheet changes. For example, to perform the calculation 33-31, you could enter **33** in cell B4 and **31** in cell B5 and then enter this formula in cell B6:

    =B4-B5

This tells Excel to subtract the contents of cell B5 from the contents of cell B4. Now you can change the data in cells B4 and B5, and Excel will automatically recalculate the values and show the result in cell B6.

When you're referring to the current worksheet in a formula, you can use cell references without specifying the worksheet name: Excel will assume you mean the current sheet. To reference cells on another worksheet, enter the worksheet name and an exclamation point before the cell reference:

    =Sheet11!B4-Sheet11!B5

If you rename a worksheet, Excel will automatically change the references in your formulas. For example, if you renamed Sheet11 **Dresden China**, Excel would change the above formula as follows:

    ='Dresden China'!B4-'Dresden China'!B5

Notice that Excel encloses the name of the worksheet in single quotation marks.

One of the easiest ways to enter the references to a formula is to use range names, which we looked at in Chapter 14. For example, if you've assigned the name **TotalIncome** to one cell and the name **TotalOutgoings** to another, you could use this formula to calculate the net income:

    =TotalIncome-TotalOutgoings

By using range names, you avoid having to specify which sheet the information is currently residing on.

Operators

The *operator* is the way in which you tell Excel which operation to perform with the data you've supplied by using constants and references. As we mentioned earlier, Excel uses four types of operators: arithmetic, logical, text, and reference.

Arithmetic Operators

Excel's six *arithmetic operators* are the old standbys from math adapted slightly for the computer keyboard:

Operator	Action	Example
+	Addition	=D4+E4
/	Division	=20/E4
^	Exponentiation	5^2
*	Multiplication	=E5*24
%	Percent	20%
-	Subtraction	=D4-E4

As you will remember from that math class, exponentiation raises the specified number to the given power (for example, $2 \wedge 2$ is 2 to the power of 2—2x2, or two squared). The percent operator divides the number preceding it by 100 to produce a percentage, so 20% is expressed as 0.2.

Logical Operators

Straight math is all very well, but you also need to be able to compare values, and for this you need to use Excel's *logical operators* (also known as *comparison operators*):

Operator	Meaning	Example
=	Equal to	=D5=6
>	Greater than	=D5>6
<	Less than	=6<5
>=	Greater than or equal to	=Sheet4!A33>=250
<=	Less than or equal to	=88<=10000
<>	Not equal to	=A5<>"Penguin"

As you can see from the examples, these operators compare one value or text string (such as *Penguin* in the sixth example) to another. They return a result of TRUE if the condition is true and a result of FALSE if the condition is false; TRUE is represented as a mathematical 1 and FALSE as a mathematical 0. This means that, while a cell will display TRUE or FALSE, if you use the result of the cell in a formula, it will be treated as a 1 or a 0.

Text Operator

Excel uses one *text operator*—the *ampersand* (&)—for joining two labels together. For example, if cell C47 contains the label *1994* and cell D47 contains the label *Results* (with a blank space before it), you could use the formula **=C47&D47** to produce the result *1994 Results* in another cell. You can use the & operator with a value and a text string, as in the example here; with two values; or with two text strings. If you use & to *concatenate* (which is computer Latin for "slam together") two values, bear in mind that Excel joins the two values together rather than adding them: If cell A11 contains the value **50** and cell B11 contains the value **100**, the formula **=A11&B11** will produce the result 50100 rather than 150.

Reference Operators

Excel uses three *reference operators* for defining references:

Operator	Meaning	Example
:	Range—refers to the cells between (and including) the two reference cells	A1:A3
,	Union—for combining two or more references into one	SUM(A1:A3,A5:A7)
(space)	Intersection—indicates a reference to a cell or cells shared by two references	SUM(A3:B10 A4:D4)

The *range operator* and *union operator* are straightforward, but the *intersection operator* needs a word or two of explanation. The intersection operator refers to the cells shared by two references—in this example, cells A4 and B4, because both are in the range A3:B10 and the range A4:D4.

How Excel Uses Operators

So far the examples we've looked at have been agreeably simple, using only one operator apiece; but when any formula contains more than one operator, the order in which Excel evaluates the operators becomes important. For example, **=50*100-40** could mean that either you multiply 50 by 100 and then subtract 40 from the result (giving you 4960), or you subtract 40 from 100 and then multiply 50 by the result (60), to get 3000—figures distinct enough to make an appreciable difference to the bottom line.

Excel evaluates operators in the order of precedence shown in the following list. When two operators have the same precedence, Excel evaluates them from left to right:

Operator	Action
-	Negation (negative numbers)
%	Percent
^	Exponentiation
* and /	Multiplication and division
+ and -	Addition and subtraction
=, >, <, <=, >=, <>	Comparison

You'll see from this that in the example above (**=50*100-40**), Excel will evaluate the multiplication operator before the negation operator, giving you a result of 4960.

If you want to perform the calculation the other way, read the next section for instructions on how to use parentheses to change the order in which Excel evaluates operators.

Changing Precedence in a Formula

Memorizing Excel's operator precedence list and applying it effectively can be tricky. To alleviate this, Excel lets you use parentheses to change the order in which it evaluates the operators in a formula. Excel evaluates the contents of parentheses in a formula first, ignoring its otherwise slavish devotion to operator precedence. For example, you could change our example formula from **=50*100-40** to **=50*(100-40)** to force Excel to evaluate the contents of the parentheses before the multiplication (and thus produce the result 3000).

Excel insists on your using parentheses in pairs—each left (opening) parenthesis must be matched by a right (closing) parenthesis. If you try to enter a formula that's missing a parenthesis, Excel will display a message box suggesting a way to fix the problem by adding a missing parenthesis or removing an extra one. You can click the Yes button to have Excel fix the formula along the lines it indicated. If you click the No button, Excel will display a message box telling you that the formula contains an error and suggesting possible recourses.

To help you in pairing your parentheses, Excel flashes each opening or closing parenthesis you enter in bold, together with its matching parenthesis if it has one. When you enter a closing parenthesis and see no opening parenthesis flash in acknowledgment, look closely for a missing opening parenthesis. When you enter it correctly, you should see its paired closing parenthesis flash.

Pairing parentheses becomes even more important when you *nest* parentheses, putting one pair of parentheses inside another. Excel will evaluate the nested parentheses first. For example, in the formula **=400-(44/A2)+(3*(C3+1))**, Excel will evaluate C3+1 first. Each level of nested parentheses flashes in a different color as you enter them.

If you find that entering grouped values in parentheses helps you understand what your formulas are doing, you can use parentheses even when they are not strictly necessary for telling Excel how you want a formula to be calculated.

Creating a Formula

You can simply type a formula straight into the active cell or the reference area of the formula bar, and then click the Enter button (or press Enter, or click in another cell) to enter the formula. But you can also use the mouse to quickly indicate references (cells and ranges).

To enter a reference in a formula, you can simply point to the cell or range with the mouse and click on it. To do so, start typing the formula as usual, or click the Enter Formula button. Then, when you've reached the point where you want to enter the first reference, move the mouse pointer to the cell you want to reference and click on it. To reference a range, click and drag through it. To reference a cell or range on another worksheet, click on the worksheet tab to move to the worksheet first. Excel will enter the reference in the formula, display a shimmering dotted border around the referenced cell or range, and display *Point* in the status bar to indicate that you've just used Point mode. You can then continue typing your formula in the reference area.

TIP You can also use the keyboard to enter a reference in a formula by using ↑, ↓, ←, and → to navigate to the cell. To select a range, hold down Shift and use the arrow keys to select the range.

To enter a range name in a formula, you can either type it in or press F3 to display the Paste Name dialog box; then choose the range name from it and click OK. (Pressing F3 won't display the Paste Name dialog box if the workbook contains no range names.)

When you click the Enter Formula button, Excel displays the Formula Palette, in which it then displays the result of the formula as you enter it. Use this as a tool to make sure you're not creating any bizarre values as you go along. Click the OK button on the Formula Palette to enter the formula, or click the Cancel button to cancel it. Either way, Excel will remove the Formula Palette.

Working with Functions

As we discussed at the beginning of this chapter, a function is one of Excel's built-in formulas. For example, the SUM formula mentioned earlier adds the contents of the specified range. To add the contents of cells B5 through B10, you could use the function **=SUM(B5:B10)** rather than the formula **=B5+B6+B7+B8+B9+B10**.

Each function consists of a *name* and one or more *arguments* indicating the data to be used. In the above example, the name is SUM and the single argument it uses is B5:B10. The arguments for a function can be constants, references, range names, or other functions; for functions that use multiple arguments, the arguments are separated by commas. A function returns a *result*.

NOTE   I just lied: Excel has a few functions that take no arguments at all. One is NA, which returns #N/A, an error value indicating that a result is not available. (In case you're wondering, this can be useful for troubleshooting problems in your formulas.)

Entering a Function by Hand

As with formulas, you can enter functions in your worksheets by simply typing them in. You can use Point mode to select references, and you can enter range names by pressing F3 and using the Paste Name dialog box. But for most functions, you will do better to use the help provided by the Function Wizard, as described in the next section.

The main exception to this is the SUM function, for which Excel provides an AutoSum button on the Standard toolbar. To quickly create a sum with AutoSum:

1. Click the cell that will contain the function.
2. Click the AutoSum button. Excel will enter the function =SUM() and will suggest within the parentheses the cells in the current row or column that it identifies as most likely contenders for summing. For example, if the active cell is immediately below a column of figures, AutoSum will suggest summing that range; if the active cell is to the right of a row of figures, AutoSum will suggest summing that range.
3. If the range is not correct, click and drag with the mouse to indicate the correct range.
4. Press Enter, click the Enter button, or click elsewhere in the worksheet to enter the function.

Entering a Function with the Function Wizard

Excel's Function Wizard provides an easy way to select the function you need and supply it with the arguments it wants:

1. Click the cell that you want to contain the function.
2. Click the Paste Function button on the Standard toolbar to display the Paste Function dialog box (see Figure 16.1).

> **NOTE** If you don't have the Standard toolbar displayed, type = or click the Edit Formula button to start the function, and then click the Function drop-down list on the Formula bar and choose More Functions to display the Paste Function dialog box.

3. In the Function Category list box, choose the category of functions you want.
   - Click the Most Recently Used item at the top of the list to see which functions you've used most recently.
   - Choose All if you're not sure which category the function you're looking for fits into.
4. Choose the function from the Function Name list. Use the description at the bottom of the Paste Function dialog box to check that this is the function you want.

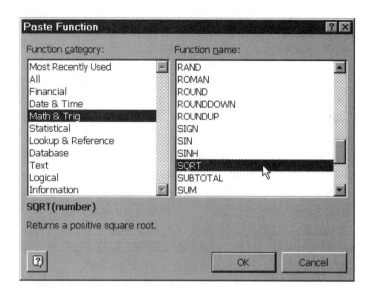

FIGURE 16.1:
To enter a function, click the Paste Function button to display the Paste Function dialog box.

5. Click the OK button to close the Paste Function dialog box and enter the function you chose on the Formula Palette (see Figure 16.2). The Formula Palette shows different information for each function—a description of the function and the arguments required for it and boxes in which to enter the arguments.

6. Choose the arguments for the function in the appropriate text box or text boxes. The number of text boxes will match the number of arguments the function needs; as you can see in Figure 16.2, the SQRT function needs only one argument.

   • Type in a constant, a reference, a range, or a function.
   • Use Point mode to enter a reference or a range by clicking (and dragging if necessary) in the worksheet. The Formula Palette will collapse itself out of your way as necessary, but you can click any Collapse Palette button first if you prefer. (The Collapse Palette button is the button with the red arrow that you'll find at the right-hand end of each text box.)
   • To enter a range name, press F3 and select the name in the Paste Name dialog box.

7. Click the OK button to close the Formula Palette and enter the function in the worksheet.

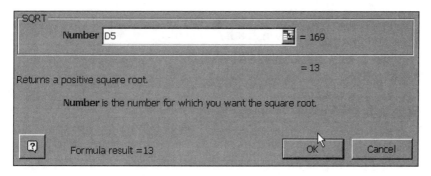

FIGURE 16.2:   Choose arguments for the function on the Formula Palette.

Copying and Moving Formulas

You can copy or move formulas about a workbook by using the regular Cut, Copy, and Paste commands. But with formulas that contain cell references, you need to consider the effect that copying or moving the formula will have on the references.

First, you need to know what absolute references and relative references are and the distinction between the two.

Absolute, Relative, and Mixed References

By default, Excel uses *relative references*, which work relative to the cell containing the formula. For example, say you have three columns of numbers—A, B, and C—and you want to subtract the value in each B cell from the value in the corresponding A cell and then multiply the result by the value in the corresponding C cell. You could enter in cell D1 the formula **=(A1-B1)*C1**, copy it, and paste it into the remaining cells in column D. With relative references, Excel will adjust the formula it enters in each cell so each performs the same relative operation: Subtract the value in the cell three columns to the left by the value in the cell two columns to the left, and multiply the result by the value in the cell one column to the left. So cell D2 will contain the formula **=(A2-B2)*C2**, cell D4 will contain **=(A4-B4)*C4**, and so on.

TIP   **You can also copy a formula by using the AutoFill handle, as discussed in Chapter 13.**

Relative references are useful in creating worksheets quickly, but sometimes you'll want to use absolute references instead. An *absolute reference* refers to the same place in a workbook no matter where you copy or paste it to. For example, suppose you wanted to add your beloved state sales tax to the calculation in the previous example, and cell E10 held the current tax rate. If you used the relative reference **E10** in the first formula (**=(A1-B1)*C1*E10**), Excel would change E10 to E11, E12, and so on, when you pasted the formula into another cell. But when you use an absolute reference, Excel will not change the reference: Cells D2, D3, and so on will still use E10 as the reference.

Excel uses the dollar sign (*$*) to denote absolute references, so the absolute reference for cell E10 would be **E10**. As you can see, both the column and the row need the dollar sign for the reference to be absolute. This is because you can also create *mixed references*—references with either the column fixed and the row relative (**$E10**), or with the column relative and the row fixed (**E$10**).

To quickly create an absolute reference or a mixed reference from a relative reference, select the reference using Point mode, and then press F4 once, twice, or thrice:

- Once produces an absolute reference (**A1**).
- Twice produces a mixed reference relative in the column and absolute in the row (**A$1**).
- Thrice produces a mixed reference absolute in the column and relative in the row (**$A1**).

Pressing F4 a fourth time returns you to a relative reference. If you start with an absolute reference or a mixed reference, each press of F4 moves you on to the next type of reference listed above.

NOTE **Two quick notes here: First, when you use Cut and Paste to move a formula (rather than Copy and Paste to copy it), Excel does not change its references. Second, when you move a range of data referenced in a formula, Excel modifies the reference in the formula (whether absolute, mixed, or relative) to reflect the new location. (This happens when you move the whole range of data referenced, not if you move just part of it.)**

Recalculating Formulas

Every time you change the numbers in a workbook that contains formulas, Excel needs to recalculate them. By default, Excel recalculates all formulas whenever you change the workbook, keeping everything up-to-date. Usually this will happen fast enough not to slow down your work, so you'll have no reason to change it. But if you're regularly working with large spreadsheets or with a slow computer, you can turn automatic recalculation off (or back on) as follows:

1. Choose Tools ➤ Options to display the Options dialog box.
2. Click the Calculation tab to bring it to the front of the Options dialog box.
3. In the Calculation group box, choose the option you want:

   Automatic   Turns automatic recalculation on (as described above).

   Automatic Except Tables   Calculates all dependent formulas except data tables.

   Manual   Recalculates formulas only when you choose to do so by pressing F9 in the workbook or clicking the Calc Now button on the Calculation tab of the Options dialog box.

   Recalculate before Save   Recalculates the workbook when you save it.

4. Click the OK button to close the Options dialog box and save your choices.

TIP   **When you're using manual calculation, Excel will display Calculate in the status bar when the workbook contains a change that requires recalculation. At the time of this writing (Fall 1997), it has been reported that a bug inExcel causes it to occasionally fail to recalculate some formulas in complex worksheets. If you suspect that this is happening in your worksheets, press F9 to force manual calculation.**

Viewing Formulas

As we've seen so far in this chapter, Excel, by default, displays the result of any formula in the cell the formula occupies, letting you view and work with the result as if it were a regular number and displaying the formula only in the reference area when the cell that contains it is active.

For working out problems in your workbooks, use the Ctrl+` toggle (that's the single left quotation mark found to left of 1 on full-size keyboards and in weird places on notebook keyboards, *not* the single-quote key) to display all formulas in the worksheet instead of their results.

Dealing with Errors in Formulas

As you'll have guessed from reading this chapter, the power and flexibility that Excel's formulas offer give you plenty of latitude for getting things wrong. Here are the top eight error messages that you'll see when you've done something wrong in a formula and Excel doesn't like it:

Message	Meaning	What to Do
#####	The formula result is too long to fit in the cell.	Increase the column width.
#DIV/0!	The formula is trying to divide by zero.	Locate the reference or formula that provides the zero and change it.
#N/A	No value is available for the value to which the formula refers.	Nothing. (Enter **#N/A** in cells that do not have data yet to mark the lack of data.)
#NAME?	The formula references a range name that Excel cannot find, or a function name is misspelled.	Make sure the range exists and that its name is correctly spelled. Redesignate the range if necessary. Check function names for misspellings.
#NULL!	The formula references a range incorrectly.	Check that the range is specified correctly. Use a comma (,) to refer to two areas that do not intersect.
#NUM!	The formula cannot use the number supplied. For example, a function that requires a positive number cannot use a negative number.	Check for unsuitable numbers and correct them.

Message	Meaning	What to Do
#REF!	The formula refers to an invalid cell. For example, you may have deleted a cell that the formula refers to or pasted something over it.	Change the formula to correct the invalid reference.
#VALUE!	The formula uses the wrong type of argument—for example, if you specify text where Excel expects to find a number.	Make sure all arguments are valid.

Chapter 17

CREATING MACROS AND CUSTOMIZING EXCEL

- **Creating a macro**
- **Editing a macro**
- **Choosing environment options**
- **Creating templates**

Excel offers almost as many customization features as Word does to make your everyday work smoother, faster, and simpler. In this chapter, we'll first discuss Excel's macro-recording and macro-editing features before moving on to look at how you can customize Excel to provide a suitable working environment for yourself. Finally, we'll look at how you can use templates in Excel to create workbooks quickly.

Macros

As we mentioned in Chapter 2, Excel uses the Visual Basic for Applications macro language (VBA for short), as does Word. Excel lets you record a macro simply by switching on the macro recorder, performing the actions you want to record, and then turning the recorder off. Once you've recorded a macro, you can open it in the Visual Basic Editor and edit it by adding, deleting, or altering the instructions it contains.

Recording a Macro

To record a macro:

1. Choose Tools ➤ Macro ➤ Record New Macro to display the Record Macro dialog box (see Figure 17.1).

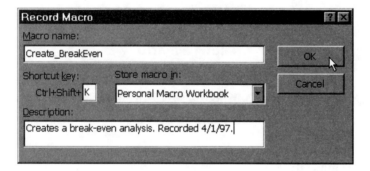

FIGURE 17.1:
In the Record Macro dialog box, enter a name and description for the macro, choose a shortcut key, and specify where to store the macro.

2. Enter a name for the macro in the Macro Name box. The name must begin with a letter and can be up to 255 characters long; it can contain underscores, but cannot contain spaces or punctuation marks.

3. Enter a description for the macro in the Description box. Excel will propose by default a description involving your user name and the date: *Macro recorded 6/28/97 by Rikki Nadir* or something similar. You can enter several lines of text here, but later you will thank yourself for being concise and providing a coherent description of what the macro does.

4. To assign the macro to a shortcut key, click in the Shortcut Key check box and press the key that you want to use with Ctrl as a shortcut key. Press Shift if you want to add that to the key combination: You can use Ctrl+k and Ctrl+Shift+K to run different macros in the same workbook if you want.

5. If you want to store the macro somewhere other than in the current workbook (This Workbook), choose Personal Macro Workbook or New Workbook in the Store Macro In group box. Storing the macro in your Personal Macro

Workbook means that you will be able to use the macro in any workbook. Storing the macro in the current workbook means that you will be able to use the macro only in this workbook, and any shortcut key you create will apply only to this workbook.

6. Click OK to close the Record Macro dialog box and start recording the macro. Excel will display the Stop Recording toolbar, and the status bar will display *Recording*.

7. If you want the macro to use relative references rather than absolute references, click the Relative References button on the Stop Recording toolbar so that it appears pushed in, as shown here. A *relative* reference is a reference relative to where the active cell currently is, whereas an *absolute* reference is fixed no matter where the active cell happens to be. If you choose to use relative references, the macro will record which direction and how far you move the active cell from the cell you start recording in (rather than recording the identities of the cells you make active) and will work from whichever cell is active when you start replaying it. If you do not use relative references, the macro will use absolute references and will record the specific cells that you use when recording the macro; when you play back the macro, it will use those cells, no matter which cell is active. Use relative references for any macro that you want to be able to use on different worksheets; use absolute references for any macro that will always work with the same cells.

8. Perform the actions that you want to record in the macro.

9. Click the Stop Recording button on the Stop Recording toolbar to stop recording.

Running a Macro

Once you've recorded a macro, the first thing to do is to make sure that it works as you intended. If you didn't assign a shortcut key to the macro when you recorded it, you can quickly run it by making the appropriate cell active, choosing Tools ➤ Macro ➤ Macros to display the Macro dialog box (see Figure 17.2), selecting the name of your macro, and clicking the Run button. Excel will perform the actions you recorded.

Assigning a Macro to a Shortcut Key

If you didn't assign a shortcut key to a macro when you recorded it, you can assign one afterwards easily enough:

1. Choose Tools ➤ Macro ➤ Macros to display the Macro dialog box.

2. Select the macro in the Macro Name list box.

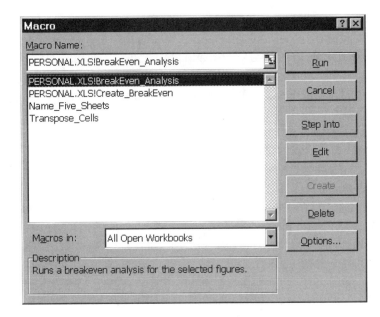

FIGURE 17.2:
The Macro
dialog box

3. Click the Options button to display the Macro Options dialog box (see Figure 17.3).

4. In the Shortcut Key box, select the shortcut key you want. Press Shift if you want to add that to the shortcut key combination.

5. Click the OK button to close the Macro Options dialog box and return to the Macro dialog box.

6. Repeat the process for another macro, or click the Close button (into which the Cancel button will have changed) to close the Macro dialog box.

NOTE You can quickly assign a macro to a menu item by following the procedure described in Chapter 2 in "Adding and Removing Toolbar and Menu Commands."

Assigning a Macro to a Toolbar Button

You can also run a macro by assigning it to a toolbar button:

1. Choose Tools ➤ Customize to display the Customize dialog box.

2. Make sure the toolbar to which you want to add the macro is displayed. If it's not displayed, select its check box in the Toolbars list box on the Toolbars tab.

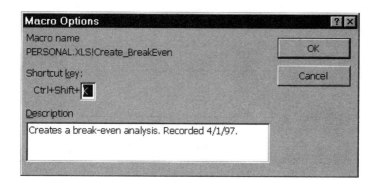

FIGURE 17.3:
In the Macro Options dialog box, you can quickly add (or change) the shortcut key for a macro.

3. On the Commands tab, click the button you want to use to run the macro and drag it to the toolbar.
    • If you don't want to reuse one of the buttons assigned to Excel's commands, select Macros in the Categories list box and choose Custom Button in the Commands list box.
    • If the toolbar already contains the button you want to add, skip this step.
4. Right-click the toolbar button you want to use and choose Assign Macro from the context menu to display the Assign Macro dialog box (see Figure 17.4).
5. Select the macro in the Macro Name list box. (If necessary, choose the workbook containing the macro from the Macros In drop-down list.)
6. Click the OK button to assign the macro to the toolbar button. Excel will return you to the Customize dialog box.
7. Repeat steps 4 through 6 as appropriate, or click the Close button to close the Customize dialog box.

Running a Macro from a Graphic Object

You can also run a macro from a graphic object in a worksheet. By using a graphic object rather than a toolbar button, you can make sure a macro is available right where you need it. This is especially useful if you share worksheets with your colleagues.

To assign a macro to a graphic object:

1. Click on the object to select it and display selection handles around it.
2. Right-click on a handle and choose Assign Macro from the context menu to display the Assign Macro dialog box.
3. Select the macro in the Macro Name list box. (If necessary, choose the workbook containing the macro from the Macros In drop-down list.)
4. Click the OK button to close the Assign Macro dialog box.

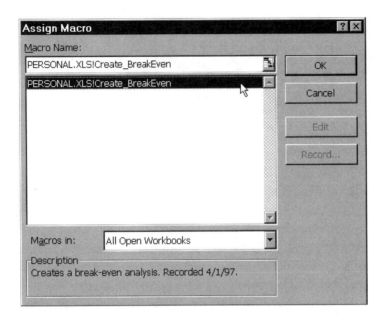

FIGURE 17.4:
In the Assign Macro dialog box, choose the macro you want to assign to the toolbar button, and then click the OK button.

The graphic object will now act as a button for the macro you assigned: When you move the mouse pointer over the graphic object, you'll see the upward-pointing-finger mouse pointer shown here (in the lower-left corner of the graphic object) to indicate the graphic object is a *hot spot* (an area associated with an action), and when you click the graphic object, the macro will run.

To select a hot spot, Ctrl+click it. To assign a different macro to it, right-click the button, choose Assign Macro from the context menu, select the macro in the Assign Macro dialog box, and click OK.

Editing a Macro

If you make a mistake when recording one of your macros, you have the choice of recording the macro again from scratch or braving the rigors of VBA and editing the macro to fix the problem. All the macros you create in a workbook in any one editing session are stored in modules attached to the workbook; you can get to them by choosing Tools ➤ Macro ➤ Macros to display the Macro dialog box, selecting the name of the macro in the Macro Name list box, and clicking the Edit button to display the Visual Basic Editor with the macro displayed.

When you look at the macros within a module, you will see that each macro is prefaced by *comment lines* (indicated by a comment character, the single quotation mark) consisting of the macro name and the description you gave it.

```
'Integrate_Data_from_Access Macro
'Incorporates Access data in the daily report for Head Office
```

Beyond that, each macro starts with a Sub statement and ends with an End Sub statement:

```
Sub Integrate_Data_from_Access()
     ActiveCell.FormulaR1C1 = "Daily Report for Head Office"
End Sub
```

The instructions between the Sub and End Sub statements are what you can edit, add, or delete. As a simple example, in the above macro you could rewrite the text within quotation marks to change what the macro enters in the active cell.

Global Macros

As we mentioned in "Recording a Macro" earlier in the chapter, Excel can store macros either in a workbook (so that the macros are available only in that workbook) or in the personal macro workbook, Personal.xls. Once the personal macro workbook is created, it is always loaded when you run Excel, but it's in the background so you don't see it unless you deliberately display it. Because the personal macro workbook is always loaded, any macros you create in it will be available in any workbook you have open.

To record a macro in the personal macro workbook, in the Record Macro dialog box, select the Personal Macro Workbook option button in the Store Macro In drop-down list when recording a macro. Excel creates the personal macro workbook automatically the first time you choose to store a macro there, so you don't need to worry about creating it or finding it.

You can edit your global macros by displaying the personal macro workbook. To do so, choose Window ➤ Unhide to display the Unhide dialog box, select Personal in the Unhide Workbook list, and click the OK button. Excel will display Personal.xls. Edit the macros in the Visual Basic Editor as described in the previous section, and then choose Window ➤ Hide to hide the personal macro workbook again.

Choosing Environment Options

In this section, we'll look at the various environment options Excel offers. As you might guess, some of these are more important than others.

View Options

The View tab of the Options dialog box offers a number of options that can make Excel easier to read—or give you more screen real estate to work in.

- In the Show area, choose whether to display or hide the Formula bar and the status bar. Usually, you'll want to keep these on screen.
- In the Comments area, choose whether to have no comments or comment indicators displayed, the comment indicators only (the small red triangles in the upper-right corner of a cell to which a comment is attached), or the comments and the indicators.
- In the Objects area, choose whether to show all objects (which is usually best), to show placeholders for them, or to hide all objects.
- In the Window Options area, you can choose to display or hide various items, from page breaks to the horizontal scroll bar and vertical scroll bar. Select the check boxes for the items that you want to have displayed. If you display gridlines, you can choose a color for them in the Color drop-down list.

Calculation Options

On the Calculation tab of the Options dialog box, the most important options are in the Calculation area, which we looked at in Chapter 16. Usually, you'll want to keep the Automatic option button selected, so Excel automatically recalculates all parts of the worksheet whenever necessary.

Edit Options

The Edit tab offers a number of important options:

- Edit Directly in Cell lets you edit the contents of a cell by double-clicking inside it, rather than having to work in the formula bar.
- Allow Cell Drag and Drop enables drag-and-drop copying and AutoFilling of cells. If you select Allow Cell Drag and Drop, you can select the Alert before Overwriting Cells check box to have Excel warn you when a drag-and-drop generation will overwrite existing cell contents.
- The Move Selection after Enter drop-down list lets you choose the direction in which Excel moves the active cell after you press Enter. The default setting is Down, but you can choose Right (which is often useful), Up, or Left if that's the way you prefer to work.
- The Provide Feedback with Animation check box controls whether Excel shows worksheet changes with animation or without. For example, select

several columns in an empty worksheet and choose Edit ➤ Delete. With animation on, you'll see Excel slide the other columns across to replace them; with animation off, the other columns will just blink into place. Turn animation off to improve performance on slow computers.

- The Enable AutoComplete for Cell Values check box controls whether AutoComplete (which we looked at in Chapter 13) displays suggestions or not. If AutoComplete annoys you, clear this check box.

General Options

The most important options on the General tab are the following:

- The Macro Virus Protection check box controls whether Excel checks each workbook you open for macro viruses when you open it. *Macro viruses* are malevolent programs written in a macro language (here, VBA) and concealed within harmless-looking files (here, Excel spreadsheets and templates). So far, most of the excitement about macro viruses has taken place in Word, but macro viruses have surfaced in Excel as well, and unless you know precisely where your workbooks are coming from, you may do well to make sure this feature is turned on. Be aware that Excel templates, such as those used in the Small Business Financial Manager, use macros and will trigger a macro-virus warning.

- The Prompt for Workbook Properties check box controls whether Excel displays the Properties dialog box when you save a file. If you find the Properties dialog box useful, select this check box.

- The Provide Feedback with Sound check box controls whether Excel plays sounds when you perform actions, such as saving or printing a file. The sounds can quickly become tedious, so this check box is a prime candidate for clearance.

- The Zoom on Roll with IntelliMouse controls whether the IntelliMouse zooms. If you're not using an IntelliMouse (or a mouse that mimics it), make sure this check box is cleared.

- Adjust the Entries box next to the Recently Used File List to have Excel show more of the most recently used files at the foot of the File menu (from 1 to 9), or clear the check box to turn off the display of the files (for example, for security).

- Change the Sheets in New Workbook number to have Excel place more or fewer worksheets in each new workbook you create.

- Use the Standard Font and Size drop-down lists to set the standard font that Excel uses.

- Set the folder in which you most frequently work with Excel workbooks in the Default File Location text box. This is the folder in which Excel will propose saving new files and in which it starts looking for files when you choose File ➤ Open.
- Make sure your name is correctly spelled in the User Name text box. Excel will use this name for file property information.

Transition Options

The Transition tab contains options for moving to Excel 97 from another spreadsheet program:

- In the Save Excel Files As drop-down list, you can choose to save files as a format other than Excel 97. For example, if your colleagues are still using Excel 95 (a.k.a. Excel 7) and Excel 5, you could choose Microsoft Excel 97 & 5/95 Workbook to make sure your colleagues can open your files.
- If you're moving to Excel from Lotus 1-2-3, you may want to investigate the options in the Settings area and the Sheet Options area to help you make the transition to Excel.

Custom Lists

The Customs Lists tab lets you define new custom lists, which are especially useful with AutoFill. For example, if you have offices in Los Angeles, Oakland, San Francisco, and Petaluma, you could create a custom list containing those location names so that you could quickly enter them in adjacent cells in your spreadsheets.

To create a custom list:

1. Click the NEW LIST item in the Custom Lists list box.
2. Enter the entries in the List Entries list box. Alternatively, either type the entries into the List Entries list box; or click the Collapse Dialog Box button in the Import List from Cells text box to collapse the Options dialog box; then drag through the cells that contain the list entries, click the Collapse Dialog Box button again to restore the Options dialog box, and click the Import button to enter the contents of the cells in the List Entries list box.

You can then use AutoFill to enter your custom list by typing the first entry into a cell and then dragging the AutoFill handle.

Chart Options

The most useful options on the Chart tab are the two in the Chart Tips area: Show Names and Show Values. Show Names displays the name of each part of a chart when you move the mouse pointer over it; Show Values displays the value of a data marker. You'll probably want to leave these selected, as they are by default.

Color Options

The Color tab lets you define custom colors for use with Excel. To define a custom color, select the color you want to change in the Standard Colors palette, the Chart Fills palette, or the Chart Lines palette, and click the Modify button to display the Colors dialog box. Select the color you want on either the Standard tab or the Custom tab, and click the OK button to return to the Options dialog box. Click the Reset button if you want to reset Excel's colors to their defaults.

Using Templates to Save Time

By creating a template from a workbook that you've painstakingly set up, you can reuse the workbook's setup and formatting and save yourself time and effort.

First, make sure the workbook is set up perfectly for reuse. This may mean removing from it data that you'll enter for each new workbook you create based on the template or entering date formulas into cells rather than specific dates. Once the workbook is ready:

1. Choose File ➤ Save As to display the Save As dialog box.
2. In the Save As Type drop-down list, choose Template. Excel will switch to the Templates folder.
    - Templates you save in the Templates folder will appear on the General tab of the New dialog box. Alternatively, you can save your templates in the Spreadsheet Solutions folder by double-clicking that folder at this point.

    - You can also create a new folder for your templates by clicking the Create New Folder button, entering a name for the folder in the New Folder dialog box, clicking OK, and then selecting that folder. This new folder will appear as another tab in the New dialog box.
3. Enter the name for your template in the File Name box.
4. Click the Save button to save the template.
5. If Excel displays the Properties dialog box, enter property information in it if you want. Select the Save Preview Picture check box if you want your template to be able to display a preview in the New dialog box.
6. Choose File ➤ Close to close your template.

To create a new workbook based on the template, choose File ➤ New and select the template in the New dialog box.

Chapter 18

SMALL BUSINESS FINANCIAL MANAGER

FEATURING

- **Understanding what Small Business Financial Manager is and what it does**
- **Importing accounting data into Small Business Financial Manager**
- **Creating financial reports**
- **Performing what-if analyses**
- **Updating your accounting data**

Small Business Financial Manager is a decision-making tool for manipulating accounting information to view and analyze the financial history and condition of a business. In this chapter, I'll explain how to use Small Business Financial Manager (which I'll refer to as simply "Financial Manager") to create financial reports and perform what-if analyses.

What Is Financial Manager?

Financial Manager works with your existing financial information. You can import accounting information from a variety of widely used accounting applications, such as One-Write Plus, Peachtree Accounting, and Quick Beans.

Once you've imported the information into Financial Manager, you can run various types of reports to analyze it in order to help you establish and understand your current situation, and to make tactical and strategic business decisions that will determine the future of your business. For example, you can create cash-flow reports to assess your company's current financial predicament, or you can perform what-if analyses to see what would happen if you fired two employees, raised the price of your product by 18 percent, and gave up gourmet coffee.

Before You Use Financial Manager...

Financial Manager is implemented as a set of Excel 97 templates and add-ins, so you need to have Excel 97 installed on your computer in order to be able to install and use Financial Manager. (If Office 97 Small Business Edition came preinstalled on your computer, you should have no problem here.)

You also need to have accounting information available in a format that Financial Manager can use. Financial Manager supports the following formats:

- BusinessWorks for Windows, version 9.0
- CA Simply Accounting for Windows, versions 3.0 and 4.0
- CA ACCPAC Plus for DOS, version 6.1a
- DacEasy Accounting for DOS, version 5
- Great Plains Accounting for DOS, version 8.0 and 8.1
- Intuit QuickBooks for Windows, versions 3.1 and 4.0
- Intuit QuickBooks Pro for Windows, version 4.0
- M-A-S 90 Evolution/2 for DOS, version 1.51.
- One-Write Plus Accounting for DOS, version 4.0
- Peachtree Accounting for Windows, versions 3.0, 3.5, and 4.0
- Peachtree Complete Accounting for DOS, version 8.0
- Platinum Series for DOS/Windows, version 4.1
- Timeline MV Server, versions 2.3 and 2.4

To use Financial Manager, you need a working knowledge of Excel (you can get that "working knowledge" by working through the previous five chapters) and an understanding of accounting practices. In this chapter, I'll assume that you have a fair understanding of business and accounting practices. If you're not comfortable with concepts such as bad debt, cash flow, and liquidity, you probably don't need to use Financial Manager.

Starting Financial Manager

You can start Financial Manager by double-clicking the Small Business Financial Manager icon that the installation program created on your Windows Desktop. If Excel is not running, Financial Manager will start it up automatically. Alternatively, you can start Excel as you usually do (for example, by choosing Start ➤ Programs ➤ Microsoft Excel, or by using a shortcut). You can then use the Accounting menu that Financial Manager adds to Excel to access the Financial Manager functions.

When you start Financial Manager from the Desktop, Excel will warn you that the workbook you are opening contains macros that might contain viruses. This is nothing to worry about; Financial Manager runs largely as macros and does not contain viruses. Click the Enable Macros button to open Financial Manager, which starts up with a new workbook named Report Workbook 1. Once Financial Manager is up and running, your screen should look like Figure 18.1.

NOTE   **If you've disabled macro virus protection, as described in Chapter 17, Excel will not display the dialog box warning you about macros.**

Importing Information

Once you've started up Financial Manager, you can import your accounting information from your accounting application. To import information:

1. If you started Financial Manager from the Desktop, click the Import button on the Financial Manager opening screen. If you've simply opened Excel, choose Accounting ➤ Import Wizard. Financial Manager will display the first Import Your Accounting Data dialog box.

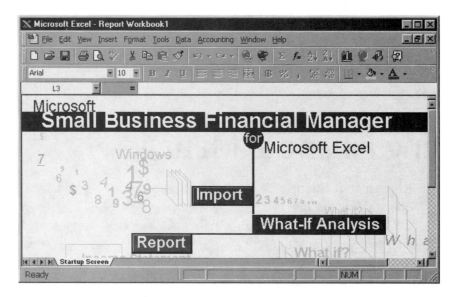

FIGURE 18.1: The opening screen of Financial Manager provides quick access to its three main features: importing information, creating reports, and performing what-if analyses.

2. Choose the Import option button if you're importing data for the first time. Choose the Update option button if you're updating data. (I'll discuss how to update data later in this chapter.)

3. Click the Next button to move on to the second stage of the import process. Financial Manager will display the second Import Your Accounting Data dialog box (see Figure 18.2).

4. Tell Financial Manager where to look for your accounting data:

   • If you're not sure where the accounting data is located on your computer, leave the Look on My Computer option button selected.

   • If you know the approximate location of your accounting data, select the In Specific Folders option button and choose the drive in the drives drop-down list and the folder or folders in the tree box. Once you've navigated to the appropriate folder, click the Add Folder to List button to add it to the list of folders in the list box to the right.

   • If your accounting data is in multiple folders, keep adding to the list of folders until you've selected all the folders. (If you add a folder that doesn't contain accounting data, select it and click the Remove from List button.)

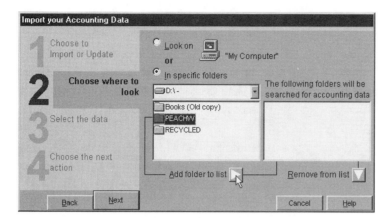

FIGURE 18.2:
In the second Import Your Accounting Data dialog box, select the location or locations that Financial Manager should search to find your accounting data.

NOTE   **If you click the drives drop-down button and see no action for a minute or so (and no Windows hourglass either), be patient—Financial Manager is slow to identify the drives on some computers (your computer probably has not crashed).**

5. Click the Next button to have Financial Manager search for your accounting data. When Financial Manager finds the data, it will display the third Import Your Accounting Data dialog box.

6. In the list box in the third Import Your Accounting Data dialog box, select the data you want to import. (If you have only one company, you won't have a choice here.) Then click the Next button to proceed.

7. Financial Manager will display a message box warning you that the import process can take a long time—from several minutes to several hours. Click the Yes button to proceed.

NOTE   **If you want to defer the import process, click the No button to return to the third Import Your Accounting Data dialog box, where you can click the Cancel button to exit the Import Wizard. (You'll need to repeat the whole identification procedure when you decide to import your data.)**

8. Financial Manager will now import your data. As it just warned you, the process may take a while. You'll see a progress indicator near the bottom of the dialog box, along with a description of the process currently under way.

9. When Financial Manager has finished importing your data, it will display the fourth Import Your Accounting Data dialog box, offering you the choices Create a Financial Report, Perform a What-If Analysis, and Remap Your Accounting Data.

10. The first time you import data into Financial Manager, choose the Remap Your Accounting Data option button and click the Finish button. Financial Manager will display the Map Your Accounts dialog box (see Figure 18.3).

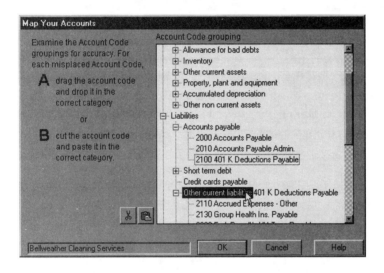

FIGURE 18.3:
In the Map Your Accounts dialog box, check that Financial Manager has mapped your accounts correctly when importing your accounting data.

11. Check the mapping of your accounting data to make sure all the information is in the right place:
    - Click the + sign next to a collapsed category to expand it; click the – sign next to an expanded category to collapse it.
    - Move categories and items by using either drag-and-drop or the Cut and Paste buttons in the dialog box.

12. Click the OK button to close the Map Your Accounts dialog box.

You can also remap your accounting data at any point by choosing Accounting ➤ Remap Data, selecting the company in the dialog box, and clicking the OK button to display the Map Your Accounts dialog box.

Creating Financial Reports

You're now ready to use Financial Manager to generate a variety of reports from your accounting data. In this section, I'll walk you through the creation of a cash-flow report, one of the reports that you're likely to want to generate.

1. Start Financial Manager and click the Report button, or choose Accounting ➤ Report Wizard. Financial Manager will display the first Create a Financial Report dialog box (see Figure 18.4).

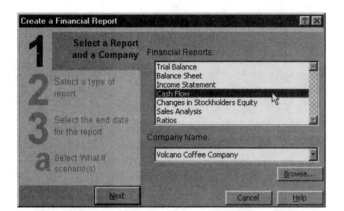

FIGURE 18.4:
In the first Create a Financial Report dialog box, select the type of report to create and the company for which to create it.

2. In the Financial Reports list box, select the type of report to create. For this example, choose Cash Flow.
3. In the Company Name drop-down list, choose the company for which to create the report.
4. Click the Next button to display the second Create a Financial Report dialog box (see Figure 18.5).
5. Select the subtype of report to create. For this example, select One Period & YTD with Comparisons to get an up-to-date picture of the cash flow.
6. Click the Next button to display the third Create a Financial Report dialog box.
7. In the End Date for the Report list box, choose the end date with which to work. (For some report types, you'll need to choose a start date as well.)
8. If you chose a report that involves scenarios, click the Next button to proceed; otherwise, click the Finish button to have the Report Wizard generate the report. Figure 18.6 shows a sample cash-flow report for a fictional company.

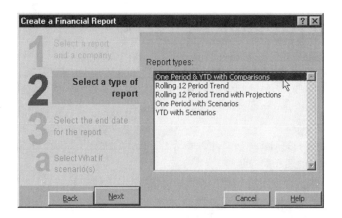

FIGURE 18.5:
In the second Create a Financial Report dialog box, select the subtype of report.

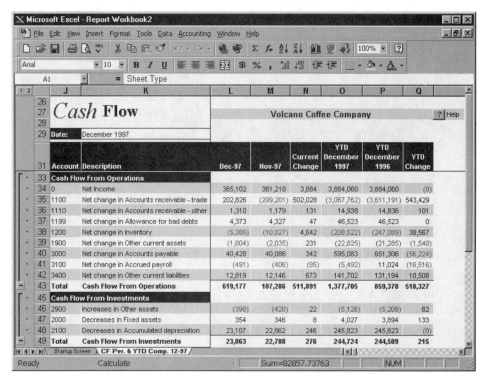

FIGURE 18.6: A sample cash-flow report generated by the Report Wizard

Performing What-If Analyses

What-if analyses are a powerful decision-making tool, letting you explore the likely consequences of multiple courses of action in theory before deciding which of them (if any) to try in practice. Financial Manager provides templates and macros for generating what-if analyses from your accounting information.

Creating a What-If Scenario

To work with what-if analyses, you typically create a what-if scenario using your existing accounting information. You then perform what-if analyses to factor in possibilities and gauge the results.

To create a what-if scenario:

1. From the Financial Manager Startup Screen, click the What-If Analysis button. Alternatively, from Excel, choose Accounting ➤ What-If Wizard. Financial Manager will display the first Perform a What-If Analysis dialog box.
2. Choose the company for which to create the what-if scenario, then click the Next button to display the second Perform a What-If Analysis dialog box.
3. Select the New option button and enter a name of up to 50 characters for the new what-if scenario in the New text box. (After you've created what-if scenarios, you can open an existing one by selecting the Existing option button and choosing its name from the Existing drop-down list.)
4. Click the Finish button. Financial Manager will display the Save Scenario Workbook As dialog box, which you'll recognize as a mutant version of the Save As dialog box. Adjust the suggested name and location for the new what-if scenario file as necessary, and then click the Save button. Financial Manager will display the What-If Overview worksheet for the scenario. (If you're opening an existing what-if scenario, Financial Manager will display it rather than the dialog box for saving the workbook.)

Working with Your What-If Scenario

Once you've created a what-if scenario, it should be open on-screen (see Figure 18.7) so that you can work with it. (If not, choose Accounting ➤ What-If Wizard, select the company and click the Next button, and then select the existing scenario to work with, as described in step 3 of the previous section.)

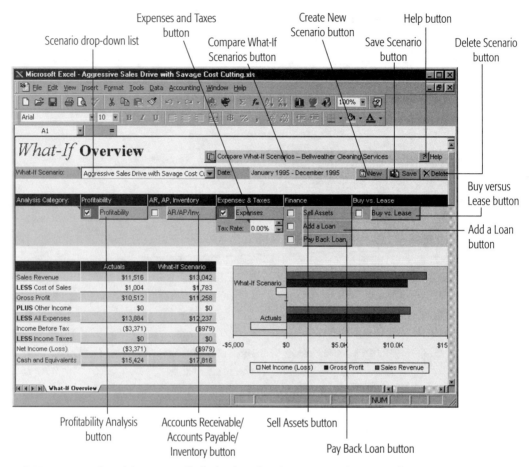

FIGURE 18.7: Financial Manager will display the What-If Overview worksheet for the scenario.

Here's what the elements of the What-If Overview worksheet do:

- Use the Scenario drop-down list to select a different scenario to work with (if you've created more than one).
- Click the Compare What-If Scenarios button to display a summary worksheet showing all the what-if scenarios you've created.
- Click the Create New Scenario button to create a new scenario. Enter a name for the scenario in the Enter a Name for the New What-If Scenario dialog box, and click the OK button. Financial Manager will create the new scenario and will automatically save it under the chosen name with an .xls file extension.
- Click the Save Scenario button to save changes you've made to the current scenario. It's a good idea to save changes to the current scenario before creating a new scenario or comparing what-if scenarios.

- Click the Delete Scenario button to delete the current scenario. Financial Manager will display a confirmation message box; click the OK button to proceed with the deletion.
- Click the Help button to display the Financial Manager Help file. (You can use the Tutorial choice to get an overview of Financial Manager.)
- Click the Profitability Analysis button to create a profitability analysis. Financial Manager will display the Profitability Analysis dialog box; choose the category you want to analyze and then click the OK button. Use the drop-down list at the top of the page to analyze profitability from a different viewpoint (Revenue View, Cost View, Mix View, or Price View) and the drop-down lists that head the columns to display different items of information. Use the Graphical View drop-down list to choose the item you want to have graphed. Click the Breakeven button to produce a Breakeven Analysis worksheet for the currently selected item or customer.
- Click the Accounts Receivable/Accounts Payable/Inventory button to display the Accounts Receivable, Accounts Payable, and Inventory Analysis worksheet (AR, AP, & Inv. Analysis for short). Adjust the Scenario Days and Scenario End Balance figures as necessary by clicking the spin buttons or dragging the sliders.
- Click the Expenses button to display the Expense Analysis worksheet. You can then adjust your expenses by clicking the spin buttons or dragging the sliders in the To a Value Of column. You also can choose By Difference or By Percentage in the drop-down list at the top of the sheet to change the expenses by difference (for example, by a specified dollar value) or by percentage (such as by 2.39%).

NOTE **Each of the supporting worksheets shows only the values for that topic. The worksheets all feed to the Overview and Summary worksheets, but they do not feed to each other.**

- Enter the appropriate tax rate in the Tax Rate text box, either by selecting the cell and typing in a value or by using the spinner buttons.
- Click the Sell Assets button to display the Finance Analysis worksheet and the What If I Sell Plant, Property, or Equipment? dialog box. Enter the details for the item in the dialog box and click the OK button to have Financial Manager enter them in the worksheet.

- Click the Add a Loan button to display the Finance Analysis worksheet and the What If I Take Out a New Loan? dialog box. Enter the details for the putative loan in the dialog box and click the OK button to have Financial Manager add the loan to the mix. Click the Payment Schedule button to view the Payment Schedule worksheet (return by clicking the Go Back button), or click the What-If Overview button to return to the What-If Overview worksheet.

- Click the Pay Back Loan button to display the Finance Analysis worksheet and the What if I Pay Back and Remove All, or Part of a Loan? dialog box. Enter the details for the loan and its repayment in the dialog box and click the OK button to have Financial Manager factor in this information. If you do not have enough cash on hand to pay back the loan, Financial Manager will warn you and ask you how you want to proceed. Usually, you'll want to adjust your payment schedule to fit your pocketbook. Click the Payment Schedule button to view the Payment Schedule worksheet (return by clicking the Go Back button), or click the What-If Overview button to return to the What-If Overview worksheet.

- Click the Buy vs. Lease button to start the Analyze Buy versus Lease Wizard. In the first dialog box, enter the details of the asset and click the Next button. In the second dialog box, enter the data for buying the item with a loan and click the Next button. In the third dialog box, enter the data for leasing the item and click the Finish button. Financial Manager will display a Lease Analysis for the item showing you how the lease, purchase with loan, and purchase with cash compare. You can click any of the buttons in the worksheet to adjust the values they refer to.

Most of the supporting worksheets provide several common buttons:

What-If Overview   Returns to the What-If Overview worksheet. Financial Manager will select the check box for the item you worked with to indicate that the data it contains will be factored in, and will darken the cell around the check box. You can exclude this item by deselecting its check box; the cell will remain darkened to indicate that information is available.

Restore Actuals   Displays the Display Actual Values dialog box, which lets you restore the actual values to the whole worksheet or to selected items (replacing what-if values you've used). Click the OK button to proceed.

Calculator   Displays the Windows Calculator so that you can quickly perform calculations.

Help   Displays context-sensitive help for the worksheet.

When you've finished working in your what-if scenario, save your changes as necessary and close the workbook as normal.

Updating Your Accounting Data

Depending on the nature of your business, you may need to update the accounting data you put into Financial Manager frequently. For example, if you're working with financial results or sales figures, you might want to update the data once a month, once a week, or even every time you open Financial Manager.

To update your accounting data, choose Accounting ➤ Import Wizard and select the Update Existing Accounting Data option button in the first Import Your Accounting Data dialog box. Then follow the Wizard's instructions to update your data.

Part 5

Publisher

Chapter 19

GETTING STARTED WITH PUBLISHER

FEATURING

- **Understanding what Publisher is and what it does**
- **Navigating the Publisher interface**
- **Creating, saving, and opening publications**
- **Choosing options for Publisher**

In this chapter, I'll start by discussing what Publisher is and what it does. After that, we'll look at the Publisher interface and its built-in Help application. Finally, we'll look at how to create publications using Publisher's wizards and how to save the results.

What Is Publisher?

Publisher is a full-featured desktop-publishing and Web-publishing application that lets you create professional-looking publications, Web pages, and Web sites with a minimum of effort and fuss.

You can use Publisher to create your own publications from scratch, but if you start trying to do this with no instruction or experience, chances are you'll be forcefully reminded why design professionals can command salaries inflated enough to put management consultants to shame: It's very easy to design something so unattractive that nobody will look at it, let alone read it. (If you doubt this, check out the signs for lost cats and garage sales in your neighborhood this weekend.)

To help you avoid such design mishaps, Publisher provides a number of templates driven by PageWizards that guide you through the steps of creating a publication, automating much of the process. Here, I'll assume that you're less interested in enrolling in a design class at your local college than in producing businesslike brochures, flyers, or Web pages. So we'll be approaching Publisher in the easiest possible way—using all the automatic features and help it provides. In the following chapters, I'll show you how to adjust your publications manually. Let's begin by starting Publisher and then examining its interface.

Starting Publisher

To start Publisher, choose Start ➤ Programs ➤ Microsoft Publisher, or click any shortcut for Publisher that you've created on your Desktop.

The first time you start Publisher, you'll see the Introduction to Publisher dialog box, which provides a brief, 11-screen overview of what Publisher is and what you can do with it. Click the Next button to move forward through the series of dialog boxes, and click the Close button to close the final dialog box when you've finished viewing it. (Alternatively, click the Cancel button to dismiss the Introduction to Publisher without viewing it.)

NOTE   **If Publisher has already been run on the computer you're using, you can choose Help ➤ Introduction to Publisher to display the Introduction to Publisher: What Would You Like to See? dialog box, then choose the Introduction to Publisher option button and click the OK button to run the Introduction to Publisher.**

Once you've finished with the Introduction to Publisher, Publisher will display the Startup dialog box, offering you a choice of templates and wizards. For the moment, click the Cancel button to dismiss the Startup dialog box so that you can examine the Publisher interface.

> **TIP**
>
> **If you don't want Publisher to display the Startup dialog box when you start it, you can easily turn it off. Choose Tools ➤ Options to display the Options dialog box, clear the Use Startup Dialog Box check box on the General tab, and click the OK button. To turn the display of the Startup dialog box back on, select the Use Startup Dialog Box check box again.**

Working with the Publisher Interface Elements

Once you've started Publisher, watched (or dispensed with) the Introduction to Publisher, and dismissed the Startup dialog box, you should see a screen similar to Figure 19.1.

> **NOTE**
>
> **You'll notice that a publication in Publisher takes up the entire window. You can't work with multiple publications open at the same time in Publisher.**

Working with Toolbars and Rulers

Like the other Office applications, Publisher provides toolbars and rulers to help you work using the mouse. But Publisher offers less flexibility with its toolbars than the other Office 97 applications: You can't alter the toolbars, other than choosing whether to display or hide them, whether to have their buttons display in color, and whether to display large buttons or regular-size ones. Also, you can't get rid of the Publisher toolbar that appears at the left side of the screen.

Rulers

Layout guides

Scratch Area

Menu bar

Standard toolbar

Format toolbar

Publisher toolbar

Previous Page button

First Page button

Change Pages button and text box

Status bar

Next Page button

Last Page button

Select Zoom Mode button and text box

Zoom Out button

Zoom In button

Show Index button

Show Help button

Scroll bars

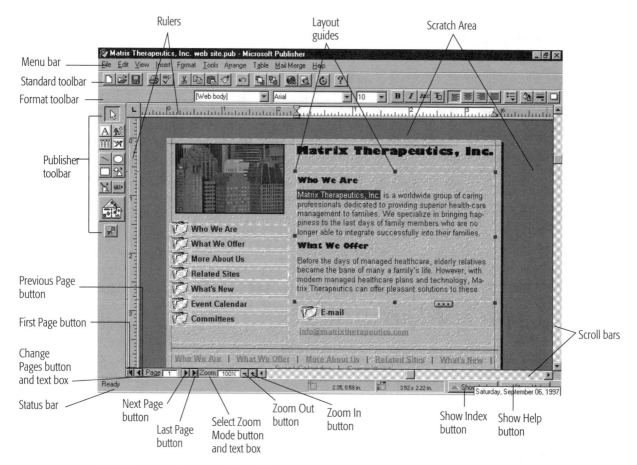

FIGURE 19.1: Elements of the Publisher screen

Displaying the Toolbars and Ruler

By default, Publisher displays the Standard toolbar and Format toolbar and the horizontal and vertical rulers. The Standard toolbar contains buttons for regular operations such as Open, Save, and Print; Cut, Copy, and Paste; and so on. The Format toolbar contains buttons for formatting the currently selected object. If a particular button does not apply to the current object, Publisher will not display it. With no objects selected in a publication, you'll see no buttons at all on the Format toolbar, which can be initially disconcerting.

To change the display of the toolbars and rulers, choose View ➤ Toolbars and Rulers to display the Toolbars and Rulers dialog box. Select the check boxes for the items you want to display and the options you want to have active, and clear the check boxes for the items you want to hide and the options you want to have inactive.

Then click the OK button to close the Toolbars and Rulers dialog box. (Alternatively, right-click in a toolbar and select or deselect Standard Toolbar, Format Toolbar, Rulers, or Status Line from the context menu.)

Using the Toolbars

Most of the buttons on Publisher's Standard toolbar need little or no introduction (see Figure 19.2). I will explain the function of four buttons:

- The Bring to Front button and Send to Back button are used for manipulating layers of objects. (See "Working with Layered Objects" in Chapter 20.)
- The Rotate button displays the Rotate Objects dialog box, which you use to adjust the rotation of an object. (See "Rotating an Object" in Chapter 20.)
- The Help button displays the last-used Help topic. (See "Getting Help in Publisher," later in this chapter.)

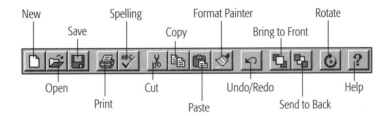

FIGURE 19.2:   Publisher's Standard toolbar provides file-management and editing tools.

Publisher's Format toolbar displays only buttons relevant to the current object, so you'll see several different variations of the Format toolbar.

The Format Toolbar for Text Objects   Figure 19.3 shows the Format toolbar you'll see when a text object is selected. You'll find most of the buttons familiar from the other Office applications, but note the following:

- The Bulleted or Numbered List button displays a drop-down list of bullet styles. You can click the More item at the bottom of the list to display the Indents and Lists dialog box, which offers a full range of indentation formats, bulleted lists, and numbered lists.
- The Object Color button displays a drop-down palette of colors that you can apply to the current object. You can click the More Colors button to display the Colors dialog box, which provides a fuller set of colors, or the Patterns and Shading button to display the Fill Patterns and Shading dialog box, which offers a variety of tints and shades, patterns, and gradients.

- The Border button displays a drop-down list of borders. You can select from the list or click the More item to display the BorderArt dialog box, which offers line borders and decorative borders made of objects such as gingerbread men or baby pacifiers.
- The Add/Remove Shadow button adds or removes a drop shadow to or from the current object.

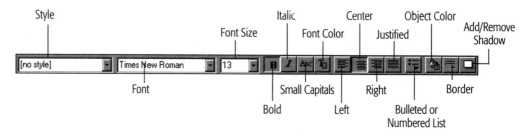

FIGURE 19.3: With a text object selected, you'll see this Format toolbar.

The Format Toolbar for Graphical Objects   With a graphical object (for example, a custom shape) selected, you'll see the Format toolbar shown in Figure 19.4, which offers the following different buttons:

- The Flip Horizontal button flips the object horizontally about its midpoint.
- The Flip Vertical button flips the object vertically about its midpoint.
- The Rotate Right button rotates the object clockwise in 90-degree increments.
- The Rotate Left button rotates the object counterclockwise in 90-degree increments.

NOTE   **The Rotate Right and Rotate Left buttons appear for pictures as well as graphical objects, but the Flip Horizontal and Flip Vertical buttons do not appear for pictures.**

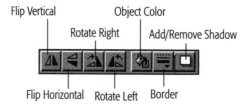

FIGURE 19.4: These buttons appear on the Format toolbar when you have a graphical object selected.

The Toolbar for Frames, Shapes, and Other Design Elements   The toolbar along the left side of the Publisher screen (see Figure 19.5) offers tools for creating frames, lines, and shapes; for invoking the PageWizards; inserting OLE objects; and displaying the Design Gallery. We'll look at how to use these features in the next chapter.

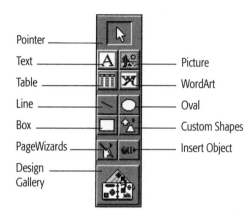

Pointer

Text — Picture

Table — WordArt

Line — Oval

Box — Custom Shapes

PageWizards — Insert Object

Design
Gallery

FIGURE 19.5:   Use the tools on the left-hand toolbar to create frames..

Zooming the View

To zoom the view, click the Select Zoom Mode button or the Zoom indicator box to the left of the horizontal scroll bar to display the pop-up menu, then choose the type of view or zoom percentage you want. Publisher offers zoom percentages from 10% to 400%, together with an Actual Size view and a Full Page view.

If you have one or more objects selected, Publisher will also offer a Zoom to Selection option. This zooms the view to the largest zoom percentage that will display the selected object or objects in the available space in the Publisher window.

You can quickly zoom the view to the previous or next preset zoom percentage by clicking the – and + buttons to the right of the Zoom indicator box. For example, if the current zoom percentage is 50% and you click the + button, Publisher will zoom the view to 66%, the next larger preset zoom percentage; if you click the – button, Publisher will zoom the view to 33%, the next smaller preset zoom percentage.

TIP   **You can press the F9 key to toggle between the current view and Actual Size (100%) view. This is useful for toggling between a full page to position a text box, for example, and a zoom view, so that you can read or edit the text that the text box contains.**

Getting Help in Publisher

Publisher includes a full-featured built-in Help application that works differently from the Help in other Office applications.

To show the top level of Help, choose Help ➤ Microsoft Publisher Help Topics. Publisher will display Help as a panel at the right side of the Publisher window. Click on the topic you want to view, and follow the subtopics until you reach the information you want. In the Help panel, Publisher will display a How To tab; if more information is available, Publisher will also display a More Info tab containing additional information. Click the < button at the bottom of the Help panel to move back to the previous level of Help, and click the Contents button to get back to the top level of Help.

To search for help on a specific topic, you work with the Help Index (see Figure 19.6). To display the Help Index, click the Show Index button on the status bar, choose Help ➤ Show Index, or press Ctrl+F1. Then, in the 1 Type a Keyword text box, start typing the keyword you want to look up. Help will scroll to display entries starting with the letters you type. In the main list box, click the appropriate topic to display it in the How To panel.

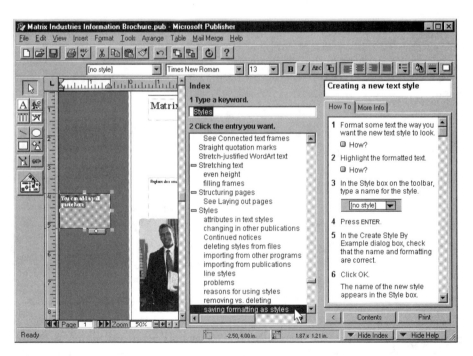

FIGURE 19.6:   Use the Help Index to search for specific help topics.

To display the last help topic again, click the Help button on the Standard toolbar or the Show Help button on the status bar, choose Help ➤ Last Help Topic, or press Shift+F1. To adjust the size of the text in the Help panel, choose Help ➤ Help Text Size and choose Smaller, Normal, or Bigger from the submenu.

To hide the Help Index again, click the Hide Index button on the status bar. To hide Help, click the Help button again, or choose Help ➤ Hide Help, or click the Hide Help button on the status bar.

Creating a Publication

You can create a publication with Publisher in several ways:

- Publisher provides a team of PageWizards to help you design publications. You can quickly create even complex publications, with the assurance that the elements will work together.
- You can create a blank page of a shape and size that suit you by choosing File ➤ Create New Publication to display the Publisher 97 dialog box, clicking the Blank Page tab, and choosing the type of publication from it.
- You can create a new, blank page of the default size and shape by clicking the New button on the Standard toolbar.
- You can create a custom type of publication, either as a one-time piece or as a template on which you can then base future publications, by choosing File ➤ Create New Publication to display the Publisher 97 dialog box, then clicking the Custom Page button.

The easiest way to create publications is with Publisher's PageWizards. However, if you need to create a number of publications that follow the same design and content, your best bet is to create a custom template and base the publications on it. Both of these methods are described in the following sections.

Using the PageWizards

To create a new publication with Publisher's PageWizards:

1. Choose File ➤ Create New Publication to display the Publisher 97 dialog box.
2. If the PageWizard tab isn't displayed, click the tab to display it.
3. Select the type of publication you want to create (scroll to see items further down the list box) and click the OK button. Publisher will start up the appropriate PageWizard. For example, if you select the Newsletter item, Publisher will display the first Newsletter PageWizard Design Assistant dialog box (see Figure 19.7).

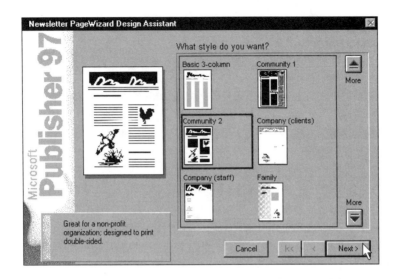

FIGURE 19.7:
Use the PageWizard Design Assistants to quickly put together a publication using Publisher's templates.

4. Choose the appropriate option or options in the first PageWizard Design Assistant dialog box and click the Next button to move to the next dialog box.

5. In the second and subsequent dialog boxes, select options as appropriate and click the Next button to proceed. If you need to move back, you can click the < button to return to the previous dialog box or the << button to return to the first dialog box.

6. In the final dialog box, click the Create It! button to have the PageWizard create the publication you've chosen. Publisher will display a Creating Your Publication dialog box that shows you the PageWizard's progress, and then display the publication.

Creating a Custom Page Layout

If none of the blank pages that Publisher provides are suitable for the publication you want to create, you can create a custom page layout:

1. Choose File ➤ Create New Publication to display the Publisher 97 dialog box, select the Blank Page tab if it isn't already displayed, and then select the Custom Page button to display the Page Setup dialog box (see Figure 19.8).

2. In the Choose a Publication Layout group box, select the layout for the publication: Normal, Special Fold (for folded publications such as brochures or menus), Special Size (for custom sizes of paper), or Labels. The rest of the Page Setup dialog box will change to display the appropriate set of options.

3. Choose options for the publication (for example, for Special Fold publications, you get to choose the type of fold, the width and height of the publication, and the orientation of the paper) and click the OK button.

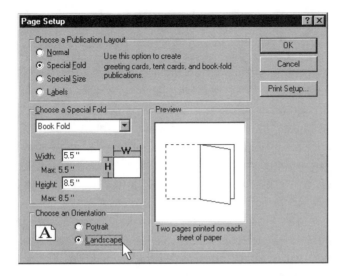

FIGURE 19.8:
In the Page Setup dialog box, enter the specifications for the type of page you want to create.

4. If your publication requires multiple pages, Publisher will prompt you to automatically insert more pages. Click the Yes button to have Publisher insert the correct number of pages automatically.

You can now work with the publication. If you want to save it as a template so that you can reuse it, when you save the publication (as described in the next section), select the Template check box in the Save As dialog box.

Saving and Closing a Publication

In Publisher, you save publications using the standard Windows techniques discussed in Chapter 2:

- To save a publication, click the Save button on the Standard toolbar, choose File ➤ Save, or press Ctrl+S. When saving a publication for the first time, enter the name and choose the folder in the Save As dialog box, and then click the OK button.
- To save a publication under a different name, choose File ➤ Save As, specify the name and folder in the Save As dialog box, and click the OK button.

Publisher offers the following options when you're saving a publication:

- To save all the text in a publication as a separate file (for example, so that you can work with it in another application), select the Save All Text as File check box and choose the file type you want in the Save as Type drop-down list.
- To save a preview of the publication, select the Save Preview check box. A preview—a miniature picture of the beginning of the publication—lets you

quickly identify a publication on the Existing Publication tab of the Publisher 97 dialog box without opening it. This option becomes unavailable when you select the Save All Text as File check box.

- To save the current publication as a template—a design on which you can base other publications—select the Template check box. For example, if you create a Web page that you can use to display different information by filling in a few fields of text, you might want to make it into a template so that you could quickly create other Web pages based on the same design.

The Save As dialog box also contains a Backup check box, which you can select to create a backup copy of the publication the second or subsequent time you save it. Use this option in case something goes wrong with the current version. For example, you might delete the current version by mistake or make ill-advised changes to it, or it might become corrupted by a power problem. In each case, you would probably want to revert to the backup version of the file. Here's how it works: The first time you save a publication, Publisher saves it under the name specified. The second time you save the publication, Publisher renames the previously saved version to "Backup of" and the file name, and saves the new version under the original file name. For example, suppose you save a publication under the name Industry Trends.pub. The first time you save it, Publisher creates a file with that name. The second time you save it, Publisher renames Industry Trends.pub to Backup of Industry Trends.pub and then saves the second version under the name Industry Trends.pub. When you save it after that, Publisher renames the version on disk to Backup of Industry Trends.pub (discarding the current file with that name) and saves the current version as Industry Trends.pub.

TIP If you make backups to protect your Publisher publications from computer accidents, you'll probably want to make sure that your backup files are as up-to-date as possible. To do so, when you save a publication, save it twice in rapid succession. On the other hand, if you want to be able to revert to the backup if your make a disastrous mistake in your work on the current version, you'll probably want to save conventionally—once at a time.

By default, Publisher reminds you to save your work every 15 minutes that pass without your saving it. You can turn off the reminder by clearing the Remind to Save Publications check box on the Editing and User Assistance tab of the Options dialog box (choose Tools ➤ Options to display this dialog box), as discussed in "Choosing Options for Publisher" later in this chapter.

To close a publication, choose File ➤ Close Publication. If the publication contains unsaved changes, Publisher will prompt you to save them; choose Yes or No. Publisher will then close the publication and will open a new, blank publication.

Opening a Publication

Publisher adds a wrinkle to the regular Office procedure for opening a file. To open a publication you've worked with recently, choose File ➤ Open Existing Publication to display the Existing Publication tab of the Publisher 97 dialog box. Choose the publication from the Most Recently Used Files list box (which lists only recently used Publisher files, not those from other applications) or from the list of files in the Files list box, which lists Publisher files located in your Publisher folder. Then click the OK button.

If neither the Most Recently Used Files list box nor the Files list box contains the publication you want to open, click the Click Here to Open a Publication Not Listed Above button to display the Open Publication dialog box.

You can also open a publication in the usual way: click the Open button on the Standard toolbar or press Ctrl+O to display the Open Publication dialog box, then select the file to open and click the Open button.

Finding a Publication

Publisher also provides a different Find File dialog box for finding publications you've lost. To find a publication:

1. Choose File ➤ Find File, or click the Find File button in the Open Publication dialog box, to display the Find File dialog box.
2. In the Search Options group box, leave the Find All Files of This Type option button selected if you want to find all Publisher files, or select the Find This File option button and enter the file name to find in the text box.
3. In the Search on Drive drop-down list, select the drive on which to search. Select the All Drives option to search on all currently connected drives.
4. Click the Start Search button to begin the search. Publisher will display the files found in the Files Found list box.
5. Select the file you want in the Files Found list box. Click the Preview button to display a preview of the file, or click the Open File button to open the file.

Choosing Options for Publisher

Publisher offers a number of options that you can use to customize its interface and its behavior. Choose Tools ➤ Options to open the Options dialog box.

General Options

The following options are on the General tab of the Options dialog box:

- The Start with Page text box lets you specify a starting page number for the publication. For example, if you needed to start the second chapter of a book at page 20, you could enter 20 in the Start with Page text box.
- The Measurement Units drop-down list lets you choose Inches, Centimeters, Picas, or Points for the ruler and the measurement features. (As you may remember from Chapter 6, points and picas are typesetting measurement units: A point is $\frac{1}{72}$ inch, and a pica is 12 points, or $\frac{1}{6}$ inch.)
- The "Greek" Small Text check box controls whether Publisher displays gray bars in place of text in fonts smaller than 7 points at zoom factors that make the text too small to read on screen. Displaying the gray bars lets Publisher update the screen more quickly, giving better performance, for example, when you move the view to a different part of the publication. (Technically, "greeking" means using rubbish text in bastardized Latin to show how text in a design will look.)
- The Preview Fonts in Font Lists check box controls whether Publisher displays the font names in the Font drop-down menu and other font lists in their fonts rather than in the Windows system font. On a slow computer, or on a computer with a minimal amount of memory, previewing the fonts may result in slow performance, so you may want to turn the preview off. Also, symbol fonts, such as Wingdings and Transport MT, will appear as symbols, so it's difficult to work out their names (except by guessing from where they appear in the alphabetical list of fonts).
- The Use Startup Dialog Box check box controls whether Publisher displays the Publisher 97 Startup dialog box when you start the application.
- The Print with Print Troubleshooter check box controls whether Publisher runs the Print Troubleshooter each time you print. The Print Troubleshooter slows down printing a bit, but it can save you a great deal of frustration by helping you avoid printing problems.

- The Preview Web site with Preview Troubleshooter check box controls whether Publisher runs the Preview Troubleshooter after you preview a Web site. The Preview Troubleshooter helps you resolve problems that you identify when previewing a Web site. (We'll look at creating and previewing Web sites in Chapter 21.)
- The Improve Screen and Printer Color Matching check box controls whether Publisher attempts to match the colors you see on screen more closely with the colors you'll see in your printouts.
- The Single-Click Object Creation check box controls the behavior of the tools in the Publisher toolbar. When this check box is selected, you can click in a publication to create a standard-sized object of the type selected in the Publisher toolbar. When this check box is cleared, you click in a publication and drag to the size you want the object to be. (When the check box is selected, you can still click and drag to the size of object you want to create, but you have the single-click, standard-size option as well.)
- The Show Rectangle for Text in Web Graphic Region check box controls whether Publisher displays a warning rectangle when you create a text frame in an area where it will be interpreted as a graphic on the resulting Web page. (Text frames that overlap with graphics or that appear very close to graphics are treated as graphics, which means that they will download slowly on a Web page, rather than appearing rapidly as straight text does.)
- The Use Helpful Pointers check box controls whether Publisher displays different mouse pointers when you move the mouse pointer over different objects. For example, when you move the mouse pointer over a sizing handle, Publisher changes the mouse pointer into a Resize pointer. Use Helpful Pointers is a useful feature, but it may slow down an underpowered computer.

Editing and User Assistance Options

On the Editing and User Assistance tab of the Options dialog box, Publisher offers options for text editing, hyphenation, and user assistance. The four text-editing options will be familiar if you've worked with Word:

- The Typing Replaces Selection check box controls whether any current selection is overwritten when you start typing. If the check box is selected, Publisher overwrites the selection with what you type; if the check box is cleared, Publisher deselects the selection, positions the insertion point at the beginning of the selection, and inserts what you type.

- The Automatically Use Smart Quotes check box controls whether Publisher automatically inserts smart quotes (curved quotation marks: " " and ' ') when you type straight quotation marks (" and ').
- The Drag-and-Drop Text Editing check box controls whether you can drag and drop text to move it in your publications. In general, this feature is useful, but it may slow down an underpowered computer.
- The Kern Character Pairs Above text box lets you specify the font size above which you want Publisher to adjust the kerning of pairs of characters. The default setting is 15 points, above which the spacing between letters may need adjustment.

Publisher's hyphenation options will also seem familiar if you've worked with Word:

- The Automatically Hyphenate by Default check box lets you choose whether to have Publisher automatically hyphenate your publications. (You can override automatic hyphenation manually if you wish.)
- The Hyphenation Zone text box lets you specify the width of the area at the right margin in which Publisher will automatically hyphenate words. The default setting is 0.25", which works well for columns of a moderate width. For narrow columns, you'll probably want to reduce the hyphenation zone.

Publisher's user-assistance options are as follows:

- The Show Tippages and First-Time Help check box controls whether Publisher offers advice and demonstrations of features the first time you access them. When you're starting to use Publisher, you may find these helpful; if you already know your way around Publisher, or prefer to find your own way without help, you may find them irritating.

TIP Publisher tracks your use of features and tries not to offer you help on the same feature twice. You can reset Publisher's record of your use of features by clicking the Reset All button. You might want to reset the record, for example, if you know someone new to Publisher will be using it instead of you.

- The Remind to Save Publications check box and its associated Every *XXX* Minutes text box control whether Publisher prompts you to save your work regularly when you don't do so. You can enter any value between 1 minute and 999 minutes in the Every *XXX* Minutes box; an interval between 10 and 30 minutes for this reminder is practical if you elect to leave this feature turned on.

Making Publisher Run Faster

If Publisher runs slowly on your computer, there are a couple of things you can try to speed it up.

First, clear the check boxes for those options (in the Options dialog box) that can slow down a computer: Preview Fonts in Font Lists, Use Helpful Pointers, Drag-and-Drop Text Editing, and Automatically Hyphenate by Default. Then turn on the "Greek" Small Text option, which helps speed things up a bit.

Second, choose View ➤ Picture Display to display the Picture Display dialog box. Select the Fast Resize and Zoom option button to have Publisher resize and zoom pictures with lower detail. (This is primarily useful for working with large or complex graphics.) Alternatively, select the Hide Pictures option button to have Publisher suppress the display of all pictures and graphical objects in your publication. You'll see only the frames for the pictures and graphics objects—no pictures at all—but the screen will redraw much faster; and when you print, the pictures will print as normal. This option is most useful for checking the flow of text in a publication.

Chapter 20

WORKING IN PUBLICATIONS

- **Inserting and deleting pages**
- **Working with objects**
- **Adding and manipulating text**
- **Inserting tables**
- **Working with pictures, WordArt, and shapes**
- **Printing your publications**

In this chapter, I'll discuss the actions you're most likely to take regularly in Publisher. These include inserting and deleting pages, arranging and sizing objects, and working with common publication elements: text, pictures, and tables. I'll also explain how to create WordArt and use the Design Gallery and Design Checker. Finally, I'll show you how to print your publications.

> **NOTE** In Publisher, you use *frames* to position elements. Each type of element has its own type of frame: Text goes in a text frame, text (or other items) in a table goes in a table frame, WordArt objects go in WordArt frames, and pictures go in picture frames. To create a frame, you use the appropriate tool on the left-hand toolbar in the Publisher window, as described in this chapter.

Working with Pages

Your publications consist of one or more pages, and Publisher provides tools for working with them. You can insert and remove pages, design a page's foreground and background, and add guides to your pages.

Inserting and Deleting Pages

To insert one or more pages in the current publication:

1. Choose Insert ➤ Page to display the Insert Page dialog box (see Figure 20.1).

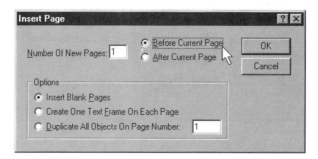

FIGURE 20.1:
Use the Insert Page dialog box to insert one or more pages in your publication.

2. In the Number of New Pages text box, enter the number of pages you want to insert. If you want to insert the new page or pages before the current page, select the Before Current Page option button; otherwise, leave the After Current Page option button selected.

3. In the Options group box, you can choose to insert blank pages (the default), create one text frame on each page, or duplicate all objects on a page of your choice. Duplicating objects on a particular page is useful for quickly adding pages to a publication that uses a standard layout on each page.

4. Click the OK button to insert the page or pages.

To delete the current page, choose Edit ➤ Delete Page. If you're viewing a two-page spread, Publisher will warn you and will suggest that you delete two pages instead to prevent text from moving from a right-hand page to a left-hand page. Click the OK button to delete the page.

The Foreground and the Background

Publisher considers a publication to have a foreground and a background. The background contains information that appears on each page, and it is overlaid by the foreground, which contains the information on a particular page. To have an object appear on each page, you place it in the background. (This is similar to using headers and footers in Word, as discussed in Chapter 7, but the background provides more flexibility than the header and footer area.)

To work with the background, display it by choosing View ➤ Go to Background or pressing Ctrl+M. You can then adjust the background as necessary—for example, by inserting frames or graphics. When you're finished, choose View ➤ Go to Foreground or press Ctrl+M again.

When the background is displayed, Publisher replaces the page controls on the status bar with a background symbol to the left of the Zoom button, as shown here. (For facing-page designs, Publisher displays a left background page symbol and a right background page symbol.)

TIP **You can suppress the background for a selected page by choosing View ➤ Ignore Background. The background for that page will not display on the screen, and will not appear when you print the publication.**

Using Layout Guides and Ruler Guides

To help you lay out your publications, Publisher provides on-screen layout guides and ruler guides that you can use to align objects horizontally or vertically.

Layout Guides

Publisher's layout guides serve as a visual reference for when you're placing objects manually, and they also do some of the work for you—Publisher will automatically snap an object to a layout guide when you bring the object close to the guide.

When you start a new publication, you'll see margin guides, which are the pink and blue dotted lines around the page. By default, Publisher places these margin guides one inch from the edge of 8½ × 11-inch paper, but you can move them to positions that suit your publication better.

You can change the position of layout guides by entering measurements in the Layout Guide dialog box or by going to the background and dragging them. Both of these methods are explained here.

To adjust the placement of layout guides using measurements:

1.   Choose Arrange ➤ Layout Guides to display the Layout Guides dialog box.
2.   In the Margin Guides group box, use the Left, Right, Top, and Bottom text boxes to specify the placement of the margin guides from the edge of the page.
3.   In the Grid Guides group box, use the Columns and Rows text boxes to specify how many columns and rows you want to divide the page into.
4.   If your design involves two-page spreads that have different inside and outside margins, select the Create Two Backgrounds with Mirror Guides check box to have Publisher create facing-page guides.
5.   Click the OK button to apply your choices.

To adjust layout guides quickly and visually, display the background by choosing View ➤ Go to Background. Then move the mouse pointer over a guide, hold down the Shift key to display the Adjust mouse pointer, and drag the guide to where you want it. Choose View ➤ Go to Foreground when you're finished working in the background.

Ruler Guides

Publisher's ruler guides help you with horizontal and vertical object alignment. To display a ruler guide, move the mouse pointer over one of the rulers (the horizontal ruler for a vertical ruler guide, and the vertical ruler for a horizontal ruler guide) and hold down the Shift key so that the mouse pointer changes into an Adjust pointer. Then drag a ruler guide out to where you want it. It will appear as a green line on the Publisher page. When you drag objects near the ruler guide, they will snap into place.

To move a ruler guide, move the mouse pointer over it and hold down the Shift key to display an Adjust pointer. Then click and drag the guide to where you want it. To get rid of a ruler guide, drag it off the page and drop it on the workspace.

NOTE   To hide layout guides and ruler guides, choose View ➤ Hide Boundaries and Guides. To display them again, choose View ➤ Show Boundaries and Guides.

Working with Objects

Publisher provides a variety of ways to work with objects on a page. You can layer objects and place them precisely how you want them to appear on the page.

Layering Objects

In either the foreground or the background, you can layer objects, placing them on top of each other. This allows you to create complex effects, to present more information in a smaller area, or to make your publications exceptionally difficult to decipher. For example, you could put a graphic behind a table to add visual appeal, but doing so might make the text in the table harder to read. Alternatively, you could layer several graphical objects so that they appeared to work together as one object.

To layer objects, place them on top of each other by dragging them to the appropriate position. You will then see the objects in the lower layers through (or past) the topmost objects.

To arrange layers of objects, you use the Bring to Front, Bring Closer, Send Farther, and Send to Back commands on the Arrange menu, or the Send to Back button and Bring to Front button (shown here, from right to left) on the Format toolbar. Select the object and issue the appropriate command. In complex arrangements, you may need to send the uppermost objects to the back in order to select an object midway down the layers, then bring the other objects forward again when you've finished working with the object.

To display the layer under an object, you can make the object transparent by pressing Ctrl+T. This is especially useful for text frames that you place on top of graphical objects. By making the text frame transparent, you can have the text appear to float on the object (rather than appearing in a rectangular text frame that shows against the object). Press Ctrl+T again if you need to toggle the transparency off.

Lining Up Objects

To line up objects quickly, select them and choose Arrange ➤ Line Up Objects to display the Line Up Objects dialog box. In the Left to Right group box or the Top to Bottom group box, select the way that you want the objects to line up. For example, you might choose No Change in the Left to Right group box and Top Edges in the Top to Bottom group box to have Publisher line up the objects by their top edges. To have Publisher align the objects along the margin, select the Align Along Margin check box. Then click the OK button to apply your choices and close the Line Up Objects dialog box.

Moving an Object

To move a selected object, move the mouse pointer over it (or over its border) so that Publisher displays the Move mouse pointer, then click and drag the object to where you want it. To move the object to another page, drag it off the source page and onto the scratch area outside the page (the gray area that surrounds the page), then display the destination page and drag the object from the scratch area onto it.

If you need to move an object just a tiny amount, use the Nudge command. Select the object, hold down the Alt key, and press the appropriate arrow key. For example, to move a selected object down a fraction, press Alt+↓. You can also select the object, choose Arrange ➤ Nudge Objects to display the Nudge Objects dialog box, and use the controls to nudge the object. Select the Nudge By check box and adjust the increment by which to nudge the object in the text box. Click the Close button to close the Nudge Objects dialog box when you've positioned the object where you want it.

Resizing an Object

To resize a selected object visually, move the mouse pointer over one of its handles so that it becomes a Resize pointer. Then click and drag the handle to resize the object. Drag a side handle to resize the object only in that dimension; drag a corner handle to resize the object in both dimensions.

You can also resize a object proportionally and about its midpoint:

- To resize a object proportionally, hold down Shift as you drag a corner handle.
- To resize a object about its midpoint, hold down Ctrl as you drag the handle.
- To resize a object proportionally about its midpoint, hold down Ctrl and Shift as you drag a corner handle.

Rotating an Object

To rotate an object, click the Rotate button on the Standard toolbar to display the Rotate Objects dialog box. Then click either the counterclockwise button or the clockwise button to rotate the object in five-degree increments, or enter an angle in the Angle box, and click the Close button. (To restore a rotated object to zero rotation, click the No Rotation button in the Rotate Objects dialog box.)

You can also rotate a selected object manually by moving the mouse pointer over one of the object's handles, holding down the Alt key, and dragging clockwise or counterclockwise.

Grouping Objects

If you need to keep several objects together while working on them, you can group them. To group objects, select the first object, then hold down the Shift key and click each object you want to have in the group. (If the objects are adjacent to one another, you can click the Pointer button on the Publisher toolbar and drag a rectangle around them instead.) Then click the Group Objects button that Publisher displays below the last object you selected or below the rectangle you dragged. You can now work with these objects as if they were a single object.

To ungroup objects, select the group and then click the Ungroup Objects button that Publisher displays.

Adding an OLE Object

Along with inserting graphics in your publications, you can also insert other OLE objects. For example, you might want to insert a chart or an equation in a math publication. To do so, click the Insert Object button on the Publisher toolbar  and choose More from the context menu to display the Insert Object dialog box, then insert the object as discussed in Chapter 4 (see the "Embedding" section).

Working with Text

Before you type any text into a publication, you need to place a text frame for it. Click the Text button on the Publisher toolbar, then click in your publication and drag to place and size the frame (or click once to place a standard-size frame).

To add content to a text frame you've placed, start typing with the insertion point in the frame. Lines of text will wrap automatically at the right edge of the frame. Once the text reaches the bottom of the frame, it will disappear from view into the overflow area. You can continue to add text, but you won't be able to see more of it than will fit in the frame. If necessary, you can connect other text frames to display this text (see "Connecting Text Frames" a little later in this chapter).

As long as you can see all the content in a text frame, the Connect Frame button below the frame shows a white diamond (as shown here, on the left). When a frame contains more text than it can display, the Connect Frame button displays three dots (an ellipsis), as shown here on the right.

TIP You can work with the text in Publisher's text frames using most of the same editing and navigation techniques as you use in Word. For example, you can double-click to select a word, press Ctrl+, to move to the beginning of the next paragraph, and use drag-and-drop to move or copy text.

Importing Text

Typing and editing text in Publisher is straightforward, but you may want to bring in text from other sources as well. Publisher can import text from Word for Windows versions 2 through 97, Microsoft Works 3.0 for Windows, Microsoft Write, WordPerfect versions 5.0, 5.1, and 6.0, text (.TXT), and rich-text format (.RTF).

To import text, right-click in a text frame and choose Insert Text File from the context menu, or select a text frame and choose Insert ➤ Text File, to display the Insert Text File dialog box. Select the file you want and click the OK button to import it.

If the text you imported does not fit into the frame you specified, Publisher will ask if you want it to automatically flow the text through your publication. If you choose the Yes button, Publisher will check with you before using existing text frames, and will insert extra text frames and extra pages as needed to contain the text. Alternatively, you can choose the No button if you want to connect the frames yourself.

Connecting Text Frames

By connecting text frames, you can have text flow from one text frame to another text frame, on the same page or on another page, so that you don't need to break up an item (such as the article or feature) into a number of different segments, one for each frame.

 To connect one text frame to another, click the Connect Frame button on the first frame. Publisher will change the mouse pointer to a pitcher overflowing with text, as shown here. Then click the next frame in the sequence to connect the text to it. Publisher will automatically flow the text from the end of the first frame into the second frame.

When a frame is connected to another frame, Publisher displays a chain symbol on the Connect Frame button to indicate the connection and one or more Frame Jump buttons (each with an arrow pointing forward or back, as appropriate). Click the Connect Frame button to break the connections to the current frame. Click the Frame Jump button to move to the next or previous connected frame. Figure 20.2 shows a text frame connected to a frame before it and a frame after it.

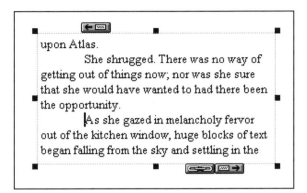

FIGURE 20.2:
Publisher displays a chain symbol on the Connect Frame button to indicate that a text frame is connected to another text frame, and Frame Jump buttons to indicate the direction of the connected text frame or frames.

To add a *Continued on* or *Continued from* notice to a linked frame, right-click the frame and choose Text Frame Properties from the context menu to display the Text Frame Properties dialog box. In the Options group box, select the Include "Continued On Page" check box and the Include "Continued From Page" check box as appropriate, then click the OK button. You can edit the resulting *Continued on* and *Continued from* notices in the text frame as you would other text.

NOTE   The *Continued on* and *Continued from* notices appear only when the next or previous linked frame is on a different page than the current frame. For example, if the previous frame is on the same page as the current frame, the current frame will not display a *Continued on* notice.

Formatting Text

Formatting text in Publisher is very straightforward. Your primary tool is the Format toolbar, discussed in the previous chapter, which offers a full complement of formatting options, including styles.

Using Styles

If you're familiar with Word's styles (discussed in Chapter 7), you'll find Publisher's styles easy to use. Like Word's styles, Publisher's styles contain complete formatting information for a paragraph, and you apply them by using the Style drop-down list on the Format toolbar. You can even use Word styles in Publisher by importing them.

To work with styles (including to import them), choose Format ➤ Text Style to display the Text Styles dialog box (see Figure 20.3).

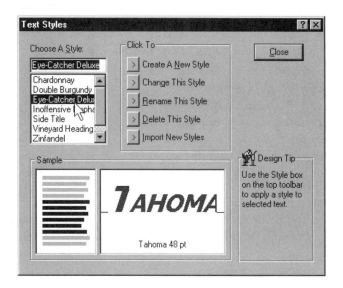

FIGURE 20.3:
The Text Styles dialog box is your headquarters for working with styles in Publisher.

- To create a style, click the Create a New Style button to display the Create New Style dialog box (see Figure 20.4). Type the name for the style into the Enter New Style Name text box, then use the five buttons in the Click to Change group box. Each of these displays a dialog box that lets you set attributes of the style. Use the Sample boxes to judge how the style will look. When you're finished, click the OK button to close the Create New Style dialog box.

- To change a style, select it in the Choose a Style list box in the Text Styles dialog box, then click the Change This Style button to display the Change Style dialog box, which you'll recognize as the Create New Style dialog box in disguise. Modify the style using the five buttons in the Click to Change group box, and click the OK button to close the Change Style dialog box when you're finished.

- To delete a style, select it in the Choose a Style list box and click the Delete This Style button. Publisher will display a confirmation message box; click the Yes button to delete the style.

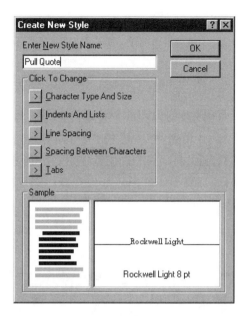

FIGURE 20.4:
Creating a new style
in the Create New
Style dialog box

- To rename a style, select it in the Choose a Style list box and click the Rename This Style button. In the Rename Style dialog box, make sure the correct style is selected in the Rename Style drop-down list box, then enter the new name for the style in the To text box and click the OK button.
- To import styles from another publication, click the Import New Styles button in the Text Styles dialog box. Publisher will open the Import Styles dialog box. Select the document that contains the styles and click the OK button. Publisher will convert the file and will import the styles. If any style name is used in both the current publication and the document from which you're importing styles, Publisher will warn you and will give you the choice of keeping the existing style or overwriting it with the newcomer.

Working with Pictures

Publisher provides a wide array of pictures for enlivening your publications and conveying your message. The Complete installation (which is the default) places many of the pictures on your hard disk, but leaves a reservoir of extra pictures on the CD; so to use the full range of pictures, you'll need to have your CD-ROM loaded when you're using Publisher. Microsoft also makes more pictures available on its Web site, as I'll discuss later in this section. (For information about installing Publisher, see the Appendix.)

Publisher's PageWizards place graphics automatically in your publications, but you can change, move, and resize the graphics as needed, as well as add graphics of your choice wherever you want them.

Inserting or Removing a Picture

To insert a picture:

1. To insert a picture frame where you want the picture to appear, click the Picture button on the Publisher toolbar, then either click once to place a standard-size picture frame or click and drag to place and size the frame.

2. Right-click in the frame and choose Insert Clip Art from the context menu (or select the frame and choose Insert ➤ Clip Art) to display the Microsoft Clip Gallery dialog box (see Figure 20.5).

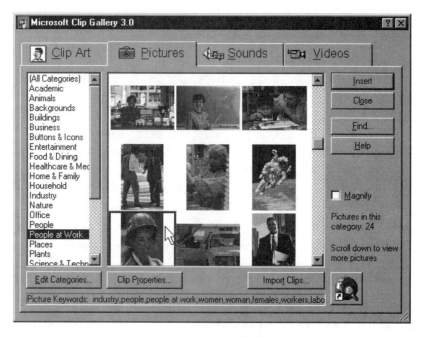

FIGURE 20.5:   In the Microsoft Clip Gallery dialog box, select the picture and click the Insert button.

3. Click the Clip Art tab or the Pictures tab to display it.
4. In the left list box, select the category of picture you want to see.
5. In the right list box, select the picture to insert. You can select the Magnify check box to enlarge the preview slightly and display its file name.

6. Click the Insert button to insert the picture. If the proportions of the frame do not fit the picture, Publisher will display the Import Picture dialog box (see Figure 20.6). By default, Publisher selects the Change the Frame to Fit the Picture option button, which adjusts the frame to the proportions of the picture so that the picture is not cropped or distorted. But you can select the Change the Picture to Fit the Frame option button to have Publisher distort the picture so that it fits exactly in the frame. Then click the OK button to insert the picture.

WARNING The Change the Picture to Fit the Frame option is mostly useful for decorative or artistic effects with abstract images. If you use it on a photograph, it will look horrible.

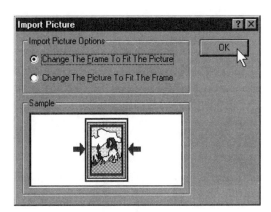

FIGURE 20.6: In the Import Picture dialog box, choose whether to change the frame to fit the picture or the picture to fit the frame.

To get more pictures, click the Connect to Web for Additional Clips button in the lower-right corner of the Microsoft Clip Gallery dialog box. Publisher will launch or activate your Internet connection and Web browser and will connect with the Microsoft Clip Gallery Live Web site. After you accept the End User License Agreement, you can browse and download clips.

To remove a picture from a publication, right-click it and choose Delete Object from the context menu, or select it and press the Delete key.

Resizing a Picture

You can resize a picture by eye, as described in "Resizing an Object" earlier in the chapter. To resize a picture by a specific percentage, right-click the picture and choose

Scale Picture from the context menu to display the Scale Picture dialog box. (For some types of pictures, the menu item and dialog box are named Scale Object rather than Scale Picture.) Enter the percentages in the Scale Height and Scale Width text boxes and click the OK button. To restore a picture to its original size, select the Original Size check box and click the OK button.

Cropping a Picture

By *cropping* a picture, you can hide the parts of it that you don't want to display, or make it fit exactly in a given space. To crop a selected picture, click the Crop Picture button on the Format toolbar, then move the mouse pointer over a picture handle. Publisher will change the mouse pointer to the Cropper (which has the same two overlapping-scissors icon as the Crop Picture button). Click and drag the handle to crop the picture. To crop a picture on two or four sides at once, hold down the Ctrl key as you drag a side handle (for two-sided cropping) or a corner handle (for four-sided cropping). Click the Crop Picture button again when you're finished to restore the mouse pointer.

To uncrop a cropped picture, click the Crop Picture button and drag the appropriate handle.

Replacing a Picture

To replace a picture with another one from the Microsoft Clip Gallery, right-click the picture and choose Microsoft Clip Gallery Object ➤ Replace to display the Microsoft Clip Gallery dialog box (see Figure 20.5). Select the replacement picture and click the Insert button. If the proportions of the frame do not fit the new picture, Publisher will display the Import Picture dialog box (see Figure 20.6) so that you can choose whether to adjust the frame to fit the picture or the picture to fit the frame.

Working with Tables

Publisher makes it easy to add tables to your publications. You can insert formatted or blank tables, type or paste entries into table cells, adjust the rows and columns, and change the margins and borders.

Inserting a Table

To insert a table in your publication:

1. Click the Table button on the Publisher toolbar. The mouse pointer will change to a crosshair.

2. Click once where you want the upper-right corner of the table to appear in the publication, or click and drag to indicate the location and size of the table. Publisher will display the Create Table dialog box (see Figure 20.7).

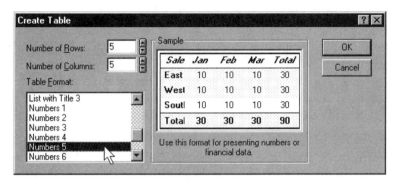

FIGURE 20.7:   Use the Create Table dialog box to quickly create a table.

3. Use the Number of Rows and Number of Columns text boxes to specify the number of rows and columns in the table.
4. In the Table Format list box, select the type of table you want to create. Watch the Sample box to get an idea of how the table will look. Choose the [None] format to create a plain table without special formatting.
5. Click the OK button to have Publisher create the table in the publication.

NOTE   In Publisher, a table cell will automatically expand downward when you enter more material than will fit in the cell. To prevent a table from automatically expanding, select it and choose Table ➤ Grow to Fit Text to remove the check mark from this item. Repeat the procedure to turn Grow to Fit Text back on.

Entering Text in a Table

Enter text in the table as you would in Word. As with Word, you use Tab to move forward cell by cell through a table, and Shift+Tab to move backward, → and ← to move right and left one character, and ↑ and ↓ to move up and down. To select a column, click the column heading; to select a row, click the row heading; and to select the whole table, click the Select Entire Table cell (the junction of the column heading row and the row heading row). In general, you'll find that tables in Publisher work in a very similar way to tables in Word (see Chapter 9).

You can paste in tabular material—a tabbed or comma-separated list, or table cells, from Word; or spreadsheet cells from Excel directly into a Publisher table. To transfer the material, copy it from its source, switch to Publisher, right-click in the upper-right destination cell, and selecting Paste Cells from the context menu.

To quickly fill a number of cells with the contents of an existing cell, select the cell and the cells to its right or below it that you want to fill, then choose Table ➤ Fill Right or Table ➤ Fill Down. Be aware that these commands will overwrite any existing text in your chosen cells.

Working with Rows and Columns

To insert one or more rows or columns, select the cell next to which the new row or rows, or column or columns, should appear, and choose Table ➤ Insert Rows or Columns to display the Insert dialog box (see Figure 20.8). In the Insert group box, select the Rows option button or the Columns option button, then specify the number of rows or columns to insert using the Number of Rows or Number of Columns text box. In the Options group box, leave the After Selected Cells option button selected if you want the new rows or columns to appear below the current row or to the right of the current column, or select the Before Selected Cells option button to have the new rows appear above the current row or to the left of the current column. Then click the OK button to insert the rows or columns.

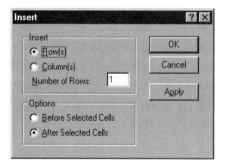

FIGURE 20.8:
Use the Insert dialog box to add rows or columns to a table.

To delete one or more rows or columns, click the row headings or column headings, then choose Table ➤ Delete Rows or Table ➤ Delete Columns.

To resize a row or a column, move the mouse pointer over the row or column border in the row or column heading so that Publisher displays an Adjust pointer, then click and drag the border to where you want it.

Adjusting Margins and Borders

To adjust the margins of a cell, right-click in it and select Table Cell Properties from the context menu to display the Table Cell Properties dialog box. Adjust the margins in the Left, Right, Top, and Bottom text boxes, and click the OK button.

To change the border around selected cells, right-click and choose Border from the context menu (or choose Format ➤ Border) to display the BorderArt dialog box. Select the borders you want and click the OK button.

Creating WordArt

Publisher coyly describes WordArt as "fancy text"—words distorted into graphics, or graphics built from text, depending on your viewpoint. Used within reason, WordArt can provide dramatic text to give your publications impact and can enhance readability. Used excessively, WordArt can make your publications hard on the eyes and difficult to read.

To insert a WordArt object in your publication, click the WordArt button on the Publisher toolbar. Create a frame with the resulting cross-hair pointer, either by single-clicking (to place a standard-size frame) or clicking and dragging to the dimensions you want. Publisher will automatically display the WordArt toolbar and text-entry box.

Enter the text for the WordArt in the text-entry box, and click the Update Display button to have Publisher show your changes on screen. Then work with the buttons on the WordArt toolbar (see Figure 20.9) to make the WordArt appear as you want it.

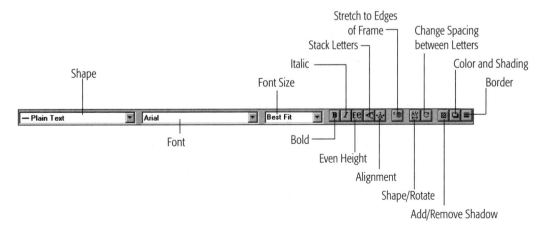

FIGURE 20.9: Use the buttons on the WordArt toolbar to manipulate your WordArt objects.

Here's the lowdown on what the buttons do:

- The Shape drop-down palette contains predefined shapes for WordArt objects.

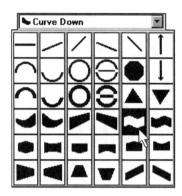

- The Font drop-down list, Font Size drop-down list, Bold button, and Italic button work as they do in other Windows applications.
- The Even Height button makes all the letters in the object the same height (regardless of their capitalization).
- The Stack Letters button changes the letters to a vertical orientation, producing one column for each line of text.
- The Stretch to Edges of Frame button stretches the letters to reach the edges of the frame.
- The Alignment drop-down list offers left alignment, right alignment, and center alignment, together with three types of justification: Stretch Justify (stretching the letters to implement justification), Letter Justify (altering the space between letters to implement justification), and Word Justify (altering the space between words to implement justification).
- The Change Spacing between Letters button displays the Spacing between Characters dialog box, which lets you specify how narrow or wide the space between characters should be.
- The Shape/Rotate button displays the Special Effects dialog box, which lets you change the rotation and shape of the WordArt object.
- The Color and Shading button displays the Shading dialog box, which lets you choose the shading style and foreground and background colors of the WordArt object.
- The Add/Remove Shadow button displays the Shadow dialog box, which offers a choice of shadows in an assortment of colors.

- The Border button displays the Border dialog box, which provides a variety of borders in your choice of colors.

When you're finished working on the WordArt, click outside the WordArt frame to enter it in your publication. To edit the piece of WordArt further, double-click in it to display the WordArt toolbar and text-entry box again.

Adding Lines, Boxes, and Custom Shapes

Publisher provides straightforward and intuitive tools for creating boxes and custom shapes—everything from straight lines and arrows to squares, ovals, and jagged explosions:

- To insert a line, click the Line button on the Publisher toolbar, then click and drag where you want it to appear. To change the appearance of a line, right-click it and choose Line Properties from the context menu to display the Line dialog box.
- To insert an oval, click the Oval tool, then click and drag where you want the oval to appear. To draw a circle, hold down Shift as you click and drag.
- To insert a rectangle, click the Box button, then click and drag in the publication. To draw a square, hold down Shift as you click and drag.
- To insert a custom shape, click the Custom Shapes button and choose the type of shape from the panel that appears. Then click and drag in the publication to create the shape you want. As usual, you can hold down Shift to constrain the shape proportionally, or hold down Ctrl to draw it about its midpoint.

Adding Objects from the Design Gallery

Publisher's Design Gallery provides a collection of predesigned objects that you can quickly insert in your publications. You can also add objects that you've created to the Design Gallery.

Inserting an Object from the Design Gallery

To add a predesigned object from Publisher's Design Gallery:

1. Click the Design Gallery button on the Publisher toolbar, or choose Tools ➤ Design Gallery, to display the Design Gallery dialog box (see Figure 20.10).

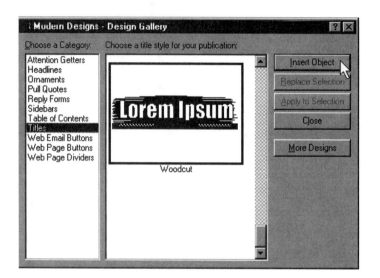

FIGURE 20.10:
Use the Design Gallery to quickly insert predesigned objects into your publications.

2. The first part of the name of the Design Gallery dialog box will indicate the style of items the dialog box is displaying. For example, the dialog box will identify itself as "Jazzy Designs–Design Gallery" or "Classic Designs–Design Gallery." To change to a different set, click the More Designs button and select the type of design from the drop-down list:
   - The three CD Deluxe items are available only on the Publisher Deluxe CD.
   - The Other Designs item displays the Other Designs dialog box, which allows you to open a publication that contains design objects you want to reuse.
   - The last item on the list lets you choose designs from the current publication.
3. In the Choose a Category list box, choose the category of item you want.
4. In the main list box, select the item you want (scroll down to see more items).
5. Click the Insert Object button to insert the object in your publication. Publisher will close the Design Gallery dialog box.

Adding an Object to the Design Gallery

To add an object you've created (or adapted) to the Design Gallery:

1. Select the object in the publication and choose Tools ➤ Add Selection to Design Gallery.
2. If you currently have one of Publisher's built-in sets of designs open, Publisher will invite you to add the object to one of your own design sets (if you have one or more) or to start a new design set in which to put the object (if you have no design sets of your own). Click the Yes button.
3. Publisher will display the Adding an Object dialog box, in which you assign the object a name and a category. (Here, you can choose an existing category if you have one.) Click the OK button to close this dialog box.
4. If you entered a name for a new category, Publisher will display the Create New Category dialog box. Enter the description for the category in the Type a Description text box and click the OK button. Publisher will add the object to the category and return you to your publication.

Using the Design Checker

Publisher includes a built-in Design Checker to help you avoid making any of nine design errors. These include errors such as empty frames (which have no use), text in the overflow area of unlinked frames (that text will not print), too many special effects, too many fonts, and too many colors (all errors of overenthusiasm that are apt to put the reader off rather than turn them on).

To run the Design Checker, choose Tools ➤ Design Checker to display the beginning Design Checker dialog box.

- Choose the All option button to check all pages, or select the Pages option button and specify in the From and To text boxes which pages to check.
- Leave the Check Background Pages check box checked if you want Publisher to check background pages as well as foreground pages (this is usually a good idea).
- To choose which types of problems the Design Checker should look for, click the Options button to display the Options dialog box. To check only for some problems, select the Check Selected Features option button and select the appropriate check boxes in the group box. To check for all problems, select the Check All Problems option button. Click the OK button to close the Options dialog box.

When you've chosen the options, click the OK button to start checking the design. The Design Checker will warn you of problems it finds in the Design Checker dialog box (see Figure 20.11). Use the Ignore button to ignore the current instance of the problem, the Ignore All button (when available) to ignore all instances of the problem in the publication or section you're checking, or the appropriate action button (for example, the Delete Frame button) to take action. Click the Close button to stop checking the design.

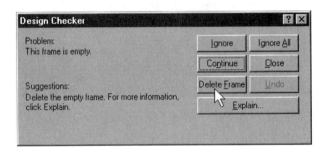

FIGURE 20.11:
Use the Design Checker to check for common problems in your publications. Here, the Design Checker has caught an empty frame and is recommending that I delete it.

Printing a Publication

Once your publication is finished, you'll probably want to print it. To print a publication, choose File ➤ Print to display the Print dialog box, select options (described below), and click the OK button.

Publisher offers several options that are not available in the Print dialog boxes in the other Office applications:

- Select the Use Print Troubleshooter check box if you want Publisher to run the Print Troubleshooter helper application after you print each publication. The Print Troubleshooter displays a message box asking whether the publication printed correctly; if you choose the No button, it walks you through some ways to improve printing performance. Whether the Use Print Troubleshooter check box appears selected or cleared is controlled by the Print with Print Troubleshooter check box on the General tab of the Options dialog box (Tools ➤ Options).

- Select the Print Crop Marks check box if you want Publisher to print crop marks to indicate where to cut the paper on the publication to its correct size (or, if you are shooting film from it, the corners of the page).

- Select the Do Not Print Pictures check box if you want Publisher to print your publication without the pictures in it. You might use this option if you want to proof the text of your publication, and you need to print it out quickly without worrying about any pictures it contains.

TIP

To speed up printing of drafts of a complex publication, you can choose not to print the pictures and other graphical objects it contains. Before you print, choose View ➤ Picture Display to bring up the Picture Display dialog box, select the Hide Pictures option button, and click the OK button to close the dialog box. Now when you print, Publisher will display a message box asking if you want to print the pictures. Click the Yes button to include the pictures with your publication; click the No button to print the publication without its pictures. (Click the Cancel button to cancel the Print command.) This option is especially useful for checking the text in your publication quickly.

Chapter 21

CREATING WEB PAGES AND WEB SITES

- **Creating Web sites and Web pages**
- **Converting an existing publication into a Web site**
- **Customizing your Web site**
- **Previewing your Web site**
- **Publishing your Web site**

Publisher provides PageWizards that make it easy to create Web sites, ranging from single-page personal sites up to fairly complex, multiple-page community or company sites. In this chapter, I'll discuss how you can use Publisher to create Web pages and Web sites, to tweak the results, and to publish them to your corporate intranet (an internal Web site) or the Web. We'll start with using the Web Site PageWizard, because this is the easiest way of creating reasonable-looking Web pages and Web sites, but we'll also look at how you can create Web pages from your existing documents and specify custom page designs.

Creating a Web Site with the PageWizard

Publisher's Web Site PageWizard Design Assistant makes it easy to create both individual Web pages—documents that contain text and graphics, and maybe sound files and video clips—and Web sites, collections of Web pages organized behind a home page.

Here's how to create a Web site:

1. Choose File ➤ Create New Publication to display the Publisher 97 dialog box.
2. If the PageWizard tab is not displayed, click it to display it.
3. Select the Web Site item and click the OK button.
4. In the first Web Site PageWizard Design Assistant dialog box, choose the main purpose of the Web site: Business, Community, or Personal. The three choices offer different categories of pages you can add. For example, for a Business site, you may add information about the company; for a Community site, you may add information about committees. After you choose the purpose, click the Next button to continue.
5. In the second Web Site PageWizard Design Assistant dialog box, choose whether you want to create a one-page site or a multiple-page site. Generally, you'll want to create a multiple-page site, because a single page of conventional length contains too little information for a satisfactory Web presence, and an overlong page is likely to deter visitors. Click the Next button to continue.

NOTE   At any point in the following procedure, you can click the |<< button to return to the first Web Site PageWizard Design Assistant dialog box or the < button to return to the previous Web Site PageWizard Design Assistant dialog box.

6. If you selected to create a multiple-page site, in the third Web Site PageWizard Design Assistant dialog box, select the check boxes for the additional pages you want to include in your Web site. (If you're creating a single-page Web site, you'll skip this step.) For example, for a Business Web site, you can choose from Company Profile, Directory, Company Update, Event Calendar, and so on (Community and Personal Web sites have different choices). The PageWizard will create a linked page for each selected check box. Click the Next button when you've made your selections.

7. In the fourth Web Site PageWizard Design Assistant dialog box, choose the style of Web pages you want: Basic, Bold, Classic, Jazzy, or Modern. Click the Next button to move on.

8. In the fifth Web Site PageWizard Design Assistant dialog box, choose the type of background for the site: Plain, Solid, or Texture. For Business sites, you'll often want to choose a relatively sober background to avoid distracting the reader from the information you're presenting; for a Community site or a Personal site, you may want to give a warmer feel at the expense of some visual clarity. Click the Next button after you've made your choice.

9. In the sixth Web Site PageWizard Design Assistant dialog box, choose the type of navigation buttons you want to have on your pages: Text Only, Buttons and Text, or Icons and Text. The Icons and Text choice is usually best; the icons provide a graphical representation of the link, and the text provides a straightforward text link for anyone browsing without viewing graphics. Click the Next button to proceed.

10. In the seventh Web Site PageWizard Design Assistant dialog box, type the heading for your home page (the front page for the site, or if you're creating a one-page site, the only page). For example, if you're creating a Business site, you might enter the company name; for a Personal site, you will probably want to enter your own name. Publisher allows you to enter up to 30 characters for the name. Click the Next button to continue.

11. In the eighth Web Site PageWizard Design Assistant dialog box, choose whether to add a postal address or street address to your home page. For a business, an address is usually important; for an individual user, an address is usually a mistake (for reasons of security and privacy). If you choose the Yes, Please! button, the Web Site PageWizard Design Assistant will display another Web Site PageWizard Design Assistant dialog box for entering the address. Choose the option button for the type of address: My Business Address, My Personal Address, My Organization, or Other Address. Then enter the name and address in the Name and Address text boxes. (Leave blank any of the address text boxes that you don't need.) Click the Next button to move on.

12. In the next Web Site PageWizard Design Assistant dialog box, enter your phone number, fax number, and e-mail address in the text boxes as appropriate. (If you don't want to include any of the three, clear the relevant check box.) Once again, click the Next button to move on.

13. In the final Web Site PageWizard Design Assistant dialog box, click the Create It! button to have the PageWizard create your Web site. This may take several minutes for complex Web site designs with many pages and graphics.

14. When the PageWizard has finished creating your Web site, it will display a Web Site PageWizard Design Assistant dialog box asking if you want step-by-step help as you work on the Web site. Choose the Yes option button or the No option button as appropriate, and then click the OK button. Publisher will display your Web site. If you chose the Yes option button, Publisher will display the Help panel showing information about working with Web sites.

15. Save your Web site under an appropriate name by clicking the Save button or choosing File ➤ Save.

After you've had the PageWizard create your Web site design according to your specifications, you're ready to add your own content. Skip ahead to "Customizing Your Web Site" for instructions.

Creating a Web Site from an Existing Publication

If you have the material for your Web site already in a publication, you can create a Web site from it:

1. Open the publication you want to use for the Web site.

2. Choose File ➤ Create Web Site from Current Publication. Publisher will convert the publication to Web format. If the publication has not been saved, or contains unsaved changes, Publisher will prompt you to save changes before closing it. Usually, you'll want to choose Yes, and to name the publication if it's never been saved.

3. Publisher will ask if you want to run the Design Checker on the publication; choose Yes or No. (It's usually a good idea to run the Design Checker to remove from your publication any features that will not convert properly to Web pages.) If you choose Yes, specify the pages to check in the Design Checker dialog box and click the OK button, then use the Design Checker's advice to fix any problems that the publication contains. (For details on what the Design Checker checks on Web sites, see "Checking the Design of Your Web Site," later in this chapter.)

4. Publisher will then prompt you to have the Design Checker test whether the publication will download quickly. Choose Yes or No.

5. When the design check is complete, save the publication as a Web page.

NOTE When converting an existing publication to a Web site, Publisher turns each page of the publication into a separate Web page. This means that, for example, an article that spans text boxes on multiple pages will become multiple Web pages. You'll need to add hyperlinks to navigate from one page to another. So when planning a publication that you'll turn into a Web site, divide the text into logical sections—one per text box—rather than simply flowing it as normal from one page to the next.

Customizing Your Web Site

Once you've created a Web site using the PageWizard, you'll need to change its default contents to something appropriate. Invariably, you'll need to change the default explanatory text and greeked text that Publisher uses to lay out the pages, and you'll often want to change the pictures as well. You may also want to add pages to your Web site or remove pages that turn out to be superfluous.

Here are the main actions you're likely to take:

- To replace the text in a text box, click once in the text box. Publisher will highlight all its contents. You can then type in new contents; or press Delete to delete the contents, right-click, and choose Insert Text File from the context menu to insert a text file in the text box.

- To resize, reposition, copy, or delete an element, or to add other elements, use the techniques discussed in Chapter 19. For example, to replace a picture, right-click the picture and choose Microsoft Clip Gallery Object ➤ Replace to display the Microsoft Clip Gallery dialog box. Select the replacement picture and click the Insert button.

- To add one or more pages to the Web site, choose Insert ➤ Page (or press Ctrl+Shift+N) to display the Insert Page dialog box, and specify the number of pages and where to add them, as discussed in the previous chapter. You'll then need to add one or more hyperlinks from the home page or the other pages to allow the viewer to move to that page (see "Working with Hyperlinks" later in this chapter).

- To delete a page, display it and choose Edit ➤ Delete Page. Publisher will display a confirmation dialog box warning that you'll also be deleting all the objects on the page. Click the OK button to proceed. After deleting a page, be sure to remove any hyperlinks that lead to it.

- To change the page size for your Web page, choose File ➤ Page Setup to display the Web Page Setup dialog box, choose the page width you want (Standard, Wide, or Custom), choose the height and (for Custom) the width of the page, and click the OK button. (See "Creating a Custom Web Page" later in the chapter for information about the page width settings.)

- To change the background color and texture of a Web page, choose Format ➤ Background and Text Colors to display the Background and Text Colors dialog box. To use a preset color scheme or texture, select it in the Available Selections list box on the Standard tab; the Preview box will display a preview of the color scheme or texture. To create a custom texture, select the Custom tab of the Background and Text Colors dialog box. In the Custom Background group box, select the background color you want from the Color drop-down palette. Select the texture by clicking the Browse button to display the Insert Picture dialog box, choosing the texture, and clicking the OK button. To remove a texture from the color scheme, click the No Texture button. Click the OK button to apply your choices to the Web page.

Saving Your Web Site

Saving a Web site in Publisher is not quite intuitive, because the standard procedure is to save the site as a Publisher publication as you are working on it, and then *publish* it in HTML format to a folder or to the Web when you've finished.

To save your Web site as a Publisher publication, choose File ➤ Save to display the Save As dialog box, and then save your publication as usual. I'll discuss how to publish the site in "Publishing Your Web Site" at the end of the chapter.

Working with Hyperlinks

A *hyperlink* is a link for navigating between documents on an intranet or on the Web. Each hyperlink contains an address to an intranet or Web location, typically in a different document, although a hyperlink can also link to a different location in the same document. When you click a hyperlink, your Web browser moves to the address that the hyperlink indicates.

Adding a Hyperlink

As you probably know from surfing the Web, a hyperlink can be presented as either text or a graphic object, such as a picture. Text hyperlinks usually use underline, boldface, or a different font color (or a combination of these, such as blue underlined text). When you move your mouse pointer over a hyperlink in a Web page, the mouse pointer typically changes to a pointing finger to indicate the link.

To insert a hyperlink:

1. Select the text or graphical object that you want to create the hyperlink with.
2. Click the Hyperlink button on the Standard toolbar to display the Hyperlink dialog box (see Figure 21.1).

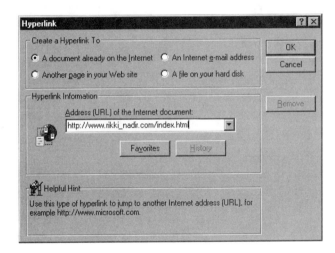

FIGURE 21.1:
In the Hyperlink dialog box, select the options for your hyperlink and click the OK button.

3. Choose the type of hyperlink to create:
    *   A Document Already on the Internet requires you to enter the full URL (Uniform Resource Locator, which is the Internet address) of the document in the Address (URL) of the Internet Document drop-down list box in the Hyperlink Information group box. You can simply type in the URL; select the URL from the drop-down list of recently used URLs; choose the URL from your Favorites folder by clicking the Favorites button, selecting it in the Favorites dialog box, and clicking the Open button; or, if you use Internet Explorer as your browser, choose the URL from your History folder by clicking the History button, selecting it in the History dialog box, and clicking the Open button.

- Another Page in Your Web Site lets you create an internal link to a page in your Web site. Once you've selected this option button, select the page in the Hyperlink To area in the Hyperlink Information group box: First Page, Previous Page, Next Page, or Specific Page (choosing the appropriate page number from the drop-down list).

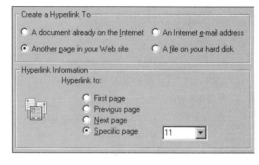

- An Internet E-Mail Address lets you provide a hyperlink that enables visitors to your Web page to quickly send messages to your e-mail address (or another address of your choice). Select this option button and enter the e-mail address in the Internet E-mail Address drop-down list box in the Hyperlink Information group box.

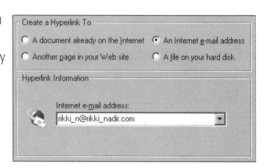

- A File on Your Hard Disk lets you provide a hyperlink to a local file (either on your hard disk or on a hard disk to which you have access). This is primarily useful when you're working with an intranet. Select the option button and specify the file in the Path of the File text box in the Hyperlink Information group box. Use the Browse button and resulting Browse Files dialog box to navigate to the file if necessary.

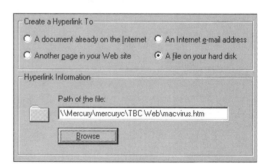

4. Click the OK button to create the hyperlink and close the Hyperlink dialog box.

Changing or Deleting a Hyperlink

From time to time, you'll find you need to change a hyperlink, either because the location or file to which it pointed has changed or because you want it to point to a different location or file. To change a hyperlink:

1. Right-click the hyperlinked text or graphical object and choose Hyperlink from the context menu to display the Hyperlink dialog box. (Alternatively, select the hyperlink by clicking the graphical object or the text, and then choose Insert ➤ Hyperlink or press Ctrl+K.)
2. Change the information in the Create a Hyperlink To group box and the Hyperlink Information group box as appropriate. For example, if you need to change a hyperlink to a URL, enter the new URL in the Address (URL) of the Internet Document drop-down list box.
3. Click the OK button to apply your changes and close the Hyperlink dialog box.

To delete a hyperlink, right-click the hyperlinked text or graphical object and choose Hyperlink from the context menu to display the Hyperlink dialog box. Click the Remove button to remove the hyperlink from the text or graphical object. Publisher will close the Hyperlink dialog box automatically.

TIP

Few things are more frustrating to a visitor to your Web site than hyperlinks that either are broken or that point to the wrong location. To make sure your hyperlinks are functional and accurate, you need to test them. You do so in Publisher by previewing your Web site. I'll discuss previewing in "Previewing Your Web Site" a little later in the chapter.

Creating a Custom Web Page

For specific purposes that the PageWizard and the default Web page can't serve, you may want to create a custom Web page:

1. Choose File ➤ Create New Publication to display the Publisher 97 dialog box. If the Blank Page tab is not displayed, click it to display it.
2. Click the Custom Web Page button to display the Web Page Setup dialog box (see Figure 21.2).
3. In the Page Width group box, choose the page width you want:
    *   The Standard width works for all video displays. Viewers will be able to see the full width of the Web page at 640 × 480 resolution, the minimum resolution of a modern monitor. This is a good choice when you don't know what equipment visitors to your Web page will be using (for example, for pages you post on the World Wide Web).

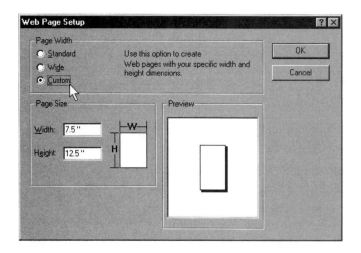

FIGURE 21.2:
In the Web Page Setup dialog box, choose the type of Web page you want to create.

TIP   When creating a Web page, keep in mind the type of monitor that visitors to the Web site are likely to be using. Usually, it's best to plan your Web site for the lowest quality of hardware that you expect people to be using, so that nobody who visits your site is unable to view its contents.

- The Wide width works for higher-resolution video displays—800 × 600 pixel resolution or higher. The extra width allows you to present more information at once, but any visitor using 640 × 480 resolution will not be able to see the full width of the page at once; they will need to scroll from side to side to view the margins. The Wide width is a reasonable choice if you know that all the visitors to your page will be using high-resolution displays (for example, if you're posting your pages on a corporate intranet).
- The Custom width allows you to specify a width of your own choice for the Web page. Use the Custom width if your Web page has special width requirements.

4. In the Page Size group box, you can set a height for a Web page of Standard or Wide width; for a Custom width page, you set the width as well. Watch the Preview box to get an approximate idea of the shape of the page you're creating.

TIP   For most purposes, it's better to create multiple Web pages of a reasonable length than to create fewer pages of epic length. Try to break up the information into easily accessible and browsable portions, and provide hyperlinks to let people jump quickly to the topics they're interested in.

5. Click the OK button to close the Web Page Setup dialog box and apply your choices.

Checking the Design of Your Site

In the previous chapter, I discussed how to run the Design Checker (Tools ➤ Design Checker) to identify common problems in publications. The Design Checker also works for Web sites, but with a modified set of options. In addition to checking for empty frames and text in the overflow area of frames, the Design Checker can also check for the following:

Disproportional Pictures   The Design Checker checks for pictures modified from their original proportions (for example, squashed or stretched). If you're mangling pictures for artistic effect, deselect this check box.

Objects Partially Off Page   The Design Checker alerts you to objects that are partially off the Web page. You can choose to expand the Web page to include the whole object.

Text Becomes a Graphic   In a Web site, when text overlaps another object, or if it uses BorderArt, Publisher creates it as a graphic rather than as text. Because graphics download much more slowly than text, the Design Checker warns you of text that will be converted to a graphic so that you can adjust it if you wish.

Blank Space at Top of Page   Blank space at the top of a page works well in many paper-based publications, but it may confuse the viewer on a Web page. The Design Checker alerts you to pages with more than an inch and a half of blank space at the top.

Page Unreachable by Hyperlinks   In a multiple-page publication, the Design Checker will identify pages that do not have links to the home page and will suggest adding hyperlinks to them to make them accessible from the home page.

Long Download Time   Over a slow connection, graphics take a significant amount of time to load. To help you avoid having a slow Web site, the Design Checker will identify graphics more than 20KB in size and suggest reducing their size or removing them. If you're checking the design of intranet pages accessed at network speeds, consider turning off this option.

Previewing Your Web Site

Before you publish your Web site, preview it to make sure that it looks as you intended, ensure no hyperlinks are broken, and that all the hyperlinks point to suitable locations.

TIP | **When previewing your Web site, use a variety of Web browsers if possible, unless you know that all visitors to your site will be using a particular browser (as might be the case with a corporate Web site). Because different browsers interpret HTML codes differently, a Web page that looks great in one browser can look horrible in the other. At the very least, try to preview your Web site in both Internet Explorer and Netscape Navigator.**

To preview your Web site:

1. Click the Preview Web Site button or choose File ➤ Preview Web Site. Publisher will convert the publication to Web pages (which it stores in the Windows temporary folder), and then display the Preview Web Pages dialog box telling you that you are about to preview the Web site in your browser.
2. Click the Continue button. Publisher will start the browser configured in Windows as your default browser and will open the site in it.
3. Browse your site. Try to use as many hyperlinks as possible to make sure they're working and that they take you to the proper locations. To make changes to the publication containing the site, you can switch back to Publisher (by using Alt+Tab or the Taskbar) and make the changes as usual. Note that your changes will not be reflected in the Web site unless you choose File ➤ Preview Web Site again.
4. When you're finished previewing, close your Web browser to return to Publisher.

Publisher offers a Preview Troubleshooter to help you resolve problems with your Web site before you publish it to the Web. The Preview Troubleshooter appears as a Help panel at the right side of the Publisher window when you choose File ➤ Preview Web Site. If you identify a problem when previewing your site—for example, a border does not appear where it should—click the appropriate topic in the Preview Troubleshooter panel to see the suggestions that Publisher has to offer. To remove the Preview Troubleshooter pane, click the Hide Help button.

TIP To turn the Preview Troubleshooter off so that it does not run when you preview a Web site, choose Tools ➤ Options to display the Options dialog box, clear the Preview Web Site with Preview Troubleshooter check box on the General tab, and click the OK button.

Publishing Your Web Site

Once you've created a Web site, you'll want to make it available to your audience, be it your colleagues on your company's intranet or the millions of people on the World Wide Web. In this section, we'll look first at publishing the Web site to a folder on a local network, and then at publishing to the Web itself.

Publishing to a Folder on Your Network

To publish your Web site to a folder on either your computer or on your network:

1. Choose File ➤ Publish Web Site to Folder to display the Select a Folder dialog box (see Figure 21.3).
2. In the Drive drop-down list box, select the drive to which to publish the Web site. To publish your Web site to a folder on a network drive that is not currently mapped (identified to your computer by a drive letter), click the Network button to display the Map Network Drive dialog box. In the Drive drop-down list, select the drive letter you want to map. In the Path drop-down list, select the map to which to map the drive. Select the Reconnect at Logon check box if you want your computer to reestablish the drive mapping every time you log on to the network. Then click the OK button to map the drive and close the Map Network Drive dialog box.
3. In the Folder list box, select the folder to which to publish the Web site. To create a new folder for your Web site, select the folder in which you want the new folder to be created. (Change drives if necessary before selecting the folder.) Then click the New Folder button to display the Create New Folder dialog box. Enter the name for the new folder in the Name text box and click the OK button.

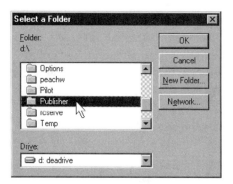

FIGURE 21.3:
In the Select a Folder dialog box, choose the drive and folder to which you want to publish your Web site.

4. Click the OK button. You'll see the Save Web Site to Folder dialog box for a few seconds as Publisher publishes your Web site to the folder. If the folder already contains a Web site, Publisher will ask if you want to overwrite it. When it's finished, Publisher will return you to your publication.

NOTE **Publisher will name the first page of the publication index.html, and the other pages page2.html, page3.html, and so on.**

Now you can start your browser and check that the site contains what it should.

Publishing to the Web Using the Web Publishing Wizard

Microsoft provides a Web Publishing Wizard to help you publish your Web site to the World Wide Web. The Web Publishing Wizard works with Microsoft applications other than Publisher and is not installed on your computer under the default or custom installation of Publisher; you usually need to install it yourself.

Downloading the Web Publishing Wizard

The easiest way to find out if the Web Publishing Wizard is installed on your computer is to try to run it. If the Web Publishing Wizard is not installed on your computer, you'll see a message box telling you so and offering to download it for you. If your computer has an Internet connection and a Web browser, click the Yes button.

Publisher will start or activate your Internet connection and Web browser and connect to the Web Publishing Wizard page at the Microsoft Web site (depending on how your computer is configured, you may need to start your Internet connection manually). Click the download link for the appropriate version of the Web Publishing Wizard (this may depend on the version of Internet Explorer that you have), choose a download site (geographically closer sites should run faster and use fewer Internet resources), and save the file to your hard disk when prompted. (The Web Publishing Wizard file is approximately 750KB and takes about three to five minutes to download over a typical 28.8Kbps connection.) Then, in Windows Explorer, double-click the executable file you downloaded. Agree to the setup license and let the Web Publishing Wizard install itself.

NOTE **To publish your Web site on the World Wide Web, you'll need to know what services your Internet service provider (ISP) supports. You'll also need the URL (Web address) that your ISP uses to identify your site.**

Running the Web Publishing Wizard

Once you've installed the Web Publishing Wizard, you're ready to publish to the Web:

1. Open the publication you want to publish to the Web.
2. Choose File ➤ Publish to Web. You'll see the Generating Web Pages dialog box while Publisher builds your Web pages. Publisher will then display the first Web Publishing Wizard dialog box, which displays general information. Click the Next button.
3. On the Name the Web Server screen of the Web Publishing Wizard dialog box, enter a descriptive name for the Web server you'll be using. This is just the name you use to identify it, so name it whatever is easiest for you. Click the Next button.
4. In the Select Your Service Provider screen of the Web Publishing Wizard dialog box, choose your ISP's name from the Service Provider drop-down list. If your ISP is not listed, leave the default Automatically Select Service Provider item chosen. Click the Next button.
5. On the Specify the URL or Directory screen of the Web Publishing Wizard dialog box, enter the Web address for your site. Click the Next button.
6. Follow the subsequent prompts (which will vary) to publish your Web site to the Web. For example, if you choose to use FTP to publish your Web site, you'll see the Specify the FTP Server and Subfolder screen of the Web Publishing Wizard dialog box. Enter the name of the FTP server in the FTP Server name text box and the subfolder for your Web pages in the Subfolder Containing Your Web Pages text box, and then click the Next button.

Once you've published your Web site to the Web, fire up your Web browser and visit the site to double-check that the site is fully functional.

Chapter 22

MAIL MERGE WITH PUBLISHER

- **Understanding mail merge in Publisher**
- **Creating a merged document**
- **Using existing data sources**
- **Creating and editing address lists in Publisher**
- **Disconnecting a merge document from its data source**

In Chapter 10, we looked at the features that Word offers for producing a variety of merged documents—anything from letters to forms to catalogs. Publisher offers similar features for creating merged documents. As with Word, you can use data files from other applications; you can also use data files that you create in Publisher.

Before creating any merge documents in Publisher, make sure that you couldn't create them more easily in Word. As a general rule of thumb, use Publisher to create merge documents that require the design features that Publisher offers and Word does not. If you can create the same merge documents more easily in Word, you should probably do so.

The Basics of Mail Merge

As you'll remember from Chapter 10, to create merged documents, you need a *main document* and a *data source*:

- The main document contains the information that remains constant for each of the merged documents—for example, the information in the catalog or brochure, or the content of the letter.
- The data source contains the sets of information that will go into the merged documents to make them different—for example, the data source will often contain a list of addresses and their associated data, so that each merged document receives a different address.

When you're merging with Publisher, the main document will always be a Publisher publication. The data source can be a Publisher address list, a Word document, an Excel spreadsheet, or a file from a non-Office Small Business Edition application, such as an Access, FoxPro, or dBASE database, or even an ASCII text file.

NOTE   **The data source doesn't need to be an address list; it can be a file that holds any other variable information that you need to be able to enter in your merged documents. For example, when creating a catalog or brochure, you could keep the prices in a data source so that you could quickly update them each time you needed to print an up-to-date catalog.**

Performing a Mail Merge

Here's how to perform a mail merge in Publisher:

1. Open the publication that will be your main document, and then choose Mail Merge ➤ Open Data Source to display the first Open Data Source dialog box.

2. Click the Merge Information from a File I Already Have button. Publisher will display a second Open Data Source dialog box. Select the file by navigating to the folder as usual and, if necessary, using the Files of Type drop-down list to display the appropriate type of file, such as Microsoft Word Address Lists (*.doc). Then click the Open button.

   - If you do not have an existing data source, click the Create an Address List in Publisher button in the Open Data Source dialog box, and go to step 2 in the next section.

- If Publisher cannot identify the type of file you've chosen, it will display the Choose File Type dialog box. Select the type of file in the File Type list box and click the OK button. If Publisher cannot handle the file, it will tell you so and will terminate the merge operation. Try converting your file to a different form (for example, a Word table).

3. Publisher will display the Insert Fields dialog box (see Figure 22.1). If the data source contains field headings, Publisher will list them in the Fields list box; otherwise, Publisher will list the contents of the first record as fields.

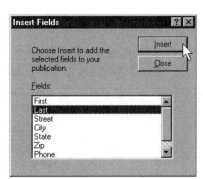

FIGURE 22.1:
Use the Insert Fields dialog box to choose the fields to insert in your publication.

4. Click in the publication to place the insertion point in the text frame that will hold the merge information. (Click the Text button in the Publisher toolbar and create a frame if necessary.) Then select a field and click the Insert button (or double-click the field name). Publisher will insert the field and will leave the text frame active (rather than the Insert Fields dialog box), so that you can enter text or punctuation as necessary.

5. Continue inserting fields as appropriate, adding spaces, punctuation, and text as you go. You can also format the fields as necessary by selecting them in the text box and applying formatting using the regular methods.

6. Click the Close button when you're finished inserting fields. (If you find you need to insert more fields, choose Mail Merge ➤ Insert Field to display the Insert Fields dialog box again.)

7. Choose Mail Merge ➤ Merge to display the Preview Data dialog box.

8. Use the First, Previous, Next, and Last buttons (from left to right in the dialog box) to move through the merge documents that will result. (Alternatively, click in the text box, enter the number of the record you want to see, and press Enter.)

9. Click the Close button when you're finished previewing your records.

Now skip ahead to "Filtering and Sorting the Merge" if you want to rearrange or select records, or go directly to "Printing the Merged Documents" if you're ready to print your final documents.

Creating an Address List in Publisher

If you don't have an existing data source that you want to use, you can create an address list in Publisher. The main advantage to creating the address list in Publisher is that you can edit the address list in Publisher even when the main document is open. When you use a data source from another application, such as a Word document or an Excel table, you won't be able to edit the data source while the main document linked to the data source is open in Publisher; you'll need to close the main document in Publisher and edit the data source in its source application (such as Word or Excel) Publisher saves its address lists in Access database format (*.mdb, which Publisher slyly describes as Publisher Address List format), so you can use Publisher address lists for mail merge in Word as well.

To create an address list in Publisher:

1. Choose Mail Merge ➤ Create Publisher Address List to display the New Address List dialog box (see Figure 22.2).

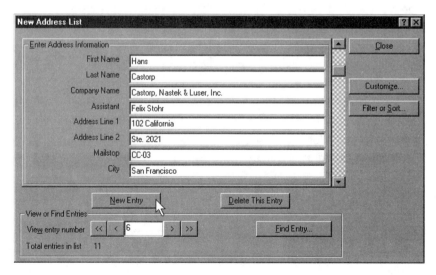

FIGURE 22.2: In the New Address List dialog box, create the records for the address list.

2. Check the fields in the Enter Address Information group box to see if they suit your needs for the address list (use the scroll bar to view the lower part of the list of fields).

3. If you need fields other than the default fields that Publisher provides for the address list, click the Customize button in the New Address List dialog box to display the Customize Address List dialog box (see Figure 22.3). Then adjust the list as necessary:

   - To add a field, select the field before or after which you want to place the new field, and click the Add New Field button. Publisher will display the Add Field dialog box. Enter the name for your field in the Type a Name for Your Field text box. In the Add This Field group box, select the After the Currently Selected Field option button if you want the new field to be added after the current field rather than before it (the default choice). Then click the OK button to close the Add Field dialog box.

   - To delete a field, select it in the list box and click the Delete Field button. Publisher will display a confirmation message box to make sure that this is what you want to do; click the Yes button.

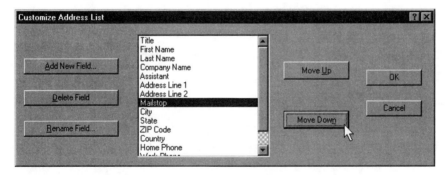

FIGURE 22.3: Use the Customize Address List dialog box to add, delete, rename, and rearrange fields until the fields in the address list meet your needs.

WARNING   **When you delete a field, any information that it currently contains will be deleted as well. This isn't a concern when you're creating a new address list and haven't entered any information in the fields, but it's something to watch out for when you're editing an existing address list.**

   - To rename a field, select it in the list box in the Customize Address List dialog box and click the Rename Field button. Publisher will display the Rename Field dialog box. Enter the new name for the field in the To box, then click the OK button.

- To adjust the order of fields, select the field to move and use the Move Up and Move Down buttons to position it where you want it to appear in the list of fields.
- When you've finished customizing the list of fields, click the OK button to close the Customize Address List dialog box and return to the New Address List dialog box.

4. Enter the information for the data source in the fields in the Enter Address Information group box.
   - Click the New Entry button to create a new entry in the data source (for example, for another customer).
   - Use the buttons in the View or Find Entries group box to move through entries in the database.
   - Use the Find Entry button (which displays the Find Entry dialog box) to search for specific text in either a given field or all fields in the data source.

5. Click the Close button when you're finished creating your data source. Publisher will display the Save As dialog box.

6. Specify a name and folder for the data source and click the Save button to save it.

7. If you entered this list at step 2 after clicking the Create an Address List in Publisher button in the Open Data Source dialog box, Publisher will display a message box asking if you want to merge information from this address list in your publication. Click the Yes button and go to step 3 in the previous section.

You can now use the address list in a mail merge by following the procedure described in the previous section.

To edit an address list that you created in Publisher, select Mail Merge ➤ Edit Publisher Address List to display the Open Address List dialog box. Select the address list and click the Open button. Publisher will open the data source in a variation of the New Address List dialog box named after the data source. You can then add, edit, and delete entries as described in the previous steps. Click the Close button to close the address list. Publisher will save it automatically under its current name.

Filtering and Sorting the Merge

After you've performed a mail merge in Publisher, you can filter or sort your merge. Choose Mail Merge ➤ Filter or Sort to display the Filtering and Sorting dialog box.

The settings in Publisher's Filtering and Sorting dialog box work in almost exactly the same way as the Query Options dialog box in Word (see "Sorting the Records to Be Merged" and "Filtering the Records to Be Merged" in Chapter 10). For example, to sort a merge by zip code and then city to make things easier for your mailroom, click the Sort (Change the Order of Entries) tab in the Filtering and Sorting dialog box, specify the field containing the zip code in the Sort by This Field drop-down list, and specify the field containing the city in the Then by This Field drop-down list.

To remove a sort, click the Remove Sort button. To remove a filter, click the Remove Filter button.

Printing the Merged Documents

After you've finished creating the main document and specifying the data source and fields for it to use, you can print the merged documents:

1. Choose File ➤ Print Merge to display the Print Merge dialog box.
2. Choose printing options as appropriate:
   - In the Print Range group box, select the All Entries option button to have Publisher print all the merged documents, or click the Entries option button and specify starting and ending numbers in the From and To text boxes.
   - Click the Test button to print one publication as a test to make sure nothing horrible has happened during the merge.
   - Leave the Don't Print Lines that Contain Only Empty Fields check box selected if you want Publisher to suppress blank lines where fields contain no information. (This is usually a good idea.)
3. Click the OK button to print your merged documents.

TIP	**To preview your merged documents again, choose Mail Merge ➢ Show Merge Results, and navigate through the merged documents using the Preview Data dialog box.**

Changing Data Sources

To disconnect a publication from its data source so that you can return it to normal use, choose Mail Merge ➤ Cancel Merge. Publisher will display a confirmation message box; click the Yes button to proceed. Publisher will convert any field codes in the publication to text.

NOTE A publication can be attached to only one data source at a time; you cannot create a merge document that draws data from two or more data sources. If you need records from more than one data source, you'll need to create a single data source that contains the relevant information from each of the data sources that you want to use.

To attach an open publication to a different data source, choose Mail Merge ➤ Open Data Source. Publisher will display a message box identifying the data source to which the publication is currently attached and asking whether you want to attach it to a different data source. Click the Yes button. Publisher will display the Open Data Source dialog box, and you can proceed as usual. Note that fields you've inserted in the main document may not match the fields in the new data source.

Part 6

Automap
Streets Plus

Chapter 23

GETTING STARTED WITH AUTOMAP STREETS PLUS

- **Understanding what Automap Streets Plus is and what it does**
- **Moving and zooming the view**
- **Finding addresses and places**
- **Highlighting routes**
- **Printing Streets Plus maps**

In this chapter, we'll look at the Automap Streets Plus (which I'll refer to as simply "Streets Plus") interface and how to use Streets Plus to find locations. We'll also discuss how to highlight routes on a map, use Streets Plus maps in other applications, and print maps.

What Is Streets Plus?

Streets Plus is a mapping software package that provides detailed coverage of the United States and general coverage of adjacent countries. Streets Plus can display a view that encompasses anywhere from the width of the United States to a single block, enabling you to choose the area and the amount of detail you want to see.

Mapping software sounds unexciting to many, but Streets Plus offers strong functionality. You can use Streets Plus to perform a number of tasks. Here are some examples:

- Find an address (for example, to plan a visit to a customer).
- View a set of addresses (for example, to work out the best route between several appointments).
- Highlight and measure a route between two or more places.
- Find places of interest (such as historical monuments or Laotian restaurants).
- Paste Streets Plus maps into other documents (such as a Word document).
- Use Streets Plus's WebLinks feature to access online information about several hundred United States cities.

As you'll see when you fire it up, Streets Plus gives you an overview of North America, with detailed information about the United States, including Alaska and Hawaii. Streets Plus provides an overview of the countries near the United States; for example, you can see where Toronto is, but you won't be able to zoom in for a block-by-block view.

Starting Streets Plus

Unlike the other Office 97 Small Business Edition applications, Streets Plus needs to be run from the CD-ROM. It does not offer an option for hard-drive installation because of the space needed for the amount of information it contains—a full CD-ROM's worth. However, if you have the space available on your hard disk, you can back up the full CD-ROM to your hard drive and run the Streets Plus installation routine from there. (See the Appendix for details on this and on regular installation.)

You can start Streets Plus in several ways:

- If you're running Streets Plus from your CD-ROM drive, and the AutoPlay feature is enabled on your computer, Streets Plus will start automatically when you insert the Streets Plus CD-ROM in the drive.

- If the CD-ROM is already in the drive (for example, if you haven't removed it since the last time you closed Streets Plus), select Start ➤ Programs ➤ Microsoft Reference ➤ Automap Streets Plus.
- If you've created a shortcut on your Desktop or in another folder for Streets Plus, double-click that shortcut.

When Streets Plus starts, you'll see the startup screen (or *home screen*) shown in Figure 23.1. To continue, you can click any of the active buttons. For example, when you click the View the Map button, you'll see the map of the United States (see Figure 23.2).

FIGURE 23.1:   The Streets Plus startup screen. Choose the action you want to take.

NOTE   **The Find Yellow Page Listings feature, which you'll see is grayed out in Figure 23.1, is available only in the Deluxe version of Streets Plus, not in the regular version included in Office 97 Small Business Edition.**

FIGURE 23.2: When you click the View the Map button in the Streets Plus startup screen, Streets Plus displays the map of the 48 contiguous states.

Working with Streets Plus Views

In this section, I'll discuss how you can get around with Streets Plus. We'll cover how to move and zoom the view; the various insertion points you see at different times and what they mean; and how to navigate with the Forward and Back buttons on the menu bar.

Moving the View

While using Streets Plus, you'll spend a lot of time moving the view so that it displays exactly what you want to see. You can move the view by using either the mouse or the keyboard.

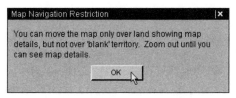

Whichever method you use, if you move the map into an area with nothing to show, Streets Plus will display the Map Navigation Restriction dialog box, telling you to zoom out until you can see map details. Zooming out works, but you can also simply move back to an area for which Streets Plus has information to display.

Moving the View with the Mouse

There are several ways to move the Streets Plus view with the mouse:

- To scroll the view, move the mouse pointer to the side or to a corner of the Streets Plus window, where it will change to a fat white arrow pointing toward that side or corner. You can then click and hold down the mouse button to scroll the view toward that side or corner of the window. For example, if you move the mouse pointer to the upper-right corner of the Streets Plus window, the pointer will turn into an arrow pointing northeast. You can then click and hold down the mouse button to scroll the view to the northeast.

- To nudge the view just a fraction, move the mouse pointer to the side or corner of the Streets Plus window as described in the previous bullet point, and click once. Streets Plus will nudge the view one step in that direction. For example, if you move the mouse pointer to the left side of the Streets Plus window and click once, Streets Plus will move the view one step to the left (west).

- To move the view more freely, click the Move Map button (the one that shows a hand) on the toolbar. Streets Plus will change the mouse pointer to a hand with a finger pointing upwards (as shown here on the right). Click and drag to move the map so that it displays the area you want to view.

- To move quickly to a place or route you see on the map, move the mouse pointer to it and click. Streets Plus will display a context menu of cities, routes, and rivers (if any), as shown here. If there are no nearby cities or routes, the context menu will list only the state and the United States choices. Choose the city or route (or state) you want to view from the context menu, and Streets Plus will display it. (At the bottom of the context menu, Streets Plus displays an entry for Points of Interest, which is covered in the next chapter.)

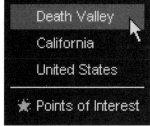

TIP You can move to the item that would appear at the top of the context menu by double-clicking instead. This is useful when you click a specific item (such as a town or a highway), because Streets Plus places it at the top of the context menu. So if you can predict which item will appear at the top of the context menu, you can move quickly to it by double-clicking.

- To move quickly to an area, click the rectangular button on the toolbar (if it isn't already selected), then click and drag a rectangle that approximately encloses the area you want to see. Streets Plus will display a dotted rectangle around the area. Move the mouse pointer into the rectangle so that it displays a magnifying glass with a plus (+) sign, and then click to zoom in on the area.

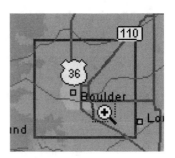

Moving the View with the Keyboard

To move the view with the keyboard, you use the arrow keys—either the set on the numeric keypad (with the Num Lock setting at Off) or the separate set of arrow keys. The numeric keypad is more flexible, because the 1, 3, 7, and 9 keys allow you to move the map diagonally: 1 moves the map southwest, 3 southeast, 7 northwest, and 9 northeast. Each press of an arrow key moves the view one step in the direction specified by the key. For example, pressing → moves the view one step to the right (east). You can hold down an arrow key to scroll the map in the direction of the arrow key.

Moving the map with the arrow keys works well in conjunction with zooming the view with the F5 and F6 keys, which I'll discuss in the next section.

Zooming the View

Streets Plus allows you to zoom the view from a height of 8700 miles above the earth's surface to a height of 1 mile. From the former, you can see the whole of North

America; from the latter, you can see only a few city blocks. Usually, you'll want to work with zoom factors in between the two.

You can zoom the map in several ways:

- Press the F5 key or the – key on the numeric keypad to zoom out, and the F6 key or the + key on the numeric keypad to zoom in.
- Right-click your target and choose Zoom ➤ In or Zoom ➤ Out from the context menu.
- Click the Select Area button on the toolbar, drag the area on the map, and then click in the area, as described in the previous section.
- Click the Zoom Slider button on the toolbar to display the Zoom Slider, then drag the slider to the degree of zoom you want. Click elsewhere to close the Zoom Slider.

Changing the View

Streets Plus offers four different views and a number of view options that you can use to optimize the Streets Plus display for your needs. For example, when you are viewing a large area, you may want to see only the major cities; when you are mapping a route, you may want to look at just the roads and not the terrain shading.

To choose views and view options, select View ➤ Map Display to open the Map Display dialog box (see Figure 23.3). On the Map Styles tab, choose the view you want. Detailed Terrain View and Terrain View both show topographical information; Detailed Road Map View and Road Map View do not. Use the Detailed views when you want to see the full set of information that Streets Plus has available. To reduce the display to its essentials, use the nondetailed views.

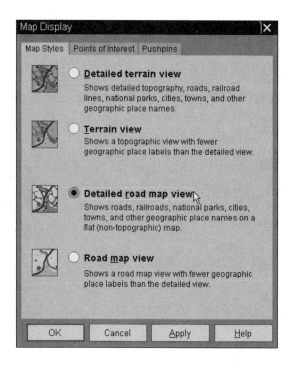

FIGURE 23.3:
Use the Map Display dialog box to optimize the Streets Plus display for your needs.

Finding an Address

Streets Plus can take you to nearly any street address in the United States (including Alaska and Hawaii). To find an address:

1. Display the Find: Find an Address dialog box (see Figure 23.4) by choosing Find ➤ Address, pressing Ctrl+D, clicking the Find Address button on the toolbar, or choosing Find an Address from the startup screen.

2. In the Street Address box, enter the street address you want to find. Streets Plus supports most standard abbreviations (to see the full list in the Help file, search for "abbreviations"). Note that Streets Plus doesn't pay much attention to capitalization: You can type in all capitals, all lowercase, propercase, or a mixed bag of cases, and you'll get the same results.

Don't enter a suite or apartment number for an address you're looking up, because Streets Plus assumes that any apartment or suite is at the main address, and ignores any number (such as #2) that you enter. If you enter a word such as *Apt* for *apartment* or *Ste* for *suite*, Streets Plus will understand it to be a part of the address and will search for it (often confusing the search).

3. In the City text box, enter the city if you know it.

4. In the State text box, enter the state if you know it. You can either click the drop-down list button with the mouse and choose the state from the drop-down list or use "type-down" to reach the state you want—for example, press **C** once to get California, twice to get Colorado, three times to get Connecticut, and so on.

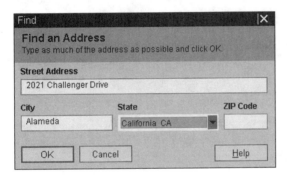

FIGURE 23.4:
In the Find: Find an Address dialog box, enter the address that you want to find.

If the city name is unique, you can skip the state. But you might be surprised to find how many city names in the United States are not unique. For example, there are more places named Saratoga than you could shake a stick at, and any number of places called San Jose.

5. In the ZIP Code text box, enter the zip code for the address. Note that if you know the zip code for the address, you can skip the city and state in most instances. If you've entered the city and state, in many cases, you won't need to enter the zip code.

6. Click the OK button to find the address.

If you've entered enough of the address to identify it uniquely, Streets Plus will move to the relevant part of the map, zoom to a three-mile view to show you a useful size area, and insert a pushpin marking the address. Figure 23.5 shows an example of an address that Streets Plus located. (Chapter 24 discusses how to work with pushpins.)

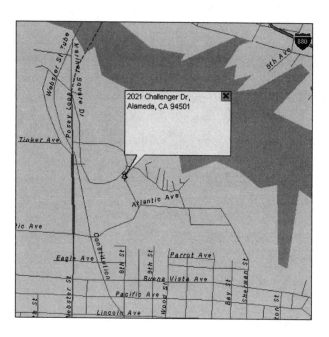

FIGURE 23.5:
Streets Plus will move and zoom the view to show the relevant part of the map, and will insert a pushpin marking the address.

If you haven't entered enough of an address for Streets Plus to identify it uniquely, Streets Plus will display the Find: Address Match dialog box (see Figure 23.6), which lists the similar addresses that Streets Plus found. Select the address you want from the list box and click the OK button to have Streets Plus display it with a pushpin, or click the Cancel button to return to the Find: Find an Address dialog box, where you can enter more details for the search.

If Streets Plus has found more than 100 possible matches for the address you entered, you'll see this message box telling you so and asking you to supply more details to narrow the search. Click the OK button to dismiss the message box. Then enter more information in the Find dialog box and click the OK button again.

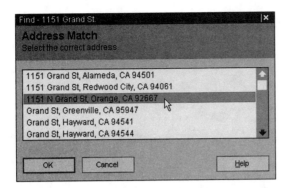

FIGURE 23.6:
In the Find: Address Match dialog box, choose the correct address and click the OK button to have Streets Plus display it.

Finding a Place

If you know the name of a place but not the address, or just need to find a town, use Streets Plus's place-finding feature:

1. Click the Find a Place button on the toolbar, or choose Find ➤ Places, or press Ctrl+G, to display the Find: Find a Place dialog box (see Figure 23.7).

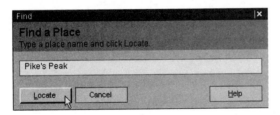

FIGURE 23.7:
In the Find: Find a Place dialog box, enter the name of the place you want to find, and then click the Locate button.

2. Enter the name of the place in the text box and then click the Locate button. Streets Plus will display the Select a Place dialog box (see Figure 23.8) showing the places it found that match or approximate the name.
3. From the list box, choose the place you want, and then click the OK button to close the Select a Place dialog box. Streets Plus will move the map and zoom to show the place.

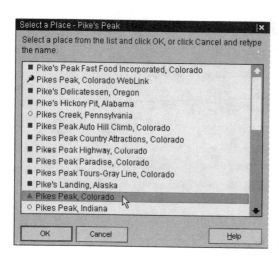

FIGURE 23.8:
In the Select a Place dialog box, choose the place you want from Streets Plus's listing of matching places.

Getting Your Bearings

Streets Plus provides tools for helping you understand what you're seeing on the map, where it is, and the distance between locations:

- If you're not sure what you're seeing, you can display the map legend in the Map Legend dialog box (see Figure 23.9) by choosing Tools ➤ Map Legend. Scroll down through the dialog box to see the full legend. You can either leave the Map Legend dialog box on-screen or click its close button in its upper-right corner to close it.

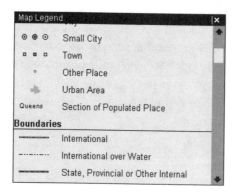

FIGURE 23.9:
The Map Legend dialog box displays Streets Plus's legend.

- To get a quick reading on the part of the map over which you're moving the mouse pointer, display the Location Sensor dialog box by choosing Tools ➤ Location Sensor. To close the Location Sensor dialog box, click its close button or choose Tools ➤ Location Sensor again.

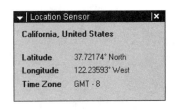

- To see where the area you're viewing appears on the larger map, or to navigate on a grander scale, display the Locator Map by choosing Tools ➤ Locator Map. Click a place on the locator map to move the main map to display it, or click and drag to move the map. To close the Locator Map dialog box, click its close button or choose Tools ➤ Locator Map again.

- To measure the distance between locations on a map, choose Tools ➤ Measuring Tool or press Ctrl+E. Streets Plus will display the Measuring Tool dialog box and change the

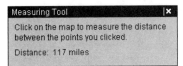

mouse pointer to a crosshair with a ruler. Click each point of the distance you want to measure; Streets Plus will display the result in the Measuring Tool dialog box. To close the Measuring Tool dialog box, click its close button, press the Esc key, or choose Tools ➤ Measuring Tool again.

Working with Routes

Streets Plus lets you highlight a route on a map, which is especially useful when you want to print directions, either for yourself or for someone visiting you.

Highlighting a Route on a Map

To highlight a route on the map, navigate to the area that contains the route and zoom to a distance where you can easily pick out your starting point. The size of the area and the degree of zoom will vary considerably depending on whether you're highlighting a route street by street or choosing a route from city to city.

To highlight a route:

1. Click the Highlight a Route button on the toolbar, choose Route ➤ Highlight a Route, right-click and choose Highlight a Route from the context menu, or press Ctrl+H. Streets Plus will display the Highlight a Route dialog box and change the mouse pointer into a pen with a crosshair at its business end.

2. Click your starting point to begin highlighting the route, then click on the series of points that delineates the route. For example, if you're highlighting a route along streets, click at the turning points; if you're highlighting a route from city to city, click at each city and at each turn of the route. While highlighting the route, you can zoom and scroll the display as usual. The Highlight a Route dialog box will display the current total distance of the route.

3. When you reach the end of the route, click the close button in the Highlight a Route dialog box to stop highlighting the route.

4. If you need to keep a route you've highlighted, choose Route ➤ Save a Route (or press Ctrl+S) to display the Save As dialog box. Save the file as usual. Streets Plus routes are saved as the file type Automap Streets Plus Routes and with the .asr extension. To save a previously saved route under a different name, choose Route ➤ Save As to display the Save As dialog box again. Choose a different name or location (or both) for the route and click the Save button.

Opening a Saved Route

You can open a saved route by choosing Route ➤ Open (or by pressing Ctrl+O) to display the Open dialog box. Select the route you want to open, and click the Open button.

You can have only one route open at a time. If you have a route with unsaved changes open when you choose to open an existing route, Streets Plus will prompt you to save changes to the open route.

To extend an open route, choose Route ➤ Highlight a Route, click the Highlight a Route button, or press Ctrl+H.

Clearing or Deleting a Route

To clear the open route, choose Route ➤ Clear Route or press Ctrl+L. Streets Plus will wipe the route from the screen, but will not delete any copy of it saved to disk.

To delete a route from the disk, choose Route ➤ Open Route (or press Ctrl+O) to display the Open dialog box. Select the route you want to delete, right-click, and choose Delete from the context menu. If Windows displays a message box asking you to confirm the deletion, choose the Yes button.

Using Streets Plus Maps in Other Applications

You can include part of a map from Streets Plus in another document. For example, you could copy the relevant section of a map into an e-mail message in Outlook and send it to someone, or you could use a road map as part of a company information sheet.

WARNING **Remember that a copyright applies to the use of the maps: You're supposed to keep the copyright information with the map, and you're not supposed to sell the map.**

To copy the currently displayed area from Streets Plus, choose Options ➤ Copy or press Ctrl+C. Streets Plus will copy the currently displayed area to the Clipboard. You can then switch to the recipient application and file and paste in the information using the Paste command. Note that Streets Plus does not support object linking and embedding (OLE); you're essentially pasting the map in as a picture.

Printing Maps from Streets Plus

To print the currently displayed map directly from Streets Plus:

1. Choose Options ➤ Print or press Ctrl+P to display the Print dialog box.
2. If you want to add a title or two to your printout, leave the Yes option button selected and enter the title or titles in the two Map Title text boxes. If not, select the No option button.
3. Click the Print button to print the map.

TIP
If the map prints poorly, display the Print dialog box and click the Optimize button to display the Print Optimization dialog box, which allows you to try four different printing methods for computers configured with small and large amounts of memory.

Exiting Streets Plus

You can exit Streets Plus in several ways:

- Click the Windows 95 Close button at the upper-right corner of the Streets Plus window.
- Choose Options ➤ Exit Streets Plus from the menu bar.
- Press Alt+F4, the standard Windows key combination for closing an application.
- Click the control-menu box in the upper-left corner of the Streets Plus window and choose Close from the control menu.
- Right-click the title bar of the Streets Plus window and choose Close from the control menu.

Chapter 24

PUSHPINS, POINTS OF INTEREST, AND WEBLINKS

FEATURING

- **Creating and manipulating pushpins**
- **Importing pushpins from other applications**
- **Locating points of interest**
- **Using WebLinks to access Web pages**
- **Choosing Streets Plus options**

In this chapter, I'll start by showing you how to work with Streets Plus's push-pins—electronic versions of the pushpins you might poke into a real map—to mark addresses in Streets Plus. Then I'll discuss how to find points of interest, from Mexican restaurants to museums, and how to use Streets Plus's WebLinks. Toward the end of the chapter, I'll discuss the options that Streets Plus provides and how to get Streets Plus to run faster on your computer.

Working with Pushpins

Streets Plus provides electronic pushpins for marking places on its maps. These virtual pushpins have several advantages over real ones:

- You can display and hide them at will.
- You can search for lost pins without pricking your fingers.
- Pushpins can have notes, pictures, and even Internet addresses attached to them.

Streets Plus organizes pushpins into sets. You can manipulate sets of pushpins, displaying and hiding them as you wish. For example, you can display a set of pushpins marking your child's newspaper-delivery route, then hide that set and display a set marking the customers you needed to visit on a certain day. Streets Plus also automatically creates pushpins for addresses you find, and it uses pushpins to coordinate WebLinks, which we'll look at later in this chapter.

Creating a Pushpin

To mark a spot on the map in Streets Plus, you create an electronic pushpin:

1. Click the Pushpin button on the toolbar. The mouse pointer will change to a crosshair with a pushpin attached. Click to place the pushpin on the map. Streets Plus will display the Pushpin Properties dialog box (see Figure 24.1).

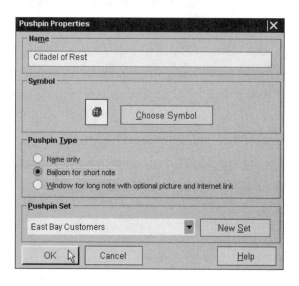

FIGURE 24.1: In the Pushpin Properties dialog box, enter the name for the pushpin and choose the details you want for it, then click the OK button.

2. In the Name text box, enter the name you want for the pushpin. Pushpin names can contain letters, numbers, symbols (such as #, $, and %), and punctuation; and they can be up to 53 characters long. But you'll usually find that short, unique pushpin names are best. Don't make them too short, though. As you'll see in a minute, you can use the Find: Find a Place dialog box to find stray pushpins, but not if they are shorter than three letters. Also, it helps to have names long enough to easily distinguish them from place names that start with the same letters.

3. In the Symbol group box, you can choose a different symbol for the pushpin to help you identify it easily and locate it quickly—a No Entry symbol for an area that's off limits, perhaps, or a ship symbol for a jetty or dock. To change the pushpin, click either the pushpin symbol currently displayed or the Choose Symbol button to display the Choose Symbol dialog box. Select a symbol (scroll if necessary to reach the nether regions of the dialog box) and click the symbol you want. Streets Plus will return you to the Pushpin Properties dialog box with the symbol you chose displayed in the Symbol group box.

4. In the Pushpin Type group box, select the type of pushpin you want to create: Name Only, Balloon for Short Note, or Window for Long Note with Optional Picture and Internet Link.

5. In the Pushpin Set group box, choose the set of pushpins to which you want to add the pushpin you're creating. Either select an existing set from the drop-down list or create a new set. To create a new set of pushpins, click the New Set button to display the New Set dialog box. Enter the name for the new set of pushpins in the text box and click the OK button to create it. Streets Plus will create the new set of pushpins with the name you specified, return you to the Pushpin Properties dialog box, and select the new set in the drop-down list.

6. Click the OK button to create the pushpin.

7. If you chose to create a balloon pushpin, the balloon appears on the map with the pushpin; if you chose a window pushpin, a window opens.

   - Type in text as usual. Balloon pushpins can include up to about six lines of text. Window pushpins can contain a number of pages' worth.

   - To format characters or paragraphs, select them, click the down-arrow button, and choose formatting options from the Format Characters or Format Paragraphs submenu. Alternatively, right-click and use the commands on the context menu.

- To cut, copy, or paste text or a picture, use the commands on the Edit submenu or on the context menu.
- To add an Internet link to the pushpin, click at the end of the Enter a World-Wide Web Link Here area (to select the dummy text) and enter the address. Click the Connect button to connect to the Internet address.

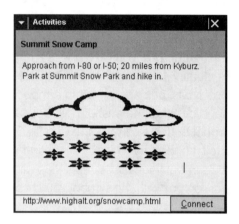

- Click the close button to close the pushpin balloon or window.

TIP　**To change a balloon pushpin to a window pushpin, right-click the pushpin to display the Pushpin Properties dialog box, then change the pushpin designation in the Pushpin Type group box.**

Manipulating a Pushpin

Streets Plus makes it easy to manipulate pushpins you've created on the map. Right-click a pushpin and use the context menu items:

- Choose Display Label or Hide Label to display or hide the label for a pushpin.
- Choose Open to open a pushpin. To close the pushpin again, click the close button on its label or window.
- Select Pushpin Properties to display the Pushpin Properties dialog box. Change the properties as appropriate, and then click the OK button.
- Select Move Pushpin to move a pushpin. Streets Plus will remove the pushpin and display the pushpin pointer. Move the pointer to where you want to place the pushpin and click.

- Choose Delete Pushpin to delete a pushpin from the map. Streets Plus will display a message box identifying the pushpin and asking you to confirm that you want to delete it; click the Yes button.

Finding a Pushpin

If you lose a pushpin, the easiest way to find it is to choose Find ➤ Places to display the Find: Find a Place dialog box. Enter the name of the pushpin in the text box and click the Locate button. Streets Plus will display the Select a Place dialog box listing the pushpin and any similar items. Select the pushpin and click the OK button to display that pushpin on the map.

Working with Sets of Pushpins

To work with sets of pushpins, choose Tools ➤ Pushpins ➤ Pushpin Explorer to display the Pushpin Explorer dialog box (see Figure 24.2). You can then do the following:

- To go to a pushpin, select its set in the Sets list box, right-click the pushpin in the Pushpins list box, and choose Go To from the context menu.
- To rename a pushpin, select its set in the Sets list box, right-click it in the Pushpins list box, and choose Rename from the context menu. Streets Plus will display a renaming box around the name. Edit the old name or type a new one, and press Enter or click elsewhere in the dialog box to register the change.
- To delete a pushpin, select its set in the Sets list box, right-click it in the Pushpins list box, and choose Delete from the context menu. (Alternatively, select the pushpin and press the Delete key.) Streets Plus will display a confirmation message box; click the Yes button to delete the pushpin.
- To delete a set of pushpins, right-click the set in the Sets list box and choose Delete from the context menu. (Alternatively, select the pushpin set and press the Delete key.) Streets Plus will display a confirmation message box; click the Yes button to delete the set of pushpins.
- To create a new set of pushpins, click the down-arrow button and choose New Set, or right-click in the Sets list box and choose New Set from the context menu, to display the New Set dialog box. Enter the name for the new set and click the OK button.
- To export a set of pushpins (for example, to give them to a colleague), right-click the set of pushpins in the Sets list box and choose Export from the context menu to display the Export Pushpin File dialog box. Specify the file

name and folder to which you want to export the pushpins and click the Save button. Streets Plus will display a message box confirming that the pushpins were exported successfully.

- To import pushpins from pushpin files (for example, from a network), click the down-arrow button and choose Import Pushpin File to display the Import Pushpin File dialog box. Select the file to import (pushpin files have a .pin extension) and click the Open button to display the Import Pushpin Set dialog box. Choose the pushpin set into which to import the new pushpins and click the OK button. You can create a new set by clicking the New Set button and specifying the name in the New Set dialog box. Streets Plus will display a message box telling you the pushpins were imported successfully.

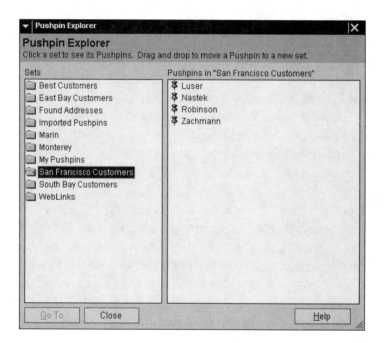

FIGURE 24.2: Use the Pushpin Explorer (Tools ➤ Pushpins ➤ Pushpin Explorer) to manipulate sets of pushpins.

Importing Pushpins from a Text File or Comma-Separated File

For business owners, Streets Plus's ability to import pushpins from outside data sources is one of its strongest features. For example, you can grab a list of your customers from a spreadsheet and import the information as a set of pushpins into Streets Plus, where you can locate each of them swiftly on the map.

To get data into Streets Plus, you need to have it in a file saved in one of the two formats that Streets Plus can import: *comma-separated value files* (.csv—data separated into fields delimited by commas) or *text files* (.txt—ASCII text files with fields of information separated by tabs, commas, semicolons, or other unique separator characters).

Most word-processing applications can create text files; most spreadsheet applications can create comma-separated value files. Here's how to create them with Word and Excel:

- To use a Word document as a source for pushpins, save it as a text file by selecting File ➤ Save As and choosing Text Only (*.txt) in the Save as Type drop-down list in the Save As dialog box.
- To use an Excel spreadsheet as a source for pushpins, save it as a comma-separated value file by choosing File ➤ Save As and choosing Comma Separated Value (*.csv) in the Save as Type drop-down list in the Save As dialog box. Excel will warn you that you can save only the active sheet this way; click the OK button to proceed.

To import pushpins from a text file or comma-separated value file:

1. Choose Tools ➤ Pushpins ➤ Import Text File to display the Find Your Text File dialog box.
2. Select the file from the list. To use a comma-separated value file, choose Comma Delimited Files (*.csv) from the Files of Type drop-down list, then select the file. Then click the Open button. Streets Plus will display the first Text File Import dialog box.
3. Choose the pushpin type (Name Only, Balloon, or Window), the symbol, and the set into which you want to import the pushpins. (You can click the New Set button and create a new set of pushpins in the New Set dialog box.)
4. Click the Next button to display the second Text File Import dialog box (see Figure 24.3).
5. In the Separator group box, select the character used to separate the fields in the text file. Select Comma, Tab, or Semicolon, or click the Other button and enter another separator character (such as |) in the Other text box. Streets Plus will adjust the information shown in the Data Preview box to reflect the separator character you chose. Make sure that the information appears to be separated correctly.
6. If the first row of the text file contains field names (such as First Name, Last Name, and so on), make sure that the Skip the First Row check box is selected. Then click the Next button to display the third Text Field Import dialog box.

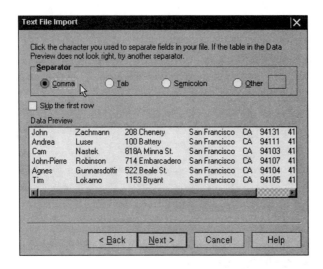

FIGURE 24.3:
In the second Text File Import dialog box, choose the separator character for the text file.

7. In the Data Preview box, assign the fields that you want to use to name and place your pushpins. Click the heading for the appropriate field to select it, and then choose a category for it in the Category drop-down list. Select the [Not Used] category for fields you 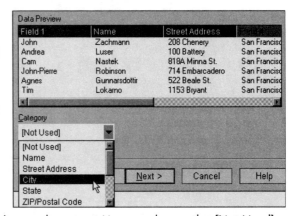 don't want to use for naming or placement. You can choose the [Not Used] category for as many fields as you want, but each other category can be assigned to only one field. Streets Plus will update the column headings in the Data Preview box to reflect your choices. After you've assigned fields, click the Next button to display the fourth Text Field Import dialog box.

8. Select the check boxes for the fields you want to have appear in your pushpins, then click the Next button to display the fifth Text Field Import dialog box.

9. To prevent the pushpins you're importing from being edited, select the No, Do Not Allow Them to Be Edited option button. Otherwise, leave the Yes, Allow Them to Be Edited option button selected. Then click the Finish button to finish importing your pushpins.

If Streets Plus can parse all the addresses, it will create pushpins for them. If there are problems with an address, Streets Plus will display the Find: Address Match dialog box, in which it lists possible variations on that address. Choose the correct address and select the OK button to proceed, or click the Skip button to skip that particular address. (You can click the Automatic button to have Streets Plus automatically fix any irregularities it can, but if Streets Plus cannot fix them, it will display the Import Unsuccessful dialog box.)

Finally, Streets Plus will display the Import Text File Results dialog box, which shows your score of successfully processed and failed records and indicates the log file that contains more information. Click the OK button to dismiss the dialog box.

Finding Points of Interest

Streets Plus includes a listing of points of interest throughout the United States. These points of interest include lodging (hotels, motels, and so on), restaurants, museums, and tourist information.

Streets Plus includes your pushpins along with the points of interest, enabling you to work with both at the same time. For example, you could easily locate the nearest Mexican restaurant within a few miles of a client's office.

To display points of interest by category, choose View ➤ Map Display to display the Map Display dialog box and click the Points of Interest tab. Select the categories of points of interest that you want the map to display, such as Bed and Breakfast, Museums, and Restaurants – Greek.

To display points of interest located near a place you choose:

1. Click the Nearby Points of Interest button on the toolbar, or choose Find ➤ Points of Interest. (Alternatively, click the place in the map and choose Points of Interest from the context menu.) Streets Plus will change the mouse pointer to an animated circle containing a star.

2. On the map, click the place you're interested in. Streets Plus will display the Points of Interest: Nearby Points of Interest dialog box (see Figure 24.4).

3. In the left panel of the dialog box, select the check boxes for the types of points of interest you want to find. For example, if you want to find seafood restaurants and steak houses only, select the Restaurants – Seafood and Restaurants – Steak Houses check boxes and clear all the other check boxes. If Streets Plus finds any matching items, it displays them in the list box on the lower-right side of the dialog box, along with their distance from the place you chose, listed by proximity.

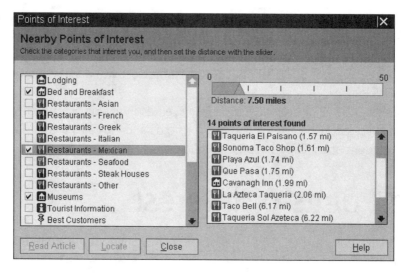

FIGURE 24.4: In the Points of Interest: Nearby Points of Interest dialog box, select the types of points of interest you want to locate.

4. You can adjust the distance slider on the upper-right side of the dialog box to change the range in which Streets Plus should look for points of interest. You can set any range from 0.5 mile to 50 miles, in half-mile increments. As you drag the slider left or right to decrease or increase the distance from the default 5 miles, Streets Plus will update the list box of matching items.

5. To see what information Streets Plus has on a point of interest, select it and click the Read Article button to display the Travel Guide dialog box. Most of the articles provide minimal information, giving just the address and phone number of the point of interest.

   • You can copy the information from the Travel Guide dialog box by right-clicking the down-arrow button at the upper-left corner of the Travel Guide dialog box and choosing Copy from the context menu. You can then paste the information into another Windows application.

   • You can print the information by clicking the down-arrow button at the upper-left corner of the Travel Guide dialog box and choosing Print from the context menu. Streets Plus will display the Print dialog box; make your choices and click the OK button.

   • You can click the Locate button to display the location of the point of interest on the map.

   • Click the Close button to close the Travel Guide dialog box and return to the Points of Interest: Nearby Points of Interest dialog box.

6. To display the location of a selected point of interest on the map, click the Locate button in the Points of Interest: Nearby Points of Interest dialog box.

Using WebLinks

Streets Plus provides WebLinks, which are links to Web pages containing information about 450 cities and locations throughout the United States. To use WebLinks:

1. Choose Find ➤ WebLinks to display the Find: Find WebLinks dialog box.
2. Select the place name for the WebLink in the list box, or type the first few letters of the name, and then use ↓ and ↑ to navigate to it.
3. Click the OK button. Streets Plus will display the Web Link: Connect to the Web dialog box.
4. If you don't want to see this dialog box each time you use a WebLink, select the Don't Show This Message Again check box.
5. Click the OK button. Streets Plus will activate your default Internet connection, start or switch to your default browser, and display the appropriate WebLink information.

When you're finished viewing the WebLink information, close your browser. Also, if you're paying for your Internet connection time, you may want to disconnect from the Internet before you continue with your work.

Choosing Streets Plus Options

To customize Streets Plus's behavior, choose Options ➤ Streets Plus Options to display the Streets Plus Options dialog box. All the check boxes are selected by default when you install Streets Plus:

Menus Fly Out Automatically   Pops up menus automatically when you move the mouse pointer over a menu. Clear the check box if you would rather have the menu wait for you to click it before it appears.

Always Show Tooltips   Displays Tooltips whenever you move the mouse pointer over items that have them. Clear this check box if you don't want to see the Tooltips.

Play Button and Menu Sounds   Plays sounds when you select a button, a menu, or a menu item. Clear the check box if you prefer peace and quiet.

Show Home Screen when Streets Plus Starts   Shows the home screen each time you start Streets Plus. If you prefer to go directly to the map without stopping at the home screen, clear this check box.

Play Startup Sound   Blasts Streets Plus's fanfare when you start it up. Clear the check box if you would like to retain your sanity.

Finally, you can switch the display of distances between miles and kilometers by selecting the Miles option button or the Kilometers option button in the Show Distances In area of the Streets Plus Options dialog box.

Click the OK button to apply your selected options and close the Streets Plus Options dialog box. Alternatively, click the Reset button to return the options to their default settings.

Making Streets Plus Run Faster

Because Streets Plus is such a large and complex application, and it typically runs off a CD-ROM, it's prone to run slowly on older computers, particularly those with slow CD-ROM drives and small amounts of RAM. For example, if you have a 486-based computer with 12–16MB of RAM and a 2x or 4x CD-ROM drive, Streets Plus will probably be frustratingly slow.

Short of upgrading your hardware or optimizing your Windows settings for the CD-ROM drive (which I'm assuming you've already done), there are a number of things you can do to improve the speed at which Streets Plus runs. You'll notice that each way of improving speed has one or more disadvantages, so you'll need to decide which tradeoffs make sense for you.

- Close any programs that you don't need to run at the same time as Streets Plus to make more memory available.
- Adjust your display to use a lower resolution or fewer colors. For example, if Streets Plus is grindingly slow at 1024x768 resolution, try 800x600 resolution or even 640x480 resolution. If you're using High Color or True Color color depths and find Streets Plus is slow, reduce the number of colors to 256. (Streets Plus will not run at 16 colors.) 256 colors at 640x480 resolution provides the best performance, but you'll see a much smaller area of the map at any one time. To adjust the display, choose Start ➤ Settings ➤ Control Panel to display the Control Panel, then double-click the Display icon to open the Display Properties dialog box. On the Settings tab, adjust the Desktop Area and Color Palette settings as necessary, then click the Apply button.
- If your CD-ROM drive is slow (for example, a 2x or 4x drive), and you have 650MB of hard disk space free, you can back up the full Streets Plus CD-ROM to your hard drive, and then install and run it from there. This will make it run much faster. See the Appendix for details on installing Streets Plus.

Part 7

Outlook

Chapter 25

GETTING STARTED WITH OUTLOOK

FEATURING

- **Understanding what Outlook is and does**
- **Navigating the Outlook interface**
- **Scheduling appointments**
- **Scheduling meetings**
- **Working with tasks and task requests**
- **Using Notes**

In this chapter, we'll look at what Outlook is, what it does, and how to navigate its interface. Because of its wealth of apparently disparate features, Outlook takes a little getting used to; it integrates e-mail, a calendar, group scheduling, and desktop information management into a complex interface.

We'll start by discussing what Outlook does. To get technical for a second, Outlook is a *desktop information manager*—DIM for short, an unfortunate acronym but one you'll probably remember. The DIM is Microsoft's idea of the next stage of evolution for the *personal information manager* (PIM) that has become a staple of the organized electronic office.

If you've used a previous version of Office, you'll see that Outlook integrates features from the Schedule+ personal information manager and from the Exchange client that ships with Windows 95 and Windows NT.

We'll also look at how to manage your schedule by using Outlook's Calendar, Tasks, and Notes. The Calendar is your main tool for planning and scheduling your appointments, arranging and tracking meetings, and generally managing your time. Outlook's Tasks feature lets you not only define tasks and track your progress, but also assign them to your colleagues over the network to spread the workload. Finally, Outlook's Notes are an efficient temporary storage of information—the electronic equivalent of sticky notes.

What Outlook Does

Here's a brief rundown on what Outlook does and what its components are. Once we've looked at the big picture, we'll zero in on what each component does.

- Most of Outlook's calendaring capabilities will be familiar if you've used a personal information manager before. You can view your schedule for one day or for a number of days; you can create appointments for yourself and set reminders for them a convenient length of time beforehand. The Calendar also shows the TaskPad, which provides a quick overview of the tasks assigned to you.

- If your colleagues use Outlook, and your company uses Microsoft Exchange Server (or a compatible messaging product) as its messaging system, you can use Outlook to schedule meetings with your colleagues, avoiding tedious back-and-forth phone and e-mail tag. Using Outlook's scheduling capabilities, you can consult your colleagues' calendars and pick what looks like a suitable time for a meeting before inviting them to it. Your colleagues can then reply by clicking the appropriate button on the meeting request they receive—Accept, Tentatively Accept, or Decline—and adding an explanatory note if they want.

- Outlook provides full facilities for keeping as much information as you need for each contact. As we'll see in Chapter 26, you can customize the fields contained in the contacts database, so you can store the data you need for your business. For example, if you need to store the names of your contacts' spouses, children, and dogs, you can create fields specially for these, and you can search on whatever information you retain.

- Outlook's Tasks feature lets you create and monitor tasks; you can track the progress of the task, make notes about it, and assign it to various categories for filing and billing. As we'll see later in this chapter, you can assign tasks to your coworkers (and they can assign tasks to you). Once you've done that, the task is their responsibility, but you can track the progress of the task to make sure they're on schedule.

- Outlook provides a full e-mail client for sending and receiving messages, either on their own or with attached files, and for receiving faxes. In the mail boxes, you can display the first few lines of each e-mail message to help you identify its topic without opening it fully. We'll look at e-mail in detail in Chapter 27.

- The Other category on the Outlook Bar provides quick access to the files on your computer and computers to which yours is connected via an Explorer-style window. For sharing information with your colleagues, you can create public folders on a networked drive; this is useful for setting up informal arrangements for collaborating on projects.

- Outlook's Journal feature enables you to track the actions you perform in the Office applications and record them on a timeline. In addition to any entries you make manually, the Journal can list the Office files you worked on by date, giving you not only a record of what you worked on when but also direct access to the files involved. You can also choose which Office operations you want the Journal to record. For example, you could choose to record every Excel or PowerPoint file you work with, but not every Word document. You can also track every conversation and meeting with a contact, which can prove invaluable for accurate billing of projects.

- Outlook's Notes pages let you take quick notes on projects. For example, you might take notes during a phone call on a Note page rather than on a sticky note or a pad of paper. You can then transfer the information from the note into one of the other areas of Outlook—for instance, to create a new contact, to update your notes for a contact, or as part of an e-mail message or meeting request. We'll look at Notes at the end of this chapter.

Navigating the Outlook Interface

The Outlook interface is straightforward to navigate once you know what all its components are. Each of the components of Outlook has its own layout. These components are tied together by a shared menu structure, shared toolbar buttons, and the Outlook Bar on the left side of the Outlook window.

- To go to one of the components of Outlook, click its icon on the Outlook Bar. To switch the Outlook Bar from displaying the main set of Outlook items to the set of Mail items or Other items, click the Mail, Other, or Outlook button at the bottom or top of the Outlook Bar.
- You can customize the size of the panes in any of the Outlook windows by moving the mouse pointer over the division between the panes so that it turns into a double-headed arrow; then click and drag the division to where you want it.
- You can toggle the display of the Outlook bar by choosing View ➤ Outlook Bar.
- If you hide the Outlook Bar, you can navigate among the components of the Outlook display by using the Folder List drop-down list or the Folder List pane. To toggle the display of the Folder List pane, choose View ➤ Folder List.
- You can click the Forward and Back buttons on the Standard toolbar to move forward and backward through the different items you've been working on in Outlook. For example, if you're working in the Calendar and you decide to create a note and then check your Journal, you can click the Back button to move from the Journal back to the note and then back to the Calendar. At this point, clicking the Forward button will take you to the note and then to the Journal.

Using the Calendar

As you might guess, the Calendar is for keeping your schedule organized. The Calendar recognizes a number of different items: appointments, events, annual events, meetings, meeting requests, tasks, task requests, contacts, journal entries, notes, and Office documents. In the following sections, we'll look at what these are—and how they differ from one another.

To switch to the Calendar, click the Calendar icon on the Outlook Bar.

Using Views in Calendar

Calendar provides six predefined views for viewing the information in your calendar: Day/Week/Month view, Active Appointments view, Events view, Annual Events view, Recurring Appointments view, and By Category view. We'll look at these in the next sections.

To move between the different views, use the Current View drop-down list on the Outlook toolbar.

Using Day/Week/Month View

Day/Week/Month view (see Figure 25.1) provides a traditional calendar view consisting of appointments, meetings, and events, together with a display of two months and a list of tasks.

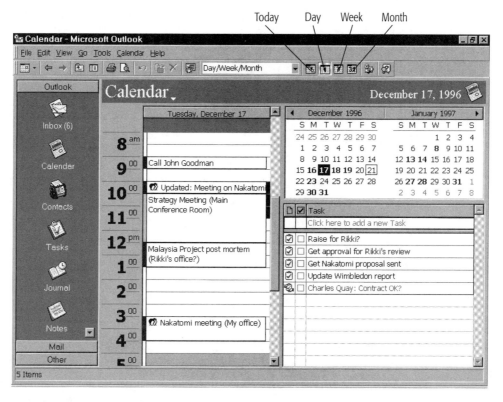

FIGURE 25.1: Use Day/Week/Month view to get a quick look at a day's business.

By default, the view starts by displaying the current day's calendar, but you can change this by using the toolbar buttons or by clicking and dragging in the month area:

- To display the current day, click the Today button.
- To display just the day currently selected in the Calendar, click the Day button.
- To display the week for the day currently selected, click the Week button.
- To display the month for the day currently selected, click the Month button.
- To select another day, click on it in the month area.
- To select several days, a week, or several weeks, click and drag through them in the month.
- To move to the month before the earlier month shown, click the left-arrow button beside the month's name. To move to the month after the second month shown, click the right-arrow button beside the month's name.
- To move to a month farther from the displayed months, click on one of the months and choose the month you want to move to from the pop-up list. The pop-up list will display six months, but you can drag up and down through it to reach other months.

Other Views

The other calendar views work as follows:

Active Appointments View   Lists all appointments entered in your calendar from the current day forward (see Figure 25.2).

Events View   Shows you a list of all events (one-shot or recurring) you have defined, together with all the details you've entered for them (see Figure 25.3).

Annual Events View   Llists the annual events you have defined, together with their details.

Recurring Appointments View   Lists the recurring appointments you have defined, together with their details.

By Category view   Lists the Outlook items that you have assigned to a particular category (see Figure 25.4). For example, by assigning a variety of items to a project for a client, you can track them together in By Category view, rather than scrabbling to pull together assorted e-mail messages, appointments, meetings, and so on.

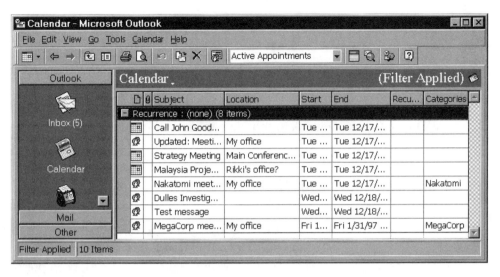

FIGURE 25.2:   Use Active Appointments view to see what you've got lined up for the foreseeable future.

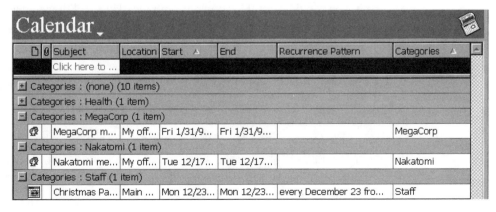

FIGURE 25.3:   Use Events view to see your list of events.

FIGURE 25.4:   Use By Category view to manage the Calendar items you have assigned to the categories you use.

Scheduling Appointments

One of Outlook's strengths is in scheduling appointments and reminding you of them. You can set up one-shot appointments or recurring appointments; you can use alarms to remind you of impending appointments; and (if you're using Exchange Server) you can use Outlook to schedule meetings by manipulating other people's schedules.

Creating an Appointment

To create a one-shot appointment:

1. If you're not already in Day/Week/Month view, switch to it by choosing it in the Current View drop-down list. Alternatively, choose View ➤ Current View and select Day/Week/Month from the submenu. (This isn't compulsory, but Day/Week/Month view makes it far easier to see what you're doing.)

2. Click in the time slot for the appointment. If your appointment is for more than 30 minutes, drag through the time slots it will occupy.

3. Right-click in the time slot or time slots you selected and choose New Appointment from the context menu to display an Appointment window with the Appointment tab displayed (see Figure 25.5). Alternatively, click the New button and choose Appointment from the drop-down list, or choose File ➤ New ➤ Appointment.

4. Type a cogent description for the appointment in the Subject box. (This is what you'll see in the Calendar.)

5. If you want, enter the location for the meeting in the Location box.

6. Verify the dates and times shown on the Start Time and End Time lines. If you've chosen the time for the appointment by clicking and dragging in the calendar, these should reflect your choices; otherwise, you'll need to set them manually. For each, use the drop-down calendar to set the date and the drop-down list to set the time.

7. To have Outlook remind you of the appointment, select the Reminder check box. Specify the interval (in minutes, hours, or days) before the appointment that the reminder should occur.

8. To set a sound for the reminder, click the sound icon to display the Reminder Sound dialog box. Make sure the When Reminder Comes Due, Play This Sound check box is selected, and then click the Browse button to display the Reminder Sound File dialog box. Choose the sound file you want

to hear; then click the Open button to return to the Reminder Sound dialog box. Click the OK button to set the sound and close the dialog box.

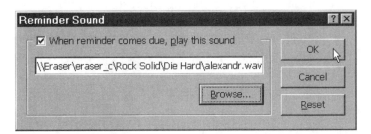

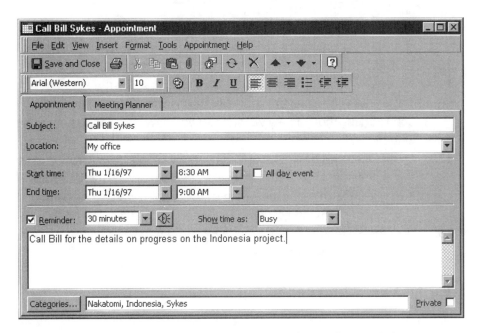

FIGURE 25.5: Set up the details for your appointment in the Appointment window.

TIP   You can set a reminder sound for all your appointments by choosing Tools ➤ Options from the main Outlook window (not from an Appointment window) to display the Options dialog box. On the Reminders tab, select the Play Reminder Sound check box; then click the Browse button to display the Reminder Sound File dialog box. Choose the sound file you want to hear, and click the Open button to return to the Options dialog box. Click the OK button to close the Options dialog box.

9. In the Show Time As drop-down list, choose how you want the time period for this appointment to appear on your calendar: Free, Tentative, Busy, or Out of Office. (If you're sharing your calendar with your colleagues, this can help them schedule appointments with you.) Appointments marked as Busy appear in the Calendar with royal-blue shading in the bar beside the time span; appointments marked as Tentative appear with gray shading and are shown to others as free; appointments marked as Out of Office appear with light-blue shading; and appointments marked as Free appear without shading.

10. Enter any notes for the appointment in the main text box.
11. If you want to mark an appointment as private, select the Private check box. This allows you to prevent your colleagues from seeing the details of the appointment, though they will see that you have an appointment scheduled at the time.
12. In the Categories box, enter any categories with which you want to associate this appointment. Click the Categories button to display the Categories dialog box, select the check boxes for the categories you want in the Available Categories list box, and click the OK button to close the Categories dialog box.
13. Click the Save and Close button to close the Appointment window and record the details in the Calendar.

Creating a Recurring Appointment

If only all appointments were one-time, life would be eternally entertaining—but no, recurring appointments are a fact of life. Outlook can help you deal with those weekly (or biweekly) progress reports, those monthly strategy meetings, and even those bi-annual visits to the dentist. You can create a recurring appointment either from scratch or from an existing appointment.

To create a recurring appointment from scratch:

1. Right-click in the time slot and choose New Recurring Appointment. Outlook will display an Appointment window and the Appointment Recurrence dialog box (see Figure 25.6).
2. In the Appointment Time group box, specify the starting time, ending time, and duration of the appointment.

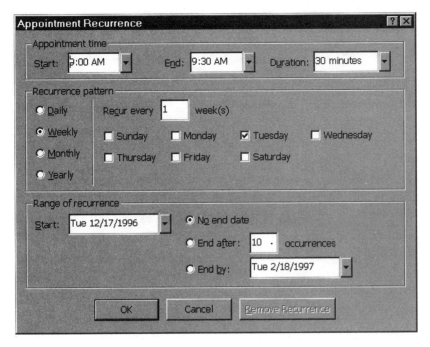

FIGURE 25.6: In the Appointment Recurrence dialog box, specify details for a recurring appointment.

3. In the Recurrence Pattern group box, specify how often and when the appointment will recur:

- First, select the Daily, Weekly, Monthly, or Yearly option button. The dialog box will display the appropriate set of options in the right-hand panel.
- Then specify the details of the recurrence in the right-hand panel. For example, if you chose the Monthly option button, you could choose The Third Wednesday of Every 1 Month, as shown here.

4. In the Range of Recurrence group box, adjust the start date in the Start box if necessary, and then specify an end date if the recurring appointment has one in sight. Often you'll want to leave the No End Date option button selected, but you can also select the End After option button and specify a number of occurrences, or select the End By option button and specify a date in the drop-down calendar.

5. Click the OK button to close the Appointment Recurrence dialog box. You can then create the appointment as usual in the Appointment window. When you save and close the appointment, it will appear at every recurrence you set, marked by a circular-arrow icon, as shown here.

| 10 ⁰⁰ | ↻ Strategy Session (Conference Room) |
| 11 ⁰⁰ | |

To turn an existing appointment into a recurring appointment, create a regular appointment as described in "Creating an Appointment," but don't click the Save and Close button; instead click the Recurrence button or choose Appointment ➤ Recurrence to display the Appointment Recurrence dialog box, and specify the details of the recurring appointment as discussed in the steps above.

Deleting an Appointment

Deleting an appointment is straightforward and painless: In the Calendar, right-click in the appointment and choose Delete Item from the context menu. If the appointment is open in an Appointment window, click the Delete button or choose File ➤ Delete.

When you delete a recurring appointment, Outlook will display a message box asking if you want to delete all occurrences of the recurring appointment. Select the Delete All Occurrences option button to delete all occurrences or the Delete This One option button to delete just this occurrence, and then click the OK button.

TIP   If you accidentally delete the wrong appointment, choose Edit ➤ Undo immediately (or press Ctrl+Z).

Moving an Appointment

The easiest way to change the time of an appointment is to drag it in the Calendar, as shown here. This also works well for moving an appointment by a number of days:

Display a suitable number of days in the Calendar, and then click in the appointment and drag it to where you want it to be. If the Calendar is displaying days and hours, you 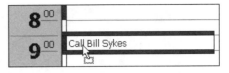 can change both the time and date at the same time; if the Calendar is displaying only days, the appointment will retain its current time when you drag it to a different date. You can also drag an appointment to a date displayed in the months area.

You can also move an appointment by opening it in an Appointment window and then changing the date and time on the Start Time and End Time lines.

Scheduling a Meeting

Outlook thinks a meeting is an appointment that requires at least one other person. (In reality, of course, this is true for most appointments.) If your office is using Outlook with Microsoft Exchange Server as your messaging system, you can use Outlook's automatic features to schedule meetings: You specify the time for the meeting and who (and what resources) you want to attend, and then Outlook checks the attendees' calendars and lets you know if they can attend.

To schedule a meeting:

1. Right-click in the Calendar and choose New Meeting Request from the context menu, or click the New button's drop-down list and choose Meeting Request, or choose Calendar ➤ New Meeting Request. Outlook will open a Meeting window (see Figure 25.7).

2. Click the To button to display the Select Attendees and Resources dialog box (see Figure 25.8).

   • Choose the appropriate address book in the Show Names From The drop-down list.

   • In the Type Name or Select from List list box, select the name and click the Required button, the Optional button, or the Resources button to add the selected name to the appropriate box. When you mark a person as required for a meeting, Outlook will try to resolve any scheduling conflicts so the person can attend the meeting; when you mark a person as optional, Outlook will not try to resolve any scheduling conflicts. Resources are items such as conference rooms or presentation equipment.

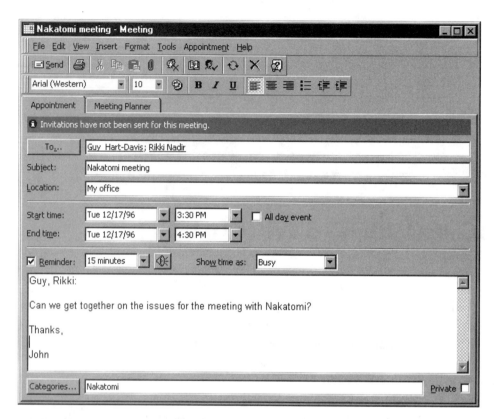

FIGURE 25.7: On the Appointment tab in the Meeting window, arrange the details for the meeting.

NOTE Depending on what kind of e-mail system you're using Outlook with, you'll have different address books available to you. For example, if you're using Outlook with an Exchange Server messaging system, you should have access to a Global Address List of all the people and resources on the network. You probably won't be able to add addresses to the Global Address List, but you can keep a Personal Address Book, which you can add to by clicking the New button in any of the dialog boxes that allow you to select names (Select Names, Select Task Recipient, and so on) or by choosing Tools ➤ Address Book and working in the Address Book dialog box.

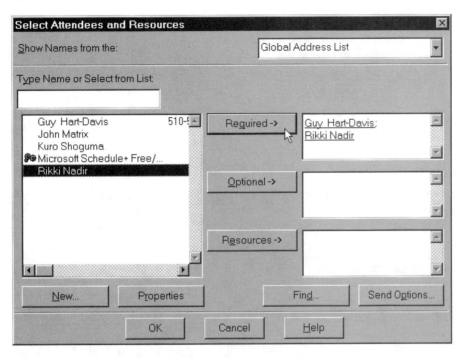

FIGURE 25.8: In the Select Attendees and Resources dialog box, invite the people you want (or need) to attend the meeting.

3. In the Subject text box on the Meeting Window, enter a description of the meeting.

4. In the Location text box, enter the location for the meeting, or choose it from the drop-down list.

5. Set the date, starting time, and ending time for the meeting in the Start Time and End Time lines.

6. Set a reminder for the meeting if you want one, and then choose an option in the Show Time box and categories in the Categories box. (For details, see "Creating an Appointment," earlier in this chapter.)

7. Click the Meeting Planner tab to display it (see Figure 25.9). Click the Show Attendee Availability option button to show the calendar for each of the attendees for the day in question and a day or two after it. You can scroll to different days using the horizontal scroll bar.

8. Drag the meeting selection bars to a mutually convenient time for the meeting. The green bar indicates the start of the meeting and the scarlet bar the end of the meeting. Alternatively, click the AutoPick button to have Outlook automatically pick the next vacant time slot for the meeting; click the << button to move to the previous vacant time slot.

9. Click the Send button to send the meeting request to the prospective attendees.

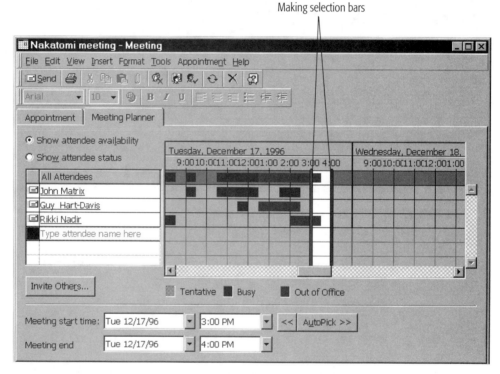

FIGURE 25.9: On the Meeting Planner tab, schedule the best time for the meeting by consulting the schedules of those attending.

Receiving Replies to a Meeting Request

When your colleagues reply to a meeting request (we'll look at replying in "Responding to a Meeting Request" in a moment), the reply will come to your Inbox.

Double-click the reply to open it. Outlook will display a Meeting Response window (see Figure 25.10) and will update your calendar with the acceptance, tentative acceptance, or refusal.

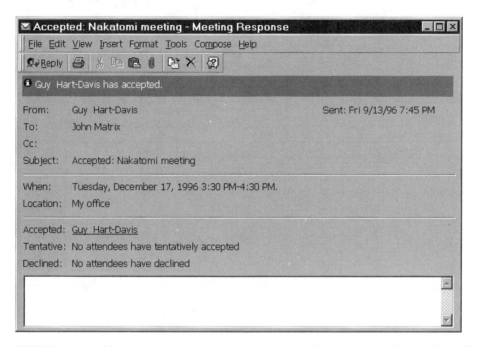

FIGURE 25.10: When you open a meeting response in a Meeting Response window, Outlook will automatically update the meeting status in your calendar.

Checking Attendee Status

You can track responses to a meeting request by using the Show Attendee Status option button on the Meeting Planner tab of the Meeting window (see Figure 25.11). (Open the Meeting window by double-clicking the meeting in question on the Calendar.) The Attendance column shows the person's or item's status for the meeting (Meeting Organizer, Required Attendee, Optional Attendee, or Resource), and the Response column shows whether they have responded to the meeting request and (if they have) what their answer was.

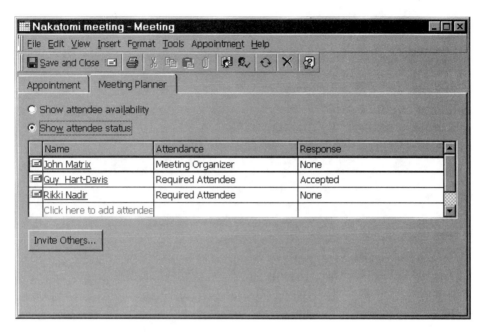

FIGURE 25.11: Use the Show Attendee Status option button to track who has responded to your meeting requests.

Responding to a Meeting Request

When you receive a meetingrequest, it will show up in your Inbox marked with a meeting request icon, as shown here.

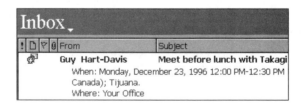

To respond to the meeting request, double-click the request to open it in a Meeting window (see Figure 25.12). The Standard toolbar will display Accept, Tentatively Accept, and Decline buttons so that you can respond quickly.

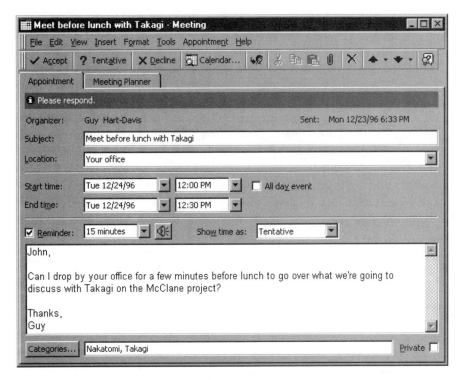

FIGURE 25.12: When you receive a meeting request, open it in a Meeting window.

To respond quickly, click the Accept, Tentatively Accept, or Decline button on the Standard toolbar. Outlook will display a Microsoft Outlook dialog box to confirm your choice.

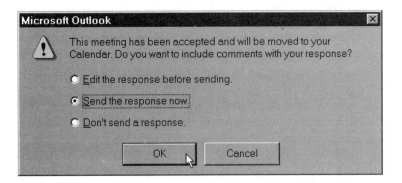

Choose one of the option buttons:

- Edit the Response before Sending opens a Meeting Response window in which you can add your comments to the response. Enter your comments in the main text box as usual, and then click the Send button to send the response. This is useful for suggesting a new time for a meeting that you have to decline for reasons not apparent from your published calendar.
- Send the Response Now sends the response you gave without your adding any comments to it. If you're accepting a meeting, you may not need to add any comments.
- Don't Send a Response closes the message without sending a response. This isn't a great choice unless you're making a mental note to send a firm response later.

If you choose to send a response (with or without adding comments to it), it will show up in the Meeting organizer's Inbox, as discussed in the previous section.

Tasks

Outlook's task-management capabilities can help you get your work life organized. A task in Outlook, as in life, is something that you need to get done. You can set alarms and reminders for tasks; for example, you could set a reminder to alert you three days before a task was due. You can also track the status of each task so deadlines don't creep up on you by surprise.

Tasks can belong to one or more *categories*. By assigning each task to the appropriate categories, you can quickly pull together all the tasks for a particular project, along with the meetings, appointments, and other details for that project.

You can sort and filter tasks so Outlook presents to you only the ones you need to see at any given point. For example, you might want to filter tasks so you see only the tasks needing to be completed in the next week or two; you could then sort that list by priority to see what you absolutely had to do first.

You can work with tasks in the Tasks window (see Figure 25.13) or in the TaskPad in the Calendar. To display the Tasks window, click the Tasks icon on the Outlook Bar.

You can create one-time tasks or recurring tasks. Recurring tasks can recur either at scheduled intervals (such as distributing paychecks on the last day of the month) or at a set interval after the completion date of the previous instance of the task (such as going to the dentist—you want to go six months *after* you actually visit the dentist, *not* six months after that first appointment you missed because of a business trip to Cancun).

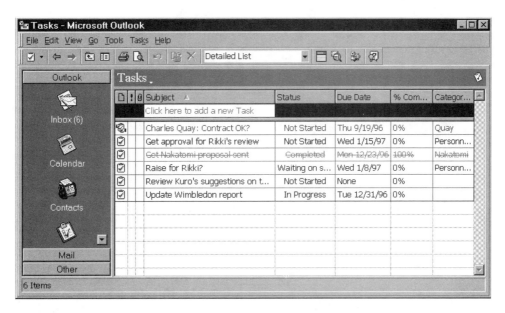

FIGURE 25.13:   Working with tasks in the Tasks window.

Creating a Task

You can create a task quickly in the Tasks window or TaskPad, or if you need, you can create a more detailed task in the Tasks window. To create a task quickly, click in the Click Here to Add a New Task box. Enter the name for the task; then (in the Calender Only) click in the Due Date column box, click the drop-down list button that will appear, and choose the due date from the drop-down calendar. Click elsewhere in the Task list to enter the task.

To create a task with more detail:

1.   Right-click in the Task list and choose New Task from the context menu, or click the New button and choose Task from the drop-down list, or choose File ➤ New ➤ Task. Outlook will display a Tasks window (see Figure 25.14).

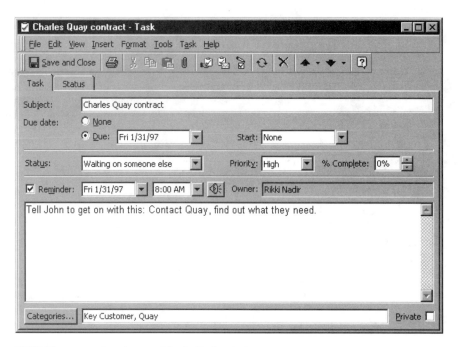

FIGURE 25.14: Creating a task in the Tasks window

2. In the Subject text box, enter a description of the task. This is what you will see in the Task list, so the more cogent and concise it is, the more comprehensible your list will be.

3. If the task has a due date, select the Due option button in the Due Date area, and then select a date from the drop-down calendar. If appropriate, select a start date in the Start drop-down calendar.

4. If you're recording a task you've already started, adjust the selection in the Status drop-down list from Not Started to In Progress or Waiting on Some-one Else, and set the percentage of the task completed so far in the % Complete box.

5. Adjust the priority for the new task in the Priority box as necessary.

6. If you want, set a reminder for the task by selecting the Reminder check box and specifying a date.

7. In the main area, enter notes about the task. You can use the buttons on the Formatting toolbar to format this text.

8. If appropriate, assign the task to one or more categories by clicking the Categories button and selecting the check boxes for the categories in the Available Categories list box in the Categories dialog box. Click the OK button to close the Categories dialog box.

9. If necessary, select the Private check box to mark the task as private.

10. Click the Save and Close button to save the task and close the Tasks window.

Tracking the Status of a Task

You can adjust the status of each task to reflect your progress on it:

1. In the Task list or the TaskPad in the Calendar, double-click the task to open it in a Tasks window.

2. Click the Status tab to display it (see Figure 25.15).

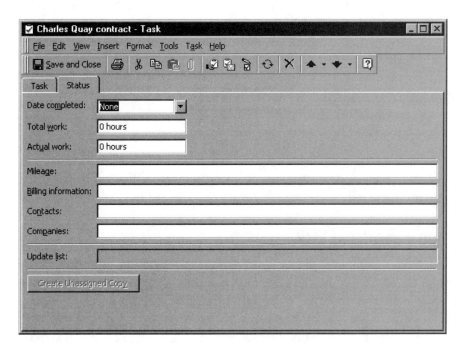

FIGURE 25.15: On the Status tab of the Tasks window, track the status of the task, your contact and billing information, and more.

3. If you've completed the task, you can select the date when you completed it in the Date Completed drop-down calendar. The Date Completed box will automatically be filled in when the % setting on the Task tab reaches 100%.

4. In the Total Work and Actual Work text boxes, enter the number of hours spent on the task.
5. Enter mileage, billing information, contacts, and companies as appropriate.
6. Click the Save and Close button to save the changes and close the Tasks window.

Marking a Task as Completed

You can mark a task as completed in three ways:

- In the Task list, click in the Completed column (the column headed with the check mark) for the task.
- On the Task tab of a Tasks window, change the percentage completed to 100%.
- On the Status tab of a Tasks window, choose a completion date, as discussed in the previous section.

Completed tasks are marked with a check mark in the Completed column and are shown in strikethrough text.

☑		Get approval for Rikki's review	Not Started	Wed 1/15/97	0%	Personnel...
☑		~~Get Nakatomi proposal sent~~	~~Completed~~	~~Mon 12/23/96~~	~~100%~~	~~Nakatomi~~
☑		Raise for Rikki?	Waiting on so...	Wed 1/8/97	0%	Personnel...

To mark a task as incomplete again, click once more in the Completed column for the task or set the percentage completed to less than 100%.

Adding a Recurring Task

In Outlook, you can set recurring tasks, such as submitting timecards. As we saw earlier in this section, you can create both tasks that recur regularly at set intervals and tasks that recur a set interval after the previous task was completed.

To turn a task into a recurring task:

1. Double-click the task in the task list or the TaskPad to open it in a Tasks window.

2. Click the Recurrence button or choose Task ➤ Recurrence to display the Task Recurrence dialog box (see Figure 25.16).

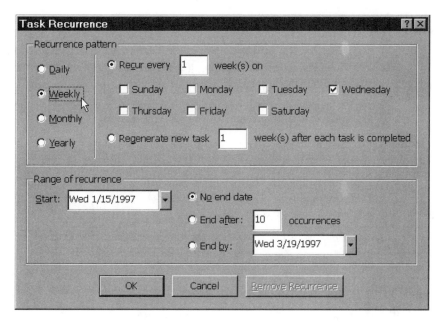

FIGURE 25.16: Arrange your recurring tasks in the Task Recurrence dialog box.

3. In the Recurrence Pattern group box, specify how often the task will recur:
- Select the Daily, Weekly, Monthly, or Yearly option button. The dialog box will then display the appropriate set of options in the right-hand panel.
- If you want the task to recur at regular intervals, specify the details of the recurrence in the right-hand panel. For example, if you chose the Weekly option button, you could choose Recur Every 1 Week and Thursday.
- If you want the task to recur based on when the previous instance was completed, select the Regenerate New Task option button and specify the number of days, weeks, months, or years to pass.

4. In the Range of Recurrence group box, adjust the start date in the Start box if necessary, and then specify an end date if the recurring task has one in sight. Often you'll want to leave the No End Date option button selected, but you can also select the End After option button and specify a number of occurrences, or select the End By option button and specify a date in the drop-down calendar.

5. Click the OK button to close the Task Recurrence dialog box.

Deleting a Task

To delete a task, right-click in it and choose Delete Item from the context menu or click the Delete button on the Standard toolbar. If the task is a recurring task, Outlook will ask if you want to delete all instances of it or just this one; choose the appropriate option and click the OK button.

To change the view of your tasks, select a view from the Current View drop-down list on the Standard toolbar:

- Simple List shows all tasks with just their subject and due date.
- Detailed List shows all tasks with their subject, due date, status, percent complete, and categories.
- Active Tasks shows tasks that have not been completed.
- Next Seven Days shows tasks marked as due within the next seven days.
- Overdue Tasks shows tasks that have not been completed and that are past their due date.
- By Category displays tasks broken down into the categories to which they are assigned.
- Assignment displays tasks listed with the person to whom they are assigned.
- By Person Responsible displays a list of the people to whom tasks are assigned.
- Completed Tasks displays tasks marked as complete.
- Task Timeline displays a timeline view of when tasks are due.

Sorting Tasks

You can quickly sort tasks in Outlook by clicking the displayed column headings in any Tasks view. For example, to sort tasks alphabetically in ascending order by the Subject column, click the Subject column heading once. Outlook will sort the tasks alphabetically and will display an upward-pointing arrowhead in the column heading. To sort tasks alphabetically in descending order, click the Subject column heading; Outlook will sort the tasks and will display a downward-pointing arrowhead.

You can apply finer sorting by choosing View ➤ Sort and choosing sorting options for one, two, three, or four fields in the Sort dialog box. For each field, you can specify Ascending or Descending sort order.

Using Task Requests

Not only can you set tasks for yourself to perform, but you can send task requests to your colleagues. These function in a similar way to meeting requests, except that there's no need to work out a meeting time.

Creating and Sending a Task Request

To create a task request:

1. Click the New button and choose Task Request from the drop-down list, or choose File ➤ New ➤ Task Request, or right-click in the TaskPad in the Calendar and choose Task Request from the context menu to display a Tasks window.
2. On the Task tab, use the To box and To button to specify the recipient or recipients, and enter a subject for the task in the Subject box.
3. Specify the other task details as discussed in "Creating a Task."
4. Choose how you want to track the status of the tasks by selecting the Keep an Updated Copy of This Task on My Task List check box and Send Me a Status Report When This Task is Complete check box.
5. Click the Send button to send the task request.

Responding to a Task Request

When you find a task request sitting in your Inbox smiling at you, here's what to do:

1. Double-click it to open it in a Tasks window.
2. Accept the task by clicking the Accept button or decline the task by clicking the Decline button. Outlook will display the Accepting Task dialog box, shown here, or the Declining Task dialog box.

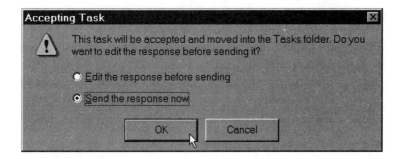

3. If you want to add comments to the response, select the Edit the Response Before Sending option button, click the OK button, enter your comments, and then click the Send button to send the response. Otherwise, select the Send the Response Now option button and click the OK button to send the response.

4. If you accepted the task, Outlook will add it to your Tasks list. If you declined the task, Outlook will move it to your Deleted Items folder.

Notes

Outlook's notes are simple and intuitive to work with. You can work with them either in the Notes window or by opening a note on top of any other Outlook window.

To work with notes in the Notes window, display the Notes window by clicking the Notes icon on the Outlook Bar. You can then create a note by clicking the New Note button or choosing File ➤ New ➤ Note. Outlook will open a new note in its own window and will stamp it with the date and time. Enter the text of the note by typing and editing as usual (see Figure 25.17). When you're finished, close it by clicking its close button.

FIGURE 25.17:
Creating a note in the Notes window

If you want to create a new note while working in another Outlook window, click the New drop-down list button and choose Note from it, or choose File ➤ New ➤ Note. Outlook will display a Note window on top of the window you're working in.

To open an existing note, double-click it in the Notes window. Once you've opened a note, you can drag and drop or copy and paste its contents into any of the Outlook windows or into any Office application. For example, by dragging the contents of a note and dropping them in a time slot in the Calendar window, you can have Outlook start a new appointment for you, open it in an Appointment window, and enter the dropped text into it.

Chapter 26

CONTACTS, THE JOURNAL, AND YOUR DATA

- **Working with contact information**
- **Using the Journal to track your activities**
- **Importing and exporting data**
- **Using the backup, archive, and restore features**

Apart from scheduling appointments, projects, and tasks, Outlook offers a powerful contact-management database that you can integrate with the other Office applications. In this chapter, we'll also look at how you can import into Outlook information from other personal information management applications, and how you can streamline Outlook and protect your data by archiving it.

Contacts

Depending on your business, you may find Outlook's contact-management features even more useful than its scheduling capabilities. To work with the contacts database, click the Contacts icon in the Outlook Bar to display the Contacts book (shown in Figure 26.1), and then follow the instructions in the following sections for adding contacts and working with the contact information.

FIGURE 26.1: Working with contacts in the Contacts book

First, we'll look at how you can use Outlook's default contact form to add information for a contact. Then we'll look at how you can create custom contact forms that contain the fields you need.

Adding a Person to Your Contact List

To add a person to your list of contacts:

1. Click the New Contact button, or right-click in the Contacts window and choose New Contact from the context menu, or choose File ➤ New ➤ Contact, to open a Contact window with the General tab displayed (see Figure 26.2).

2. Enter the person's name in the Full Name text box.

    - If you're not sure that Outlook will identify the components of the name correctly, click the Full Name button to display the Check Full Name dialog box (see Figure 26.3), in which Outlook will show you how it thinks the components of the name fit together. Add a title as necessary in the Title text box, either by typing or by choosing it from the drop-down list, and verify the entries in the First, Middle, and Last text boxes. You can also choose a suffix (I, II, III, Jr., Sr.) as needed from the Suffix drop-down list. Click the OK button to close the Check Full Name dialog box.

    - Alternatively, you can simply click the Full Name button and enter the name as you want it in the Check Full Name dialog box.

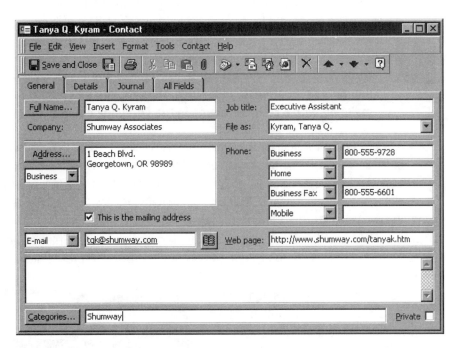

FIGURE 26.2: Enter all the details for your contact in the Contact window.

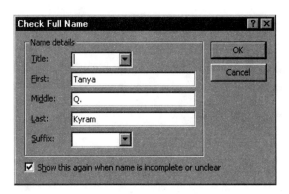

FIGURE 26.3:
You can use the Check Full Name dialog box to make sure that Outlook has understood a name correctly or to enter the name manually.

- The Show This Again When Name Is Incomplete or Unclear check box controls whether Outlook automatically displays the Check Full Name dialog box when you enter a name it cannot separate into its components in the Full Name text box. For example, if you enter just a first name and move to another field, Outlook will display the Check Full Name dialog box to prod you to enter the rest of the name. On the other hand, if you enter something off-kilter, such as **Francis the Talking Mule**, Outlook will simply divide it (with *Talking* as first name, *Mule* as the last name, and *Francis the* as the title) and let you proceed, so don't trust it too much. (I agree, that wasn't a fair test of its capabilities.)

NOTE	Outlook craves first names and last names, and it will try to make you enter one of each. In a pinch, though, you can persuade it to make do with a company name in the Company box.

- As soon as you move from the Full Name text box to another text box (by pressing Enter or Tab to move to the Job Title text box or by clicking elsewhere in the Contact window), Outlook will divide the name and enter it in the File As drop-down list in filing order. For example, if you enter **Tanya Q. Kyram** in the Full Name text box, Outlook will enter **Kyram, Tanya Q.** in the File As drop-down list.

3. Enter the contact's job title in the Job Title text box and press Enter or Tab.
4. Enter the contact's company in the Company text box and press Enter or Tab.
5. If necessary, change the setting in the File As drop-down list. Outlook offers various permutations of name and company name, as shown here.

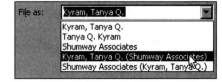

6. Enter an address in the Address box. As with the Full Name, you can do this in a couple of ways:

- First, select the type of address in the drop-down list: Business, Home, or Other.
- Then either enter the address in the Address box by typing it in, or click the Address button to display the Check Address dialog box (see Figure 26.4).

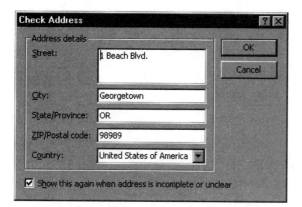

FIGURE 26.4:
You can use the Check Address dialog box either to check that Outlook has divided an address correctly or to enter the address manually in the appropriate boxes.

- The Show This Again When Address Is Incomplete or Unclear check box in the Check Address dialog box controls whether Outlook automatically displays the Check Address dialog box if you enter an address that confuses it. For example, if you enter something idiotic like **The other side of town** in the Address box, Outlook will display the Check Address dialog box to query you (unless you've switched this feature off by clearing the check box).
- Back in the Contact window, select the This Is the Mailing Address check box if this is the address you want to use by default for mailings to this contact.

7. To enter another address (of a different type) for the contact, repeat step 6, choosing a different type of address in the drop-down list. For example, if you already entered a business address in step 6, you might now enter a home address.

8. Enter phone numbers for the contact in the Phone area. Outlook provides storage for up to 19 phone numbers for each contact, of which you can display up to four at any one time.

- In the top box, choose the type of phone number from the drop-down list, and then enter the number in the text box. When you move from that text box, Outlook will format the number for you in the (510) 555-1212 format, so you can enter it without any separators as **5105551212** or with spaces as **510 555 1212**.

- Repeat for the other three boxes as necessary. If you have more numbers than that for the contact, select another type of phone number from one of the drop-down lists and enter the number.

9. Enter one to three e-mail addresses for the contact by selecting E-mail, E-mail 2, or E-mail 3 in the E-mail drop-down list and entering the address in the text box. If you already have the e-mail address stored in one of your address books, you can click the Select Name button to display the Select Name dialog box. Choose the address book to use from the Show Names From The drop-down list, select the name in the Type Name or Select from List list box, and click the OK button.

10. In the Web Page text box, enter the URL for the contact's Web page.

11. In the Categories text box, use the Categories button to choose any categories you want to be associated with this contact.

12. If this is a private contact, select the Private check box.

13. If you want to have the Journal automatically record your dealings with this contact, select the Automatically Record Journal Entries for This Contact check box on the Journal tab.

14. When you've finished entering the details for your contact, click the Save and Close button to close the Contact dialog box and to enter the details in your contact database.

Customizing Your Contact Forms

You can create customized contact forms that contain the fields you need for working most efficiently with your contacts. For example, if you want to include your contacts' birthdays in your database, or the names of any administrative assistant they may have, you can add fields for these on a tab in the Contact window.

Choose Tools ➤ Design Outlook Form to display the Contact form in Design View. Outlook will display *(Design)* in the title bar of the Contact window.

Click on the page you want to modify. You can modify the pages identified as P.2, P.3, P.4, P.5, and P.6; you cannot modify the General tab or any of the other pages. At first, P.2 and so on will appear in parentheses. This means that Outlook will not display them in Form view (the view you use for working in them) until you tell it to.

As an example, let's add a page named Personal to the Contact window:

1. Click on one of the Page tabs to display it. Here, I'll click on P.2. Outlook displays a blank page and the Field Chooser dialog box (see Figure 26.5).

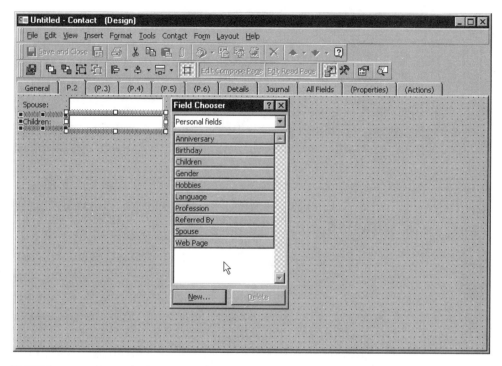

FIGURE 26.5:   Use Outlook's Design View to customize a contact form to suit your needs.

2.   Choose the category of fields you want from the drop-down list at the top of the Field Chooser dialog box. Here, I'll choose Personal Fields to display a list of personal fields in the Field Chooser dialog box.

3.   Click and drag the fields you need to where you want them to appear on the page.

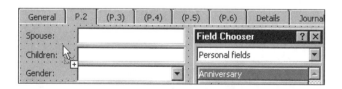

• By default, Outlook sets three options that will help you lay out your form. These are Show Grid, which shows the grid of dots that you see in Figure 26.5; Snap to Grid, which aligns the edges of any field you drag and drop with the grid; and Auto-Layout, which automatically lays out items at a sensible spacing interval from each other and rearranges fields you drop on top of other fields. You can toggle any or all of these options off (or back on) by pulling down the Layout menu and selecting the relevant item. (Snap to Grid and Show Grid are also on the context menu.)

- To delete a field you've placed, select it and press the Delete key.
- To move a field you've placed, select it and drag it to where you want it.
- To choose fields from a different category, choose the category in the drop-down list.

4. To create a new field of your own, click the New button in the Field Chooser dialog box to display the New Field dialog box (see Figure 26.6):

- In the Name text box, enter the name for the field. In the figure, I'm creating one named Spouse's Birthday.
- In the Type drop-down list, choose the field type: Text, Number, Percent, Currency, Yes/No, Date/Time, Duration (a number of hours), Keywords, Combination, or Formula. For the Spouse's Birthday field, I'll choose Date/Time.
- In the Format drop-down list, choose an appropriate format for the field. For the Spouse's Birthday field I'm creating here, I'll choose a date format that doesn't include a time.
- Click the OK button to create the field. Outlook will list it among the User-Defined Fields in Folder and will change the drop-down list in the Field Chooser dialog box to show these new fields. You can now drag and drop the field you just created.
- To delete a field you've created, select it in the Field Chooser dialog box and click the Delete button. Outlook will display a confirmation dialog box; click the Yes button.

5. To rename the page you're working on, choose Form ➤ Rename Page to display the Rename Page dialog box. Enter a new name in

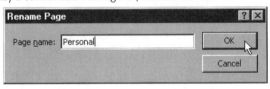

the Page text box and click the OK button. Here, I'll name the page Personal.

6. Make sure Outlook will display the page by verifying that Outlook has selected the Display This Page item on the Form menu. If not, select this item to display a check mark by it.

FIGURE 26.6:
In the New Field dialog box, you can create new fields to meet your special needs.

7. When you've finished customizing this page (and other pages as needed), choose Tools ➤ Design Outlook Form to switch back to Form view.

8. To save this form in a reusable format, choose File ➤ Publish Form As to display the Publish Form As dialog box. Enter a name for the form in the Form Name text box, and then click the Publish button.

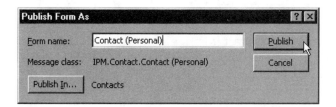

9. Choose File ➤ Close to close the Contact window.

To create a new contact based on the form you created, choose File ➤ New ➤ Choose Form to display the New Form dialog box (see Figure 26.7). Make sure Personal Forms is selected in the drop-down list; then choose the form in the list box and click the OK button.

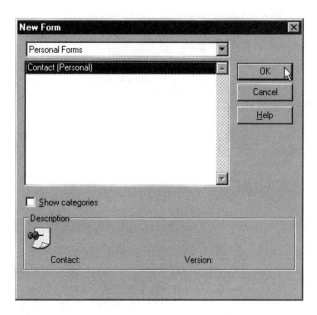

FIGURE 26.7:
To create a new contact based on a custom form, select the form in the New Form dialog box.

Using Your Contact Information

Outlook makes using your contact information especially easy. If you have specified birthdays and anniversaries for your contacts, Outlook will even add those to your calendar as appointments so that you can deliver timely congratulations or commiserations.

Creating a New Contact from the Same Company as an Existing Contact

To create a new contact from the same company as an existing contact, right-click on the existing contact in the Contact window, and choose New Contact from Same Company from the context menu. Outlook will open a new window and will copy the company name, business address, and any business phone numbers from the existing contact to the new contact.

Dialing a Contact

If you've got a modem, you can dial a contact:

1. Right-click on the contact's information and choose AutoDialer from the context menu to display the New Call dialog box (see Figure 26.8).

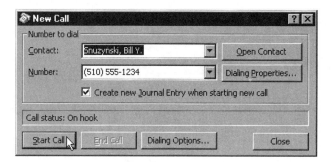

FIGURE 26.8:
In the New Call dialog box, verify the contact you're dialing, and then click the Start Call button.

2. If you want to log the call in your Journal, select the Create New Journal Entry When Starting Call check box.

3. Click the Start Call button to start the call. Outlook will display the Call Status dialog box.

4. Pick up the telephone handset and click the Talk button to take the call, or click the Hang Up button to disconnect.

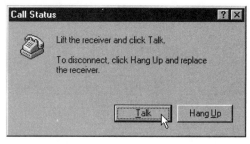

Forwarding a Contact to a Colleague

You can forward a contact to a colleague by right-clicking on the contact and choosing Forward from the context menu. Outlook will create a new message titled *FW:contact's name* and will include the contact's information as an icon in the message. Address it to the recipient and click the Send button to send it.

Exploring a Contact's Web Page

To quickly go to a contact's Web page, right-click anywhere in the contact and choose Explore Web Page from the context menu. Outlook will start your default Web browser and will connect to that page. (If you're not currently connected to the Internet, Outlook will start your connection.)

Sending a Message, Letter, Meeting Request, or Task Request to a Contact

To quickly send a message, letter, meeting request, or task request to the contact currently selected in the Contacts list or currently open in the Contact window, click the New Message to Contact button to send a message (the button shown here on the left) or the New Meeting with Contact to set up a meeting (the button shown here on the right) or choose Contacts ➤ New Message to Contact, Contacts ➤ New Meeting with Contact, Contacts ➤ New Task for Contact, or Contacts ➤ New Letter to Contact. Outlook will start a new message, meeting request, or task request with the contact's name entered in the To box; if you choose New Letter to Contact, Outlook will start the Word Letter Wizard (and will start Word if it isn't already running). Proceed from there as usual.

Updating Contact Information

To update information for a contact, double-click the contact name in the Contacts list to open a Contact window. Change the information in the fields; then click the Save and New button to save the information and display a new record. Click the Close button to close the Contact window. Alternatively, choose File ➤ Save and then File ➤ Close.

Displaying Your Contact Information

Outlook provides a number of views for working with your contacts:

- Address Cards and Detailed Address Cards display contact information as a series of address cards on tabbed pages. Address Cards display the contact's name, address, phone numbers, and e-mail addresses, while Detailed Address Cards (illustrated here) also include information, such as the contact's job title, company, Web page (if any), and categories (again, if any).

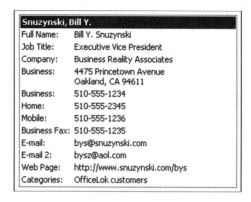

- Phone List displays a spreadsheet-like list of contacts, their companies, their File As names (for quick reference), and their phone numbers.

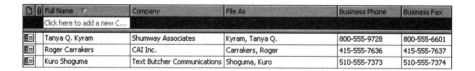

- By Category displays a breakdown of contacts by category. You can click the plus sign by a category name to expand the list under it and click the resulting minus sign to collapse the category again.

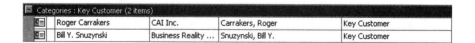

- By Company displays a breakdown of contacts by company. Click the plus sign by a company name to expand the list under it, and click the resulting minus sign to collapse the company list again.
- By Location displays a breakdown of contacts by location. Again, you can expand or collapse the list under each location.

NOTE	For the Phone List, By Category, By Company, and By Location views, you can customize the columns by dragging the column headings to where you want them or by dragging the borders of the column headings to widen or narrow the columns. You can quickly sort your contacts into ascending order by clicking a column heading so it displays a downward-pointing arrowhead or into descending order by clicking the column heading again so it displays an upward-pointing arrowhead.

To choose the view, use the Current View drop-down list on the Standard toolbar or choose View ➤ Current View and choose the view you want from the Current View submenu.

Using the Journal

Outlook's Journal ties together the many actions you can take in Outlook and in the other Office applications. Using the Journal, you can have Outlook automatically record activities as you perform them—for example, you can automatically record every file you work with in the Office applications, and you can record your meetings and conversations with contacts, which can help with billing. You can also manually record activities—for example, if you gave an item to a contact (or received one from a contact), you could add a Journal entry about that.

By recording the actions you take, the Journal creates a timeline that you can use to quickly find and open files you worked on at a given time or to identify meetings and conversations you had. Furthermore, you can sort items by type in the Journal, so that you can quickly pull together all the actions you took on a given project.

Recording Your Activities Automatically

You can automatically record your e-mail messages, meeting requests and responses, task requests and responses, and any documents you create in the Office applications on your computer:

To choose which activities and files to record:

1. Choose Tools ➤ Options to display the Options dialog box, and then click the Journal tab to bring it to the front (see Figure 26.9).

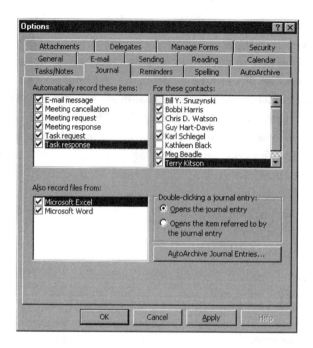

FIGURE 26.9:
Choose which activities and files to record in the Journal on the Journal tab of the Options dialog box.

2. In the Automatically Record These Items list box, select the check boxes next to the items you want to record.

3. In the For These Contacts list box, select the contacts with whom you want to record your activities.

4. In the Also Record Files From list box, select the check boxes next to the appropriate applications.

5. In the Double-Clicking a Journal Entry group box, select the action you want Outlook to take when you double-click a Journal entry. Select the Opens the Journal Entry option button if you want Outlook to open a Journal window containing information about the journal entry; select the Opens the Item Referred To by the Journal Entry option button if you want Outlook to open the item in the appropriate application.

6. Click the OK button to close the Options dialog box and apply your choices.

Creating a Journal Entry Manually

To manually record an activity, you create a Journal entry for it:

1. Click the New button and choose Journal Entry, or choose File ➤ New ➤ Journal Entry, to open a Journal Entry window (see Figure 26.10). (If you're already working in the Journal, click the New Journal button, or right-click in the Journal and choose New Journal Entry from the context menu.)

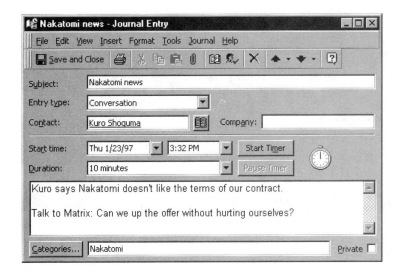

FIGURE 26.10:
In the Journal Entry window, enter the details of what you want to record.

2. Enter the subject of the Journal entry in the Subject box.

3. Specify the type of entry—phone call, conversation, letter, or whatever—in the Entry Type drop-down list.

4. In the Contact text box, enter the name of any contact involved in this activity, either by typing the name in or by clicking the Select Names button and choosing the name from the Select Names dialog box.

5. Enter the contact's company in the Company box if appropriate.

6. Use the Start Time and Duration text boxes to specify the time and duration of the activity. You can also use the Start Timer and Pause Timer buttons to record the length of an activity.

7. Enter notes about the activity in the main text box.

8. Enter any categories for the activity in the Categories box.

9. Click the Save and Close button to add the entry to the Journal.

Viewing Your Journal

To display the Journal (see Figure 26.11), click the Journal button on the Outlook Bar.

- Use the Go to Today, Day, Week, and Month buttons on the Standard toolbar to display the time frame you want to see.
- Use Outlook's views to display the Journal items: Click the Current View button on the Standard toolbar and choose By Type, By Contact, By Category, Entry List, Last Seven Days, or Phone Calls.

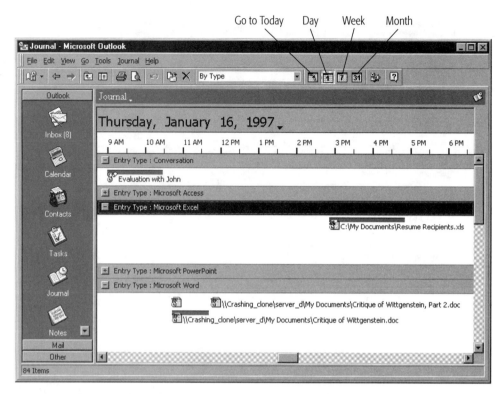

FIGURE 26.11: The Journal gives you an easy way to find what you did when.

- In the By Type, By Contact, and By Category views, you can expand and collapse the types, contacts, or categories so you can see the information you need.

> **NOTE** Use the By Category view to bring together all the activities you've performed in a certain category—for example, everything you've done to win or fulfill a particular contract.

- To open a Journal entry in a Journal Entry window, right-click the entry and choose Open Journal Entry from the context menu.
- To open the item listed in the Journal entry, right-click the entry and choose Open Item Referred To from the context menu. Outlook will activate the appropriate application, starting it if necessary, and will open the item.
- To delete a Journal entry, click it in the Journal and click the Delete button, or right-click it and choose Delete from the context menu.

Importing and Exporting Data

You can import data into Outlook either from one of the other Microsoft Office applications or from just about any contact-management application. Outlook can read files from the other Office applications without converting them, but information from non-Office applications needs to be saved in comma-delimited format.

First, run the other application and save the data in comma-delimited format. For example, in Sidekick, you would choose Tools ➤ Export Cardfile to display the Export Cardfile dialog box, and then choose the Comma Delimited (*.csv) format.

Now you can import the data into Outlook. Choose File ➤ Import and Export to start the Import and Export Wizard. In the first Import and Export Wizard dialog box, select the appropriate action from the Choose an Action to Perform list box. For example, to import a .csv file, choose Import from Schedule+ or Another Program or File. After that, the actions you need to take will depend on the type of file you're importing, but the procedure is relatively straightforward with the Wizard: You identify the file to import and select a destination folder for it (for example, the Contacts folder if you're importing contact information or one of your mailboxes if you're importing Microsoft Mail files); Outlook does the rest.

To export data, choose one of the export options from the Import and Export Wizard dialog box, and then choose the destination and follow the instructions that Outlook provides.

Archiving Your Old Data

If you use Outlook as extensively as its capabilities allow, you'll rapidly amass a large quantity of valuable information. Sooner or later, you'll probably need to archive the old information so your Outlook files do not grow too large and slow down your computer.

You can archive your data whenever you want to, or you can have Outlook's AutoArchive feature automatically archive any data that's more than a certain number of months old. AutoArchive comes with preset values that you can easily change.

Setting AutoArchive to Archive Data

To choose settings for AutoArchive to automatically archive Outlook information:

1. Choose Tools ➤ Options to display the Options dialog box, and then click the AutoArchive tab to display it (see Figure 26.12).

2. Choose settings for AutoArchive:
- Select the AutoArchive Every check box to enable automatic archiving, and specify the interval in the Days at Startup box.

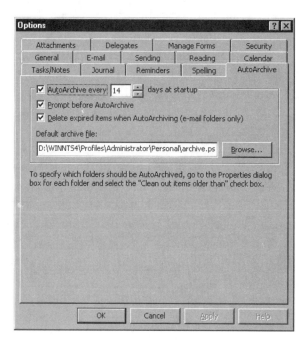

FIGURE 26.12: Choose settings for automatic archiving on the AutoArchive tab of the Options dialog box.

- Select the Prompt before AutoArchive check box if you want Outlook to check with you before automatically archiving material.
- Select the Delete Expired Items When AutoArchiving (E-Mail Folders Only) check box if you want AutoArchive to delete e-mail messages that have passed their specified expiration date.
- Change the Default Archive File if necessary. (For example, you might want to archive your Outlook information on a different drive or on a different computer.)

3. Click the OK button to close the Options dialog box and apply the choices you made.

You now need to specify the folders on which you want to run AutoArchiving. You need to do this folder by folder.

1. In the Outlook Bar, right-click on the folder you want to affect and choose Properties from the context menu to display the Properties dialog box.

2. Click the AutoArchive tab to bring it to the front.

3. Select the Clean Out Items Older Than check box to enable AutoArchiving for this folder, and then use the number box and the time unit drop-down list to specify a number of days, weeks, or months.

4. Select the Move Old Items To option button if you want to archive your old items, and change the archive folder in the text box if necessary. Select the Permanently Delete Old Items option button if you want to have Outlook get rid of them instead of archiving them.

5. Click the OK button to apply the AutoArchiving for this folder.

6. Repeat this procedure for other folders as necessary.

Archiving Your Data Manually

To archive your old data manually:

1. Choose File ➤ Archive to display the Archive dialog box.

2. Select the Archive This Folder and All Subfolders option button.

3. In the list box, select the folder to archive.

4. In the Archive Items Older Than drop-down list box, enter the cut-off date for items. Use the drop-down calendar to change the date.

5. Select Include Items with "Do Not Archive" Checked if you want to archive even items that were set not to be archived.

6. Specify the archive file in the Archive File text box.

7. Click the OK button to archive your material.

Chapter 27

WORKING WITH E-MAIL

FEATURING

- **Reading e-mail**
- **Creating and sending e-mail**
- **Organizing your e-mail**
- **Filtering your e-mail**
- **Sending files via e-mail**

Outlook integrates with the messaging client built into Windows and with messaging systems such as Microsoft Exchange Server to provide full e-mail capabilities. You can send and receive plain messages or messages with attachments, maintain an elaborate hierarchy of folders to organize your e-mail to the *n*th degree, and even use rules to specify special treatment for messages that might be of special interest to you (or to delete messages that you do not want to receive). Finally, you can use Outlook's capabilities to send files via e-mail directly from Word and Excel.

To work with e-mail, you use the Mail section of the Outlook Bar. To display the Mail section, click the Mail button at the bottom of the Outlook Bar.

Reading E-Mail

To read your e-mail, first display the Inbox by clicking the Inbox icon on the Outlook Bar. The Inbox shows you the messages and faxes you've received (see Figure 27.1), while the Inbox icon shows in parentheses the number of unread messages in your Inbox.

Outlook offers the following views for the Inbox (and for its other folders) from the Current View drop-down list on the Standard toolbar (or the View ➤ Current View submenu):

- Messages displays a list of messages with their sender, subject, date and time received, and any flags or attachments they have. Messages with AutoPreview displays the first few lines of each message to help you identify the messages you want to read.
- By Message Flag displays messages ranked by their flag for priority or status.
- Last Seven Days displays messages from only the last seven days.
- Flagged for Next Seven Days displays messages flagged for action over the next seven days.

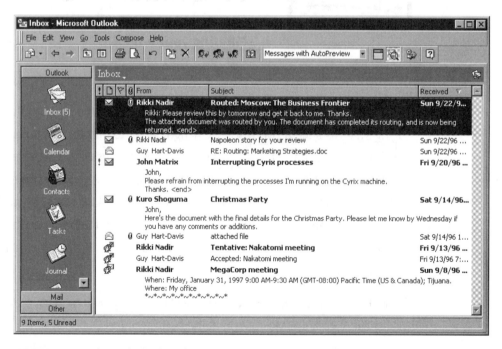

FIGURE 27.1: The Outlook Inbox gives you quick access to your incoming messages and faxes.

- By Conversation Topic sorts messages by topic or *thread*, so you can quickly find related messages.
- By Sender sorts messages by their sender.
- Unread Messages displays only unread messages.
- Sent To groups messages by their addressee and is more useful in the Outbox and the Sent Items folder.
- Message Timeline displays a journal-style listing of when you sent or received messages.

To read the whole message, double-click it. Outlook will display it in a separate window.

Setting AutoPreview Preferences

Outlook's AutoPreview feature lets you view the first few lines of text in messages. By default, it shows you the first few lines of unread messages and only the title lines of messages you've read, but you can choose to view the first few lines of messages you've read as well. To do so:

1. Choose View ➤ Format View to display the Format View dialog box.
2. In the AutoPreview group box, choose the appropriate option button: Preview All Items, Preview Unread Items (the default), or No AutoPreview.
3. Click the OK button to close the Format View dialog box.

You can then toggle AutoPreview on and off by clicking the AutoPreview button or choosing View ➤ AutoPreview. If you chose Preview All Items, this will toggle the view between Preview All Items and No AutoPreview; if you chose Preview Unread Items, this will toggle the view between Preview Unread Items and No AutoPreview.

When your Inbox contains new unopened items, you'll see an icon of a sealed envelope in the tray on the Windows Taskbar.

NOTE Outlook provides full e-mail editing features, but you can also use Word as your e-mail editor, which allows you to use many Word features and commands when creating your mail. This option is called WordMail. To toggle between using Word as your e-mail editor and using Outlook's editor, choose Tools ➤ Use Word as the E-Mail Editor (if this command is available) or choose Tools ➤ Options to display the Options dialog box, select the Use Microsoft Word as the E-Mail Editor check box on the E-Mail tab, and click the OK button.

Using Message Flags

You can use message flags to indicate message priority or status, either to yourself on messages you receive or to the recipients of messages you send.

Working with Message Flags in Your Mailboxes

The Flag Status column in the message list displays any flag set for the message. You'll see a red flag for flagged items and a grayed-out flag for completed items. You can easily change the flagging for a message in a mailbox:

- To flag a message, right-click on it and choose Flag Message from the context menu.
- To flag a flagged message as complete, right-click on it and choose Flag Complete from the context menu.
- To clear a flag from a message, right-click on it and choose Clear Message Flag from the context menu.

Working with Message Flags in a Message

When you have a message open in a message window, you can use the following flags, whose meanings are self-explanatory: Call; Do Not Forward; Forward; Follow Up; For Your Information; No Response Necessary; Read; Reply; Reply to All; and Review. Flags for the current message appear in the information bar across the top of the Message tab in the message window.

To set a flag, click the Message Flag button on the toolbar of the message window to display the Flag Message dialog box. In the Flag drop-down list, select one of the message flags. Use the By drop-down calendar panel to specify a completion date for the action. Select the Completed check box if you want to flag a message as completed.

TIP **You can create your own customized flags by typing them into the Flag text box in the Flag Message dialog box.**

Moving Read Messages to a Different Folder

Once you've read a message, you'll probably want to move it from the Inbox to a suitable folder for storage. To move an open message to a folder, choose File ➤ Move to Folder to display the Move Item To dialog box. To move a message from the Inbox to a folder, right-click in the message (or in its AutoPreview) and choose Move to Folder from the context menu to display the Move Items dialog box (see Figure 27.2).

In the Folders list box, select the folder to which to move the message or fax, and then click the OK button to move it there.

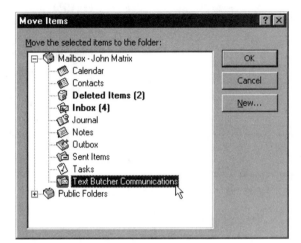

FIGURE 27.2:
In the Move Items dialog box (or Move Item To dialog box), select the folder where you want to move the message or fax; then click the OK button.

Creating a New Folder for Messages

To create a new folder for messages:

1. Click the New button in the Move Items dialog box (or Move Item To dialog box) to display the Create New Folder dialog box (see Figure 27.3).

2. In the Name text box, enter the name you want the folder to have.

3. In the Folder Contains drop-down list, specify the type of item that the folder will contain; in this case, select Mail Items.

4. In the Make This Folder a Subfolder Of list box, select the folder under which you want to place the new folder. You may need to navigate through several layers of folders to reach the appropriate one.

5. In the Description group box, enter a description for this folder if you want. (For example, if you were creating a folder to contain e-mail about a particular project, you might enter details about that project.)

6. Click the OK button to create the folder and close the Create New Folder dialog box.

7. In the Move Items dialog box (or Move Item To dialog box), click the OK button to move the item to this new folder.

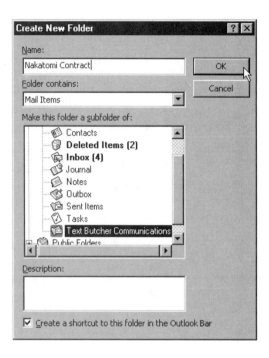

FIGURE 27.3:
In the Create New Folder dialog box, enter the name for the folder, specify what it contains, enter a description if you want, and click the OK button to create the folder.

Sending E-Mail

You can generate e-mail in Outlook by creating new messages, replying to messages you've received, or forwarding messages you've received (or messages you've created and sent before).

Composing a New Message

To create a new message:

1. Click the New drop-down list button on the Outlook toolbar and choose Mail Message from the drop-down list. If you're working in the Inbox, this button will be the New Mail Message button, shown here, and you can simply click it to create a new message. (Alternatively, choose Compose ➤ New Mail Message.) Outlook will open a message window with the Message tab displayed (see Figure 27.4).

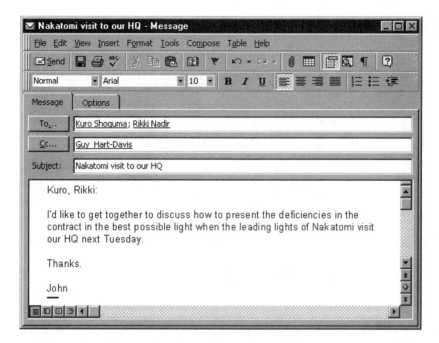

FIGURE 27.4:   Create your message in the message window.

2. Enter the e-mail address of the recipient or recipients in the To text box and the names of cc. recipients in the Cc text box. Separate multiple addresses with semicolons. You can either type each address in or choose it from your address books:

   - Click the To button to display the Select Names dialog box (see Figure 27.5).
   - Choose the appropriate address book in the Show Names From The drop-down list.
   - In the Type Name or Select from List list box, select the name and click the To button, the Cc button, or the Bcc button to add the selected name to the appropriate box of message recipients.
   - Add further names to the To, Cc, and Bcc lists as appropriate, and then click the OK button to close the Select Names dialog box.

3. In the Subject text box, enter a subject line for the message. The more descriptive, informative, and concise the subject line is, the more useful it will be to the recipients of the message—and the more likely they will be to read the message.

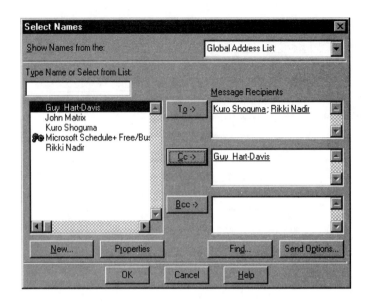

FIGURE 27.5:
Choose the names of recipients for the message in the Select Names dialog box.

4. In the message box, enter the text of the message. You can enter and edit the text using standard Office features (such as cut and paste, and drag and drop) and format it using the buttons on the Formatting toolbar (see Figure 27.6).

5. Click the Options tab of the message window to display it (see Figure 27.7).

6. Choose options in the General Options group box:
   - In the Importance drop-down list, choose Low, Normal, or High to indicate to the recipient the message's priority.
   - In the Sensitivity drop-down list, choose the level of sensitivity you think it rates: Normal, Personal, Private, or Confidential. If you mark a message Private, it cannot be modified once you've sent it.

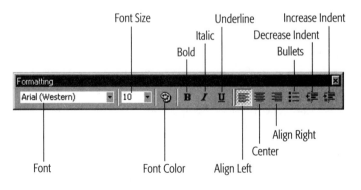

FIGURE 27.6:
Use the buttons on the Formatting tool-bar to quickly format the text of a message.

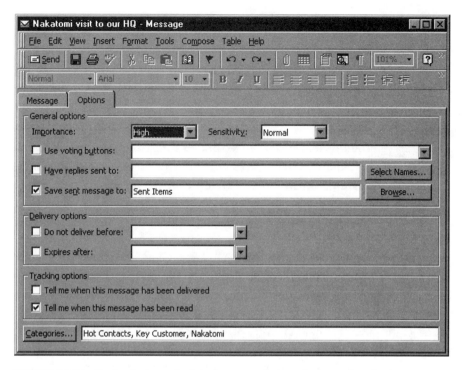

FIGURE 27.7:   On the Options tab of the message window, choose options for the message.

- If you want people to be able to give you a quick thumbs-up or thumbs-down to a message, select the Use Voting Buttons check box and select the button names you want from the drop-down list: The choices are Approve and Reject; Yes and No; or Yes, No, and Maybe.

- To specify where the replies to this message should be sent (if you want them to go to someone other than yourself), select the Have Replies Sent To check box. Outlook will display your address in the text box. To change this, click the Select Names button to display the Have Replies Sent To dialog box, which works like a stripped-down version of the Select Names dialog box: Choose the appropriate address book in the Show Names From The drop-down list; then type or select the names in the Type Name or Select from List boxes, and click the Reply To button to add the names to the Message Recipients list box. Click the OK button when you've finished selecting recipients.

- If you want to save a copy of the message for your records, make sure the Save Sent Message To check box is selected. This option will be selected by default, and in the text box, Outlook will suggest Sent Items as the destination folder for sent messages. To change the folder, click the Browse button to display the Select Folder dialog box; then select the folder in the Folders list box and click the OK button.

7. Set delivery options in the Delivery Options group box:
- To specify the earliest delivery date allowable for the message, select the Do Not Deliver Before check box. Outlook will suggest an earliest delivery date of 5:00 PM on the next day; you can change this by clicking the drop-down list button and choosing a date from the calendar panel.

NOTE   **The Do Not Deliver Before and Expires After features work only with Microsoft Exchange Server. If you're using a different e-mail system, these features won't work. (If you're not sure which e-mail system you're using, check with your e-mail administrator.)**

---

8. To set an expiration date for this message, select the Expires After check box. Again, Outlook will suggest a date that you can change by using the drop-down list button and the calendar panel. This can be useful for messages whose information may become embarrassingly out-of-date if they are not read in the time span you envision.

9. In the Tracking Options group box, choose whether you want to receive notification when a message has been delivered and when it has been read. Under most circumstances, delivery notification has little value—for example, in a corporate e-mail system, messages will typically be delivered within seconds of your sending them, and you will usually receive a warning if a message is *not* delivered. Reading notification, on the other hand, can be very useful: Once you know the recipient has read (or at least opened) the message, you can reach for the telephone to follow up while the iron is hot.

10. If you want to assign this item to a category, click the Categories button to display the Categories dialog box (see Figure 27.8). In the Available Categories list box, select the check boxes for the categories; then click the OK button.

11. Choose to include your AutoSignature if appropriate by selecting Tools ➤ AutoSignature. (See "Creating an AutoSignature" for details on AutoSignatures.)

12. You're now ready to send the message. Read through the message quickly to make sure it conveys what you want it to and that you haven't written anything ambiguous or rash; then click the Send button or choose File ➤ Send to send it on its way.

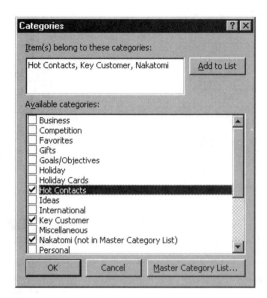

FIGURE 27.8:
In the Categories dialog box, choose which categories you want to assign this item to, and then click the OK button.

Creating an AutoSignature

An *AutoSignature* is a predefined chunk of text that you can have added automatically to messages you send or forward or to replies you send. A typical use for an AutoSignature is to include your full name, your position, your company's name, and so on.

NOTE   If you're using WordMail as your e-mail editor instead of Outlook, the procedure for creating an AutoSignature is a little different. Start a new message, and then enter the text for the AutoSignature and format it as appropriate. Then choose Tools ➤ AutoSignature to display the AutoSignature dialog box, which provides a couple of options for the AutoSignature.

To create an AutoSignature:

1. Choose Tools ➤ AutoSignature to display the AutoSignature dialog box (see Figure 27.9).

2. In the text box, enter the text that you want to have added to the end of your messages.

   • To format the selected text's font, click the Font button to display the Font dialog box, choose the font formatting, and click the OK button.

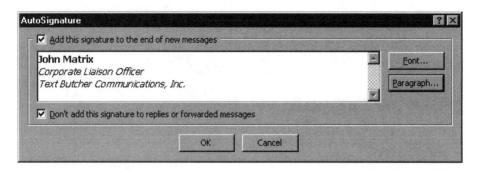

FIGURE 27.9: Specify your AutoSignature in the AutoSignature dialog box.

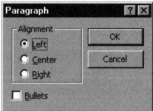

- To format the paragraph alignment of selected text, or to add bullets, click the Paragraph button to display the Paragraph dialog box. Select the option button for the alignment you want; select the Bullets check box if you want to add bullets; and click the OK button.

3. Choose whether to add the AutoSignature to your messages automatically by clearing or selecting the Add This Signature to the End of New Messages check box. If you choose to add the Auto-Signature automatically, you have the choice of using the AutoSignature for replies or forwarded messages by clearing or selecting the Don't Add This Signature to Replies or Forwarded Messages check box.

4. Click the OK button to close the AutoSignature dialog box.

If you chose to have your AutoSignature inserted automatically, Outlook will insert it in messages as you specified. Otherwise, you can insert it manually at the insertion point in an open message by choosing Insert ➤ AutoSignature.

Once you've created an AutoSignature, you can easily change it as needed:

- To change your AutoSignature for all messages, choose Tools ➤ AutoSignature again and change your signature in the dialog box.
- To change your AutoSignature for a single signature, insert it (or have it inserted automatically) and change it in the message.

Replying to a Message

To reply to a message from the Inbox, click the Reply button on the Outlook toolbar, or right-click in the message or message header and choose Reply from the context menu.

To reply to a message from a message window, click the Reply button on the toolbar in the Message window.

 If you were not the only recipient of a message, you can use Outlook's Reply to All feature to reply quickly to all the recipients of that message (and to cc everyone on the Cc list). From the Inbox, click the Reply to All button on the Outlook toolbar, or right-click and choose Reply to All from the context menu. From a message window, click the Reply to All button on the Message Window toolbar.

When you reply to a message, Outlook adds RE: to the subject line so the recipient can easily see that the message is a reply.

Forwarding a Message

You can easily forward a message to someone who did not receive it.

To forward a message from the Inbox, click the Forward button on the Outlook toolbar, or right-click and choose Forward from the context menu.

To forward a message from a message window, click the Forward button on the toolbar in the window.

When you forward a message, Outlook adds FW: to the subject line so the recipient can easily see that the message was forwarded.

Inserting an Office File in an Outlook Message

If you're sending a message to someone else who is using Outlook, you can insert a file created in an Office application in a message to transfer it easily. To do so, start the message and then do the following:

1. Click in the text box for the message and choose Insert ➤ File to display the Insert File dialog box (see Figure 27.10).
2. Select the file you want to insert.
3. In the Insert As group box, select the appropriate option button:
    - Text Only inserts the text of the file in the message.
    - Attachment adds the file to the message as an attachment. This is the best way to transfer a whole file to someone so the recipient can open it and work with it.
    - Shortcut inserts a shortcut to the file (rather than inserting the file itself). This is useful for giving others quick access to a file by telling them its location—for example, you could send them a shortcut to a Web page or to a file on a network to which you and the recipients have access.

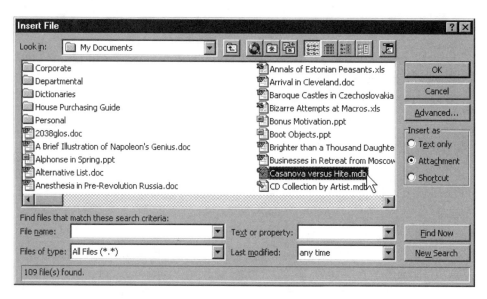

FIGURE 27.10: In the Insert File dialog box, select the file, choose how to insert it, and click the OK button.

4. Click the OK button.
5. Finish the message, and then send it by clicking the Send button or choosing File ➤ Send.

Recalling or Replacing an Unread Message

Before a message is read, you can recall it from the person you've sent it to or replace it with another message. Once a message has been read, you cannot recall it or replace it.

You can recall or replace only local messages—you can't recall or replace messages that you have sent over the Internet.

To recall or replace a message:

1. Display the Mail section of the Outlook Bar.
2. Click the Sent Items icon to display the Sent Items box.
3. Double-click the message you want to recall or replace to open it in a message window.
4. Choose Tools ➤ Recall This Message to display the Recall This Message dialog box (see Figure 27.11). The top line of the dialog box tells you whether any of the recipients have reported reading the message yet.

FIGURE 27.11:
In the Recall This Message dialog box, choose whether to delete or replace unread copies of the message.

5. Use the option buttons to decide whether to simply delete unread copies of the message or to delete them and replace them with a new message.

6. If you want Outlook to monitor the success or failure of the recall or replace operation, select the Tell Me If Recall Succeeds or Fails for Each Recipient check box.

7. Click the OK button to close the Recall This Message dialog box. Outlook will return you to the message window and will add to the top of the window an information bar detailing the recall or replace operation.

> ⓘ You attempted to recall this message on Thursday, January 16, 1997 8:43 PM.
> This message was sent with High importance.

8. If you chose to replace the message with a new one, compose the replacement message from the original, and send it by clicking the Send button. Otherwise, simply close the message window that you had opened.

Routing Files to Your Colleagues

You can also e-mail or route a file to your colleagues from within Word or Excel. Here's how to do so:

1. Start the application and open the file.

2. Choose File ➤ Send To ➤ Routing Recipient to display the Routing Slip dialog box (see Figure 27.12).

3. First, choose the recipients. Click the Address button to display the Address Book dialog box.

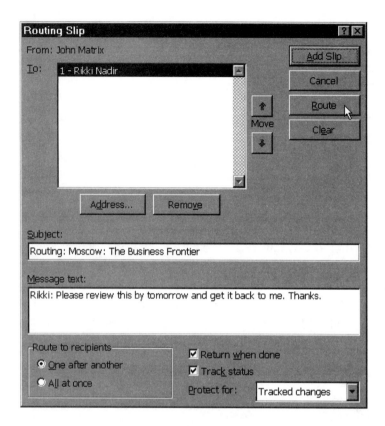

FIGURE 27.12: Choose recipients for the open document, specify a subject, enter message text, and decide how to route the message in the Routing Slip dialog box.

4. Select the names of the recipients and click the To button to add them to the list.
   - You can Shift+click to select a range of recipients or Ctrl+click to select a group of recipients one by one.
   - If need be, choose another address book from the Show Names drop-down list.
5. Click the OK button when you've finished selecting your recipients. The application will return you to the Routing Slip dialog box.
6. Check the Subject line that the application has automatically entered from the subject set in File ➤ Properties. Change it if necessary.
7. Enter any message text in the Message Text box.
8. Choose how to route the message to recipients: One after Another, or All at Once. If you choose One after Another, Word or Excel will send out only one copy of the document, and it will be passed on from one recipient to the next (we'll look at how they pass the document on in "Receiving a Routed

File"). Each will see the comments that have been added, so you may want to arrange the To list carefully. (Highlight a name and use the Move buttons to move it up or down the To list.)

9. Choose from among the options in the lower-right corner of the Routing Slip dialog box:

   - Leave Return When Done selected if you want the document to come back to you after it has been routed.
   - Check the Track Status box if you want to have an electronic message sent to you each time one of the recipients in a One after Another routing sends the message on to the next recipient.
   - In Word only, you can choose how to protect the document in the Protect For drop-down list: None, Tracked Changes, Comments, or Forms.

10. To route the document now, click the Route button.

    - To save your recipient list, subject, and message before routing it so you can return to the document to do more work, choose Add Slip. You can then choose File ➤ Send To ➤ Next Routing Recipient to send the document on its way. The application will display the Send dialog box, in which you can choose whether to send the document with the routing slip or without. Click the OK button when you've made your choice.

Receiving a Routed File

Here's what to do when you receive a routed file:

1. Open the document in the appropriate application by double-clicking the document icon in the message in Outlook.

2. Review and revise the file as appropriate. If the file is a Word document protected for tracked changes, change marks will appear automatically whenever you alter the file; if it's protected for comments, you will only be able to insert comments.

3. When you're finished, choose File ➤ Send To ➤ Next Routing Recipient to send the document either on to the next recipient or back to the sender (depending on what the originator chose on the routing slip). The application will display the Send dialog box showing you where the document is headed and telling you that it contains a routing slip, as shown here. Click the OK button to send the document on its way.

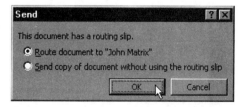

Organizing Your Messages

You can organize your messages into a hierarchy of folders within your mailbox. By moving messages into the appropriate folder for the project or client, you can keep your Inbox and Sent Items folders uncluttered and your messages neatly organized.

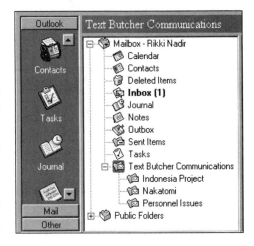

When working with folders, it's easiest to use the folder list pane (shown here). To display this, choose View ➤ Folder List.

To create a subfolder, right-click its prospective parent folder and choose Create Subfolder from the context menu, and then specify the details for the new folder in the Create New Folder dialog box as discussed in "Creating a New Folder for Messages" earlier in this chapter.

To add a folder to the Outlook Bar, right-click the folder in the Folder List pane and choose Add to Outlook Bar from the context menu.

To remove a folder from the Outlook Bar, right-click the folder in the Outlook Bar and choose Remove from Outlook Bar from the context menu.

NOTE No matter how superbly you've organized your messages in Outlook, you'll eventually need to find a message whose sender, subject, or contents you can't quite remember. You can use the Journal to find such messages, as discussed in the previous chapter. Failing that, you can use the Windows Find feature to find messages that contain specific words that you can remember.

Creating and Using Rules

Outlook offers rules to streamline your handling of the material that arrives in your Inbox, along with two Assistants to help create and manage rules. A *rule* is a set of actions to be taken when the specified conditions are met. For example, you could create a rule that identifies messages coming from your boss and notifies you immediately, or you could create a rule that automatically deletes messages from a tiresome coworker either after you've read them—or before. The Inbox Assistant is designed for creating general-purpose rules. The Out of Office Assistant is designed to make it easy to create rules notifying people that you are out of the office.

Creating a Rule

To create a rule:

1. Choose Tools ➤ Inbox Assistant to display the Inbox Assistant dialog box (see Figure 27.13).

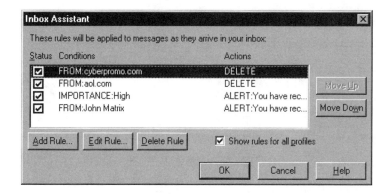

FIGURE 27.13:
The Inbox Assistant helps manage rules.

2. Click the Add Rule button to display the Edit Rule dialog box (see Figure 27.14).

3. In the When a Message Arrives That Meets the Following Conditions group box, specify criteria for the type of message that this rule should affect:
- You can enter the sender's name in the From text box, either by typing it in or by clicking the From button and specifying the name in the Choose Sender dialog box.
- You can enter the recipient's name (for example, your own) in the Sent To text box, again either by typing it in or by clicking the Sent To button and specifying the name in the Select Recipient dialog box. Select the Sent Directly to Me check box or the Copied (Cc) to Me check box as appropriate. For example, if you want to delete all messages that are cc'ed to you (a worthy cause), you would select the Copied (Cc) to Me check box.
- You can enter a subject or partial subject for the message in the Subject box. If any part of the subject line of an incoming message matches the contents of this box, the rule will take effect.

- You can enter text in the Message Body text box. If any part of the body text of an incoming message matches the contents of this box, the rule will take effect. This is a powerful capability; use it carefully.
- You can choose advanced options, such as specifying items above a certain size, or items received during a certain time period, or items with attachments, by clicking the Advanced button and specifying criteria in the Advanced dialog box.

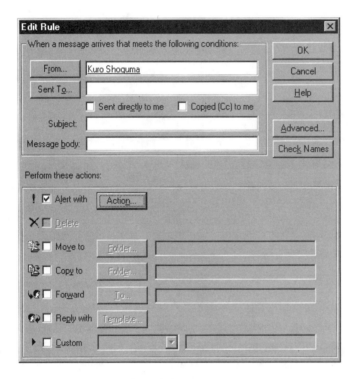

FIGURE 27.14:
In the Edit Rule dialog box, specify the conditions and actions for the rule.

4. In the Perform These Actions group box, choose what Outlook should do when a message matches the criteria you chose:
   - Select the Alert With check box to have Outlook alert you to a message's arrival. Click the Action button to display the Alert Actions dialog box, and specify what you want Outlook to do. To receive a text notification in the New Items of Interest dialog box, shown here, select the Notify with the Text check box and enter the text you want to see in the text box. To have a sound played, select the Play check box and use the Sound button to browse for a sound. Click the OK button to close the Alert Actions dialog box.

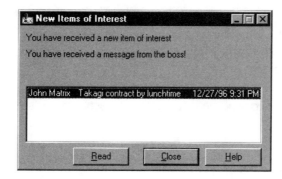

- Select the Delete check box to have the message automatically deleted. (You cannot choose both the Alert With check box and the Delete check box because the actions are incompatible.)
- Select the Move To check box and specify a folder to have the message automatically moved there.
- Select the Copy To check box and specify a folder to have the message automatically copied to a folder.
- Select the Forward check box and specify a recipient in the To box to have the message automatically forwarded.
- Select the Reply With check box and choose a message template to have an automated reply sent to the sender of the message.
- Select the Custom check box to apply custom rules available on your messaging system.

5. Click the OK button to close the Edit Rule dialog box and return to the Inbox Assistant dialog box.

6. Create more rules by repeating these steps, or click the OK button to close the Inbox Assistant. Outlook will then put the rules into effect.

Using Rules

Once you've created rules, you can work with them in the Inbox Assistant:

- To turn a rule off, display the Inbox Assistant and clear the check box in the Status column for the rule. To turn the rule back on, select the check box again.
- To modify a rule, select it in the Inbox Assistant and click the Edit Rule button to display the Edit Rule dialog box. Then modify the rule using the same methods as you used for creating it.

- To delete a rule, select it in the Inbox Assistant and click the Delete Rule button. Click the Yes button in the confirmation dialog box.
- To reorder your rules, use the Move Up and Move Down buttons in the Inbox Assistant. Place your most important rules at the top of the list: The first rule that a message matches will take effect; other rules that a message matches may not apply if the first rule takes drastic action (such as deleting the message).

Using the Out of Office Assistant

The Out of Office Assistant lets you set up automatic replies for when you are out of the office. Here's how to use it:

1. Choose Tools ➤ Out of Office Assistant to display the Out of Office Assistant dialog box (see Figure 27.15).

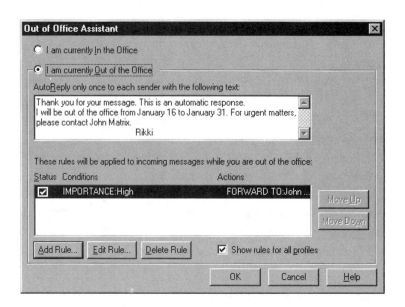

FIGURE 27.15:
Use the Out of Office Assistant to set up automatic replies for when you're out of the office.

2. In the AutoReply Only Once to Each Sender with the Following Text box, enter the text of the message you want to have sent in reply to messages you receive while you are out of the office. Outlook will track the messages it sends and will make sure that, even if one person sends you multiple

messages, they receive only one out-of-office message in reply. (Beyond applying common sense and common courtesy, this feature helps make sure that your copy of Outlook doesn't get stuck in an endless loop of automatic replies with someone else's e-mail program.)

3. In the These Rules Will Be Applied to Incoming Messages While You Are Out of the Office box, create rules as described in the previous two sections.

4. When you are about to leave the office, select the I Am Currently Out of the Office option button to apply the rules. (Otherwise, you can leave the rules in place and the I Am Currently In the Office option button selected.)

5. Click the OK button to close the Out of Office Assistant.

Chapter 28

OFFICE AND THE WEB

FEATURING

- **Browsing the Web with Word and Excel**
- **Creating Web pages using the Web Page Wizard**
- **Creating Web pages from Word and Excel**

Over the last few years, the surge in popularity of the World Wide Web, and of internal corporate webs or *intranets*, has left many people wishing for an easy way to create Web pages from inside their regular applications. Office 97 provides not only those capabilities but also allows you to view both local and Internet Web pages. You can browse the Web (or your company's intranet) with Word and Excel moving easily from page to page. You can open Web pages or intranet pages, alter them, and (if you have the necessary rights), save the changes to the page on the Web site.

At the risk of stating the obvious, to use the features described in this chapter, you need to have either an Internet connection or a network connection or both.

Browsing with the Web Toolbar

If you've used a Web browser before, you'll find the Office Web-browsing features very familiar indeed.

The main tool for browsing the Web with the Office applications is the Web toolbar (see Figure 28.1). You can display the Web toolbar by clicking the Web Toolbar button on the Standard toolbar, or by right-clicking the menu bar or any displayed toolbar and choosing Web from the context menu of toolbars. The Web toolbar will also pop up unsummoned when you start accessing a Web page (for example, when you click a Web hyperlink in a Word document or an Excel spreadsheet).

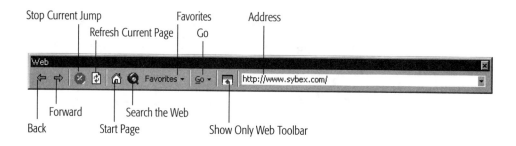

FIGURE 28.1: Use the Web toolbar for browsing the Web (and the Internet) with Word and Excel.

Here's how to navigate with the buttons on the Web toolbar:

- Click the Back button to move to the previous page you were on.
- Click the Forward button to move forward to a page you were on before you clicked the Back button.
- Click the Stop Current Jump button to stop the application from pursuing a jump that's in progress. (For example, if a jump has stalled or if a page is being dreadfully slow in loading, you might want to click this button.)
- Click the Refresh Current Page button to have the application reload the current page. You may want to do this if part of the page fails to transfer properly, or if you've had the page open for a while, and you suspect it may have been updated in the interim.
- Click the Start Page button to jump to your start page.
- Click the Search the Web button to display your chosen Web search tool.
- Click the Favorites button to display the Favorites menu. *Favorites* are pages whose address you tell Windows to store so you can return to them quickly; other browsers call them *bookmarks*. To add the current page to your

favorites, choose Add to Favorites, enter the name you want for the favorite in the File Name text box in the Add to Favorites dialog box, and click the Add button. To open a favorite, either choose it from the list of favorites on the Favorites menu or choose Open Favorites, select the favorite in the Favorites dialog box, and click the Open button to jump to it.

- Click the Go button to display a menu of actions and jumps you can make from the current page:

    Open   Displays the Open Internet Address dialog box, where you can enter a Web address to go to or click the Browse button to open a file or an address using the Browse dialog box. Select the Open in New Window check box in the Open Internet Address dialog box if you want to open the page in a new window rather than using the same window and leaving the current page.

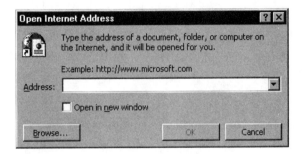

    Back and **Forward**   Move you back and forward through the series of pages you've visited.

    Start Page   Takes you to your start page.

    Search the Web   Displays your Web search tool.

    Set Start Page   Offers to set your start page to the page currently displayed. Click the Yes button to accept the offer.

    Set Search Page   Offers to set your search page to the page currently displayed. Again, click the Yes button to accept.

    The bottom of the Go menu provides a list of jumps you can take from the current page.

- Click the Show Only Web Toolbar button to toggle on and off the display of all displayed toolbars other than the Web toolbar. This quickly frees up screen real estate so that you can better view Web pages; when you need the toolbars you were using before, click the Show Only Web Toolbar button to restore them.
- Click in the Address box and enter an address to go to, or choose an address from the drop-down list of addresses you've previously visited.

Opening a Document on a Web or Intranet

To open a document at an HTTP site on the Web or on an intranet, you can use the Address box on the Web toolbar, as described in the previous section. To open the index of an HTTP site, omit the name of any file at the end of the address. (For example, if someone gives you `http://www.sybex.com/service.html` as the location of the Eighth Wonder of the Online World, you could visit the index of the Sybex Web site instead by using `http://www.sybex.com/`. To reopen a page you've visited before, choose it from the address drop-down list.

Figure 28.2 shows a Web page opened in Word. You'll see that Word has opened the page as a read-only document because I do not have rights to change it. *Hyperlinks* (jumps) to Internet locations appear as underlined red text, while hyperlinks to local files appear as underlined blue text (these colors change once you click on a hyperlink so that you can tell which ones you've tried).

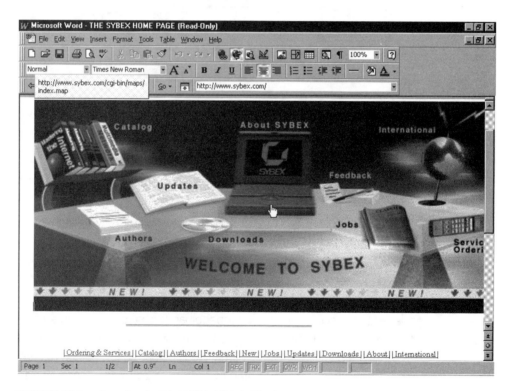

FIGURE 28.2: Browsing the World Wide Web in Word

NOTE   **You can also open Gopher documents: Simply enter the address in the format gopher://gopher.location.page in the Address box.**

Working with FTP

From within Word, you can work directly with FTP sites. In this section, you'll learn how to add the sites to your list of stored FTP sites, a step you have to take before you can actually work with them. After that, you'll learn not only how to open documents located on FTP sites, but also—if you have the necessary permissions—how to save documents to FTP sites.

Adding FTP Sites

Before you can open a file at an FTP site, you have to identify the site to Word. Here's how to do so:

1.   Choose File ➤ Open to display the Open dialog box (see Figure 28.3).

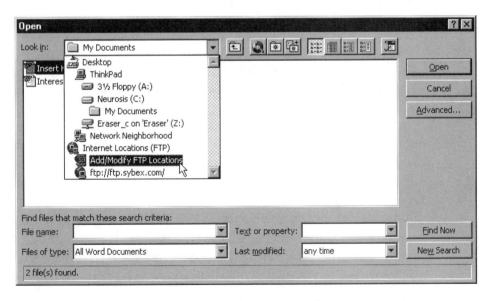

FIGURE 28.3:   Use the Open dialog box to navigate to an FTP site.

2. Select the Add/Modify FTP Locations item in the Look In drop-down list to display the dialog box shown in Figure 28.4.

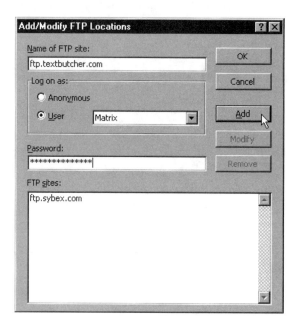

FIGURE 28.4:
Set up your FTP locations in the Add/Modify FTP Locations dialog box.

3. In the Name of FTP Site text box, enter the full address of the FTP site (for example, `ftp.sybex.com`).

4. In the Log On As group box, choose how to log on to the site. If you do not have an account at the site, leave the Anonymous option button selected. If you do have an account at the site, select the User option button and enter your user name in the text box.

5. Enter your password in the Password text box. For sites that you log onto as Anonymous, you'll typically use your e-mail address as your password; for sites where you're known by user name, you'll need to specify your personal password.

6. Click the Add button to add the site to your list of FTP sites. (Once you've created a site, you can modify it by selecting it in the FTP Sites list box, changing the information in the appropriate boxes, and clicking the Modify button; or you can remove the site from your list by clicking the Remove button.)

7. Click the OK button to close the Add/Modify FTP Locations dialog box.

Opening a File from an FTP Site

To open a file from an FTP site, use the Internet Locations (FTP) feature from the Open dialog box:

1. Choose File ➤ Open to display the Open dialog box.
2. In the Look In drop-down list, choose the FTP site from the Internet Locations (FTP) category. If you see no FTP sites listed, add sites as described in the previous section.
3. Click the Open button in the Open dialog box to open the FTP site you selected.
4. Navigate to the folder that contains the document you want to open, and then click the Open button to open it.

Saving a Document to an FTP Site

To save an Office file or an HTML file to an FTP site, choose File ➤ Save As and choose the FTP site from the Internet Locations (FTP) section of the Save In drop-down list. (If you don't see any FTP sites listed there, you need to add them as described in "Adding FTP Sites," earlier in the chapter.)

Creating Web Pages

You can create Web pages with the Office applications in three ways: First, you can use Word's Web Page Wizard to walk you through the steps of creating a Web page. Second, you can use one of Word's Web templates or Publisher's Web templates to create a particular type of page. Third, you can convert a regular Office file—a Word document, an Excel worksheet, or a Publsiher publication—to a Web page.

Web pages are formatted using the *HyperText Markup Language,* or HTML, which consists of large numbers of ugly codes each encased in angle brackets. The good news is that the Office applications not only handle the creation of, or the conversion to, HTML codes for you but also make it easy to insert hyperlinks to other documents, either on a local or networked drive or on the Web.

NOTE   **Publisher's Web site PageWizard provides as easy way to create Web pages. See Chapter 21 for details on creating Web pages and Web sites with Publisher.**

Creating Web Pages with the Web Page Wizard

To create a Web page with the Web Page Wizard in Word:

1. Choose File ➤ New to display the New dialog box.
2. Click the Web Pages tab to display it at the front of the dialog box. (If you don't see a Web Pages tab in the New dialog box, whoever installed Word on your computer probably didn't install the Web templates; see the Appendix for instructions on installing Word components.)
3. Click the Web Page Wizard icon, and then click the OK button. Word will start the Web Page Wizard and display the first Web Page Wizard dialog box (see Figure 28.5).

FIGURE 28.5:
In the first Web Page Wizard dialog box, choose the type of Web page you want to create.

4. Choose the type of Web page you want to create, and then click the Next button. (For this example, I'll choose Personal Home Page, which is a good place to start.) Word will display the next Web Page Wizard dialog box.
5. Choose the style for your Web page, and then click the Finish button to create the page. Word will display the skeleton for the type of Web page you chose in the style you selected (see Figure 28.6).
6. Save the page so that you can add hyperlinks to it. (We'll get to this in "Creating Hyperlinks" later in the chapter.)
7. Add text to the placeholders in the page by clicking in each placeholder and then typing in the text. For example, to add a heading to the Personal Home Page, click in the Insert Heading placeholder and enter the text you want. Rinse and repeat for other heading placeholders on the page (for example, for any Subheading placeholders).

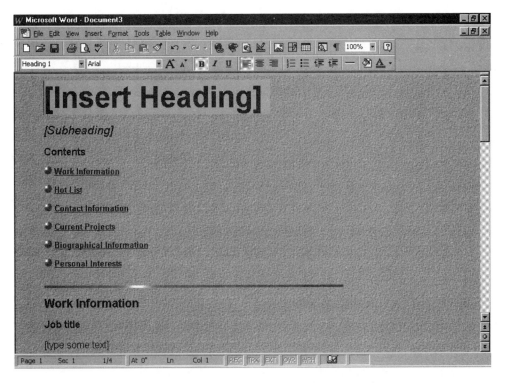

FIGURE 28.6: Word will create the skeleton for the type of Web page you chose.

8. Replace any sample text that the page includes with suitable text of your own.
9. Edit the page to suit your needs: Add, cut, and edit the text as necessary. Use any of the blue hyperlinks included on the page to move quickly to a linked part of the page.
10. Save the page when you're finished.

Using Web Templates

Instead of using the Web Page Wizard, you can start a Web file by choosing one of the templates on the Web Pages tab of the New dialog box (File ➤ New).

TIP You can download additional Web templates from the Microsoft Web site, http://www.microsoft.com.

Saving a Word Document as an HTML File

You can also save a regular Word document as an HTML file by choosing File ➤ Save as HTML and specifying a location and a file name in the Save as HTML dialog box.

WARNING **When you save a regular Word document as an HTML file, some Word elements do not translate properly to HTML. These include complex tables, bulleted and numbered lists, and graphics. If you need to include these items in your HTML documents, consider creating these documents from scratch, importing text as necessary.**

You can also save an HTML file as a Word document. To do so, choose File ➤ Save as Word Document. Specify a name for the document in the Save As dialog box, and then click the Save button.

Saving an Excel Worksheet as an HTML File

Excel provides an Internet Assistant Wizard for converting spreadsheets and charts to HTML. First, you'll need to make sure the Internet Assistant Wizard is installed on your computer. To do so:

1. Choose Tools ➤ Add-Ins to display the Add-Ins dialog box.
2. In the Add-Ins Available list box, select the check box for the Internet Assistant Wizard, and then click the OK button. Excel will install the Wizard and will add a Save as HTML item to the File menu.

To convert a worksheet or chart to HTML:

1. Open the workbook and display the appropriate worksheet or chart.
2. Choose File ➤ Save as HTML to start the Internet Assistant Wizard and display the first Internet Assistant Wizard dialog box.
3. In the Ranges and Charts to Convert list box, the Internet Assistant Wizard will list any range or chart selected when you started it. Click the Add button and click and drag in the worksheet to indicate further ranges; to remove a range or chart from the list box, select it and click the Remove button.
4. Click the Next button to display the second Internet Assistant Wizard dialog box.
5. Choose whether to create a separate HTML document from the data or to insert it into an existing HTML document.
6. Click the Next button to display the third Internet Assistant Wizard dialog box.

7. Enter any header or footer information you want in the text boxes in the dialog box. You can add a title, a header and a description, horizontal lines to separate the data from the rest of the page as necessary, and details about who last updated the page and what they did.

8. Click the Next button to display the fourth Internet Assistant Wizard dialog box.

9. In the Which Code Page Do You Want to Use for Your Web Page drop-down list, choose the *code page* (roughly translated, the set of characters) for your page: Windows Latin 1 (U.S., Western Europe) is the best choice unless you know you need another code page.

10. In the How Do You Want to Save the Finished HTML Web Page area, select the Add the Result to My FrontPage Web option button if you have an existing FrontPage Web site. Otherwise, leave Save the Result as an HTML File option button selected.

11. In the File Path text box, enter the location to which you want the document saved: Either type the location in, or click the Browse button, use the Save Your HTML Document As dialog box to select the location, and click the Save button.

12. Click the Finish button to finish saving the HTML document.

Creating Hyperlinks

A hyperlink is a jump to another location. This location can be:

- Part of an Office file (for example, part of a spreadsheet, or of another Word document, or even part of the same Word document)
- An entire Office file
- A Web page on the local computer, on a local intranet, or on the World Wide Web.

You can mix and match these different types of hyperlinks to suit yourself.

You can create a hyperlink in any of three ways in Excel; Word has a fourth way as well. (See Chapter 21 for information on inserting hyperlinks in Publisher.)

Inserting a Hyperlink Manually

To manually insert a hyperlink in a Word document or an Excel spreadsheet:

1. Enter the text or graphical object that you want to have display the hyperlink.
2. Select that text or graphical object.
3. Click the Insert Hyperlink button on the Standard toolbar, or choose Insert ➤ Hyperlink, to display the Insert Hyperlink dialog box (see Figure 28.7).

FIGURE 28.7:
In the Insert Hyperlink dialog box, specify the details for the hyperlink.

4. In the Link to File or URL text box, enter the path and name of the file for the hyperlink. Either type in the path and name, or click the Browse button, use the Link to File dialog box to select the file, and click the OK button to enter the file name and path in the Link to File or URL text box.

TIP If you're using Internet Explorer 3 or a later version, or Netscape Navigator 2 or a later version, you can quickly enter a URL by leaving the Link to File or URL text box empty and the Insert Hyperlink dialog box on screen; then use Internet Explorer or Navigator to go to the site, switch back to the application, and the site's URL will appear in the Link to File or URL text box.

5. In the Named Location in File text box, you can enter the part of the file for the hyperlink to jump to. You can jump to a bookmark in a Word document, a range in an Excel spreadsheet. Click the Browse button to display a dialog box containing a list of the objects in that file that a hyperlink could jump to.

6. Click the OK button to insert the hyperlink in your document.

Once you've inserted a hyperlink in a document, you can click the hyperlink to jump to the document or Web page to which it is connected.

Creating a Hyperlink by Dragging

You can also create a hyperlink to an Office document by dragging the object to be hyperlinked from the application to the document that should receive the hyperlink. For example, you can create a hyperlink from a range of cells in Excel or part of another Word document.

To create a hyperlink, display Word and the other application (or two windows in Word) on screen at the same time. Then right-click and right-drag the object to where you want it to appear in the Word document. Word will display a context menu; choose Create Hyperlink Here to create the hyperlink.

Creating a Hyperlink by Copying

To create a hyperlink by copying, select the material in its source application (or source file in the same application) and copy it by right-clicking and choosing Copy, clicking the Copy button, or choosing Edit ➤ Copy. Then switch to the destination application (or destination file in the same application), position the insertion point where the hyperlink should go, and choose Edit ➤ Paste as Hyperlink.

Creating Automatic Hyperlinks from File Names in Word

Word's AutoFormat feature (discussed in "Using AutoFormat" in Chapter 7) can automatically create a hyperlink when you type the name of a file into a Word document. To enable this feature, choose Tools ➤ AutoCorrect to display the AutoCorrect dialog box. Click the AutoFormat As You Type tab, and select the Internet and Network Paths with Hyperlinks check box; click the AutoFormat tab, and select the check box there, too. Then click the OK button to close the AutoCorrect dialog box. Thereafter, when you type an URL or a network path and file name into a document, Word will automatically format it as a hyperlink.

To turn URLs and file paths in an existing document into hyperlinks, use the Format ➤ AutoFormat command. Make sure the Internet and Network Paths with Hyperlinks check box on the AutoFormat tab of the AutoCorrect dialog box is selected as described in the previous paragraph.

Appendix

INSTALLING OFFICE 97 SMALL BUSINESS EDITION

FEATURING

- **System requirements for Office 97**
- **Installing the applications**
- **Installing and uninstalling components**

In this appendix, we'll look at installing the Office 97 Small Business Edition applications on your PC. We'll cover both installing the applications from scratch and installing components that whoever first installed the applications neglected to include.

System Requirements

You can install and run Office 97 Small Business Edition on any computer capable of running Windows 95 or Windows NT Workstation 4. (All the Office 97 Small Business Edition applications except Automap Streets Plus will also run on Windows NT Workstation 3.51 with Service Pack 5.)

That means, in practice, a 486 or better Intel processor (Pentium, Pentium II, Pentium Pro) or equivalent (AMD 486, 586, or K6, Cyrix 5x86 or 6x86, and so on) with 8MB or more of RAM for Windows 95 or 12MB or more of RAM for Windows NT Workstation.

Installing the Office Applications

Unlike Office 97 Standard Edition and Office 97 Professional Edition, Office 97 Small Business Edition has only a semi-integrated setup routine. Instead of being able to choose to set up all the applications at once, you need to set up each of them sep-arately. Automap Streets Plus comes on a separate CD and has its own setup routine. Internet Explorer also installs separately.

To install the Office 97 Small Business Edition applications:

1. Place the CD-ROM in your CD drive. If AutoPlay is enabled on your computer, the Microsoft Office 97 Small Business Edition window will appear automatically (see Figure A.1). Otherwise, double-click the file named Autorun.exe in the root folder of the CD to display the window.

NOTE

To enable AutoPlay, right-click the My Computer icon on your Windows Desktop. On the Device Manager tab of the System Properties dialog box, click the + sign next to the CD-ROM entry. Select the item for the CD-ROM drive and click the Properties button. On the Settings tab of the CD-ROM's Properties dialog box, select the Auto Insert Notification check box in the Options group box. Click the OK button to close the CD-ROM's Properties dialog box, and then click the OK button to close the System Properties dialog box. Windows will prompt you to restart your computer for the change to take effect.

FIGURE A.1:
In the Microsoft Office 97 Small Business Edition window, choose the application you want to install.

2. Click the button for the application you want to install.

3. The Setup program will display a Welcome dialog box inviting you to read the End User License Agreement included with the software. Click the Continue button to move on.

4. In the Name and Organization Information dialog box, enter your name (or the name of the person to whom the software belongs), and an organization if appropriate. Click the OK button to continue.

5. In the Confirm Name and Organization Information dialog box, check that you entered the name and any organization name correctly. Click the OK button to continue, or the Change button to move back to the Name and Organization Information dialog box (and to step 4).

6. Enter your Product ID number or CD Key number in the next dialog box. This number will be either on the Certificate of Authenticity in the CD-ROM's sleeve or on a sticker on the CD-ROM's jewel case. Type the ID number into the boxes (the number is divided into parts to make things more difficult) and click the OK button. You'll need to enter the CD Key for Word, Excel, and Outlook, but not for Publisher, Small Business Financial Manager, or Automap Streets Plus.

7. Write down or memorize the Product ID number that Office gives you in the next dialog box (you'll need this if you call for technical support). This number will appear in the About dialog box for the product (choose the Help ➤ About command). Click the OK button to proceed.

8. Setup will spend a little time searching for installed components, and then will suggest a destination folder for the application (for example, C:\Program Files\Microsoft Office). Accept this by clicking the OK button, or click the Change Folder button and pick a more appropriate folder in the Change Folder dialog box. Enter the name for the new folder if necessary. (If the folder doesn't exist, Setup will invite you to create it; choose the Yes button.)

9. In the next Setup dialog box, choose the type of installation you want. For most of the applications, your choice is between Typical and Custom (Small Business Financial Manager offers only a Custom installation, and Publisher offers a choice of Complete or Custom). The Typical installation installs Microsoft's predefined set of features; the Custom installation displays a dialog box that allows you to choose which features you want.

   - In most cases, it's a good idea to choose Custom so that you can tailor your installation to your needs. If you want to install all the options, choose Custom and then click the Select All button in the Custom dialog box.
   - When installing Outlook, if you will need to connect to a Microsoft Exchange server, choose the Custom installation and select the Microsoft Exchange Server Support item.
   - You must have Excel installed on your computer before you install Small Business Financial Manager. (If you don't, the Small Business Financial Manager Setup program will alert you to the problem and fail gracefully.)

10. If you choose the Typical installation, Setup will install the predefined set of features for you. If you choose the Custom installation, Setup will display the Custom dialog box for the application, in which you get to choose which options to install. Figure A.2 shows the Custom dialog box for Word. Options whose check boxes are selected will be installed wholesale; options whose check boxes are selected but grayed out will be installed but with only a part of the component; and options whose check boxes are cleared will not be installed.

    - To select all the options (for a full installation), click the Select All button.
    - To change one of the options, select it and click the Change Option button to view a list of the components of the option. Again, select the check boxes for the options you want to install, and then click the OK button. (You may need to drill down to a another layer of options for some options.)
    - When you've selected all the options you want, click the Continue button to install them.

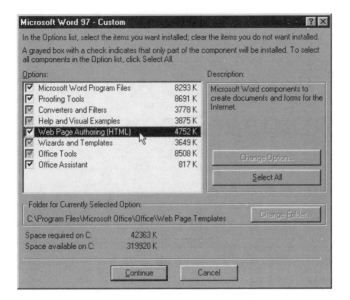

FIGURE A.2:
In the Custom dialog box, choose the parts of the application you want to install.

TIP

If you're short of disk space, try to omit features you don't need. For example, when you're installing Small Business Financial Manager, you can choose to install only the converters for the accounting package you have.

11. Setup will install the options you chose.

- At this point, the Setup program for Small Business Financial Manager displays a Financial Manager Setup dialog box that warns you that the template may not be appropriate for analysis of your business and is not a substitute for professional advice. Click the Accept button to indicate that you understand this (or click the Exit Setup button to cancel the installation). You then get to choose whether to install the United States or Canada version of the Small Business Financial Manager.

- Under Windows 95, Publisher will display the Install Windows 95 PostScript Driver dialog box asking if you want to install a PostScript driver that will enable you to have your publications printed at commercial printers and service bureaus. If you choose this option, you'll need to have your Windows 95 disks or CD-ROM on hand to install some files.

12. Once installation is complete, Setup will offer to walk you through online registration, which is handled via the Microsoft Network. If you have a modem up and running, this saves you the cost of a stamp.

13. Finally, Setup will return you to the Microsoft Office 97 Small Business Edition window, where you can choose to install another application. When you're finished installing applications, click the Close button in the upper-right corner of the window to close it.

Installing Automap Streets Plus

Automap Streets Plus comes on its own CD-ROM and is not integrated in the main setup routine, so you will need to install it separately:

1. Insert the Automap Streets Plus CD-ROM in your CD drive.
2. If AutoPlay is enabled on your computer, the Setup routine will run automatically and will display the Microsoft Automap Streets Plus Setup dialog box. Otherwise, open a Windows Explorer window and double-click the Setup.exe file in the root folder on the CD-ROM. The Setup program will display the Microsoft Automap Streets Plus Setup dialog box.
3. Click the Continue button to display the Name Information dialog box.
4. Enter your name in the Name text box, and then click the OK button to display the Confirm Name Information dialog box.
5. Double-check your name. Click the OK button to proceed, or click the Change button to return to the Name Information dialog box and step 4.
6. In the next dialog box, write down or memorize your Product ID number, and then click the OK button.
7. In the next dialog box, verify the folder that Automap Streets Plus Setup has chosen for Automap Streets Plus. It's usually the \Program Files\Microsoft Reference\Automap\ folder. Then click the Install and Run button to proceed with the installation.
8. In the Choose Program Group dialog box, select the program group to which Setup should add the Automap Streets Plus item. You can accept Setup's suggestion, or select a different group from the Existing Groups list box, or enter the name for a new group in the Program Group text box. Click the Continue button to proceed.
9. Setup will install Automap Streets Plus and will display a dialog box announcing that setup was completed successfully and inviting you to use online registration to register Automap Streets Plus. Click the Online Registration button to register, or click the OK button to run Automap Streets Plus.

Running Automap Streets Plus from Your Hard Drive

If you need to run Automap Streets Plus on a computer that does not regularly have a CD-ROM drive installed (such as a laptop), or if you need to improve Automap Streets Plus performance on a slow computer, it's possible to run Automap Streets Plus from your hard drive. You'll need 650MB of free space on the drive in question, plus approximately 10MB of free space on the drive to which you will install the Automap Streets Plus program files.

First, make a backup copy of the Automap Streets Plus CD-ROM to your hard drive. Then run the Setup.exe program from the backup copy and follow the instructions (steps 2–10) for a regular Automap Streets Plus installation.

Installing Internet Explorer

To install Internet Explorer:

1. Place the CD-ROM in your CD drive. Open Windows Explorer, navigate to the \ValuPack\IExplore\ folder on the CD-ROM, and double-click the file named Msie301.exe. (Later versions of this file will have different numbers in the name.)
2. Click the Yes button in the message box that Internet Explorer displays.
3. Read the end-user license, and then click the I Agree button to proceed. Internet Explorer will install itself on your computer.
4. Internet Explorer will display a message box telling you that you need to restart your computer for the settings to take effect. Either click the Yes button to have Internet Explorer restart your computer, or click the No button. If you choose No, you will need to restart the computer yourself before you can run Internet Explorer.

Installing and Uninstalling Office Items

Depending on how you (or whoever) originally installed Office on your computer, you may need to install extra items:

- If you need to work with text or graphics files created in another application, you may need to install extra text or graphics converter files. Office uses these files when opening a text or graphics file created in another application (or another format) and when saving Office documents in other formats for use with other applications.

TIP
If you have enough disk space, go ahead and install all the converter files. Besides exercising squatters' rights on part of your hard disk, they won't do any damage, and you'll be equipped to deal with almost any type of file your colleagues choose to throw at you.

- You may need to install extra templates or wizards.
- You may need to install specific Help files (such as the Visual Basic Help files).
- You may want to uninstall items you never use to save disk space.

To install or uninstall items in the Office applications:

1. Place the CD-ROM in your CD drive. If AutoPlay is enabled on your computer, the Microsoft Office 97 Small Business Edition window (shown in Figure A.1) will appear automatically. Otherwise, double-click the file named Autorun.exe in the root folder of the CD to display the window.
2. Click the button for the application you want to affect. The Setup routine for that application will run and will display the Setup dialog box. Figure A.3 shows the Microsoft Excel 97 Setup dialog box.

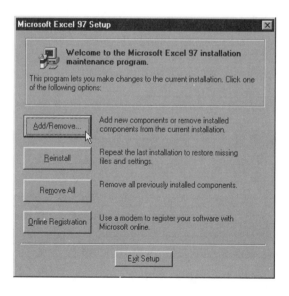

FIGURE A.3:
In the Setup dialog box for the application, click the Add/Remove button.

3.   Click the Add/Remove button to display the Maintenance dialog box for the application. This dialog box shows which Office components you currently have installed. Figure A.4 shows the Microsoft Excel 97 Maintenance dialog box.

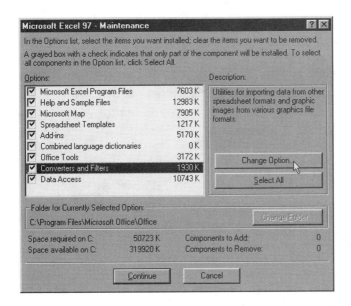

FIGURE A.4:
In the Maintenance dialog box for the application, choose which components to add and remove.

4.   Choose which components to install and which to uninstall:

- To install components, select their check boxes. You can select an option and click the Change Option button to select the components of the option to install.
- To uninstall components, clear their check boxes.

WARNING   **This dialog box is somewhat counterintuitive: Think of it not as a list of what you want to install, but a list of what you want to *have on your computer* at the end of the installation. For example, if you already have Excel's spreadsheet templates installed and want to install the data-access features, select the Data Access check box *and leave selected the check boxes for those components that were already installed and that you do not want to remove*. If you clear the check box for an item that was already installed, the Maintenance program will remove that item.**

5. Click the Continue button to continue with the installation. If you chose to uninstall components, Setup will display the Confirm Component Removal dialog box. Click the OK button to proceed.

6. When Setup is complete, you'll see a message box informing you of this. Click the OK button to return to the Microsoft Office 97 Small Business Edition window, and click the Close button in its upper-right corner to close it.

TIP

If you have an Internet connection, visit the Microsoft Office Web site at http://www.microsoft.com/office/ to check for Office Service Releases (which include bug fixes and improvements), free add-ons, and related utilities.

Index

Note to the Reader: Main level entries are in **bold**. **Boldfaced** page numbers indicate primary discussions of a topic. *Italicized* page numbers indicate illustrations.

T

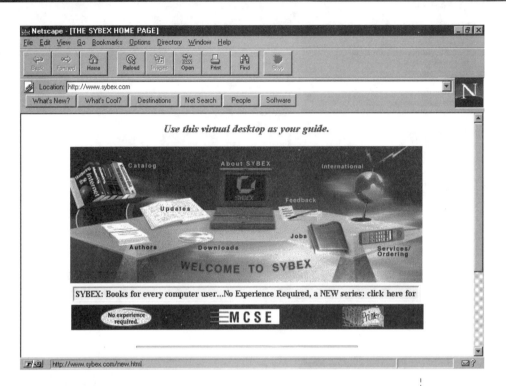